PENGUIN BOOKS
SWAMI VIVEKANANDA

Chaturvedi Badrinath was born in Mainpuri, Uttar Pradesh. A philosopher, he was a member of the Indian Administrative Service, 1957–89, and served in Tamil Nadu for thirty-one years (1958–89). He was a Homi Bhabha Fellow from 1971 to 1973. As a Visiting Professor at Heidelberg University, 1971, he gave a series of four seminars on Dharma and its application to modern times. Invited by a Swiss foundation, Inter-Cultural Cooperation, he spent a year in Europe in 1985-86. In 1985, he was a main speaker at the European Forum, Alpbach, Austria, and at a conference of scientists at Cortona, Italy. From 1989 onwards, for four years, the *Times of India* published his articles on Dharma and human freedom every fortnight. He was a Visiting Professor at the Centre for Policy Research, New Delhi, during 1990–92. He was one of the two main speakers at the Inter-Religious Federation for World Peace conference, 1994, Seoul, South Korea. In 1999, at Weimar, he gave a talk on Goethe and the Indian Philosophy of Nature; and contributed to an inter-religious conference at Jerusalem with the Dalai Lama. He was one of the two main speakers at the Sasakawa Peace Foundation symposium on 'civilizational dialogue', Tokyo, 2002.

Chaturvedi Badrinath's other published books are *Dharma, India and the World Order: Twenty-one Essays* (1993), *Introduction to the Kama Sutra* (1999), *Finding Jesus in Dharma: Christianity in India* (2000), and *The Mahabharata—An Inquiry into the Human Condition* (2006). He lives in Pondicherry and can be reached at badri9@ndf.vsnl.net.in.

Bhubaneswari Devi
(Mother of Swami Vivekananda)

To

Anna

Swami Vivekananda
The Living Vedanta

CHATURVEDI BADRINATH

With Love,
Your Sister ♥
(29/08/2015)

PENGUIN BOOKS

PENGUIN BOOKS
Published by the Penguin Group
Penguin Books India Pvt. Ltd, 7th Floor, Infinity Tower C, DLF Cyber City,
Gurgaon 122 002, Haryana, India
Penguin Group (USA) Inc., 375 Hudson Street, New York, New York 10014, USA
Penguin Group (Canada), 90 Eglinton Avenue East, Suite 700, Toronto, Ontario,
M4P 2Y3, Canada
Penguin Books Ltd, 80 Strand, London WC2R 0RL, England
Penguin Ireland, 25 St Stephen's Green, Dublin 2, Ireland (a division of Penguin
Books Ltd)
Penguin Group (Australia), 707 Collins Street, Melbourne, Victoria 3008, Australia
Penguin Group (NZ), 67 Apollo Drive, Rosedale, Auckland 0632, New Zealand
Penguin Books (South Africa) (Pty) Ltd, Block D, Rosebank Office Park, 181 Jan
Smuts Avenue, Parktown North, Johannesburg 2193, South Africa

Penguin Books Ltd, Registered Offices: 80 Strand, London WC2R 0RL, England

First published by Penguin Books India 2006

Copyright © Chaturvedi Badrinath 2006

ISBN 9780143062097

Typeset in Sabon by S.R. Enterprises, New Delhi
Printed at Repro India Ltd, Navi Mumbai

Dedicated to
Bhubaneswari Devi,
Mother of Swami Vivekananda

All expansion is life, all contraction is death. All love is expansion, all selfishness is contraction. Love is therefore the only law of life. He who loves lives, he who is selfish is dying. Therefore, love for love's sake, because it is the only law of life, just as you breathe to live. This is the secret of selfless love, selfless action, and the rest.

Swami Vivekananda

The dry Advaita must become living—poetic—in everyday life; out of hopelessly intricate mythology must come concrete moral forms; and out of bewildering Yogi-ism must come the most scientific and practical psychology—and all this must be put in a form that a child may grasp it. That is my life's work.

Swami Vivekananda

Contents

SWAMI VIVEKANANDA IN SAN FRANCISCO

Acknowledgements

Women had a central place in the life and work of Swami Vivekananda. It is, therefore, apt and artistically perfect that it should be a woman, Kamini Mahadevan, editor at Penguin India, and now managing editor, Pearson Education, who invited me to write this book on him. And just as the Swami kept expressing his eternal gratitude to what those women did for him, I wish to express my gratitude both to Kamini Mahadevan and to Penguin India.

I owe a debt of gratitude to Pravrajika Atmaprana of Sri Sarada Math, New Delhi, and I am glad to have this opportunity of expressing it. In March 1996, under the auspices of the Goethe Institute (known in India as Max Mueller Bhavan), I had spoken on 'Swami Vivekananda and Western Women—the Living Vedanta'. The Pravrajika most graciously gave me not only much of her time in discussing Sister Nivedita, of whom she has written the superb biography mentioned in this book, but also her personal copy of *Letters of Sister Nivedita* and helped me get a copy for myself. She has been ever so gracious and kind whenever I have called her.

Furthermore, I am grateful to Pravrajika Prabuddhaprana for graciously sparing an afternoon to enable me to meet her during her visit to New Delhi last year. Her two works—*Tantine, The Life of Josephine MacLeod: Friend of Swami Vivekananda* and *Saint Sara: The Life of Sara Chapman Bull, The American Mother of Swami Vivekananda*—are indispensable for understanding the Swami, and I have derived from both many facts concerning him, hitherto unknown (because concealed) but very significant. The Pravrajika truly belongs to that tradition of Swami Vivekananda in which truth was an abiding passion.

To Tulsi, my daughter, who is thoroughly familiar with the Ramakrishna–Vivekananda literature, for reading the pages of this book as they were being written and for making suggestions as regards the text that were exceedingly helpful.

I am grateful to Surendra Munshi, to his wife, Srobona, and their daughter Sharika, for finding me a copy of *Shrimat Swami Vivekanander Jibaner Ghatanabali*, written in Bengali by Mahendranath Datta, Swami Vivekananda's younger brother. Sharika went all over Calcutta (now Kolkata) looking for Mahendranath, and found him. Surendra and Srobona consulted him as regards the suicide of the Swami's (unnamed) sister, translated that portion into English for me, read some of the chapters of this book as they were being written, and offered comments that were most encouraging.

I am grateful to Irina Severin of Switzerland for reading the whole book in its first draft, and for her encouraging comments as from one who was meeting Swami Vivekananda for the first time, in the pages of this book. On reading Chapter 11, she fled to her room—to cry (as she told me later), as Sister Nivedita and Sara Bull had done a little more than a century earlier, on hearing

Vivekananda speak of his inner torments. It was not easy for me to write that chapter either.

To Peter Saeverin, for reading the book in its first draft, and for his very insightful comments, particularly on the question of simultaneity in the happenings in a person's life and the difficulty of expressing it in language, with which Chapter 10 opens.

To Gerald Daly, for the loving attention with which he read this book in its final form and for his several insightful and encouraging comments.

I am most thankful to Vijay Kumar Jain who has in Gurgaon, where I lived when this book was being written, a bookshop of old books, for quickly finding *Swami Vivekananda: Patriot-Prophet* by Bhupendranath Datta, Swami Vivekananda's youngest brother. It was a great relief when Bhupendranath arrived the day I looked for him, to know from him many details (especially some names), not found elsewhere, concerning the family in which the Swami was born, the subject of Chapter 1.

I am most thankful to the Advaita Ashrama, Kolkata, the publishers of Sister Gargi's classic six-volume *Swami Vivekananda in the West: Some New Discoveries*, for permitting me to use some historical material concerning Swami Vivekananda's work and relationships in the West, and incorporating a few quotations from her work.

I am most thankful to my Bengali cook Sumitra for helping me in many small ways during my writing this book, apart from supplying me with ginger tea through the day. Though totally illiterate, she quickly learnt to recognize—by their colour, shape, and the way in which the title of the book is printed—all the books pertaining to Swamiji and to Sri Ramakrishna in my study, and would fetch for me, unfailingly accurately, those I wanted from among them. That saved me much labour, for often they were kept in different places. Moreover, wanting to learn, she became my immediate audience on whom I daily tested, successfully, Swami Vivekananda's belief that, if conveyed in a simple language, even a child could understand the Vedanta. Sister Nivedita would have forthwith transferred Sumitra to the Nivedita Girls' School!

January 2006   Chaturvedi Badrinath

Introduction

Vivekananda is much more than the Swami Vivekananda. Few know Swami Vivekananda; Vivekananda, even fewer.

Swami Vivekananda's life is inseparable from his changing responses to the social conditions of his times in India, and of the West equally so. But this is not all. There is in all human lives the interplay of history and transcendence; in the life of a man like Swamiji even more so. The tension between the two would become a source also of his self-division; for history began to trouble him more and more. With its inner turmoil and pain, that division of the self increased very nearly in the same measure as the spectacular progress of his mission in the West. He gave expression to it in many of his letters to those American women—Mary Hale, Josephine MacLeod, Sara Chapman Bull, Christine Greenstidel (later Sister Christine)—and to Margaret Noble (later Sister Nivedita), who loved him and understood what he was. They understood that he had a mission, 'the work', rooted in the history of his times but which, simultaneously, transcended all history and touched the deepest longings of the human soul. He was concerned with both, and thus spoke two languages: the language demanded by history, and the language beyond all history, with a passion that was uniquely his. To meet Vivekananda is to float with him in these two worlds at the same time.

Furthermore, in meeting Swami Vivekananda, one necessarily meets many other persons, in India and the West, into whose lives he had come as a light and who had come into his life with *their* grace of love and care. Each of them had his or her history, of the mind and circumstance, as he had *his*. They do not constitute just a catalogue of names, only to be recited in the chanting of the Swami Vivekananda litany. Each one of them shows, in different ways, the complexities of human aspirations and character, through which alone, and not in some abstract haze of spirituality or in the beating of drums of creed and doctrine, is life *lived*. Swami Vivekananda was pointing to life where alongside its complexities is its utter simplicity, blissful joy coexisting with the pain and suffering of being human. In Vivekanandian thought, neither of the two ever remained unrelated to the other.

However, it is also true that if those who had come into his life were not to remain just names, and their life stories before and after meeting him are necessarily to be narrated insofar as they are known, the chain becomes longer and longer. Furthermore, because each of them was individually in some relationship with him, they inevitably came into relationship with each other. And those relationships were complex, not always easy, but fascinating to study. *That* chain becomes even longer. The difficulty is this: without them, Swami Vivekananda cannot be understood, but in the mass of details that have been gathered about them, the Swami is lost because the reader is overwhelmed and feels exhausted. There is no easy way

to resolve this paradox. Then the easiest thing follows—
Swami Vivekananda remains a worshipped icon. The aim
of this book is to bring to the reader the man.

The story of Vivekananda's life is inseparable from
not only that of Sri Ramakrishna Paramahamsa primarily,
but also from that of his own mother, Bhubaneswari Devi.
Thereafter come those—most of them women, women
of the West—who became central to his life and work.
That they were 'instruments of Swamiji's work' is the
notion prevalent among many of the Ramakrishna Order
and expressed easily. Not only is this wholly un-Vedantic,
it is also a complete negation of the man himself, who
never in conduct or thought ever regarded anybody as
his 'instrument'. 'Instruments' are for *use*, to be thrown
away once their *use* is over or to be put aside for future
use. Nor were those Western women empty vessels into
which an Indian saint poured enlightenment: no one can
receive enlightenment unless, in one measure or another,
one is enlightened already. That they would *feel*
Vivekananda, feel *his presence*, and talk intensely about
him, even decades later, tells us not only about *him* but
about *them* as well. Many of them were great women,
and therefore could recognize greatness where they saw
it. And this recognition and fostering of greatness with
loving care, was not limited to Vivekananda alone. Sister
Nivedita and Sara Chapman Bull also reached out to the
Indian scientist Jagadis Chandra Bose, until then
struggling alone—Nivedita, with her seemingly
inexhaustible resources of love and faith, and Sara Bull
with her considerable material resources as well. She gave
to her 'Indian son' Vivekananda her deepest love and
concern; but helped others, too, in their troubles.

Vivekananda gave a new meaning to the Vedanta, away from its dry metaphysics, and talked of 'the living Vedanta' which meant living *relationships* in a new light. Even as he expounded 'non-dualism', he lived *relationships*, and relationship implies the existence of the *other*. The sense and the feeling of oneness with the *other*, in collective relationships quite as much as in the personal, had been always inherent in the Vedanta but was thoroughly obscured in its later scholastic developments. Vivekananda brought out *in his person* that true meaning. He was, in a literal sense, the embodiment of the true Vedanta.

To all those who came into his life, took loving care of him and supported his work in one way or another, he expressed in a full-throated voice his gratitude, and gratitude implies the existence of the other. Vivekananda never turned non-dualism, or any *ism*, into some hard theory divorced from life, but brought to a world full of hatred and violence arising from religious absolutism, its deeper import, the inner unity of all life. When he spoke, it was with authority, which struck even those who were antagonistic to him. That authority and its visible majesty grew out of the sense of oneness with all he displayed in his own life, in ways natural and easy. Vivekananda's *vedanta* did not exclude the sincerest humility and gratitude for what he was receiving from others generously. And neither did it exclude a childlike capacity for merriment, fun and laughter. If university professors were attracted to his powerful intellect and conversed with him for hours, a child of six too could sit in his lap, warm and snug, and widen her eyes in wonder as he told her the stories of Indian bazaars and remember him even forty years after. Even before he began speaking about it, Vivekananda's *vedanta* was written in every line of his gorgeously handsome face and reflected in his 'midnight-blue' eyes.

Vivekananda repudiated, both in his teachings and in his conduct, the prevalent notions of *sannyasa* embodying false notions of 'renunciation'. The Mahabharata had done that in the clearest language three thousand years earlier in the voice of a woman, and lest that be regarded as the self-serving argument of a wife, also in the words of a sage. Vivekananda did likewise in so many different ways: in his deeply felt social concerns and above all in his tireless efforts to alleviate the sufferings of the poor, the oppressed, and the rejected. There had been before, and there have been since, countless sannyasis in this ageless country. But none ever spoke, much less wept, in the name of the wretched and the poor masses of India. Vivekananda did. None among the sannyasis had ever worked for *them*. Vivekananda did, driving himself relentlessly, to the point of his early death.

Above all, going beyond the false notions of renunciation and sannyasa, he remained attached to his mother, Bhubaneswari Devi, till the last day of his life. Indeed, as was known to everybody, he greatly worried about her, and never ceased to acknowledge his debt to her. Often, this aspect of Swamiji and what it teaches is ignored, particularly in the Sri Ramakrishna Order.[1] Even the names of his four sisters, one of whom had committed suicide, are not mentioned anywhere in his biographies by his followers. Their standard explanation is that, on

---

[1] There are some exceptions. Swami Nikhilananda's *Vivekananda: A Biography* (New York, 1953; first Indian edition, 1964) does mention Vivekananda's attachment to his mother, see, for example, pp. 15, 23, 333–34, 355.

renouncing the world, a sannyasi knows neither father nor mother, nor sister nor brother. But neither the true Vedanta nor true sannyasa, excepting in caricature, ever maintained that highest spirituality is incompatible with love for one's mother or, say, enjoying ice cream. Swami Vivekananda repudiated the notion that it did. For Vivekananda, as he put it to his spiritual daughter, Nivedita, it was, 'Madness of love, and yet in it no bondage. Matter changed into spirit by the force of love. Nay, this is the gist of our Vedanta'.[2] Till the very end, he remained attached to Mary Hale of Chicago, 'the sweetest note in my jarring and clashing life' as he described her and the whole Hale family, with the simple bonds of love and affection and of spiritual grace. Many of his most moving letters were written to Mary Hale. Till the very last, he retained his loving attachment to Josephine MacLeod, his 'friend', and to Sara Bull. These are only a few names given here. Permeated with his love, more than even with his formal teachings, all of them remained in Vivekananda's feelings and thought till the very last! For each of them had permeated his life with her or his love for him.

Vivekananda, and his intimate relevance to our lives and times, are to be understood not by reading his lectures alone but first by knowing how he lived his life, a perfect embodiment of love, of truth and of oneness with the other. We would have known nothing of these details of his life and relationships but for the works of Marie Louise Burke (Sister Gargi),[3] and of Pravrajika Prabuddhaprana (Leona

---

[2] Letter dated 1 October 1897.
[3] Marie Louise Burke, *Swami Vivekananda in America: New Discoveries* (1958, Advaita Ashrama, Mayavati, Almora); *Swami Vivekananda His Second Visit to the West: New Discoveries* (1963, Advaita

Katz) of Sri Sarada Math,[4] written with the scrupulous care of an honest historian seeking the truth. They are the most detailed portraits of Vivekananda's life and work in the West.[5] It is through them, not in his lectures alone, that we meet the living Vedanta.

However, Vivekananda remains his own best biographer—of his mission, of his work, of his inner life, of his self-division, of his sufferings and torments. His letters, fortunately preserved and published[6] but seldom read, much less studied, even among the Indians familiar with the Vivekananda saga, are the various portraits of himself. But they are still *his* portraits of himself. The other evidence, simply quite enormous, collected by Marie Louise Burke

Ashrama, Mayavati, Almora). Both these were later expanded into six volumes. *Swami Vivekananda in the West: New Discoveries. His Prophetic Mission*, Vol.1 (4th ed., 1992) and Vol. 2 (4th ed., 1994); *Swami Vivekananda in the West: New Discoveries. The World Teacher*, Vol. 3 (1st ed., 1985; second reprint, 2000) and Vol. 4 (2nd ed., 1996); *Swami Vivekananda in the West: New Discoveries. A New Gospel*, Vol. 5 (4th ed., 1998) and Vol.6 (4th ed., 1999). All these published by Advaita Ashrama, Mayavati, Almora. Hereafter, *SV New Discoveries*.
[4] Pravrajika Prabuddhaprana, *Tantine, The Life of Josephine MacLeod: Friend of Swami Vivekananda* (1st ed., 1990; Sri Sarada Math, Dakshineswar, Calcutta), hereafter, *Tantine*; *Saint Sara, The Life of Sara Chapman Bull: The American Mother of Swami Vivekananda* (2002; Sri Sarada Math, Dakshineswar, Calcutta), hereafter, *Saint Sara*.
[5] Both of them are Western women. The significance of *that*—pointing to a radical intellectual difference between the Indian and the Western *manas*, 'mind', even when both are imbued alike with the spirit of the Vedanta. Vivekananda himself knew that difference. Consistent with the philosophy of non-dualistic Vedanta he was propagating, although he talked of all 'differentiation' as false, an illusion, he came to respect and greatly rely upon that very difference in the progress of his work.
[6] *Letters of Swami Vivekananda*, published by Advaita Ashrama, Pithoragarh, revised edition, 1940; hereafter, *SV Letters*.

from numerous contemporary sources of every variety, shows the truth of what Vivekananda was saying about himself. And what he was saying (and indeed was) presents not only a unique portrait of ecstasy and joy in the feeling of oneness with all life, but also of the pain and suffering of the human condition.

Let us next consider whether, in the Indian context, knowledge of the historical details of a great spiritual figure's life is necessarily an aid in understanding him and the lack of it, necessarily, a hindrance. This question is best answered, I think, by contrasting the case of the Buddha with that of Swami Vivekananda. Vivekananda had the greatest reverence for the Buddha, and feelings even more intense. Excepting for a few main events in his life, we know very little of the historical Buddha; and even what little we know is not certain, and has been a subject of scholarship full of controversy.[7] But that lack of historical knowledge about him never prevented the Buddha from being a living influence through the centuries. On the other hand, there is not, as far as I know, another figure in the history of modern India whose life, work and relationships have been documented in such great detail as those of Swami Vivekananda. But that has not prevented him from remaining an icon, in front of which, along with two other sacred icons, Sri Ramakrishna Paramahamsa and Sri Sarada Devi, an arati is performed morning, noon, and evening. The two most familiar photographs of Vivekananda show him either sitting, his hands folded in his lap, his eyes closed in deep meditation, or standing, in a heroic pose,

---

[7] See Edward J. Thomas, *The Life of Buddha as Legend and History*, Routledge & Kegan Paul, London, first published 1927, chapters XV and XVI, 'Buddha and Myth', 'Buddha and History', pp. 211–36.

his eyes open and his arms firmly folded across his chest, as if delivering a challenging message. The Indian perceptions of Vivekananda are mostly limited to these two images—the one conveying tranquillity and the other, strength and power.

What does that show? It is a complex question. The least it shows is that, to the Indian *manas*, history is of little consequence. Thus, for example, it would not in the least matter to an Indian if further research concluded that the Buddha was actually born a century later, or a century earlier, than 563 BC, generally held to be the year in which he was born. There already exist Buddhist traditions that give other dates.[8] Nor would it be of any great consequence if it were now concluded that the Buddha died not when he was eighty, as generally believed, but actually when he was ninety-three or, say, when he was seventy-one. Similarly, to an ordinary Indian, it would be of little interest, for example, when exactly Vivekananda sailed from Bombay on his first journey to America; or what his life in America was like; or what his inner conflicts, generated by 'the work' and 'the organization', were. In popular perception, he is limited to 'the Vivekananda of the Parliament of Religions', where 'he defended Hinduism and Indian culture with great spiritual force' and did Hindus and India proud. Many persons may be familiar with the story of how one day when he collapsed on the roadside, tired and hungry, a kindly lady from a house opposite saw him, took him into her home, and took care of him. A few such stories, true as they are, render the legend of Vivekananda complete.

---

[8] In China and Japan, it is 1067 BC; in Tibetan schools fourteen different dates are mentioned. See Edward J. Thomas, *The Life of Buddha as Legend and History*, p. 27, *fn*.1.

But, for the most part, it is the legend of Vivekananda that fills the Indian mind and heart, not his history.

Indeed, to most Indians, not even Vivekananda's physical personality, beyond the common knowledge that he was exceedingly handsome, is of any particular interest. On this, one hears, with a sense almost of disbelief, Marie Louise Burke say:

It is curious that nowhere else does one find so detailed a description of Swamiji's personality as in the American newspapers. Although Romain Rolland gives us a general picture of him in his *Prophets of the New India*, and *The Life*[9] has reproduced a paragraph from the *Phrenological Journal* of New York in which his measurements are given and head bumps interpreted, the Indian biographies and the memoirs written by people who had known him seem with scrupulous care to avoid describing him. Unfortunately this is also true of the biographies of Sri Ramakrishna's other disciples and those of Sri Ramakrishna himself. Were it not for a few available photographs we should be left completely in the dark in regard to the personal appearance of these great souls. Possibly this oversight is due to the Hindu writers' concern with spiritual rather than physical facts. Yet the Hindu is aware that the devotee never tires of hearing detailed descriptions of the object of his devotion ...In fact, this hunger for knowledge regarding the outer characteristics of the manifestations of God and of the knowers of God is more typically Indian than Western. Why the Hindu biographies of Sri Ramakrishna and his great disciples were so unrealistic in these matters seems, therefore, an unanswerable question.[10]

---

[9] Referring to *The Life of Swami Vivekananda: By his Eastern and Western Disciples*. (Advaita Ashrama, Mayavati, Almora, first published 1912; 4th ed., 1949). Hereafter, *The Life*.

[10] Marie Louise Burke, *SV New Discoveries*, 2, pp. 333-34.

Unanswerable or not, it was left to a Western woman, Marie Louise Burke,[11] to undertake a stupendous research of the American newspapers of the times when Swami Vivekananda appeared on the American scene, and how he and his work were being perceived and reported in the public media; and follow his rich trail during his two visits to America, England and Europe, from 1893 to 1896 and then from 1899 to 1900. It was only a decade after her first volume appeared in 1958 that a corresponding work appeared in India, *Vivekananda in Indian Newspapers 1893–1902: Extracts from Twenty-two Newspapers and Periodicals*, by Sankari Prasad Basu and Sunil Bihari Ghosh,[12] and dedicated by them to her. Both of them must be honoured for producing that immense work from the Indian side and respected for their honesty in acknowledging that her work

…shamed us into a sort of moral consciousness shaking our inner minds. We felt how flagrantly indifferent we are towards our national heroes. So the latest masterpiece about Vivekananda came from the West! [In an informal meeting, Swami Nikhilananda, half-humorously remarked, 'Swami Vivekananda is America's gift to India'.] Yet we felt pride rather than shame—pride that we always feel in the universal appreciation of a great man. When a character is as great as Vivekananda, it does not matter who is presenting him as whether he is presented at all.

But our sense of guilt, nevertheless, was not to be easily wiped out. This feeling goaded us into action and led us seriously to

---

[11] Marie Louise Burke passed away on 20 January 2004 in San Francisco, aged ninety-three.
[12] First published in July 1969 by Basu Bhattacharya & Co., Calcutta.

think of setting ourselves about a work in the Swami's life in India (after his coming back from the West) just as Mary [sic] L. Burke had done about his life in America.[13]

Swami Vivekananda is wrapped in a strange paradox. So much is known about him as accurate historical record, and yet so little is understood about the man and his meaning to our own troubled times! His measure is taken in fragments. Vivekananda, the great Indian patriot, the national hero who restored in Indian society, in a people subject to a foreign rule, self-confidence and pride in their great inheritance. Vivekananda, the dominant and compelling voice of renascent Hinduism, who showed to the world that Hinduism is not a mass of evil and superstition, 'a world of darkness', as the Christian missionaries to India were saying, to be replaced with the truth and the light of Christianity. Vivekananda, the strongest voice and the champion of Indian masses, hungry and poor, exploited for centuries. Vivekananda, the most passionate voice for Indian women, they having the greatest beauty of character to be found anywhere but denied for centuries their share in education, purposely kept illiterate and backward. Vivekananda, the great Advaita philosopher, the worthiest successor of Shankaracharya, showing that all notions of duality are false, that whatever is only self is not, that the Vedanta is the future universal religion. Vivekananda, the most attractive spiritual figure of modern times, to whom his Master, Sri Ramakrishna Paramahamsa, himself among the greatest of mystic saints, had 'transmitted', even in a literal sense, *all* his spiritual energies. For Vivekananda had 'work to do': to

---

[13] Ibid., pp. ix–x.

illumine the human horizon with the truth that all religions lead to that same God that lives in all.

On each of these aspects, we have a considerable body of literature, but in which Vivekananda the man is hardly to be found. Seen through them, he very nearly vanishes. Swami Vivekananda remains for the most part a remote figure, which he never was.

Furthermore, because he said as much on several subjects that touch history as what is beyond it, Vivekananda is quoted most often selectively, for a limited purpose. That can easily be done; and it is done with supreme confidence that his message has been understood. But the truth is that anything concerning human life which he touched upon never stood alone. It formed a unity with the rest of his teachings, as we shall see later in this book. Besides, Vivekananda's thoughts, as they have come down to us, were not a revelation at birth. Nor a result of the fateful day Sri Ramakrishna Paramahamsa had, with a touch, woken him to the realization of who he was, and had transmitted to him his spiritual powers, laying upon him 'the work' he had to do for the good of mankind. Swami Vivekananda was learning all the time, with the seriousness of a scholar as in his *parivrajaka* days in India, and with the curiosity of a child wanting to know, as seen in his American years. He was 'expanding', 'growing', to use his own words, discarding his earlier prejudices, responding to the world with a childlike freshness of mind that was always, to those who knew him intimately, such a delight to watch. Swami Vivekananda 'the cyclonic monk', as some American newspapers went on to describe him, would one moment be the great sage and in the next, without any affectation whatsoever, be Vivekananda the happy, laughing, playful, dependent child.

It would be a mistake to quote only what Swami Vivekananda had said in a particular context, without relating it to the rest. But it would be an even greater mistake, because he was like a playful child, to lose sight of the immensity of what he had made his mission. That his perceptions of this mission changed as it progressed should not make us think that he was doubtful of its essence. Because, in some particular context, Swami Vivekananda had sometimes said 'I was mistaken', and at other times spoken of his progressively declining health, does not mean that he was, after all, no greater than anyone of us. For that would presuppose the common and foolish notion that the spiritually great, the enlightened, are *never* mistaken; and that the true yogi ought to be never physically ill. Thus, it can be said that there was an earlier Vivekananda as Narendranath Datta, a later Vivekananda, and the Swami Vivekananda of the middle. Yet, through them all, there was visible consistency and coherence of character.

Soren Kierkegaard (1813–55) had passionately argued that in order to be an authentic Christian, to mould one's life to the teachings of Jesus, one must feel 'contemporaneously' with Jesus; that is, feel His humiliation and suffering with Him.[14] He argued that authentic Christianity must remain at all times 'an offence', in so far as it had upset the orthodox beliefs about man's relationship with God, or lose itself in its own well-adapted, comfortable, churchy paganism which, in his dialogues with Bishop Munster, he had shown it had. Kierkegaard was expelled from the Christian Church. Swami Vivekananda felt Jesus contemporaneously.

---

[14] Soren Kierkegaard, *Training in Christianity*, 1848 (Oxford University Press, London, 1941), translated by Walter Lowrie.

Answering a question, he once said: 'Had I lived in Palestine, in the days of Jesus of Nazareth, I would have washed His feet, not with my tears, but with my heart's blood.'[15] He likewise felt the Buddha contemporaneously. He had a profound knowledge of the development of Buddhism through its various stages, and many of his lectures were devoted to that subject, examining Buddhism and Hinduism in their interrelated but complex history, talking about them as a scholar. But when he talked of the Buddha, as he did very often, he did it with the deepest *feelings*, so that those who heard him felt the very presence of the Buddha. I maintain that not until Swami Vivekananda is *felt contemporaneously* will he ever be understood in the fullness of his being. You don't simply *read* a man like Vivekananda. In reading him, you *meet* him. And if you don't *meet* him and feel him contemporaneously, you can understand little of the meaning of what he is saying. Indeed, this is true about any great thinker who keeps thinking about life and not just keeps talking metaphysics.

Josephine MacLeod once said of him: 'The thing that held me in Swamiji was his *unlimitedness*! I never could touch the bottom—or top—or sides! The amazing size of him.'[16] And she was one of those who knew him intimately. How may one presume to take the measure of such a man then?

Vivekananda had no greater passion than the passion for the truth. I believe that all summaries distort the truth in one degree or the other. They leave out the sequences,

---

[15] Sister Nivedita, *The Master as I Saw Him* (Udbodhan Office, Calcutta, 1910; 11th ed., 1972), p. 233. See also Marie Louise Burke, *SV New Discoveries*, 5, p. 231.
[16] In a letter dated 12 March 1923.

the nuances, and much else, in condensing the narration of both the inner and outer happenings that are as complex as they have many levels. That will apply to this book as well. The reader should keep this in mind throughout. In the Upanishads, concerned with comprehending Reality, one comes across the word 'neti', repeated twice. It is always translated, but wrongly, as 'it is not *this*', but the formulation of the word, na+iti, 'not yet complete' (the description), clearly shows that *neti* means 'it is not this alone'. Understood thus, *neti neti* becomes an attitude of the mind in making judgements either about oneself or about others. At the end of each chapter of this book, the reader should mentally add '*neti*', 'it is not this alone', and repeat it twice.

Neither strictly a biography of Swami Vivekananda nor a study of his philosophy, this book is written in the hope that through it the reader will *meet* Vivekananda; and in meeting him, *meet* also his or her own self.

The Beginnings: The Inheritance

To my father, I owe my intellect and compassion.
                                —Swami Vivekananda
*The love which my mother gave to me has made
me what I am and I owe a debt to her that I can
never repay.*

                                —Swami Vivekananda

Let us first meet the family in which Swami Vivekananda was born. His father, Bisvanath Datta, and mother, Bhubaneswari Devi,[1] a Bengali Hindu couple of Calcutta, had seven living children. Of these, four were daughters.[2]

---

[1] That is how their youngest son, Bhupendranath Datta, spells their names. Most of the English biographies of Vivekananda spell their names as 'Vishwanath' and 'Bhuvaneshwari', as they should be. I have adopted the spellings as given by their son.

[2] None of the biographies of Swami Vivekananda, written by his Eastern and Western disciples, mentions their names. The names of his sisters are learned from *Swami Vivekananda Patriot-Prophet—A Study*, a detailed account of the family and a study of his philosophy, by his youngest brother Bhupendranath (4 September 1880–25 December 1961). The book was first published in 1954; its second edition, revised and edited by Anuspati Dasgupta and Kunjabihari Kundu, came out in 1993 (Nababharat Publishers, Calcutta). Swami Nikhilananda, in his *Vivekananda: A Biography* speaks of 'four daughters'. The complete sentence, appearing on page 11, is as follows: 'Two sons were born to her (Bhubaneswari Devi) besides Narendranath, and four daughters, two of whom died at an early age.' That is all he

Haramoni and Swarnamayee were older than Swamiji, and Kiranbala and Jogendrabala younger.[3] The first-born of the Dattas, a son, had died in infancy.

Like most mothers, Bhubaneswari Devi longed for a son and prayed fervently to Shiva, the Lord Vishwanath of Varanasi. Her fervent prayer was answered, and a son was born to her on 12 January 1863 at her home, 3, Gour Mohan Mukherjee Lane, in a district called Simulia in north Calcutta. It was the day of the sacred festival of *makara sankranti*, when millions of Hindus bathe in the river Ganga. It was a Monday, the beginning of the week, a few minutes before sunrise, the beginning of a new day, when the child was born. Later, as Swami Vivekananda, the voice of that child was to be heard all over the world, bringing faith, strength and hope to many, proclaiming that beyond misery and pain and suffering there is a new beginning for every soul. But this is only a manner of saying it. A Vivekananda born in the dead of the night would still have brought to everybody the hope of a new beginning. Bhubaneswari Devi decided, and her husband agreed, that their son would be called Vireshwara, one of the many names of Shiva, to whose blessings they owed their second son. Later, it became Narendranath, 'Narendra' or 'Naren' to his friends.

After him, two more daughters, Kiranbala and Jogendrabala, were born and after them two sons,

---

tells us about the rest of the Datta family. The other biographies of Vivekananda, not even that. But there is an error in Nikhilananda's description. The Dattas had *six* daughters, of whom only two, the second and the fifth died in infancy.

[3] Bhupendranath, p. 295. Haramoni died at age 22, Swarnamayee at 72, Kiranbala at 16, Jogendrabala at 22. Bhupendranath provides no further information concerning his sisters.

Mahendranath and Bhupendranath. But *The Life* and the other biographies of Vivekananda do not tell us much about his two younger brothers either, just as they do not about his two elder and two younger sisters. We hear their names first from Marie Louise Burke,[4] that is, if we confine ourselves to the biographies of Swami Vivekananda written in English. Later, we hear more of Mahendranath,[5] affectionately called 'Mohin', again from the same source. And we hear more of Bhupendranath in some letters written in 1908 by Sister Nivedita, and in Pravrajika Atmaprana's superb biography of her. We will briefly meet these two younger brothers of Swami Vivekananda at different times in this book.

Bisvanath Datta was a successful lawyer at the Calcutta High Court and had a lucrative practice. That, combined with the inherited wealth, enabled the Datta family to live in the greatest of comfort, indeed, in luxury. The inherited wealth of the family came mostly from Vivekananda's great-grandfather, Rammohan Datta, who was the managing clerk and associate of an English lawyer. One of his two sons, Durgaprasad,[6] Bisvanath's father, showed such brilliance in the understanding of law that Ramachandra Datta made him his partner. Vivekananda was born in a family of three generations of highly successful and rich lawyers. Law, in the restricted sense of a profession, 'ran in the blood'.[7] What was inherited

---

[4] *SV New Discoveries*, 5, p. 19.
[5] Born, 1869; died, 1956.
[6] Bhupendranath Datta, in his book already cited, gives his grandfather's name as 'Durgaprasad'; but *The Life* mentions it as 'Durga Charan'. I am following the name 'Durgaprasad', as given by his grandson.
[7] *The Life*, p. 6.

by one generation of the Dattas from the other was not wealth alone earned by legal practice but also the intellectual acumen that the practice of law required.

What also 'ran in the blood' was dedication to Law in its deepest sense, that which governs man and the world, indeed, that which governs the whole universe. Vivekananda's grandfather, Durgaprasad, renounced the world when he was twenty-five years old, took to the ochre robe, and set forth to live a life in the light of that higher Law, leaving behind a wife and a son, as the Buddha had done. From Bhupendranath, rather than the English biographies of Vivekananda, we learn that his grandmother was called Shyamasundari and that she was strikingly beautiful. Recollecting what someone said to him about her, he wrote: 'What a beautiful woman your grandmother was! She was *Shyama* both in name and in her features; I have never seen a beautiful woman like her in any Bengalee home.'[8] *The Life* tells us that the abandoned wife was a woman of extraordinary inner spiritual strength and character. Whatever her inner feelings and thoughts might have been, Shyamasundari now dedicated herself to bringing up her son Bisvanath.[9]

Her grandson, Narendranath, also renounced the world at about the same age as her husband, and came to be known to the world as the Swami Vivekananda. But there was a spectacular difference between the *character* of the sannyasa of the grandfather and that of the grandson. Excepting a dramatic meeting of the monk

---

[8] Bhupendranath Datta, *Swami Vivekananda Patriot-Prophet—A Study*, p. 48.
[9] Of which *The Life* narrates a few instances; see pp. 4–6.

and his abandoned wife during one of his brief visits to
Calcutta, and a no less dramatic but chance meeting later
in Varanasi between him and some ladies of the family
on a pilgrimage there,[10] nothing was ever seen or heard
of Durgaprasad.[11] Much would be seen and heard of the
grandson as a monk all over the world. In their own
fashion, in their own place, Vivekananda's grandmother,
Shyamasundari, and mother, Bhubaneswari Devi, were
also devoted to the higher Law.

And so was his father. While doing his legal practice,
Bisvanath Datta lived his life believing that whatever that
higher Law might be, it did not exclude joys of music and
poetry. In fact, one of the many things the son inherited
was his father's melodious voice and joy in music. Narendra
was systematically trained in classical music. Bisvanath
also knew Persian and Arabic, and took great delight in
reading and reciting the famous *Dewan-i-Hafiz*, and also
Sanskrit poetry, having studied Sanskrit under Kali
Bhattacharya in his traditional *tol*. He took great delight
even in cooking. Besides, in his house, there were
discussions on serious subjects like history, philosophy and
religion among men of letters, eminent and otherwise,
who frequented the Datta home. Narendra, though a
small boy, was not excluded from those gatherings, which
must have been, if one knows the Bengali character, very
lively. Rather, he was quietly encouraged to take part in

---

[10] Both described by Bhupendranath, *Swami Vivekananda Patriot-Prophet—A Study*, pp. 49–50.
[11] We learn from Bhupendranath that 'The last news that was received of him was that he had become a *mathadhari* i.e. the founder of a *matha* or an abbot at a monastery at Benaras. Since then nothing more has been heard about him.' p. 50.

them; and when he did, he would question with the freshness of a child's mind what was being said, or simply express his own opinion on something or the other. As far as is known, there was seldom any attitude of condescending indulgence towards the young boy, either on the part of the father or of those who came. In brief, as his youngest son says, 'Bisvanath was a product of old Hindu-Muslim civilization and the new English culture spreading in his time.'[12] Besides, he had studied and respected the Bible. That seems to have invited much criticism. In order to understand fully what Vivekananda had inherited, it is necessary to hear what his youngest brother said about this criticism of their father:

That he was a respecter of the *Bible* and of *Dewan-i-Hafiz* has been a matter of adverse criticism of my father in certain quarters. Some disciples of Ramakrishna have made the slanting remark that Bisvanath advised his son (Vivekananda) to read the *Bible* and *Dewan-i-Hafiz* for the simple reason that he was entirely unacquainted with Hindu religious thoughts. They ignore history and jump to hasty conclusions coloured by prejudice. If it be a sin to be free from blind superstitions and to be liberal in religious outlook, the writer vicariously admits that sin on the part of his father. If it be a sin to be a student of comparative religion and to respect all cults, then Bisvanath had undoubtedly committed that sin. These monk-disciples of Ramakrishna conveniently forget that their Guru himself was a respecter of all religions and cults. That was his *forte* and that is why many people were drawn towards him. It needs to be emphasised that Ramakrishna was no blind revivalist of Brahminism. The writer is grateful to his father for bringing him along with his brothers out of the grip of priestly

---

[12] Ibid., p. 53.

superstitions and pointing out to them a new life suited to the changing times. This helped the offspring of Bisvanath to become radicals in their ways of thinking.[13]

What Bisvanath inculcated in Narendra, which he had always shown in his own life, was independence of mind but without being judgemental, hard or inconsiderate, and with an ability to see things from different perspectives. This lesson, of 'independence of mind', Narendra applied quickly. To see life from different perspectives was fine but he was puzzled by some differences he found being practised in his own home. He noticed that different hookahs were provided in his father's office at home for different castes of his clients, and a separate one for Muslims. Narendra wanted to experiment what would happen if he smoked from all of them in turn, and proceeded to do so. On being caught and scolded, it is not clear by whom, he quietly said: 'I don't see any difference.' His later passionate rejection of caste as any basis for treating people differently had undoubtedly its origin in the evidence that experiment had provided.

Bisvanath had another trait: his overwhelming generosity, whereby he was often reckless in giving. A host of his relatives, some of them good for nothing, some even drunkards, were financially supported by him and lived in his home, exploiting the giving nature of a rich and kind-hearted lawyer. When Narendra protested, his father would say to him that when he grew up he would know how much misery there was in the world, and if those who lived upon him wanted to forget their misery for some moments by drinking, what harm was there in it? But the

---

[13] Ibid., pp. 53–54.

father kept a strict eye on the son himself and on the company he was keeping without, however, exercising that oppressive but mindless discipline many parents exercise upon their children in the mistaken belief that they were doing only good to them thereby.

There was between the father and the son a close relationship of love and unspoken pride in each other. The son, who was to become one of the greatest men of our times, would later say to Sister Christine: 'To my father, I owe my intellect and my compassion.'[14] She recorded in her reminiscences of him:

And so perhaps for days we re-lived his childhood in his father's house in the Simla quarter of Calcutta. He would tell how his father would give money to a drunkard, knowing for what purpose it would be used. 'This world is so terrible, let him forget it for a few minutes, if he can,' the father would say, in self-defence. His father was lavish in his gifts. One day when he was more recklessly extravagant than usual, his youthful son said, 'Father, what are you going to leave me?' 'Go, stand before your mirror,' was the father's reply, 'and you will see what I leave you.'[15]

The relationship was even closer between mother and son and it remained so as long as he lived. While all others called him Naren, his mother called him Billeh, a colloquial usage for Vireshwara, the Shiva. To her, even when he became the great Swami Vivekananda, he would remain Billeh, her son. If the father had inculcated in the son independence of mind combined with intellectual

---

[14] Sister Christine in the *Reminiscences of Swami Vivekananda* (Advaita Ashrama, Mayavati, 1st ed., May 1961), p. 175. Hereafter, *Reminiscences*.
[15] Ibid., p. 175.

curiosity to know and to understand the substance, the mother inculcated in him devotion to truth above all. On one occasion, she is reported to have said to him: 'Always follow the truth without caring about the result. Very often you may have to suffer injustice or unpleasant consequences for holding to the truth; but you must not, under any circumstances, abandon it.'[16] And this was one lesson that had gone the deepest into the son's heart. Although full of fun and frolic to even a greater degree than children generally are, Naren was by no means an easy child; at times, because of his excessive restless energy, he was almost uncontrollable. On such occasions, which were not infrequent, the mother would pour a pot of cold water over his head, reciting 'Shiva, Shiva', and he would become quiet, for a while at least. There is this charming story of Bhubaneswari Devi (one can imagine her lifting her hands up in exasperation) complaining to Lord Shiva: 'I had asked you for a son, and you have sent me one of your demons instead.' Poetic licence does permit one to imagine Lord Shiva smiling upon her and whispering into her ears, 'Just wait, dear lady!'

Like her mother-in-law, Shyamasundari Devi, Bhubaneswari Devi was a woman of extraordinary character. Fortunately, *The Life* does provide us with a portrait of her.[17] Loving, caring, devoted to the higher Law of life as she understood it—and she understood it better than many—Bhubaneswari Devi managed a large household with the aplomb of a queen. She was regal in her appearance, commanding instant recognition and respect, almost obedience. 'Those of us who were privileged

---

[16] Swami Nikhilananda, *Vivekananda: A Biography*, p.15.
[17] *The Life*, pp. 7, 8–10.

to see his mother,' Sister Christine wrote, 'know that from her he inherited his regal bearing. This tiny woman carried herself like a queen. Many times did the American newspapers in later years refer to her son as "that lordly monk, Vivekananda". There was a virginal purity about her which it seems she was able to pass on.'[18]

Bhubaneswari Devi was regal not just in appearance but also within, refusing to be awed by the changing circumstances of life. Neither taken up by the luxuries she was surrounded with, nor broken by the poverty she and her family faced when her husband suddenly died, she seemed to have kept a distance from both, a spiritual quality of detachment. But she was deeply pained when her beloved son, like his grandfather Durgaprasad, also renounced the world and took to sannyasa. But before that, he had learnt at her knee much of what he would later draw upon as Swami Vivekananda. For him, Bhubaneswari Devi was also a portrait of Indian womanhood. And of Indian womanhood, he would speak in his American days with the deepest feelings. Vivekananda never ceased to acknowledge what he owed to his mother. Bhubaneswari Devi would one day receive another acknowledgment, this time from a land far away, from twelve women she did not know. Their letter to her said:

> Dear Madam,
> At this Christmas tide when the gift of Mary's son to the world is celebrated and rejoiced over with us, it would seem the time of remembrance. We, who have your son in our midst, send you greeting.
> His generous service to men, women and children in our

[18] Reminiscenes, pp. 174-75.

midst was laid at your feet by him the other day, in an
address he gave us on the ideals of 'Motherhood in India'.
The worship of his mother will be to all who heard him
an inspiration and uplift.
Accept, dear Madam, our grateful recognition of your life
and work in and through your son.
And may it be accepted by you as a slight token of
remembrance, to serve in its use as a tangible reminder
that the world is coming to its true inheritance from God
of Brotherhood and Humanity.
With great regard.

The letter was signed (in that order) by Sarah C. Bull, Sarah J. Farmer, Florence James Adams, Mary P. Pollett, Anne T. Shapleigh, Mary W. Wilson, Emma C. Thursby, Ruth Gibson, Elizabeth W. Bartlett, Isabel L. Briggs, Mary F. Stoddard, and Mary P. Rogers. It bore the date 'Christmas, the 25th Dec., 1894', and the place 'Cambridge, Massachusetts'.[19] The first name among them was of the woman who came to understand Swami Vivekananda, loved him dearly as a son as long as he lived, and in whose judgement and council in practical matters he would have unshakeable faith, giving her the name *Dhira-mata*, 'the Steady Mother'. Sara Chapman Bull would come to be one of the most important persons in Swami Vivekananda's life and work, both in the West and in India.

But that would be a decade later. Let us return to No. 3, Gour Mohan Mukherjee Lane. On 13 February 1884,

---

[19] It was published in the *Indian Mirror*, 23 February 1895. See Sankari Prasad Basu and Sunil Bihari Ghosh, *Vivekananda in Indian Newspapers 1893–1902: Extracts from Twenty-two Newspapers and Periodicals*, pp. 66-67.

the Datta family was struck by a disaster. Bisvanath
Datta suddenly died of heart failure.[20] When the news
was brought to Narendra, who was spending an evening
with a friend, he was stunned. He had loved his father
greatly and had admired him for the man he was. He
hastened to be by the side of his mother. But even before
the family could mourn their loss, they discovered that
Bisvanath had left behind no money; so reckless had he
been in giving that literally nothing was left to the family
with which to sustain itself. Even more serious was the
fact that in trusting others, who were borrowing money
in his name and making merry, he had run into debts
which were actually not his; now the creditors were
knocking at their door. About the same time, an aunt,
who with *her* family was living with the Dattas and whom
Bisvanath was supporting, filed a lawsuit to take
possession of the ancestral house which she claimed to
be legally hers.[21]

Narendranath was just twenty-one years old when this
calamity struck his happy and flourishing family. He had

---

[20] Bhupendranath Datta, *Swami Vivekananda Patriot-Prophet—A
Study*, p. 57. Neither *The Life* nor any other biography of Vivekananda
mentions the date, only the year 1884. The one exception seems to be
Gautam Ghosh (for that reference, see Ch. 3, p. 125, fn. 105). We find
in *The Gospel of Sri Ramakrishna* an entry dated 'Sunday, 2 March
1884', when Narendra was visiting Sri Ramakrishna, that mentions
the death of Narendra's father, p. 343.

[21] For the details of the extent to which Bisvanath's relatives were
exploiting and cheating him, and the extent of his yielding to
Kaliprasad, his father's brother, who was living with him with his
family, see Bhupendranath's account of the happenings, *Swami
Vivekananda Patriot-Prophet—A Study*, pp. 55–59. Not only his
relatives but also a friend he had trusted, and had made the manager
of his office, was borrowing large amounts in his name, p. 59.

done his graduation from what is now called the Scottish Church College in Calcutta, had enrolled himself for a degree in law but didn't complete the full course. Being the eldest son, the responsibility of taking care of the family, an old grandmother, a mother and two younger brothers,[22] fell upon his shoulders. After his father's sudden death, they were reduced to poverty, each day bringing the despair of not knowing where their two square meals would come from, or whether they would come at all. A similar responsibility, but this time of taking care of another *kind* of family to which he would then belong, would also fall on *his* shoulders. But that would be some two-and-a-half years later—after *another* death.

Narendra trudged the streets of Calcutta, going from one office to another in search of employment but only to hear one refusal after the other and return home in the evening, hungry and tired. He would say that he had eaten something outside; a lie of course, but spoken only so that what little they had somehow secured should not become even lesser by his sharing it. When pressed to eat at a friend's house, he would say he had already eaten something at home; for he could not bear the thought that while he was having a good dinner, his family was perhaps going without food. Now and then he would find some work, as once in a solicitor's office or another time in Ishwar Chandra Vidyasagar's school, to manage for his family and himself barely a hand-to-mouth existence. But

---

[22] Perhaps the two younger sisters as well, or perhaps not, because presumably they were married by that time. But we don't know anything about that. The Indian biographers of Vivekananda are silent on such details.

their financial difficulties, which were acute, continued. What an irony that there are perhaps not many offices in Calcutta today where Swami Vivekananda's photograph is not seen adorning a wall; yet many offices in the same city had once slammed their doors in his face! In Vivekananda's own words:

This first contact with the reality of life convinced me that unselfish sympathy was a rarity in the world—there was no place in it for the weak, the poor, the destitute. I noticed that those who only a few days ago would have been proud to help me in any way, now turned their face against me, though they had enough and to spare. Seeing all this, the world sometimes seemed to me to be the handiwork of the devil.[23]

None of his friends, who came from rich families, knew the extent of privation Narendra's family was suddenly reduced to; and he was too self-respecting to let any of them know. 'Only one of them came to know about my poverty without my knowledge,' he would later narrate, 'and, now and then, sent anonymous help to my mother by which act of kindness he has put me under a deep debt of gratitude.'[24] Narendra had begun to lose faith that there existed a merciful, loving God. In that state of mind, whenever he heard one of his friends sing a devotional song in adoration of some merciful, loving God, he would sternly say: 'Stop it!' The future Swami Vivekananda had known, in his own life and from experience, what hunger is, and what it is to be poor. He had known the swing of fortune. The

---

[23] *The Life*, p. 90. Vivekananda's own account of that most painful part of his life has been reproduced in *The Life*, pp. 90–96.
[24] Ibid., p. 90.

experiences he had to go through, as if given by an unseen hand, though exceedingly painful, were an inheritance too. It prepared him for his future work, for and in a world where there is hunger and poverty, and equipped him to handle the resultant pain and suffering.

Bhupendranath recounts how their mother, Bhubaneswari Devi, would complain that her daughters had failed to inherit her physical strength, which she had herself inherited from *her* mother, Raghumani Devi.[25] He tells us that their grandmother used to walk the rather long distance from Narkeldanga to the river Ganga for her *daily* morning Ganga-bath; and during her travels to sacred places, from Puri on the east coast to Dwaraka on the west, she would often walk the long distances.[26] On that account at least, Bhubaneswari Devi could not have had any complaint against her eldest son who, as a wandering monk, would walk even greater distances in India. That, too, was an inheritance: the physical strength, upon which, in all his teachings, Vivekananda would put great emphasis. His brother tells us that when Raghumani Devi fell ill at the age of seventy, the Ayurvedic physician who came to examine her and felt her pulse said: 'For a Bengalee lady of her age her pulse is extraordinarily strong. I have not seen anything like this before.'[27] Her grandson Vivekananda's *pulse* was also extraordinarily strong, so strong indeed that anyone who came to know him would say: 'I have not seen anyone like him before.'

---

[25] 'She was born around 1825 and died in 1911.' These dates are given by Bhupendranath, *Swami Vivekananda Patriot-Prophet—A Study*, p. 77.
[26] Ibid., pp. 80-81.
[27] Ibid., p. 81.

And a strong pulse is also what he had inherited from his mother and grandmother.

Many traits of Swami Vivekananda's personality were 'in the blood', so to say. They were, in brief, a questioning mind that would not accept anything merely because somebody or some book, however authoritative, had said it; a firm conviction that truth lies in self-realization and not in dogma or creed; a passionate belief that truth shall never be compromised, whatever the cost, and at the same time, an intellectual willingness, a spirit of humility, to be aware that one might be mistaken in what one believed truth was, and that it is possible to perceive a thing from other points of view, each of which might also be true; spiritual humility in not being a fanatic; giving what one has, to the point of a seeming recklessness, not asking whether the other is 'worthy' or not; renunciation of the world, sannyasa, but retaining the joy of music and poetry and literature and the sights of the world, and retaining the joys of love and friendship, for there is no incompatibility between these and sannyasa rightly understood. Most of all, it meant remaining sensitive to the pain and suffering of others, of which there is so much in the world—in other words, retaining an intuitive knowledge of, and deep concern for, the *pulse* of other human beings. All these were to be continuously seen in Vivekananda till the last day of his life; and all these were 'in the blood'.

To this legacy that he never abandoned, would be added what he inherited from his Master, Sri Ramakrishna Paramahamsa, an inheritance of the highest spiritual kind. To open one's arms, in a genuine *feeling* of the oneness of all life, even to 'the wicked', 'the terrible', 'the ugly', and then rejoice.

Enriching them even more by his own life and teachings, Swami Vivekananda shared with the world these two inheritances, only to receive from countless others what *they* had inherited, and to sing from the depths of his soul that the greatest human inheritance is love in which all are one.

2

Another Inheritance, from Another Life

That Narendranath Datta, the future Swami Vivekananda, the bearer of Sri Ramakrishna Paramahamsa's teachings to a world pitifully divided into warring religious faiths, first heard of him from an Englishman, a Christian, had a hidden irony with its meaning for the future.

It is believed that Professor William Hastie, the principal of what is now called Scottish Church College, had one day, while teaching English literature to his class, taken up for study William Wordsworth's poem, 'The Excursion'. He was explaining that the state of the mind akin to a trance, into which the poet was transported, could certainly be a real experience and was not just a flight of poetic imagination. But such a trance-like state could not be attained without the utmost inner purity. Since the one was rare, the other was rare too. William Hastie concluded: 'I have seen only one person who has experienced that blessed state of mind, and he is Ramakrishna Paramahamsa of Dakshineswar. You can understand it if you go there and see for yourself.'

While these might not have been the exact words of William Hastie, it is certain that Narendra heard of Sri Ramakrishna from him. And what he had said of Sri Ramakrishna must have been of such high praise that the young student's curiosity was roused enough to want to meet the man of Dakshineswar. Later Narendra also heard that name from a relative, Ramachandra Datta, one of the foremost householder–devotees of Sri Ramakrishna.

Meanwhile, Narendranath was being consumed by his desperate search for God. But given his questioning mind, he was no less consumed by rational doubts. He studied, and assimilated, much of Western philosophy, especially the English philosophers, David Hume (1711–76), Herbert Spencer (1820–1903) and John Stuart Mill (1808–73). What he read of them, and generally of the eighteenth-century rationalist Western philosophers, forced him to take a critical look at his own 'yearning for God'. But so forceful were their arguments that he could rationally dismiss neither them, nor his own yearning for God. Because the first was not just an exercise in intellectual argument, and the second some passing yearning of a young man, Narendranath began to feel a deep disquiet within. And it showed on his face and in his eyes. His inner disquiet was so intense that it would suddenly come to the surface, surprising, and then frightening, his friends. But Narendra would become his normal self as quickly, and laughingly tell a friend who had just narrated his belief in the existence of ghosts what a fool he was, for there *were* no such entities. And, still laughing, he would proceed to give a practical demonstration (at his own risk!) of the truth of what he was saying, that there were no such things as ghosts, and that any fear of them was irrational and unworthy of a thinking person.

But God was a different matter. Even so, if the non-existence of ghosts could be proved demonstrably, the existence of God had to have direct evidence as well. That evidence had to come from someone who could honestly, in absolute truth, say that he, or she, had seen God. Was there someone who could? Narendranath knew the most likely person who could say that—Maharshi Devendranath Tagore(1817–1905). A leader of the Brahmo Samaj, Devendranath Tagore was a revered figure in the Bengal of those days. Narendra had joined the Brahmo Samaj and often sang at their congregational prayers. He had a most attractive and melodious voice, just as his father had, and, like his parents, he was gorgeously handsome, with particularly striking eyes. One day he went up to Devendranath Tagore and, without much ado, asked him: 'Sir, have you seen God?' In answer, all that the revered man said to Narendra was: 'My boy, you have the eyes of a yogi. You should practise meditation.' That answer left him deeply disappointed, for he had not gone there to ask what his eyes looked like.

Narendra now became even more restless. The energy of his restlessness was as intense as the energy of his emotional yearning for experiencing God. Hereafter, his search was twofold: to find a person who lived in the nearness of God; and then with his or her help experience that nearness himself. But that apart, Narendra loved his father and loved his mother even more. He loved his sisters and teased them no end, as also his younger brothers. To his father, he was a brilliant open mind to talk with; to his mother, the child listening to the stories from the Ramayana and the Mahabharata which she would have narrated countless times before but each time differently; and to his sisters and brothers, great fun to be with.

Devendranath Tagore was not the only person to whom Narendra had put the question 'Have you seen God?' There were others, known for their spiritual life, he had approached in the hope of finding guidance. But invariably the answer was, 'No'. In one case the answer was: 'No, I haven't, but I hope to!' Then Narendra remembered his teacher William Hastie mention Sri Ramakrishna of Dakshineswar, a mystic saint. And he wanted to meet this man, again in the hope that *he* would guide him towards the realization of God. An opportunity arose when Narendra was invited to sing one evening at the house of Surendranath Mitra (1850–90) who was very close to Sri Ramakrishna. And there the two met. It was in November 1881. Thereafter, their lives would flow into each other. In the case of Sri Ramakrishna, from the moment he saw Narendranath and heard him sing; for the latter, only progressively, and then too not without honest doubts.

But before they meet, a very brief account of some of the historical details of Sri Ramakrishna's life is in order. Fortunately, they have been minutely recorded in *The Gospel of Sri Ramakrishna* by Mahendranath Gupta and in Swami Saradananda's superb biography of him, *Sri Ramakrishna the Great Master*.[1] *The Gospel of Sri Ramakrishna* is a daily or weekly record of his life and teachings, with exact dates given before each entry, by Mahendranath Gupta (1854–1932),[2] known only as M., who knew Sri Ramakrishna intimately and was present during most happenings from February 1882 up to 24 April 1886. It was written originally in Bengali, the language in which Sri Ramakrishna spoke, as *Sri Sri*

---

[1] First written in Bengali as *Sri Sri Ramakrishna Lila Prasanga*, and then translated into English as *Sri Ramakrishna the Great Master* (Sri Ramakrishna Math, Mylapore, Madras, 1952; 5th ed. 1978). All references are to the 5th ed., in two volumes. Hereafter, *The Great Master*.
[2] Passed away on 4 June 1932.

Ramakrishna Kathamrita, in five volumes.[3] Swami Saradananda (1865–1927), or Sarat Chandra Chakravarty, or simply 'Sharat', knew Sri Ramakrishna intimately, being one of his first twelve monastic disciples, and served him during the last days of his fatal illness.

Sri Ramakrishna was born on 18 February 1836,[4] of poor and highly traditional brahmana parents, Chattopadhyayas, in a village called Kamarpukur situated in the Hoogly district of Bengal. He was given the name Gadadhar. Saradananda provides us with clear portraits of Sri Ramakrishna's father, Kshudiram, and mother, Chandramani, or Chandradevi,[5] both of them greatly respected. Many of their spiritual characteristics, and their love and concern for others, would appear in their son Sri Ramakrishna.

Sri Ramakrishna had two elder brothers called Ramkumar and Rameswar, an elder sister, Katyayani, and a younger sister, Sarvamangala. When Ramkumar was seventeen, they lost their father, and he moved to Calcutta where, in 1850, he opened a school. Sri Ramakrishna went

---

[3] Translated by Swami Nikhilananda into English, and published as *The Gospel of Sri Ramakrishna* (Ramakrishna Math, Mylapore, Madras, 1944). Hereafter, *M—The Gospel*.

[4] A.A. MacDonell, in his article on Sri Ramakrishna in the *Encyclopaedia of Religion and Ethics*, Vol. X (ed. James Hastings, Edinburgh, 1928), pp. 567–69, gives the date of his birth as 20 February 1834. It was either a printing error or MacDonell was wrong. He was certainly wrong in giving '15 March 1886', p. 569, as the date of Sri Ramakrishna's passing away. Max Mueller (*Ramakrishna, His Life and Sayings*, first published in 1898, London) was likewise wrong in giving his date of birth as 20 February 1833.

[5] Of Kshudiram, Vol. I, pp. 27–30, 32, 36–38, 41–44; of Chandradevi, pp. 30, 34–36, 41–44, to mention only a few.

to live with him two years later. In his early years he did go to a school but showed not the slightest interest in it; nor did he go to a traditional tol. Ramkumar did his best to persuade his younger brother to have a secular education. But he would not be persuaded, his argument being that when there were great riches of an infinitely higher knowledge to be had, of what worth was the learning in a school? He was soon absorbed in his quest of God-realization. It was so emotionally intense that it told upon his delicate body and he fell ill. He was moved back to Kamarpukur. On the persistent pressure of his family that he get married, he finally agreed and, in May 1859, was married to a very young girl, Saradamani. Born on 22 December 1853, in a nearby village called Jayarambati, she was a little over six. It was actually a child marriage; but she would go to live with her husband only after she came of age; and then too she would live with him not as a 'wife'. Sri Ramakrishna returned to Calcutta after spending one year and seven months with his mother after his marriage. Sarada lived at Jayarambati with her parents, Ramachandra Mukhopadhyaya and Shyamasundari.

In a place called Dakshineswar, four miles north of Calcutta, on the east bank of the river Ganga, a very rich, pious and fearless widow, Rani Rasmani, had around the same time built a magnificent temple of Kali the Mother. She belonged to a low caste (fisherman). No brahmana would act as priest in a temple built by a shudra; nor would high-caste people accept the prasad cooked in such a temple. The problem seemed insurmountable. But Rani Rasmani was not a woman who would accept defeat so easily; in the course of her life she never had.[6] Eventually, Ramkumar was approached and he accepted, despite the disapproval of learned pandits around, and even a stronger disapproval of his younger brother Gadadhar.[7] What later became a famous temple was consecrated on 31 May 1855. The story of Rani Rasmani, who died on 19 February 1861, is in itself the story of a woman of great courage and independence of character who also had a sharp acumen in practical matters. Her story has to be told as well, not in the shadow of a great life, but independently. And of her son-in-law Mathura Mohan Biswas or Mathur Babu, too, who died in July 1871. He managed her large estate and played a notable part in the life of Sri Ramakrishna. Sri Ramakrishna always spoke with feelings of affection and gratitude of the very close relationship between Mathur Babu and himself for fourteen years. As Ramkumar grew old and somewhat infirm and could not perform his duties, Sri Ramakrishna agreed to act as the priest; for meanwhile a great change had taken place in his attitudes to the question of caste. He now lived at Dakshineswar, in a small room, as the priest to Kali, the Divine Mother.[8]

---

[6] For details, see Saradananda, *The Great Master*, Vol. I, pp. 134–38.
[7] Ibid., Vol. I, pp. 143-44, for the argument between the two brothers.
[8] In the matter of whether Sri Ramakrishna acted as a priest at the Kali temple at Dakshineswar, the versions in *The Life* and in Swami Nikhilananda, *Vivekananda: A Biography*, differ. *The Life* tells us that it was Ramkumar who was appointed as the chief priest, and says nothing of Sri Ramakrishna in that regard, see pp. 33-34. Nikhilananda speaks of Sri Ramakrishna as the priest at the Kali temple, but says nothing of Ramkumar in that regard, see p. 27. For correct facts, see Saradananda, *The Great Master*, Vol. I, pp. 153–55. Ramkumar was the priest of the newly consecrated temple; and even before his death a year after, his younger brother Sri Ramakrishna was appointed as the priest.

His own mother, Chandradevi, would later come to live in the vicinity of the Kali temple at Dakshineswar. There, eighty-five years old, she passed away on 18 February 1876; it was the birthday of her son Gadadhar who took care of her in every way and served her during her illness till her death. Sri Ramakrishna, worshipped later as an incarnation of God and considered one of our greatest mystic saints, insisted also that 'one should look after one's mother as long as she is alive. I used to worship my mother with flowers and sandal-paste. It is the Mother of the Universe who is embodied as our earthly mother. As long as you look after your own body, you must look after your mother too.'[9]

Sri Ramakrishna was already becoming known for his ecstatic joys, his trances and his suddenly beginning to sing and dance in that state, for going into deep samadhi, and for the teachings that followed. He was intoxicated with the love of Kali. He would have many conversations with her in many different attitudes, and literally feel Her *presence* in everything. He lived, both in a physical and emotional sense, in the nearness of God in the form of Kali. People came in hundreds to see this man. To some, he appeared stark mad, as he did to Narendranath, too, in his first few visits to him. To some others, he appeared divinely inspired. But soon he began being known even more for his childlike simplicity and his affection for those who came, which, like his ecstasies and trances, were no affectation. More and more people now came to Dakshineswar to see him—some still out of curiosity, others to seek his blessings. Mathur Babu, although a man of

---

[9] M—*The Gospel*, entry dated Wednesday, 15 July 1885, p. 796. See also, p. 536.

the world, was not slow in recognizing Sri Ramakrishna's mystic greatness, his divinity. He freed him from the normal duties of a priest, but continued to support him in every way. Sri Ramakrishna once said:

In that state of divine exaltation I could no longer perform the formal worship. 'Mother,' I said, 'who will look after me? I haven't the power to take care of myself. I want to listen only to talk about Thee. I want to feed Thy devotees. I want to give a little help to those whom I chance to meet. How will all that be possible, Mother? Give me a rich man to stand by me.' That is why Mathur Babu did so much to serve me.[10]

'*I want to give a little help to those whom I chance to meet*.' Vivekananda would carry all his life this inheritance from Sri Ramakrishna. To this inheritance, he would add: *I will give my life to help even those I have not met, the miserable, the wretched, and the poor of the earth.*

Meanwhile, there arose in Sri Ramakrishna's heart a sudden desire to experience the various other faiths different people lived by. Was there any difference between them and his own? But he was convinced that, to fathom this at all, it had to be done not at the level of reasoning, but by *feeling each faith in the same way as those who followed it did*. In brief, by becoming *them*. But before he started on that journey, exciting but scandalous for a priest in a Kali temple, he took the permission of the Divine Mother, almost like a young boy would his mother's before going on a somewhat long picnic. That obtained, he was assured by Mathur Babu

---

[10] Ibid., entry dated Sunday, 9 December 1883, p. 276.

of his continuous support as well. Seeing the exalted condition of Sri Ramakrishna at most times, Mathur had meanwhile very prudently arranged for the services of a few other brahmana priests to carry on the usual rituals of worship at the temple. The main priest, who was actually a saint, was now free to start on another inner spiritual journey, extending from 1856 to 1867. Saradananda gives us the historical sequence of that journey of Sri Ramakrishna, in three stages of four years each, including the one he had already experienced in the service of the Divine Mother at Dakshineswar. These were from 1856 to 1859, from 1860 to 1863, and from 1864 to 1867.[11]

First he practised the path of tantra, but without the sexual rites associated with it, under a Bhairavi Brahmani, a woman of great beauty and of learning no less, who defended him whenever the genuineness of his trances was questioned, and publicly defeated his critics. Then he took to the path of Vaishnava bhakti mainly under Vaishnavacharan and also under Gauri, or Pandit Gaurikanta Tarkabhushan. Under a monk called Jatadhari he next followed the path of the bhakti of Rama, Raghuvira, who his father Kshudiram had worshipped with the deepest emotional fervour. The previous two have been the path of worship of God with form and attributes, the *personal*, the path of *feeling*. Now, under a wandering monk called Totapuri, he walked on the path of the Vedanta, non-dualism, realization of the Absolute, the Brahman, the *impersonal*, the path of *knowledge*. It was Totapuri who gave Gadadhar Chattopadhyaya the name 'Ramakrishna', and initiated him into sannyasa. Then, under a Muslim

---

[11] Saradananda, *The Great Master*, Vol. I, p. 178.

sufi-saint, he took to the path of Islam; and then the path of Jesus. During the latter, he would have visions of Jesus, as he had had the visions of the Divine Mother earlier, and would shed tears of blissful joy, go into a trance, and then into a deep samadhi—by now the familiar sequence of various states of his God-intoxication.

Each one of these paths had its distinct colour and appeal, to which this traveller was wholly sensitive. Sri Ramakrishna even dressed like a Bengali Muslim in order to *feel* what it is to walk on the path of Islam; for there was certainly some connection between the outward dress and manners and one's faith. Swami Saradananda tells us, quoting his Master's words:

I then repeated the holy syllable 'Allah' with great devotion, wore cloth like the Muslims, said Namaz thrice daily, and felt disinclined even to see Hindu deities, not to speak of saluting them, inasmuch as the Hindu mode of thought vanished altogether from my mind. I spent three days in that mood, and had the full realisation of the result of the practices according to that faith.[12]

We learn from Swami Saradananda that 'the Master did not even once enter the inner courtyard of the Kali temple while practising Islam, but remained in the mansion of Mathur situated outside'.[13] It was the same during Sri Ramakrishna's devotion-to-Jesus days. Recalling the state of mind he was in, Saradananda tells us:

His love and devotion to the Devas and Devis vanished, and in their stead, a great faith in, and reverence for Jesus and his religion

---

[12] Ibid., Vol. I, pp. 299-300
[13] Ibid., Vol. I, p. 300.

occupied his mind. He began to see Christian worshippers offering incense and light before the image of Jesus in the Church, and his mind entered into the spirit of their longing for the Lord as expressed through their earnest prayers. He forgot altogether to go to the temple of the Divine Mother and pay obeisance to Her. He had a vision of a man, he was convinced was Jesus, and he cried out, 'Jesus the Christ! The great yogi, the loving son of God, one with the Father, who gave his heart's blood and put up with endless tortures in order to deliver man from sorrow and misery!' The man in the vision embraced him and vanished. Having attained the vision of Jesus thus, the Master became free from the slightest doubt about Christ's having been an incarnation of God.[14]

Thereafter he successively experienced the Buddha, the Jain Tirthankaras and the Sikh Gurus. Travelling on those different paths, by direct experience, Sri Ramakrishna reached the conclusion that, if lived sincerely and with true devotion, all faiths led to the same goal—realization of God, making man free. There was no difference, not in the *essence*.[15] 'I have practised all the disciplines; I accept all paths.'[16] Is it permissible to imagine that, by smoking from different pipes provided at his home for the different castes of his lawyer-father's clients, Narendra had already drawn his own conclusion '*I see no difference*' before he met his future Master in 1881?

Narendranath, as Swami Vivekananda, would one day distribute that inheritance to a world full of religious hatred. Every word of his—that all faiths lead to human

---

[14] Ibid., Vol. I, pp. 338-39.
[15] For his own words on this, see *M—The Gospel*, entries dated Sunday, 22 October 1882, p. 57, and Saturday, 5 April 1884, pp. 374-75.
[16] *M—The Gospel*, entry dated Friday, 19 September 1884, p. 497.

freedom, breaking the narrow bonds of the human condition—would ring true, for they came to him as inheritance from a man who, by following them with sincere devotion, had directly experienced the essence of different faiths. His words would not fall on deaf ears and closed minds. But *this* inheritance, in the process of being shared, would bring to him also calumny and malice.

The news of what to many people seemed insanity of the man who was her husband certainly reached Jayarambati, and the now eighteen-year-old Saradamani Devi resolved to go and take care of him. That was towards the end of March 1872. Before that, she had met him a few times when, at the end of his several journeys into different faiths, he had visited Kamarpukur in 1867 in the company of the Bhairavi Brahmani and had visited Saradamani Devi in Jayarambati.[17] When Sarada Devi arrived at Dakshineswar, he explained to her, in the most respectful words, how his life was being lived on a totally different plane and that he would not like to be drawn into the usual ways of the world. Furthermore, he said to her, the Divine Mother had shown to him that She lived in every woman and he had learnt to look upon every woman as Mother. Then he said to her, even more respectfully, 'Yet, as I have been married to you, if you wish to draw me into the world, I am at your service.' Having mystic spiritual depths in her, Sarada Devi understood and assured him that all she wanted was to be by his side and serve him.

Soon after her arrival at Dakshineswar, Sarada Devi fell ill. Sri Ramakrishna tended to her as a father would. When she recovered, she shifted from Sri Ramakrishna's

---

[17] For details, see Saradananda, *The Great Master*, Vol. I, pp. 303–10.

room to where his mother Chandradevi was lodged, the Nahabatkhana or 'the music room'. Sarada Devi now devoted herself to taking care of her husband, also her spiritual guru, and her mother-in-law now quite advanced in age. She lived at Dakshineswar for about a year and four months, and for a while returned to Kamarpukur sometime in October 1873, coming back to Dakshineswar in the middle of 1874.

Living with him, Sarada Devi quickly saw that her husband's madness, if madness it was, was of a very different kind. One day, after worshipping the Divine Mother at the temple, he entered his room which Sarada Devi had just cleaned. His eyes were red, steps unsteady, speech incoherent. Then, like one drunk, he asked her, 'Ah, have I drunk wine?' Astonished, no doubt, she said, 'No, no, why should you drink wine?' 'Why do I stagger then, why can I not speak? Am I drunk?' 'No, certainly not with wine,' she said, 'you have drunk the nectar of Mother Kali's love.' And he said, 'You are right.'[18] It was not in vain that it was *a Sarada Devi* at whose feet Sri Ramakrishna would abdicate his self.

It was a time also of being tested. Sri Ramakrishna honestly spoke about it to the special group of the young devotees around him, Saradananda being one of them. He told them how one night, massaging his feet, Sarada Devi asked him, 'How do you look at me?' His answer was unhesitating: 'The Mother who is in the temple, the Mother who has given birth to this body and is now living in the Nahabat—the same Mother is now massaging my feet. Truly, I always look upon you as a form of the blissful Divine

---

[18] Ibid., Vol. II, p. 617.

Mother.'[19] To an honest question, there was an honest answer. Sri Ramakrishna wondered, however, if that was really an honest answer to the question his young wife had honestly asked.

He spoke of another test while his young wife was sleeping by his side. He looked at her and a quick inner dialogue took place within him. Here was, beside him, a young woman, a female body; and the enjoyment of a young woman is what most men desired. He could have it too. Did he, however, want that limited pleasure or did he seek the unlimited joy of knowing and living in *sat-chit-ananda*, 'Being-Consciousness-Bliss'? But, even more important, another part of his being said to him that he should be honest and not '*harbour one thought within and a contrary attitude without*'.[20] (Here, the emphasis is mine but it is an emphasis that was of Sri Ramakrishna throughout.) And he knew that it was the limitless that he wanted.

Sri Ramakrishna always paid a particular tribute to his wife, known as 'Holy Mother' after his passing. He said, in the same context, to the same young disciples, 'Had she been not so pure, had she, losing control over herself, assailed me, who knows if my self-control would not have broken down and body-consciousness arisen?'[21] But it was not self-control against sex that both of them struggled hard to cultivate in the traditional fashion of *vairagya*. It came *naturally* to them. Being what they were, all notions of the physicality of sex and its pleasures easily dropped off, but without resentment and hatred.

---

[19] Ibid., Vol. I, p. 333.
[20] Ibid.
[21] Ibid., Vol. I, p. 334.

On a particular full moon night, 5 June 1872, Sri Ramakrishna worshipped Sri Sarada Devi as another form of the Divine Mother, during which she went into a deep tranquil trance and so did he. When they emerged from it, he placed at her feet his rosary as a profound symbol of total abdication of his self—a complete surrender, as he said to her, of all he had achieved till then. There could have been no greater spiritual humility than that.

Spiritual humility was another inheritance Narendranath would have from Sri Ramakrishna; he would enrich this further and, on the basis of all the evidence we have we can say, demonstrate it in his life as Swami Vivekananda. He would be given another equally precious inheritance: an example of living in close proximity of a young woman, taking care of her and be cared for by her, and, undisturbed by the web of sexual impulse, considering each other as friends floating together in the greatest adventure of the spirit.

Narendranath would quietly put aside, without arguing with him at least on *this* point, Sri Ramakrishna's evidently inconsistent attitude towards women. On the one hand, Sri Ramakrishna maintained, as he had said to Sarada Devi, that he saw in every woman the Divine Mother; but in the same breath he would also say:

I am very much afraid of women. When I look at one I feel as if a tigress were coming to devour me. Besides, I find that their bodies, their limbs, and even their pores are very large. This makes me look upon them as she-monsters. I used to be much more afraid of women than I am at present. I wouldn't allow one to come near me. Now I persuade my mind in various ways to look upon women as forms of the Blissful Mother.

A woman is, no doubt, a part of the Divine Mother. But as far as a man is concerned, especially a *sannyasi* or a devotee of God, *she is to be shunned* [here, the emphasis is mine; but it mostly was Sri Ramakrishna's own emphasis]. I don't allow a woman to sit near me very long, no matter how great her devotion may be. After a little while I say to her, 'Go and see the temples.' If that doesn't make her move, I myself leave the room on the pretext of smoking.[22]

Sri Ramakrishna did not live long enough to see, as Sri Sarada Devi did, that it would be mostly women who would emotionally and financially be the greatest support of his apostle Vivekananda and his world mission. The monastery called Belur Math, established in the name of Sri Ramakrishna and his Order of sannyasis, would be built mostly with the money of three of these women. *This irony teaches us something, as most ironies do.*

Far from shunning them, the spiritual growth of women in the affluent West and education for Indian women would remain the two most deeply felt concerns of Swami Vivekananda. And these would be not from condescending heights. Indeed, it is in his relationships with women during his years in the West that we can see the *living* Vedanta. But not that alone; in them we see him also as a charming, loving son or brother. Living with women, travelling with them, educating but also open to being educated, scolding but also taking a scolding, in all his loving intimate relationships with women, there was never a trace of the sexual; he had gone beyond it most naturally. That is the collective evidence left behind by all those Western women who had the greatest good fortune of knowing him, and

---

[22] M—*The Gospel*, entry dated Saturday, 4 October 1884, p. 532. See also entries dated Saturday, 11 October 1884, p. 568; Friday, 23 October 1885, p. 862; and Wednesday, 21 April 1886, p. 960.

he of knowing them, as he would acknowledge again and again.

Sri Ramakrishna, when he saw Narendranath and heard him sing at Surendranath Mitra's home, had clearly seen *who* Narendra was, a knowledge that did not in the least alter in the four-and-a-half years during which a most extraordinary relationship would develop between the two. He asked Narendra to visit him at Dakshineswar. Since Narendra felt an inexplicable inner attraction to the man, he did.

At their very first meeting, Narendranath was alarmed, and returned home certain that the man whom his teacher Hastie and Ramachandra Datta had praised so highly as a mystic saint, was on the contrary just insane. How else could anybody behave in the way Sri Ramakrishna did with him? Vivekananda later described to Saradananda and to others what happened when Sri Ramakrishna took him inside a room and closed it. It is best to hear it in his voice.

...I thought he might perhaps give me some instructions in private. But what he said and did was beyond imagination. He suddenly caught hold of my hand and shed profuse tears of joy. Addressing me affectionately like one already familiar, he said: 'Is it proper that you should come so late? Should you not have once thought how I was waiting for you? Hearing continuously the idle talk of worldly people, my ears are about to be scorched. Not having anyone to whom to communicate my innermost feelings, I am about to burst.' And so he went on raving and weeping. The next moment he stood before me with folded palms, and showing me the regard due to a god, went on saying, 'I know, my lord, you are that ancient Rishi Nara, a part of Narayana, who has incarnated himself this time, to remove the miseries and sufferings of humanity.'

I was absolutely nonplussed and thought, 'Whom have I come to see? He is, as I see, completely insane. Why should he otherwise speak in this strain to me, who am really the son of Viswanath Datta?' However, I kept silent and the wonderful madman went on speaking whatever he liked.[23]

Swami Vivekananda then described how Sri Ramakrishna brought some sweets from an adjoining room and insisted on feeding him with his own hands. Then he caught hold of his hand and extracted from him a promise that he would visit again—and next time alone. That promise made, they came out of the room and joined others who had also come with Narendranath to see the saint of Dakshineswar. Continuing his narration of the events of that first visit, his mind sharp and clear, Swami Vivekananda said to Saradananda:

I went on observing him closely and could find no trace of madness in his deportment, conversation, or behaviour towards others. Impressed by his fine talk and ecstasy, I thought that he was truly a man of renunciation who had given up his all for God and practised personally what he professed.[24]

But Narendranath not only observed him closely, but also heard with the greatest attention what he began to say; and what he said, was in a tone of absolute certainty, just as Narendranath's mind was in a state of absolute doubt. Sri Ramakrishna said: 'God can be seen and spoken with, just as I am seeing you and speaking with you; but who wants to do so?...If any one is in truth equally anxious to

[23] Saradananda, *The Great Master*, Vol. II, p. 825.
[24] Ibid., Vol. II, pp. 825-26.

see Him and calls on Him with a longing heart, He certainly reveals Himself to him.'[25]

That Vivekananda put to Sri Ramakrishna also the question he had earlier asked Devendranath Tagore, 'Have you seen God?' is now a legend and invariably a part of all biographies. That does not seem to be a fact; that is, if we rely upon the narration of Mahendranath Gupta and of Swami Saradananda, both of whom knew Sri Ramakrishna and Vivekananda closely. Neither did Vivekananda say so. It may well be that Sri Ramakrishna would very often sense what was uppermost in a person's mind—and that agonizing question certainly was in Narendranath's—and then, without being specifically asked, answer it. But that is entirely a different statement. M's *The Gospel of Sri Ramakrishna* is full of the specific questions different people asked Sri Ramakrishna and his answers to them, and the discussions that followed, which M, listening to them, recorded. It doesn't seem that Narendranath's specific question to him 'Have you seen God?' was one of them. If I bring this up here, it is only to say that the truth must not be dissolved in legend: if it is, it does not stop with only one thing.

Even more important is the strange truth that we are often most sceptical about hearing what we most want to hear as an answer to the deepest yearning of our hearts. On all accounts, his own testimony most of all, that was the conflicting inner state of Narendra when he returned from his first visit to Sri Ramakrishna. Let us hear what he felt:

When I heard these words of his, the impression grew on me that it was not mere poetry or imagination couched in fine figures of

---

[25] Ibid., Vol. II, p. 826.

speech that he was expressing like other preachers of religion, but that he was speaking of something of which he had an immediate knowledge—of an attainment which had come to him by really renouncing everything for the sake of God, and calling on Him with all his mind.

Trying to harmonize these words with his behaviour towards me a little while previously, I remembered the examples of the monomaniacs mentioned by Abercrombie and other English philosophers, and came to the sure conclusion that he belonged to that class. Although I came to that conclusion, I could not forget the greatness of his wonderful renunciation for God. Speechless, I thought, 'Well, he may be mad, but it is indeed a rare soul alone in the world who could practise such renunciation. Yes, mad, but how pure! And what renunciation! He is truly worthy of respect, reverence and worship by the human heart.' Thinking thus, I bowed down at his feet, took leave of him and returned to Calcutta that day.[26]

Narendra's promise that he would visit again was kept, but not immediately. Saradananda tells us that Narendra visited Dakshineswar the second time most probably after a month. Meanwhile, Sri Ramakrishna was restless, and with an astonishing childlike innocence candidly said to Saradananda and a few other young disciples:

Afterwards, when he (Narendranath) left, there was such an eagerness in the heart, all the twenty-four hours of the day, to see him. It cannot be expressed in words. From time to time I felt excruciating pain, as if my heart was being wrung like a wet towel. Unable to control myself, I then went running to the Tamarisk trees in the north of the garden, where people generally

---

[26] Ibid.

do not go, and wept loudly, 'O my child! Come, I cannot remain without seeing you.' It was only after weeping a little thus that I could control myself. This happened continuously for six months.[27]

Narendra was even more alarmed, almost frightened, by what happened on his second visit to Sri Ramakrishna, we don't know exactly on which day. It is best to hear *him* describe what happened.

...I reached Dakshineswar at last and went direct to the Master's room. I saw him sitting alone, merged in himself, on the small bedstead placed near the bigger one. There was no one with him. No sooner had he seen me than he called me joyfully to him and made me sit at one end of the bedstead. I sat down but found him in a strange mood. He spoke indistinctly something to himself, looked steadfastly at me, and began slowly coming towards me. I thought another scene of lunacy was going to be enacted. Scarcely had I thought so when he came to me and placed his right foot on my body, and immediately I had a wonderful experience. I saw with my eyes open that all the things of the room together with the walls were rapidly whirling and receding into an unknown region and my I-ness together with the whole universe was, as it were, going to vanish in an all-devouring great void. I was then overwhelmed with a terrible fear. I knew that the destruction of I-ness was death, so I thought that death was before me, very near at hand. Unable to control myself, I cried out loudly, saying, 'Ah! What is it you have done to me? I have my parents, you know.' Laughing loudly at my words, he touched my chest with his hand and said, 'Let it then cease now. It need not be done all at once. It will come to pass in course of time.' I was amazed to

---

[27] Ibid., Vol. II, p. 824.

see how that extraordinary experience of mine vanished as quickly as it had come when he touched me in that manner and said those words. I came to the normal state and saw things inside and outside the room standing still as before.

Although it has taken so much time to describe the event, it actually happened in a much shorter time. It produced a great revolution in my mind.[28]

Whatever it was, it left Narendranath deeply disturbed. First he thought it was some kind of hypnotism, but deep within his heart there was the clear feeling that it was not that. Then he thought it was the case of a weaker will being overwhelmed by a stronger will. But his assessment of himself could not accept that explanation either.

I have been till now feeling proud of being very intelligent and possessed of great strength of mind. It could not be that I was charmed and made a puppet in his hands, as ordinary people are when they fall under the influence of some extraordinary man. I had never allowed any such influence to gain control over me; rather I was a hostile subject in so far as I had from the start come to the certain conclusion that he was a monomaniac. Why should I then have been suddenly caught up in that state? I pondered over it but could not come to any conclusion; there it remained in my heart, an unsolved problem of great import. I remembered the words of the great poet, 'There are more things in heaven and earth than are dreamt of in your philosophy.' I thought that this might be one such...From my boyhood I could never accept any conclusion about any person or proposition as final, unless it had been arrived at after proper observation and investigation, reasoning and argumentation. That nature of mine received a severe shock that day, which created anguish in my

---

[28] Ibid., Vol. II, pp. 842-43.

heart. As a result of this, there arose a firmer determination in my mind to understand thoroughly the nature and power of that wonderful person.[29]

It took Narendranath four years to understand thoroughly the nature and power of 'that wonderful person' Sri Ramakrishna. These were also the years, especially 1884 and 1885, during which he began to understand his own nature and power as well. But despite his sharp intellect and its uncompromising honesty, a fierce combination, it did not take him long to see the purity of that man's intoxication with God in which nothing was counterfeit, his childlike simplicity which was not fake, and his selfless love for him besides.

The ways in which Sri Ramakrishna often expressed his boundless love for Narendra embarrassed the young man. Once, when he had not seen him for some days, he turned up at his house and enquired where Narendra was. On being told that Narendra was studying in his room upstairs, a kind of attic, he climbed the stairs with some difficulty and burst into the room. There followed what was by then a familiar scene: tears of joy on seeing him, and going into a trance. On another occasion, a Sunday, rightly guessing that Narendra might be singing at the congregational prayers of the Brahmo Samaj, he turned up there, astonishing everybody with his unannounced visit, creating confusion moreover by going into a trance at the altar. Nobody there greeted him on his arrival. He was completely ignored. This had something to do with the inner politics of Brahmo Samaj that had meanwhile split

[29] Ibid., Vol. II, pp. 843-44.

into two, one faction believing it was under his influence
that elder leaders like Keshab Chandra Sen (1838–84)
had deviated. Somebody switched off the lights in the
prayer hall, creating a greater confusion. Narendra was
furious at that insult to Sri Ramakrishna; but also sensed
why he had come there in the first place—to see *him*. It
was with some difficulty that he escorted Sri Ramakrishna
out of the darkened prayer hall, got him into a carriage,
and brought him to Dakshineswar. 'It is impossible to
describe the pain I felt to see the Master thus ill-treated
on my account that day. Ah! How much did I scold him
for that action of his that day!' Narendra would later
say. 'But he! He neither felt hurt at the humiliation, nor
did he give ear to my words of reproach, supremely
satisfied as he was that he had me by his side.'[30] To
Narendra's frequent protests, 'Why do you do such
things?' he would remonstrate like an innocent child, 'I
can't help it!'

Sri Ramakrishna was quite aware that his
demonstrative love might appear to be absurd, at least
strange, to most people. He spoke about it to Swami
Saradananda, and to those young seekers who had
formed a close group around him: 'What will they think
on seeing that I, a man of such advanced age, am weeping
and panting so much for him? You, however, being my
own people, I don't feel ashamed in your presence. But
what will others think when they see this? But by no means
can I control myself.' Saradananda would later write: 'We
were speechless to see the Master's love for Narendra.
We thought Narendra must be a god-like person. Why

---

[30] Ibid., Vol. II, p. 870.

otherwise should the Master be so much attracted towards him?'[31]

'I want truth,' Narendranath would say passionately in his conversations with M.[32] Devotion to truth, regardless of the consequences, was his inheritance from his mother, Bhubaneswari Devi. It was with that inheritance deeply imprinted upon his mind, and his character moulded in it, that he had met Sri Ramakrishna. Deeply moved though he was by Sri Ramakrishna's selfless love for him, he was always truthful to him, withholding nothing of what he sincerely thought to be the truth as regards his 'visions of God in the form of the Divine Mother Kali'. He brought together the full force of Western psychology to suggest that they might be nothing more than his mental states, or, in one word, 'hallucinations'. He would bring together the even greater force of the Western agnostic philosophy, that God was both unknown and *unknowable*, and also the atheistic reasoning that there *was* no God. Sri Ramakrishna would listen attentively and sometimes get disturbed. He would then rush to the Divine Mother and ask Her whether his visions of Her, and his intoxication with his love for Her, were hallucinations, as Narendranath was saying they were. Reassured by Her that they were not hallucinations, indeed, were as real as everything that could be seen with physical eyes, he would return to Narendranath with a happy face and report to him the happy news. He would repeat the equally reassuring words of the Divine Mother, 'Let him say what he likes. He will come round one day.'

---

[31] Ibid., Vol. II, p. 857. For Saradananda's analysis of what he described as 'the extraordinary relation between the Master and Narendranath', see pp. 859–82.

[32] M—*The Gospel*, p. 957, entry dated Wednesday, 21 April 1886.

Narendranath would then cite Western logic rejecting anything as 'proof' when what is put forward as 'proof' is itself in serious question.

That begets the question: Why then did Narendranath go to Dakshineswar again and again, if he was bent on not accepting, without arguing, what the Master had to say. We have here the account of M to fall back on:

Narendra: At first I did not accept most of what the Master said. One day he asked me, 'Then why do you come here?' I replied, 'I come here to see you, not to listen to you.'

  M.: What did he say to that?

  Narendra: He was very much pleased.[33]

Sri Ramakrishna was, however, confidently expressing what he *knew* to be the truth about Narendranath, which was never affected by what Narendranath was honestly saying to him about *his* visions and trances. He knew that Narendra, one of the sages countless centuries ago, or Narayana Himself, was now born to renounce the world only to dedicate himself to it in the service of man, to renounce the limited only to embrace the limitless space of humanity. Many times he said that Narendra was *nitya-siddha*, or 'forever perfect'. Indeed, he never tired of praising Narendranath in most eloquent words, and took delight in his intellect and fearless truthfulness.

Narendranath's truthfulness, which endeared him even more to the saint of Dakshineswar, would later, in his days in America and England as the Swami Vivekananda, compel respect even of those to whom he didn't particularly endear himself. One day, Narendra came and told Sri

---

[33] Ibid., Narendranath's own account in conversation with M; entry dated 8 April 1887, p. 980.

Ramakrishna that he had eaten at a hotel what was considered forbidden food. He told him because he thought he owed it to him; so that, after knowing that fact, he was free not to touch him or let him touch the cup and the plate from which he drank water and ate. Sri Ramakrishna's unhesitating response was:

No blemish will affect you on that account. If anyone eats pork and beef but keeps his mind fixed on the Divine Lord, it is like taking the sacred Havishya; on the other hand, if anyone eats greens and vegetables but is immersed in worldly desires, it is not in any respect better than eating pork and beef. I don't consider it wrong on your part—this taking of forbidden food. But had any one of them (pointing to all others) come and told me so, I could not have even touched him.[34]

If one reads the discussions on the numerous religious and philosophical questions that took place in Sri Ramakrishna's room at Dakshineswar, in the contemporary record by Mahendranath Gupta, one is struck by how genuine they were. The atmosphere was always of honest inquiry, not merely of discourse flowing from a great Master. Sri Ramakrishna, not an intellectual in the ordinary sense, enjoyed the cut and thrust of serious intellectual argument. Saradananda, who was present during many of them, tells us that Sri Ramakrishna 'had never any liking for a person of a narrow intellect or for one devoid of it. Everyone heard him say: "You should be a devotee, it is true, but why should you, therefore, be a fool?"'[35] Or 'Don't be one sided and fanatical.'

[34] Saradananda, *The Great Master*, Vol. II, p. 872.
[35] Ibid., Vol. II, p. 775.

Of the numerous examples of genuine dialogue Sri Ramakrishna had with a variety of people, let us take this one, on 28 July 1885, at the house of Nanda Bose, an aristocrat of Calcutta. Nanda Bose asked him: 'But how can we obtain God's grace? Has He really the power to bestow grace?'

In answer, Sri Ramakrishna said (*smiling*):

I see. You think as the intellectuals do: one reaps the results of one's actions. Give up these ideas. The effect of karma wears away if one takes refuge in God. I prayed to the Divine Mother with flowers in my hand: 'Here, Mother, take Thy sin; here, take Thy virtue. I don't want either of these; give me only real bhakti. Here, Mother, take Thy good; here, take Thy bad. I don't want any of Thy good or bad; give me only real bhakti. Here, Mother, take Thy dharma; here, take Thy adharma. I don't want any of Thy dharma or adharma; give me only real bhakti. Here, Mother, take Thy knowledge; here, take Thy ignorance. I don't want any of Thy knowledge or ignorance; give me only real bhakti. Here, Mother, take Thy purity; here, take Thy impurity. Give me only real bhakti.'[36]

Nanda Bose continued with his questioning, asking the very question that had been discussed in most schools of Indian philosophy throughout its history, with different answers to it. But in what Sri Ramakrishna said on that day to Nanda, the main point was not, though it seemed to be, whether God, if one took refuge in Him, could, or would, suspend the law of karma. He said with assurance

---

[36] M—*The Gospel*, entry dated Tuesday, 28 July 1885, p. 800; see also p. 762.

that He could and would. But after saying that, he went very much further, suddenly floating on to a different plane altogether. The main point in what he said was that one should transcend the workings of the opposites, sin–virtue, good–bad, dharma–adharma, knowledge–ignorance, purity–impurity, and move to a different plane of consciousness—that of bhakti. Our mind works mostly within these opposites, from which arise implacable judgements and from them, violence.

To Sri Ramakrishna, bhakti had a much deeper meaning than what it is generally believed to be. Narendranath understood that deeper meaning, and perhaps he was the only one there to do so.[37] Bhakti, not as seeking one's own salvation but as service of mankind; not in the self-virtuous attitude of 'doing good' to others, but awakening each person to his or her potential divinity beyond the play of the opposites, a consciousness in which the opposites are themselves dissolved. Bhakti is not some emotional nonsense. Nor is shedding tears on chanting and hearing the name of Lord Vishnu any sign of deep spirituality. The emotional froth of bhakti troubled Narendranath deeply, and he honestly expressed his contempt for any approach to God that lacked manliness, which the outward expressions of the Vaishnava-bhakti seemed to do. To Sri Ramakrishna, love of God meant putting oneself in the service of the suffering *other*. That would be another inheritance he would pass on to the man who was to become Swami Vivekananda. Once, in the presence of Narendranath, Sri Ramakrishna talked of the essence of Vaishnava faith, and 'compassion

---

[37] These were Swami Saradananda's words: 'It was also seen that no one could so correctly understand and express, as Narendra did, the import of the Master's wise words and extraordinary actions.' *The Great Master*, Vol. II, p. 939.

for all beings' as its integral part. Then, as a crucial postscript to his teachings, Sri Ramakrishna said, 'Talk of compassion for beings! Insignificant creatures that you are, how can you show compassion to beings? Who are you to show compassion? You wretch, who are you to bestow it? No, no; it is not compassion to Jivas, but service to them as Siva.'[38] Saradananda recounts Narendranath telling him after they emerged from Sri Ramakrishna's room:

Ah what a wonderful light have I got today from the Master's words! What a new and attractive Gospel have we received today through those words of his, wherein a synthesis has been effected of sweet devotion to the Lord with Vedantic knowledge, which is generally regarded as dry, austere and lacking in sympathy with the sufferings of others. In order to attain the non-dual knowledge, we have been told so long that one should have to renounce the world and the company of men altogether, and retire to the forest, and mercilessly uproot and throw away love, devotion and other soft and tender emotions from the heart.

...an attitude which produced in men a sort of antipathy towards society and often led them away from the true spiritual path. But from what the Master in ecstasy said today, it is gathered that the Vedanta of the forest can be brought to human habitation, and that it can be applied in practice to the work-a-day world.

Let man do everything he is doing; there is no harm in that; it is sufficient for him, first, to be fully convinced that it is God who is manifested before him as the universe and all the beings in it. Those with whom he comes in contact every moment of his life, whom he loves, respects and honours, and to whom his sympathy and kindness flow, are all His parts, are all He Himself. If he can thus look upon all the persons of the world as Siva, how can there be an occasion for him to regard himself as superior to

---

[38] Ibid., Vol. II, p. 939.

them or cherish anger and hatred for them or an arrogant attitude towards them, or even to be kind to them? Thus serving the Jivas as Siva, he will have his heart purified and be convinced in a short time that he himself is also a part of God, the Bliss Absolute, the eternally pure, wakeful and free Being.[39]

Narendranath was not merely interpreting the real meaning of what Sri Ramakrishna had said. It had kindled in him a fire that would burn till his dying day. He declared to Saradananda: 'If the divine Lord ever grants me an opportunity, I'll proclaim everywhere in the world this wonderful truth I have heard today. I will preach this truth to the learned and the ignorant, to the rich and the poor, to the Brahmana and the Chandala.'[40] Ironically, as we will see later, he would encounter not a little resistance from his brother-disciples of Sri Ramakrishna when, as Swami Vivekananda, he would proclaim that wonderful truth to *them* as well.

An equally wonderful truth that Sri Ramakrishna proclaimed, not by learned theological discourse but by his life, was that God is not '*there*' but '*here*'. As long as a man feels that God is 'there', he is ignorant. But he attains Knowledge when he feels that God is 'here': 'What a man seeks is very near him. Still he wanders about from place to place.' This he illustrated with the parable of the man who woke up his neighbour in the dead of night, asking for some fire to light charcoal to prepare the smoke

[39] Ibid., Vol. II, pp. 939-40. For the sake of more focussed reading, I have broken into three paragraphs what, in the original, is in one paragraph.
[40] Ibid., Vol. II, pp. 940-41.

he desperately needed, and the neighbour answering, 'Why, you have a lighted lantern in your hand!'[41]

It was in 1884, the year of his father's death and other disasters for the family, that Narendranath came to the definite view that God was neither 'here' nor 'there'. God just didn't exist. This conclusion of his at that time was as honest as his yearning for God was full of restless passion. Early in March that year he came to Dakshineswar. Sri Ramakrishna had a few days earlier broken his arm. Though he was in pain, his arm in splint and bandage, he was nevertheless talking with several devotees around him. Narendra was one of them. The Master said: 'The joys and sorrows of the body are inevitable. Look at Narendra. His father is dead, and his people have been put to great suffering. He can't find any way out of it. God places one sometimes in happiness and sometimes in misery.' [42]

Casting 'an affectionate glance at his beloved disciple', it seemed that Sri Ramakrishna was not particularly pleased with God, first for putting Narendra in that misery and then not helping him. Indeed, he spoke as if 'piqued'.[43] Somebody there said, 'God will be gracious to Narendra,' and Sri Ramakrishna quickly retorted, 'But when?' A quick brief dialogue followed. Narendra said, 'I am now studying the views of the atheists.' To which the Master replied, 'There are two doctrines: the existence and the non-existence of God. Why don't you accept the first?'[44]

Narendra found no rational ground for doing that. Following his father's death, his bitter acquaintance with

---

[41] M—The Gospel, entry dated Saturday, 5 April 1884, p. 377.
[42] Ibid., entry dated Sunday, 2 March 1884, p. 343.
[43] Ibid., in the same entry as mentioned above, p. 347.
[44] Ibid., p. 347.

human material had made him even less inclined to believe that God existed and, even if He did, that He was merciful. He gave expression, honestly and fearlessly, to his disbelief in a merciful God, which was not a product of his personal situation alone. Rather, he was asking, on behalf of all created beings, as it were, 'Whence has so much of evil come in the creation of a benign Creator? Why is there so much of calamity in the kingdom of one who is all bliss?' Saradananda quoted Narendra's own description of his state of mind then.

It was against my nature to do something and conceal it from others. Nor could I, from my childhood, conceal, out of fear or from any other motive, even the least shade of thought, let alone my actions. Was it, therefore, surprising that I should, in the mood that seized me then, go aggressively forward to prove to the people that God did not exist, and that even if He did, there was no need to call on Him, for it was futile to do so.[45]

The result was, Narendra continued, people thought he had become an atheist; and since the description of a person as an 'atheist' got invariably connected with his being immoral, meaning drinking and being sexually wayward, predictably the rumour spread that he was also visiting places of disrepute, namely, brothels—*if* an atheist, *then* the other as well. This simple equation was so firmly established in the minds of most people that even if there was no evidence whatsoever of sexual waywardness, it could be inferred about a person advocating atheism.

---

[45] Saradananda, *The Great Master*, Vol. II, p. 924.

Consequently, my heart, which had never been too docile from childhood, became steeled all the more on account of such false calumny. Even unasked, I was publicly telling one and all that not only had I no objection to anybody's drinking wine or going to a brothel with a view to forgetting his hard lot in this world of pain and misery, if he could feel happy thereby, but that I would myself do likewise the very day I was perfectly convinced of becoming happy for a moment like them by doing so, and that I would not retract my steps for fear of anybody.[46]

It did not take long for the rumour to reach Dakshineswar. Narendranath was worried about that, as much as he was worried about the effect it would have upon his mother. But he said to himself that if, like other ordinary men, Sri Ramakrishna believed in it, why should he worry? When the rumour about Narendranath's 'fall' was conveyed to Sri Ramakrishna, he told the person who brought it that he didn't believe a syllable of it; and if that person were again to say any such thing about Narendra, he would find that person's presence unbearable. This time, Sri Ramakrishna did not run to the Divine Mother to ask Her whether what was being said about his Narendra was true; as he had done on a previous occasion, to ask whether it was true, as Narendra said, that his visions of Her might be hallucinations.

Unable to find a satisfactory secure job that would provide his family with means of dignified subsistence, nor able to bear their suffering any more, which meant his own as well, Narendra decided to request Sri Ramakrishna to intercede on his behalf with the Divine Mother to put an

---

[46] Ibid., Vol. II, pp. 924-25

end to his misery. The scene that followed is quite well known: Sri Ramakrishna said to Narendra that he had never made any personal request to the Divine Mother, either for himself or for anyone else; so, why didn't he make that appeal to Her himself? Narendra did. But standing in front of the image of Kali, the Divine Mother, he passed into a vast consciousness where all distinctions were lost. *Everything* there appeared to him to be permeated with God. He came back with a look of ineffable bliss on his face. 'Did you appeal to the Divine Mother?' Sri Ramakrishna asked him, somewhat teasingly. 'Oh, I forgot,' Narendra answered with the innocence of a child. 'Then, go again.' And again he went—twice more. He felt the same vastness of consciousness in which everything had merged. There was the same question on his return; and the same answer, 'Oh, I forgot!' This experience would remain a singularly important part of the life of Swami Vivekananda, surfacing in many different ways, at many different levels. But that would not drown him in some 'sentimental nonsense of bhakti', 'often a mask for the weakness of character', his favourite phrases. Rather, from that all-encompassing consciousness he would feel the sufferings of others, and dedicate his life to removing them as far as he could. That was 'the work' to which Sri Ramakrishna would yoke him.

Narendra's experience was similar to the one that Sri Ramakrishna had had much earlier, as a priest in Rani Rasmani's Kali temple. In Ramakrishna's words, as recorded by M: 'The Divine Mother revealed to me in the Kali temple that it was She who had become everything. She showed me that everything was full of Consciousness. The image was Consciousness, the altar was Consciousness, the water-vessels were Consciousness, the door-still was Consciousness, the marble floor was Consciousness—all was Consciousness.'[47] That was the *sat-chit*, 'Existence-Consciousness' part; the integral third, *ananda*, 'Bliss', followed: 'I found everything inside the room soaked, as it were, in Bliss—the Bliss of Satchidananda. I saw a wicked man in front of the Kali temple; but in him also I saw the Power of the Divine Mother vibrating.'[48]

The priest then did something that was, to all ordinary eyes, scandalous for a priest to do—he fed a cat the food meant as offering to the deity.

That was why I fed a cat with the food that was to be offered to the Divine Mother. I clearly perceived that the Divine Mother Herself had become everything—even the cat. The manager of the temple garden wrote to Mathur Babu saying that I was feeding the cat with the offering intended for the Divine Mother. But Mathur Babu had insight into the state of my mind. He wrote back to the manager, 'Let him do whatever he likes. You must not say anything to him.'[49]

Neither did anyone of Narendra's family say anything to Narendra, despite their anxiety and perhaps disapproval of his spending long hours at Dakshineswar. But whatever his joy, or even bliss, Narendranath Datta also knew that he had an examination to pass for his Bachelor's degree; and for that, *sat-chit-ananda* alone would not do. But, given his capacity to comprehend even the most difficult

---

[47] *M—The Gospel*, entry dated Sunday, 16 December 1883, p. 290.
[48] Ibid., p. 291.
[49] Ibid.

subject quickly, and his immense power of concentration, that was nothing to worry about. He passed his examination with perfect ease. Then he enrolled himself for a degree in law, but did not take the final examination.

***

It would be a mistake to think that the atmosphere at Dakshineswar was that of devotees coming there just to listen to great teachings from a great Master, an assembly of people with dreadfully serious faces and no laughter. Yet, that is the image most people now have. And that is because, content with legend and images, they do not *meet* Sri Ramakrishna contemporaneously, when so much is available, in the contemporary records of his life, to enable them to do so. He remains a remote figure, only to be worshipped. But to those who came to see him—among them some eminent names in the Bengal of that time, like Keshab Chandra Sen and Girish Chandra Ghosh—he was an intimate person, loving and full of concern for others. Girish Chandra Ghosh (1844–1912) was a dramatist, poet, unabashedly a man of the world, given to heavy drinking, but utterly honest and sincere. Several other eminent persons came too. The conversations they had with Sri Ramakrishna were full of wit and good humour on both sides. Neither the visitors nor the man they visited had grim faces because they were discussing spirituality. Between them, very often, a loving relationship full of delightful banter grew, as in the case of Keshab and Girish. Moreover, Sri Ramakrishna visited other people in their homes quite as often as they visited him at Dakshineswar. His first visit to Ishwar Chandra Vidyasagar (1820–91), the famous educationist, social reformer and philanthropist, was quite an event, and equally interesting were the impressions they had of each other, which they expressed afterwards.[50] Unlike present-day gurus, Sri Ramakrishna was the first to greet with folded palms anyone who came to see him; and there was in him not a trace of self-importance, so visible in a great many gurus today. His apostle Swami Vivekananda would inherit these qualities of his Master.

It was not only eminent men, known for their high education and sophistication, who came to see Sri Ramakrishna, but also hundreds of ordinary men and women, Muslims, Christians, Sikhs, and persons of other faiths, many of them poor but earnest. To them, he was not a remote figure; he touched their hearts as much by the sincerity of his loving manners as by his teachings. And his teachings had universal meaning; he was no sectarian saint. It is of utmost importance to hear what he was saying to them; more important now than ever before, for now sectarian hatred and violence, themselves deadly, have acquired deadly weapons as well.

But I say that we are all calling on the same God. Jealousy and malice need not be. What I mean is that dogmatism is not good. It is not good to feel that my religion is alone true and other religions are false. The correct attitude is this: My religion is right, but I do not know whether other religions are right or wrong, true or false. I say this because one cannot know the true nature of God unless one realizes Him...

Hindus, Mussulmans, Christians, Saktas, Saivas, Vaishnavas, the Brahmajnanis of the time of rishis, and you, the Brahmajnanis of modern times, all seek the same object.

---

[50] For the details of his first visit on 5 August 1882, see M—*The Gospel*, entry dated 5 August 1882, pp. 25–37.

Do you know what the truth is? God has made different religions to suit different aspirants, times and countries. All doctrines are only so many paths; but a path is by no means God Himself. Indeed, one can reach God if one follows any of the paths with whole-hearted devotion. Suppose there are errors in the religion that one has accepted; if one is sincere and earnest, then God Himself will correct those errors.

If there are errors in other religions, that is none of our business. God, to whom the world belongs, takes care of that.

But dogmatism is not good. You have no doubt heard the story of the chameleon. A man entered a wood and saw a chameleon on a tree. He reported to his friends, 'I have seen a red lizard.' He was firmly convinced that it was nothing but red. Another person, after visiting the tree said, 'I have seen a green lizard.' He was firmly convinced that it was nothing but green. But the man who lived under the tree said: 'What both of you have said is true. But the fact is that the creature is sometimes red, sometimes green, sometimes yellow, and sometimes has no colour at all.'[51]

It was upon this universalism of Sri Ramakrishna, and the attitudes and feelings towards others that follow from it, that Swami Vivekananda would build the edifice of his mission both in India and the West. Sectarian arrogance and hatred were no less in India, perhaps even more, than they were in the West. The worshippers of Shiva and Vishnu have been at each other's throats for centuries; the Jainas were persecuted in some southern kingdoms for quite as long; the followers of Ramanuja and Shankara called each other names, as they do even now, although in

---

[51] Ibid., entry dated Friday, 26 September 1884, pp. 519-20.

subdued tones. Sri Ramakrishna was addressing *them* as much as he was addressing Muslims and Christians. And so would Swami Vivekananda, if only in more striking notes.

Sri Ramakrishna fell ill towards the end of April 1885. It began with his having a sore in his throat and he talked about it to M: 'I'm feeling rather uneasy. I have a sore in my throat. I suffer very much during the early hours of the morning.'[52] He was placed under the medical care of Dr Mahendra Lal Sarkar, one of the eminent doctors of Calcutta, a homeopath, who naturally consulted another doctor. By October 1885, the doctors had definitely diagnosed Sri Ramakrishna's illness as cancer.[53] Because he could not have the medical attention or nursing that his condition required at Dakshineswar, a long distance away from Calcutta where all his young disciples, including Narendranath, lived with their families, a suitable place in Calcutta had to be found and rented for him. Not happy with the place to which he was shifted first, for a while he moved to the house of Balaram Bose (1842–90), another ardent devotee who figures prominently in the story of Sri Ramakrishna's life. Soon thereafter a garden-house was rented at Shyampukur; and later, even a more spacious and comfortable garden-house at Cossipore or Kasipur.[54] Sri Ramakrishna moved there on 11 December 1885. His young disciples, who would, not long thereafter, form a monastic Order in his name, nursed him day and

---

[52] Ibid., entry dated Friday, 24 April 1885, p. 739.

[53] Ibid., entry dated 18 October 1885, p. 834.

[54] For the details of financing the rent of those two places in succession, of running the household, and the expenses of the treatment and other things, see Saradananda, *The Great Master*, Vol. II, Chapters XI–XIII, pp. 954–1021.

night. Narendranath was the leader of the loving, devoted nursing team.

Sri Sarada Devi moved from her room in the Nahabatkhana at Dakshineswar to the garden-house at Shyampukur and then to Cossipore, to take care of the diet prescribed for her husband. That undoubtedly required some major adjustments on her part. At Dakshineswar she had lived more or less in seclusion, being exceptionally shy. The male devotees of Sri Ramakrishna had hardly ever seen her, except for one or two whom Sri Ramakrishna had introduced to her. Now, in nursing her husband, she would have to be with all those nursing him likewise and 'live the whole day in the midst of menfolk in that house'.[55] She made those adjustments quickly and gracefully.

Neither Shyampukur nor Cossipore saw any difference in what Sri Ramakrishna's life had been at Dakshineswar. Neither for that matter his cancer of the throat, although at times he was in great pain. It was at these two places that a strong bonding took place among his young disciples, their different temperaments notwithstanding; and it was there, in the last year of his life, that Sri Ramakrishna carefully prepared them for a life of renunciation. That was one ideal he never tired of preaching; and on that there were endless discussions, particularly because many of those who sincerely revered him were householders. The substance of his teachings was: one can see God; for that, purity of the mind is necessary; which can come

---

[55] The testimony of Swami Saradananda, *The Great Master*, Vol. II, pp. 965–66, 970.

only with renouncing 'woman' and 'gold', the recurrent words in Sri Ramakrishna's vocabulary.[56]

It was during this period, 1885–86, that five events took place in Narendranath's life that would reverberate in him ever afterwards as Swami Vivekananda: his clear vision about the purpose of his life; his journey to Bodh Gaya, the place of the Buddha's Enlightenment, and there his deeply stirred feelings for the Buddha;[57] his experience of *nirvikalpa-samadhi*, the experience of the Absolute he had been yearning for, from which Sri Ramakrishna pulled him away saying, 'You have work to do'; Sri Ramakrishna transmitting, as it were, all his spiritual energies to him, and then saying, 'Now nothing is left with me; I have given you my all, I am now just a faqir, a penniless beggar'; and, finally, his renunciation, like that of his grandfather Durgaprasad many years earlier. All these, each a single event at the time of its happening, and each in itself an overwhelming experience, together had a mystic inner unity; but to the one experiencing each successively, that inner coherence would be known only much later. They are all mentioned in the standard biographies of Swami Vivekananda.

---

[56] Swami Nikhilananda contends that by 'woman' and 'gold', *kamini-kanchana*, Sri Ramakrishna meant only 'lust' and 'greed'. See his explanation in M—*The Gospel*, p. 6, *fn* 2. Even a quick reading of M—*The Gospel* will show that his explanation does not hold. By 'woman' Sri Ramakrishna clearly meant woman as a physical being, not just metaphorically as 'lust'. At another time he had said, 'Just see the bewitching power of women! I mean the women who are the embodiments of avidya, the power of delusion. They fool men, as it were. They take away their inner substance. When I see a man and woman sitting together, I say to myself, "Alas, they are done for!"', M—*The Gospel*, entry dated 12 April 1885, p. 725.

[57] This was at the beginning of April 1886. Tarak and Kali (later Swami Shivananda and Swami Abhedananda respectively) accompanied him.

What is left out from them all, as far as I know, is Bhubaneswari Devi's visit to Sri Ramakrishna at Cossipore, which must have become known at that time, and which is by no means an insignificant detail. Vivekananda's youngest brother, Bhupendranath, described that visit in the following words:

Due to Ramakrishna's illness, however, he (Narendra) often stayed at Cossipore and frequently absented himself from home. On account of this continued absence mother got upset and went to Cossipore to bring him back. She took the writer with her who was then only six years old. The mother and the boy were sent upstairs and ushered before the ailing Ramakrishna. In the midst of the large room he was sitting on his bed in a half-reclining position with his back resting on a big pillow. He looked at both of us and said to mother: 'The doctor has advised me not to speak. But I must speak to you. It is good that you have come. Take Naren back with you. Girish and others donned him in sannyasi's clothes. But I exclaimed—How is that? You have a widowed mother and an infant brother to look after. It is not for you to be a sannyasi!' Thereupon Narendranath accompanied mother and the writer on their way home. In the carriage, mother related to him what Ramakrishna had told her. Narendranath answered: 'He (Ramakrishna) tells the thief to steal but warns the householder at the same time.' (A Bengali idiom which means running with the hare and chasing with the hound.) On the way home, Narendranath got down at Bagbazar on the pretext of some urgent piece of work.[58]

Since this quotation cannot be concluded here without doing injury to the truth, the related part must be mentioned

---

[58] Bhupendranath Datta, *Swami Vivekananda: Patriot-Prophet*, p. 90. In another context, p. 91, he adds, 'Here it must be said that the writer heard all this from his mother when he grew older.' That applies naturally to this event as well.

too, if only briefly. According to Vivekananda's testimony, Sri Ramakrishna was somewhat alarmed when he travelled with him one day from Calcutta to Dakshineswar with the intention of telling him that he had decided to respond to what he now knew was his destiny. He had decided to renounce the world, for which he had even set a date in his mind. But he did not *say* any of that to the Master; he didn't have to. Sri Ramakrishna knew, and was immensely pleased; for he knew also that, through renunciation, Narendranath had an even greater destiny to fulfil. Then, surprisingly, Sri Ramakrishna said to him, 'Know that you have come to the world for Mother's work: you can never live a worldly life. *But remain in your family for my sake as long as I live.*'[59] (*Here* the emphasis is mine, but it was his emphasis.) 'Saying so,' Vivekananda continued his narration of the event, 'the Master immediately began shedding tears again, his voice choked with emotion.' 'That is because Sri Ramakrishna seemed to be afraid lest Narendra should leave him,' M recorded.[60] Or else the promise asked should have been 'you shall not renounce as long as you have not provided your widowed mother and young brothers with means for a dignified living'. It is true that on one or two occasions when Narendra insisted on his helping him to have the experience of *nirvikalpa-samadhi*, Sri Ramakrishna had said, 'Why don't you settle your family affairs first and then come to me? You will get everything.'[61] But he was also saying repeatedly and with great emphasis that one does

---

[59] Vivekananda's testimony quoted at length in Saradananda, *The Great Master*, Vol. 2, p. 927; read pp. 926-27.

[60] *M—The Gospel*, entry dated Sunday, 1 March 1885, p. 686.

[61] Ibid., entry dated Monday, 4 January 1886, p. 928.

not renounce *after* making calculations as regards one's family problems. That is what he had said to Narendra directly on 27 October 1885. 'But a man who feels intense renunciation within doesn't calculate that way. He doesn't say to himself, "I shall first make an arrangement for the family and then practice sadhana." No, he doesn't feel that way if he has developed intense dispassion.'[62] To say both things simultaneously had seemed to Narendranath like 'asking the thief to steal and warning the householder at the same time'.

Ironically, some years later, his spiritual daughter, Sister Nivedita, would, with equal sense of puzzlement, feel the same about Swami Vivekananda on what appeared to Nivedita the inseparable questions of 'man-making' and 'nation-making'. The Swami was talking passionately of his country and of his people, of 'man-making', but was shying away from the question of 'nation-making', which meant the politics of Indian nationalism and struggle to obtain freedom from British rule.

* * *

It may startle most people to hear that a Sri Ramakrishna, too, could feel 'very depressed', as he did one day at Dakshineswar; and that there came a point in his life when, according to his own testimony, he had wanted to commit suicide. These had much to do with Hriday, his nephew, who for many years was his personal attendant and closest to him. They were more or less of the same age and had been close since their childhood. Hridayram Mukhopadhyaya was the son of Sri Ramakrishna's cousin Hemangini Devi.

---

[62] Ibid., entry dated Tuesday, 27 October 1885, p. 887.

With a view to improving his financial prospects, he came to Dakshineswar, where his uncle was already a priest in the Kali temple of Rani Rasmani. He soon found a job as priest first in the nearby Radha–Govinda temple and was then shifted to the main Kali temple to assist Sri Ramakrishna. He became as devoted to his uncle as to the Divine Mother, and began to take care of him in every way. He attended upon Sri Ramakrishna when the latter began his journey into different faiths. In 1881, he was dismissed for doing something the owners of the estate thought was unacceptable conduct and was even forbidden to enter the estate. On 19 August 1883, M recorded Sri Ramakrishna telling him:

You see I am very much depressed today. Hriday has written (to) me that he is very ill. Why should I feel dejected about it? Is it because of maya or daya?' M could not find suitable words for a reply, and remained silent. The Master continued: 'Do you know what maya is? It is attachment to relatives—parents, brother and sister, wife and children, nephew and niece. Daya means love for all created beings. Now what is this, my feeling about Hriday? Is it maya or daya? But Hriday did so much for me—he served me whole-heartedly and nursed me when I was ill. But later he tormented me also. The torment became so unbearable that once I was about to commit suicide by jumping into the Ganges from the top of the embankment. But he did much to serve me. Now my mind will be at rest if he gets some money. But whom shall I ask for it? Who likes to speak about such things to our rich visitors?[63]

---

[63] M—*The Gospel*, pp. 214-15.

When a couple of devotees arrived in the afternoon and asked him if he was well, Sri Ramakrishna replied, 'Yes, I am physically well, but a little troubled in mind,' but did not speak of what was troubling him.[64] A little more than a year later, Hriday came and sent word from where he was—outside the estate—that he wanted to see Sri Ramakrishna desperately. 'I shall have to see Hriday,' Sri Ramakrishna said, and, accompanied by M, went to the place where the nephew was standing.[65] Seeing how very troubled Hriday was, Sri Ramakrishna cried. Thereafter he narrated to M more details of how Hriday, serving him, had also tormented him:

He tormented me as much as he served me. When my stomach trouble had reduced my body to a couple of bones and I couldn't eat anything, he said to me one day: 'Look at me—how well I eat! You have just taken a fancy that you can't eat.' Again he said: 'You are a fool! If I weren't living with you, where would your profession of holiness be?' One day he tormented me so much that I stood on the embankment ready to give up my body by jumping into the Ganges, which was then at flood-tide.[66]

M became speechless at these words of the Master. For such a man he had shed tears a few minutes before! Sri Ramakrishna continued:

Well, he served me a great deal; then why should he have fallen on such evil days? He took care of me like a parent bringing up a child. As for me, I would remain unconscious of the world day

---

[64] Ibid., p. 215.
[65] For the conversation between Hriday and his uncle, see Ibid., entry dated Sunday, 26 October 1884, p. 612.
[66] Ibid., p. 612.

and night. Besides, I was ill for a long time. I was completely at his mercy.[67]

This relationship between Sri Ramakrishna and Hridayram, between an uncle and a nephew, can be studied at many levels and many different conclusions arrived at. It could be looked at as another instance of the all-too-familiar power relationship, but in the case of Hriday it was not that alone.[68] It strengthens the view that nothing can be given and received unless what is given is in one measure or another not already present in the one who receives. Enlightenment cannot be poured into an empty vessel. Whatever it was, Sri Ramakrishna was a living example of a man capable of feeling the sorrow of one who had tormented him. This was another inheritance Narendranath would receive and live it in his life as Swami Vivekananda. For all four who were close to him and supported him greatly in his earlier days in the West, and who later turned against him, indeed, turned upon him, he had only love and blessing.

Sri Ramakrishna had once said:

The jnani experiences God-consciousness within himself; it is like upper Ganges, flowing only in one direction. To him the whole universe is illusory, like a dream; he is always established in the

---

[67] Ibid., pp. 612-13. See also p. 685, entry dated Sunday, 1 March 1885.
[68] One should salute Swami Saradananda, who knew Hriday, for giving us an honest portrait of him. See The Great Master, Vol. 1, pp. 145–48. His conclusion about Hriday: 'It is, however, true that but for Hriday, it would have been impossible for him to keep body and soul together during that period. Therefore his name remains eternally connected with the life of Sri Ramakrishna; and he deserves our heartfelt homage for ever.' p. 146.

Reality of Self. But with the lover of God the case is different. His feeling does not flow only in one direction. He feels both the ebb-tide and the flood-tide of divine emotion. He laughs and weeps and dances and sings in the ecstasy of God. The lover of God likes to sport with Him. In the Ocean of God-consciousness, he sometimes swims, sometimes goes down, and sometimes rises to the surface.[69]

A lover of God, Sri Ramakrishna laughed and wept and danced and sang in the ecstasy of God. Narendranath was a close witness of a life lived in divine emotion even when struck with deadly cancer. And that, *a living example* and not just an anthology of the great sayings of a great Master, was another great inheritance Narendranath would carry throughout his life.

But that was not all that Sri Ramakrishna did. He showed in his conduct, and in his teachings equally, that to the one floating in 'the Ocean of God-consciousness', distinctions of caste and creed vanish. Rituals drop off. The tyranny of the opposites ends. Whatever limits, and is limited, dissolves; and fears of all kinds are overcome in that freedom. He banished from his spiritual vocabulary the word 'sin'. On feeling the oneness of all that exists, expanding oneself in the consciousness that fills the universe, the one floating in 'the Ocean of God-consciousness' danced the loving dance of service to others.[70] That is what Swami Vivekananda would do.

By his childlike conduct Sri Ramakrishna showed yet another thing—*that 'God-consciousness' does not exclude fun and laughter*. That enchanted Narendranath, given his

---

[69] M—*The Gospel*, entry dated 19 August 1883, p. 217.
[70] Each of these teachings of Sri Ramakrishna, not in words alone but in his life as well, can be gathered from a study of M—*The Gospel*.

own joyous nature. It would enchant all those in America
who would come to know Swami Vivekananda intimately.
One day, Sri Ramakrishna perfectly imitated a *kirtani*, a
female singer of devotional songs, in pointing out how
the minds of most people were still on worldly things even
while telling their beads or bathing for salvation in the
river Ganga. It was so perfect that everyone present
rolled with laughter, particularly the younger ones.

The kirtani is dressed lavishly and covered with ornaments. She
sings, standing on the floor, a coloured kerchief in her hand.
Now and then she coughs to draw people's attention and blows her
nose, raising her nose-ring. When a respectable gentleman enters
the room, she welcomes him with appropriate words, still continuing
her song. Now and then she pulls her sari from her arms to show
off her jewels.

The devotees were convulsed with laughter at this mimicry
of Sri Ramakrishna. Paltu rolled on the ground. Pointing to him,
the Master said to M: 'Look at that child! He is rolling with laughter.'
He said to Paltu with a smile: 'Don't report this to your father, or
he will lose the little respect he has for me. You see, he is an
"Englishman".'[71]

Sri Ramakrishna loved the company of young people who
came to see him; for, as he said, their minds were fresh,
uncorrupted, innocent, and pure.

What Sri Ramakrishna had done at the beginning of his
career as a priest in the Kali temple built by Rani Rasmani
was, however, no mime. Everyone was aghast. The Rani
came to the temple to worship, all her staff in attendance,

---

[71] Ibid., entry dated Saturday, 7 March 1885, p. 692.

standing at a respectful distance. The priest started the
rituals of worship and the Rani, sitting on the floor in front
of the deity, seemed to be in meditation. Then suddenly
the priest interrupted the rituals, came closer to the Rani
and gently struck her cheeks with the palm of his hand,
saying, 'That thought, *here also*!' Shocked, the staff
moved threateningly to remove the young priest, but Rani
Rasmani sternly indicated to them to hold back. She quickly
understood that she was rightly being chastised. Sitting
in front of the Divine Mother, her hand moving on her
rosary, her eyes closed seemingly in meditation, she was
thinking of some lawsuits and some other business
concerning her vast estate. Hence the chastisement: 'That
thought, *here also*!' She bowed in sincere humility, the
worship was completed, and she left, one can imagine,
with joy in her heart that the Divine Mother could have
sent her no better priest than this young lad Gadadhar
Chattopadhyaya, who was no ordinary priest.

***

Between the doctor, Dr Mahendra Lal Sarkar, and the
patient, Sri Ramakrishna, a delightful relationship, which
is a beautiful story in itself, developed. It cannot be described
here in any detail.[72] Not given to demonstrating his feelings,
the doctor came to love his patient. He did not believe
that his patient was an incarnation of God, as the young
devotees were solemnly saying, but loved and revered
him all the same. The one was no prerequisite for the other.
After he had examined him, he would stay to hear what

---

[72] For that, the reader must turn both to *M—The Gospel* and *The
Great Master*.

he was teaching. Equally often the doctor would play with the patient. After giving him two globules of medicine one day, he said to Sri Ramakrishna, 'I am giving you these two globules: one is Purusha and the other is Prakriti.'[73] And everybody laughed. On another day, Girish Ghosh said to Dr Sarkar with a somewhat mischievous smile, 'You have already spent three or four hours here. What about your patients?' And the doctor replied, 'Well, my practice and patients! I shall lose everything on account of your paramahamsa!'[74] Everybody laughed; the paramahamsa chuckled, with a smile in his eyes. He knew that that remark could come only from a person who loved, without demonstrating his emotions overmuch.

One day, the doctor said to him, 'I was much worried about you last night at three o'clock. It was raining. I said to myself, "Who knows whether or not the doors and windows of his room are shut?"'[75] On hearing this, the patient felt very touched. On another occasion, when M gave a brief discourse to him on something, the doctor only asked, 'What arrangements have you made about his being nursed?'[76] Sri Ramakrishna came to love his physician and described him as 'a deep soul'; but that did not prevent him from complaining against him. When another doctor was examining his throat, the patient— referring to Dr Sarkar who was standing nearby—said to the other doctor with the charming petulance of a child, 'He is a villain! He pressed my tongue as if I were a cow!'

[73] Ibid., entry dated 18 October 1885, p. 841.
[74] Ibid., entry dated 22 October 1885, p. 854.
[75] Ibid., entry dated Friday, 23 October 1885, p. 856.
[76] Ibid., entry dated Monday, 26 October 1885, p.879.

'He didn't hurt you purposely,' the other doctor said. 'No, he pressed the tongue to make a thorough examination.'[77]

Often serious dialogues took place between the doctor and the patient, once on the classic question whether God could incarnate Himself in human form. The substance of that discussion lay in Sri Ramakrishna saying, *'He who liberates others is an incarnation of God.'*[78] What is most instructive is to see the attitude of Sri Ramakrishna in all such dialogues, and then not in them alone. If a subject were taken up at all, he would go into it at its own level, philosophically, listening attentively to all the contrary arguments being put forward if different persons sincerely believed differently on that question. He would then express his deepest conviction that God takes human forms to liberate all beings from their self-created sufferings and to bring them to the realization that they are themselves parts of God. But no sooner had he said this than he would add, 'But don't believe in God-incarnation if your reason tells you not to. It is all right. What matters is the purity of heart.'

His teachings on another classic question, of reason vs. faith, were likewise preceded and followed by a discussion. Just as there was in Sri Ramakrishna's spiritual vocabulary no such word as 'sin', there was also no such word as 'blasphemy' and, therefore, no condemnation of anybody; nor was 'reverence' to be expressed at the expense of inner truthfulness and intelligence. Given love and its truthfulness, 'reverence' was never sought by Sri Ramakrishna from anyone.

---

[77] Ibid., entry dated 2 September 1885, p. 831. See also the entry dated Tuesday, 1 September 1885, p. 830.
[78] Ibid., entry dated 18 October 1885, p. 836.

The following event, a sequel to Dr Sarkar disapproving of the devotees touching Sri Ramakrishna's feet ('Why do you allow people to take the dust of your feet?'), will throw further light both on him and on Dr Mahendra Sarkar.

Master (to Dr Sarkar): You see, you have love for this (meaning himself). You told me that you loved me.

Dr Sarkar: You are a child of nature. That is why I tell you all this. It hurts me to see people salute you by touching your feet. I say to myself, 'They are spoiling such a good man.' Keshab Sen, too, was spoiled that way by his devotees. Listen to me—

Master: Listen to you? You are greedy, lustful, egotistic.

Dr Sarkar (to the Master): If you talk that way, I shall only examine your throat and go away. Perhaps that is what you want. In that case we should not talk about anything else. But if you want discussion, then I shall say what I think to be right.

All remained silent.[79]

Dr Mahendra Sarkar continued to say to Sri Ramakrishna what he thought was right, spent even longer hours with his patient during which wide-ranging discussions took place, and the bond between the undemonstrative doctor and the patient, the latter floating in the divine ecstasy despite his painful illness, grew deeper.

There was another person there who always said to Sri Ramakrishna what he thought was right— Narendranath. Consider the following conversation between him and M.

Narendra: I want truth. The other day I had a great argument with Sri Ramakrishna himself.

---

[79] Ibid., entry dated Thursday, 29 October 1885, p. 900.

M (*smiling*): What happened?

Narendra: He said to me, 'Some people call me God.' I replied, 'Let a thousand people call you God, but I shall certainly not call you God as long as I do not know it to be true.' He said, 'Whatever many people say is indeed truth; that is dharma.' Thereupon I replied, 'Let others proclaim a thing as truth, but I shall certainly not listen to them unless I myself realize it as truth.'

M: Your attitude is that of Western savants—Copernicus and Berkeley, for instance. The whole world said it was the sun that moved, but Copernicus did not listen. Everybody said the external world was real, but Berkeley paid no heed. Therefore Lewis says, 'Why was Berkeley not a philosophical Copernicus?'[80]

This conversation took place when Narendranath was nursing Sri Ramakrishna day and night with the greatest love and reverence, had abandoned his final law examination, and had decided inwardly to renounce the world.

Simultaneously with those great conversations and intoxicating experiences, there were concrete realities of life to be taken care of: the rent of the Cossipore garden-house; the medical expenses; the expenses on running the household which by now was quite large, for the group of young devotees nursing Sri Ramakrishna lived there. '(Alongside "the Bliss of Brahman" and "God-realization") the expenses are mounting,' as Sri Ramakrishna said to Dr Sarkar and others. The doctor replied (pointing to the devotees), 'But they are ready to bear them. They do not hesitate to spend money.' Then, turning to him, said, 'Now, you see, gold is necessary'.[81] The ailing saint asked

---

[80] Ibid., entry dated Wednesday, 21 April 1886, pp. 957–58.
[81] Surendranath Mitra hired the house in his name, and paid the monthly rent of eighty rupees; see Saradananda, *The Great Master*, Vol. II, p. 1010.

Narendra to answer *that*, but Narendra remained silent. Dr Sarkar completed the thought by saying, 'Gold is necessary, and also woman.' The other doctor added, 'Yes, his (Sri Ramakrishna's) wife has been cooking his meals.' Dr Sarkar looked at his divine patient and asked challengingly, 'Do you see?' The latter replied smilingly, 'Yes—but very troublesome!'[82] It was never clear what Sri Ramakrishna meant by *that*.

Neither is there any explanation for the astonishing fact of Sri Sarada Devi remaining almost invisible in the pages of Mahendranath Gupta's most detailed contemporary account of Sri Ramakrishna's life and teachings from February 1882. All the characters in his life during that period are heard expressing *their* thoughts, *their* feelings, and *their* troubles. But nobody there, especially among those around him in his last days, seems to have cared to find out what *her* feelings were, what *she* was going through on watching the unbearable physical pain of her guru and husband daily. Except a line or two, such as 'The Holy Mother busied herself day and night in the Master's service',[83] there is nothing to enable us to feel with her, except in imagination. Saradananda attributed this to Sri Sarada Devi's extreme bashfulness so that if hardly anybody saw her at Dakshineswar, practically no one saw her at Shyampukur and Cossipore garden-house either, excepting a couple of elder devotees. But Sri Ramakrishna himself, during his last days at these two places, hardly ever mentioned her. If he did, there is no account of it.

After a long dialogue between them, on the many aspects concerning the question of God, Dr Sarkar once said to

---

[82] Ibid., entry dated Thursday, 22 April 1886, pp. 959-60.
[83] Ibid., entry dated Sunday, 14 March 1886, p. 933; see also *The Great Master* pp. 759, 970.

Sri Ramakrishna, 'The illness you are suffering from does not permit the patient to talk with people. But my case is an exception. You may talk with me when I am here.' (All laugh.) Encouraged by the physician thus, the patient said:

Your son Amrita does not believe in the Incarnation of God. What is the harm in that? One realizes God even if one believes Him to be formless. One also realizes God if one believes that God has form. Two things are necessary for the realization of God: faith and self-surrender. Your son Amrita is a nice boy.[84]

Then, referring to Amrita when Dr Sarkar said, 'He is your disciple', Sri Ramakrishna quickly said with a smile, *'There is not a fellow under the sun who is my disciple. On the contrary, I'm everybody's disciple. All are the children of God. All are His Servants. I too am a child of God. I too am His servant.'*[85]

A perspective on life in which there is neither 'sin' nor 'blasphemy', nor any one single path to God, in which truthfulness does not imply lack of love and devotion, nor is anyone anyone else's disciple, was another inheritance Narendranath would have from Sri Ramakrishna, a legacy he would blend with his own character.

At Dakshineswar, in the company of those who revered him, Sri Ramakrishna would go into ecstasy, then deep samadhi, especially after hearing a song which someone would sing, quite often Narendranath. Despite the great physical pain caused by the illness, this pattern continued at Shyampukur and Cossipore garden-house in Calcutta as well. One day, before Dr Sarkar arrived on a professional

---

[84] Ibid., entry dated 22 October 1885, pp. 854-55.
[85] Ibid., the same entry as above, p.855

visit, much had already happened in his patient's room: conversations, singing, ecstasy, deep samadhi. Sri Ramakrishna was in an exalted state. A little earlier he had said, 'Something happens to me in that state of intoxication. Now I feel ashamed of myself. In that state I feel as if I were possessed by a ghost. I cease to be my own self. While coming down from that state I cannot count correctly. Trying to count, I say, one, seven, eight, or some such thing.'[86] After a brief discussion on the nobility of medical profession if it was practised moved by another's suffering, the doctor asked, 'Will there be no singing today?' Sri Ramakrishna asked Narendra to sing. The song he sang, and the scene that followed, should neither be condensed nor paraphrased but described in the words of the one who was there, M:

> Narendra sang again.
> O Mother, make me mad with Thy love!
> What need have I of knowledge or reason?
> Make me drunk with Thy love's Wine!
> O Thou who stealest Thy bhaktas' hearts,
> Drown me deep in the Sea of Thy love!
> Here in this world, this madhouse of Thine,
> Some laugh, some weep, some dance for joy:
> Jesus, Buddha, Moses, Gauranga,
> All are drunk with the Wine of Thy love.
> O Mother, when shall I be blessed
> By joining their blissful company?

A strange transformation came over the devotees. They all became mad, as it were, with divine ecstasy. The pundit stood up, forgetting the pride of his scholarship, and cried:

---

[86] M—*The Gospel*, entry dated Sunday, 25 October 1885, p. 871.

O Mother, make me mad with Thy love!

What need have I of knowledge or reason?

Vijay[87] was the first on his feet, carried away by divine intoxication. Then Sri Ramakrishna stood up, forgetting all about his painful and fatal illness. The doctor, who had been sitting in front of him, also stood up. Both patient and physician forgot themselves in the spell created by Narendra's music. The younger Naren and Latu went into deep samadhi. The atmosphere of the room became electric. Everyone felt the presence of God. Dr Sarkar, eminent scientist that he was, stood breathless, watching this strange scene. He noticed that the devotees who had gone into samadhi were utterly unconscious of the outer world. All were motionless and transfixed. After a while, as they came down a little to the plane of the relative world, some laughed and some wept. An outsider, entering the room, would have thought that a number of drunkards were assembled there.[88]

Floating in the intoxication of divine love, Sri Ramakrishna entered into eternity on 16 August 1886.[89] Thirty-four years later, on 21 July 1920, Sri Sarada Devi, the 'Holy Mother', followed him.

---

[87] Vijayakrishna Goswami, a leading light of the Brahmo Samaj, who had moved away from it, deeply dissatisfied by its dogmatic advocacy of the Brahman as Absolute, without form. Greatly attracted by Sri Ramakrishna's life and teachings, he visited him frequently.

[88] Ibid., entry dated Sunday, 25 October 1885, pp. 873–74.

[89] Sri Ramakrishna had been exceedingly ill on 14 March 1886, and his suffering unbearable. He had called M to his side and, with great difficulty, had said to him, 'I have gone on suffering so much for fear of making you all weep. But if you will say: "Oh, there is so much suffering! Let the body die," then I may give up the body.' Ibid., p. 934.

3

The Inheritance from the Dust of India

India I loved before I came away. Now the very dust of India is holy to me, the very air is now to me holy.
— Swami Vivekananda[1]

The greatest inheritance Swami Vivekananda was to have came from the dust of India. It was from his touch of the dust of India that his anguished cry for regeneration of India arose.

Just a few days before he passed into eternity, even as he had given Narendra over to the Divine Mother, Sri Ramakrishna had entrusted Narendra with the caring of the twelve young disciples. While they were nursing Sri Ramakrishna, he was nursing *them*. Still able to talk, although with rapidly increasing pain, he was telling them from his own experience about the dangers that lurk on the path of renunciation, which are not out 'there' but in one's own mind most of all. His teaching was that both 'knowledge' and 'ignorance' are of the mind. He was teaching them how the 'I' consciousness, 'the ego', is the greatest danger of all, the greatest because it takes so many subtle, invisible

---

[1] In his Reply to the Calcutta Address, *Complete Works of Swami Vivekananda* (hereafter, *CWSV*), Vol. III, p. 309.

forms. When unable to talk, he would write something on a piece of paper, or whisper something into the ears of one of his boys. One day he wrote on a piece of paper, 'Naren will teach others.' When Narendra said, 'I won't do any such thing,' Sri Ramakrishna whispered, 'Your very bones will do it.'[2] Narendranath as Swami Vivekananda did it magnificently. Thanks mostly to a young Englishman, J.J. Goodwin, a professional stenographer, we have exceedingly rich written record of this. What most people don't know is that when he was being worshipped in India for his teachings, and had touched countless hearts and minds in the West at their deepest, Vivekananda's 'bones' got tired of it all.

Before walking to the house in Baranagore that soon became the first monastery of the first twelve monastic disciples of Sri Ramakrishna, one should ask where Sri Sarada Devi went after Sri Ramakrishna had passed away and the Cossipore garden-house could be retained no longer. This is certainly not an unimportant question, nor some minor detail. It is astonishing, therefore, that in the contemporary account by M written after Sri Ramakrishna passed away,[3] there is not a word about it. Neither is there any mention of it in *The Life of Swami Vivekananda: By His Eastern and Western Disciples*, although both these works describe in detail the life at the Baranagore Math. Nor was that question asked in any other biography of Vivekananda written in the English language. But there is a pattern to that neglect.

---

[2] Narrated in a conversation between M and Narendra, after the passing away of Sri Ramakrishna. See *M—The Gospel*, entry dated Saturday, 9 April 1887, p. 982.
[3] Ibid., pp. 971–1006.

It is from Swami Gambhirananda's book, *Holy Mother Sri Sarada Devi*,[4] that we learn that, on 21 August, four days after Sri Ramakrishna's passing away, she moved to the house of Balaram Bose, one of the most dedicated householder–disciples of Sri Ramakrishna. She stayed there till 30 August, and then set out for Vrindavan where she lived for a year. On her return to Calcutta, she again stayed with Balaram Bose and his family for a week and then went to Kamarpukur in September 1887. 'Then began the Mother's sorrowful life at that village, during which time she was practically alone.' Not only alone but extremely poor as well.[5] Much later, Swami Saradananda would devote himself to the care of Sri Sarada Devi.

The first twelve monastic disciples of Sri Ramakrishna were not some floating leaves he had gathered, but had families of their own. Generally speaking, they were brought up in Hindu middle-class homes. Some of them were still college students, one of them at the Calcutta Medical College. They had parents; and Rakhal, or Rakhal Chandra Ghosh, had a wife and a child as well. At least two of them, Narendra and Shashi (Swami Ramakrishnananda), were the eldest sons of their parents, and had inviolable obligations towards them. Narendra had to make some satisfactory arrangement for his family's upkeep and, moreover, attend to the lawsuit his aunt had slapped on his family, which was still going on in a court in Calcutta. All of them faced great unhappiness

---

[4] Published by Sri Ramakrishna Math, Mylapore, Madras, 1955. The original was written in Bengali, *Sri Ma Sarada Devi* (Udbodhan Centre, Calcutta, December 1953), and translated into English by the writer himself.

[5] For the rest of Sri Sarada Devi's story, turn to Gambhirananda.

at home; for they were completely neglecting their studies and, it was feared, progressively walking out on their families, if only to take to the ochre robe. Rakhal's wife wept inconsolably. In the previous chapter we saw Narendra's mother, Bhubaneswari Devi, walk up to Sri Ramakrishna at the Cossipore garden-house and, without her having to say a word, his asking her to take Narendra back home.

Beyond what at least two of them expressed, it is difficult to say anything definite about how sensitive those twelve were towards the unhappiness they had created in the hearts of those at home who loved them. Narendra and Shashi were the two who did. We must hear Shashi, as recorded by M:

His father, a poor brahmin, was a devout Hindu and spent much of his time in spiritual practice. Sashi was his eldest son. His parents had hoped that, after completing his education, he would earn money and remove the family's financial difficulties. But Sashi had renounced the world for the realization of God. Whenever he thought of his father and mother he felt great anguish of heart. Many a time he said to his friends, with tears in his eyes: 'I am at a loss as to my duty. Alas, I could not serve my parents; I could not be of any use to them. What great hope they placed in me! On account of our poverty my mother did not have any jewelry. I cherished the desire to buy some for her. But now all my hopes are frustrated; it is impossible for me to return home. My Master asked me to renounce "woman" and "gold". I simply cannot return home.'[6]

Some years later, on 27 January 1900, in a lecture he gave at Pasadena, California, Swami Vivekananda said, 'I had to stand between my two worlds. On the one hand,

---

[6] M—*The Gospel*, entry dated Saturday, 7 May 1887, p. 991.

I would have to see my mother and brothers starve unto death; on the other, I had believed that this man's (Sri Ramakrishna's) ideas were for the good of India and the world, and had to be preached and worked out.'[7] To another, he said that on renouncing the world and leaving his family, he had two tears in his eyes: one tear was of joy on embracing a life in the vastness of the Spirit, and the other of sorrow for his mother he was leaving behind.[8]

Given the generosity of Surendranath Mitra, another most dedicated householder–disciple of Sri Ramakrishna, a house was found in Baranagore in the suburbs of Calcutta where the young monks could live together; he paid its rent and provided them with other necessities.[9] Ironically, Surendranath Mitra is hardly known even to most of those who worship Sri Ramakrishna. M's contemporary account of those days paid him a rich tribute:

Surendra was indeed a blessed soul. It was he who laid the foundation of the Great Order later associated with Sri Ramakrishna's name. His devotion and sacrifice made it possible for those earnest souls to renounce the world for the realization of God. Through him Sri Ramakrishna made it possible for them to live in the world as embodiments of his teachings, the renunciation of 'woman' and 'gold' and the realization of God…He was the big brother of the monks.[10]

---

[7] CWSV, Vol. VIII, pp. 80-81.
[8] See Prabuddhaprana, Saint Sara, p. 309.
[9] 'For the first few months Surendra contributed thirty rupees a month. As the other members joined the monastery one by one, he doubled his contribution, which he later increased to a hundred rupees. The monthly rent for the house was eleven rupees. The cook received six rupees a month. The rest was spent for food.' See M—The Gospel, describing the scene after the passing away of Sri Ramakrishna in August 1886, p. 972.
[10] Ibid., p. 972.

Many years later, Swami Vivekananda was asked, 'Maharaj, how did you maintain yourselves at that time?' Always full of gratitude for the help others gave, Swamiji said in tribute to Surendranath Mitra, 'You have heard of Suresh Babu's name, I daresay? (Surendranath was often called 'Suresh Babu'.) Know him to be the source of this Math. It was he who helped to found the Baranagore Math. It was Suresh Mitra who supplied our needs! Who can equal him in piety and faith, my boys?'[11]

The irony is inescapable—it was the money from a man who had not renounced 'gold' that enabled the monks who had, to live together as a Brotherhood. The irony would be complete, as pointed out in the previous chapter, when the final place of the monks of Sri Ramakrishna, the Belur Math, would be built a decade later with the money of three women. During his American days, at one of his lectures when a woman asked him, 'Swami, who is it who support the monks in your country? There are so many of them', Swami Vivekananda answered, and the audience laughed, 'The same who support the clergy in your country, madam. The women.'[12]

At a ceremony called *viraja* they themselves conducted at Baranagore, the young disciples of Sri Ramakrishna took the two vows of chastity[13] and poverty, and changed to the ochre robe. That was on the night of Christmas Eve, presumably of 1886. Not planned that way, they however saw in it a meaning; for their Master, Sri Ramakrishna,

---

[11] *The Life*, pp. 161-62.
[12] Mrs Roxie Blodgett to Josephine MacLeod. *Reminiscences*, pp. 360-61.
[13] In this, 'chastity' meant 'sexual chastity', in *thought* and *deed*.

had worshipped Jesus Christ as an incarnation of God. Initiation into sannyasa is primarily of the mind, not a ritual ceremony. Sri Ramakrishna had already initiated them in spirit; they needed no other authority now, either of scripture or of person. It was a spiritual aristocracy, as it were, where one's own resolve was all that mattered. It was not wholly dissimilar to Napoleon taking the crown from the hands of the Pope and crowning himself as Emperor.

They were all more or less of the same age (excepting the elder Gopal, Tarak and Latu), and with utmost devotion had together nursed their spiritual Master in his last days, creating a strong bond among them. They were called only by their short names, by which Sri Ramakrishna called them, and by which they called each other. On entering monastic life, they gave to themselves the following monastic names[14] by which they were to be known thereafter, each name preceded by the word 'Swami'. In that they were following a tradition established for centuries. Kali (Kaliprasad Chandra), *Abhedananda* (1866–1939);[15] Latu (Rakturam), *Adbhutananda* (died, 1920);[16] Elder Gopal Sur (Gopal Sur), *Advaitananda* (died, 1909);[17] Gangadhar (Gangadhar Ghatak), *Akhandananda* (1864–1937);[18] Rakhal (Rakhal Chandra Ghosh), *Brahmananda* (1863–1922);[19] Niranjan (Nitya Niranjan Sen), *Niranjanananda* (1862–1904);[20] Tulsi

---

[14] Their monastic names are arranged here in alphabetical order, and put in the italics to highlight them. It has no other significance.
[15] Born, 2 October 1866; died, 8 September 1939.
[16] 24 April 1920.
[17] 28 December 1909.
[18] Born, 30 September 1864; died, 7 February 1937.
[19] Born, 21 January 1863; died, 10 April 1922.
[20] Born, August 1862; died, 9 May 1904.

(Tulsi Charan Dutta), *Nirmalananda* (1863–1938);
Baburam (Baburam Ghosh), *Premananda* (1861–1918);[21]
Shashi (Shashibhushan Chakravarty), *Ramakrishnananda*
(1863–1911);[22] Sharat (Sarat Chandra Chakravarty),
Saradananda (1865–1927);[23] Tarak (Taraknath
Ghoshal), *Shivananda* (1854–1934);[24] Subodh (Subodh
Ghosh), *Subodhananda* (1867–1932);[25] Sarada, called
also Prasanna, (Sarada Prasanna Mitra),
Trigunatitananda (1865–1915);[26] Hari (Harinath
Chattopadhyaya), *Turiyananda* (1863–1922);[27] Yogen
(Jogindernath Choudhry), *Yogananda* (1861–1899).[28]
Here, there are fifteen names; three of them had joined
the twelve a little later. They continued to call each other,
as before, by their short names.

Narendranath did not give himself any particular
monastic name at that time. During his wanderings as a
monk all over India, beginning from 1888, he sometimes
called himself Vividishananda, and sometimes
Satchidananda. This was intended to conceal his identity,
so that his brother-monks might not follow him. He
wanted to be alone with the dust of India. He was given
the name *Vivekananda* only a little before his departure
for America in May 1893. There is a touch of irony in the

---

[21] Born, 10 December 1861; died, 30 July 1918.
[22] Born, 13 July 1863; died, 21 August 1911.
[23] Born, 23 December 1865; died, 19 August 1927.
[24] Born, 16 November 1854; died, 20 February 1934.
[25] Born, 8 November 1867; died, 2 December 1932.
[26] Born, 30 January 1865; died, 10 January 1915.
[27] Born, 3 January 1863; died, 21 July 1922.
[28] Born, March 1861; died 28 March 1899. Among the direct disciples of Sri Ramakrishna, Yogananda was the first to pass away.

fact that the name 'Vivekananda' was given by a man who had renounced neither 'woman' nor 'gold', to a monk who had renounced both. Whereas Raja Ajit Singh of Khetri was the ruler of a small kingdom, the monk to whom he gave the name 'Vivekananda' would create a vast kingdom of the minds and hearts of men and women where there is neither ruler nor subject. And he would then say in a voice as distant as it was full of passion, and show both in his life, 'Vivekananda is much more than being the Swami Vivekananda: *neti*, I am not that *only*,'[29] and sing it many times in the joy of inner freedom.

Some important aspects of life at Baranagore Math may briefly be described next; for it was charged with a strong spiritual emotion which renunciation had brought.[30] It was charged also with a deep emotion of spiritual togetherness. Narendra did not yet live there all the time, as many of his brother-monks gradually did.[31] He would sometimes go home during the day and attend to the matters pertaining to the lawsuit and other concerns of his family, and return in the evening. However, the responsibility of looking after *this* family, to which he now belonged, fell also on *his* shoulders. Sri Ramakrishna had not only transmitted all of his spiritual energy to Narendra, but had also entrusted 'the boys' to his care; 'the boys' knew that, and felt secure. But the members of

---

[29] These words are mine, but the thoughts are his, as we will see in Chapter 11.

[30] Spiritual emotion is not incompatible with renunciation.

[31] For details, in order to get the correct sequence of who joined the monastery when, see *M—The Gospel*, pp. 972–73. Most readers may not be interested in them; but M believed them to be of sufficient importance, so that facts are not lumped together in a general statement.

this new family of monks, now living together, had very different temperaments; in that at least, it was not greatly different from any other large family.

Narendra clearly saw that, if all of them were to walk together on the path shown to them by Sri Ramakrishna, he would have to ask them to do some intelligent self-reflection, and first get rid of the deeply entrenched habit of seeing the supernatural in things that are natural. Some of them had believed that Sri Ramakrishna's illness had a divine purpose, and no sooner was that purpose fulfilled than he would be his healthy self again. Some thought that he had taken upon himself the sin of others and its punishment; some even thought that he had brought about his serious illness only to pamper the physician and his ego. Narendra saw how that tendency, if not removed, would quickly lead to a belief in the occult against which Sri Ramakrishna was warning his devotees. Narendra had argued that the human body is naturally subject to disease, decay and death, and Sri Ramakrishna's body was not exempt from that natural phenomenon any more than the physical body of the Buddha was. What he needed was good medical treatment and careful nursing. When his brother-devotees did not seem to be convinced, and still held the notion of a supernatural explanation for their Master's illness, Narendra ridiculed them mercilessly. Without spelling it out, he was saying to them what Sri Ramakrishna had said, *You should be a devotee, it is true, but why should you, therefore, be a fool?*[32]

Next, he wanted his brother-monks to open their minds to the truth that the world of spirituality is not an island,

---

[32] See Chapter 2, p. 45.

isolated from what human life had been in the past and is today. Therefore, he brought before them the history of civilization. His brother-monks were now being tutored in history and Narendra was a marvellous teacher, creating vivid images of a country's aspirations and passage through time.

Then he began to open their eyes to the wider horizons of philosophical thought. Indian philosophy was not all that there was to philosophy. In other countries, in other ages, there had been profound philosophical inquiries into the nature of Reality, the scope and the limits of knowledge, that is, the limits of the human mind and how they affected human life. A life of renunciation, even in the traditional Indian sense, was not to be lived in ignorance of what had been thought elsewhere. Therefore, alongside the Sanskrit texts of Indian philosophy, they were to study Greek philosophy, Descartes (1596–1650), Kant (1724–1804) and Hegel (1770–1831), John Locke (1632–1704), David Hume, Herbert Spencer, Jeremy Bentham (1748–1832) and John Stuart Mill. They were to study the fundamentals of the physical sciences, which at that time were extravagant claims to the allegiance of the human mind. But first those fundamentals had to be understood in their own terms before their limits could be seen. In that also, Narendranath was a brilliant teacher, himself learning all the time. In the midst of intense spiritual seeking, Narendra one day asked M, 'Can you give me a History of Philosophy?' M asked, 'By whom? Lewis?'[33] Narendra

---

[33] Actually 'Lewes', George Henry Lewes (1817–78). His *The Biographical History of Philosophy*, two vols, 1845-46.

answered, 'No, Uberweg.[34] I must read a German author.'[35]

Not all his brother-monks were enthusiastic to the same degree about the intellectual diet Narendranath was serving them. He was now putting them on the path of 'knowledge', jnana, 'reasoning'; whereas Sri Ramakrishna had taught that jnana, good in its own place, did not lead to the realization of God, it was bhakti, the devotional stirrings of the heart and surrender of the self that did. Given their different temperaments, they had different spiritual aspirations. Some were inclined to stern asceticism, others to intense meditation, and some others to reciting the many names of the Lord or concentrating on only one name. Amidst all these, Kant and Hegel, Herbert Spencer and John Stuart Mill did not quite fit in. One of them, Akhandananda, had already gone to Tibet; some others left for different places in India, with the view to undertaking the different spiritual discipline their different temperaments prompted. However, all of them not only felt fascinated by Narendra's exposition of different philosophies, including materialism and atheism, but as a Brotherhood also felt rooted in the Baranagore Math where Sri Ramakrishna's relics were now kept in a small room turned into a sort of chapel. Thus, the story of life at Baranagore Math was complex, but through it ran the binding thread of their common devotion to their Master, Sri Ramakrishna. However, not all of them understood him and his teachings in the same way. There is little evidence that they understood Narendra either.

---

[34] His *History of Philosophy*, translation (1871) from the 4th ed. of the original in German, *Grundriss der Geschichte der Philosophie*, four vols, 8th ed., pp. 1894–98.

[35] M—*The Gospel*, entry dated Wednesday, 21 April 1886, p. 958.

But in that intense flow of spiritual seeking and practice, there were moments of laughter. Recorded by M, the following are two examples.

A member of the monastery who was also lying down said teasingly, feigning great suffering on account of his separation from God: 'Ah! Please get me a knife. I have no more use for this life. I can't stand this pain any more!'
    Narendra (feigning seriousness): 'It is there. Stretch out your hand and take it.'
    Everybody laughed.[36]

Narendra was clad in a new ochre cloth. The bright orange colour of his apparel blended with the celestial lustre of his face and body, every pore of which radiated a divine light. His countenance was filled with fiery brilliance and yet touched with the tenderness of love...All eyes were fixed on him...Narendra was then just twenty-four years old.
    Narendra now began to joke like a child. He was imitating Sri Ramakrishna. He put a sweet into his mouth and stood still, as if in a samadhi. His eyes remained unwinking. A devotee stepped forward and pretended to hold him by the hand lest he should drop to the ground. Narendra closed his eyes. A few minutes later, with the sweetmeat still in his mouth, he opened his eye and drawled out, 'I—am—all—right.' All laughed loudly.
    M looked on at this wonderful mart of happiness.[37]

Narendra began to feel somewhat confined at Baranagore, and he experienced the strong urge to float in the vastness of India's spirit and feel under his feet the earth of India.

---

[36] Ibid., entry dated Saturday, 7 May 1887, p. 986.
[37] Ibid., entry dated Monday, 21 February 1887, p. 975.

Meanwhile, the lawsuit had been settled in his family's favour, but its expenses had left an already impoverished family destitute. At any rate, he was in some measure free. Sometime in 1888, he set out for Varanasi, following the course of the Ganga, on foot. His choice of Varanasi as his very first destination was not only because, as has been suggested, it was the holiest of holy places but also because it was there that, on renouncing the world, his grandfather Durgaprasad had vanished into the faceless crowd of monks. When Narendranath took to the ochre robe, he could not but have remembered the example of his grandfather, although he never spoke about it. It must have been, for that reason as well, an emotionally charged event for the grandson; as it was, for that very reason, for the whole Datta family. But, from this first journey to Varanasi, he soon returned to Baranagore, answering the call of responsibility he had towards his brother-monks, and stayed there for a few months.

From this point onwards in telling Vivekananda's story, two things are to be kept in mind. First, we should not always expect to have the dates and the exact sequence of Narendranath's journeys in his motherland. He himself was quite indifferent to recording them.[38] Some of those he met, and whose lives he touched intimately, kept a record of his visits to them, often as their houseguest, and also of the conversations he had with them;[39] but, given the general cultural indifference to date, place and time, as being of little importance (in contrast to the ancient Indian traditions where all these three were regarded as of

---

[38] As we learn from *The Life*.
[39] *The Life*, p. 170.

great importance in life), one does not always get that information from them either. As far as this is concerned, we are in Indian space. It was not Swami Vivekananda alone who was 'indifferent' to date, place, and time; his Indian biographers are no less so. However, what is known of this period of his life, 1888 to 1893, is sufficiently accurate in its general outline. Besides, Narendranath as Swami Vividishananda or as Swami Satchidananda was not wholly indifferent to saying where he was on which date. Some of his extant letters of those years, which are not many, tell us both.

More importantly, Narendra's life as a parivrajaka, a wandering monk, is a whole lifetime. It would by itself be a most ennobling story in terms of feelings, thoughts and relationships even if what followed—his years at two different times in America and England—had not followed. It is true that in that case we would not have known the Swami Vivekananda as we know him. But it is also true that the Vivekananda of the days in the West was being prepared, as it were, by his touch of the earth of India. Furthermore, each experience in human life can be said to be complete in itself at *that* moment. Each journey of Vivekananda was likewise so. For wherever he went, he *felt* intensely; there was nothing that he saw that did not find a resonance in his whole being, each such moment being complete in itself. Therefore, it is not until we feel him contemporaneously at each one of those places that we can understand him.

He travelled, often long distances, on foot, or by train when someone would buy him a ticket for his next destination, and occasionally by bullock cart. He carried with him no money, for he had none, having taken the vow of poverty. A long staff, a monk's *kamandalu* used as a water jug, a change of ochre robes, a coarse blanket with which to cover himself, and a copy each of the *Bhagvad-Gita* and *The Imitation of Christ*—these were all the physical possessions of this young monk.

Leaving Baranagore again sometime in 1888, he went to Varanasi a second time; and from there to Ayodhya, Lucknow, Agra, Vrindavan, Hathras, Haridwar and Hrishikesh. Back to Hathras, he returned to the Baranagore Math towards the end of 1888 and stayed there for almost a year.

At the end of 1889, Narendra travelled to Vaidyanath and Allahabad; and during the third week of January 1890, to Ghazipur. To Varanasi again, most likely in late March or early April, where he heard the news that Balaram Bose had died on 13 April and Surendranath Mitra was seriously ill. Narendra rushed back to Calcutta.

It was in July 1890 that Narendra cut himself loose and began to float again as an itinerant monk with the firm resolve not to return. For, he asked, how was the web of maya, 'entanglement', at a monastery any different from the web of maya at any family and home?

Before starting on a life he now yearned for, Narendra wanted to take the blessings of Sri Sarada Devi. It is said that he 'sought out the Holy Mother' at a village called Ghusuree across the Ganga.[40] When he said to her, 'Mother, I shall not return until I have attained the highest Jnana,' she asked him, 'My son, will you not see your own mother at home before leaving?' This simple question, and the concern behind it, will alone show the simple human

---

[40] Ibid., p. 192. The words 'sought out' should suggest that some searching for Sri Sarada Devi was involved.

greatness of Sri Sarada Devi. Narendra's answer was
predictable: 'Mother, you alone are my mother!' At *that*
time, in that intense flow of what he thought renunciation
was, that was an honest answer. Sri Sarada Devi gave
Narendra her blessings; and from the silence of her inner
self, from a mother's heart, a prayer for his protection. Some
three years later, before starting on a different journey, going
westwards, across the seas, on a mission that was calling
him, he would again seek her blessings through a letter he
would write to her, and receive them with great love besides.

Narendra's eyes were meantime turned mainly to the
Himalayas, but Varanasi was pulling him too. With
Gangadhar (Akhandananda), with whom he always felt
a deep bond, he set out first for Bhagalpur, then Vaidyanath
and Varanasi. From there to Ayodhya, then to Nainital and
Almora. They wanted to go to Kedarnath and Badrinath[41]
but could not, and stayed for many days at Hrishikesh
where Gangadhar fell ill. Narendra nursed him. They
came to Tehri, still in the hills (where the Dewan of Tehri-
Garhwal, then a princely state, took care of them); came
down to Dehradun; and after Gangadhar had recovered,
Narendra sent him to Allahabad (but Gangadhar decided
to get down at Meerut). Narendra himself went up to
Hrishikesh where this time *he* fell seriously ill, nearly died,
but was saved by a tribal sadhu who administered to him
an indigenous medicine. When he had recovered, he was
brought to Meerut, where many of his brother-monks had
assembled, and stayed there for five months. In the latter
part of January 1891, Narendra, or Swami Vividishananda,
set out for Delhi, alone.

---

[41] Blessed be this author's name!

Now Rajputana was calling him. Sometime early in February 1891, he arrived at Alwar where he stayed for seven weeks. Then to Jaipur, Ajmer and to Mt Abu. It was at Mt Abu that he met Raja Ajit Singh, Raja of Khetri, on whose pressing invitation he spent more than ten weeks at Khetri as his guest. Thereafter, he stayed for about two weeks at Ajmer again.

Narendra's next destination was Ahmedabad from where he made short journeys to Wadhwan, Limbdi and Bhavnagar. Next he travelled to Junagad, from where he made short visits to Bhuj, Kathiawar and Kutch. Then he came to Porbandar, the town in which Mahatma Gandhi was born. He stayed here for eleven months and made short visits to Dwaraka, Somnath and Mandvi. Then he went to Baroda, where he stayed for three weeks and from there, to Khandwa.

Narendra next arrived in Bombay about the last week of July 1892, where he stayed 'for several weeks'; one does not know how many. From there he travelled to Poona where he was a houseguest of Bal Gangadhar Tilak (1856–1920), the two having travelled together in the train from Bombay to Poona. When Tilak asked him his name, he simply said that he was a sannyasin.[42] Next he went to Kolhapur and Belgaum. From the reminiscence of Haripada Mitra, we learn that Narendra was in Belgaum in the second fortnight of October 1892 and left that place on 27

---

[42] In his reminiscence of Swami Vivekananda, Bal Gangadhar Tilak mentioned that the Swami stayed with him, at Poona, 'for eight or ten days', but no dates are given, beyond the vague 'About the year 1892'; *Reminiscences*, p. 20. Most probably it was in the first fortnight of October 1892.

October, his host putting him on the train to Marmagaon, then a Portuguese colony.[43]

Narendra now turned southward with a view eventually to go to Rameswaram, the Varanasi of southern India, as he had told Haripada. From Marmagaon he came to Bangalore and, after staying there for a few days, travelled to Mysore, Trichur, Cochin and Trivandrum where he would have arrived sometime in December 1892.[44] Before going to Rameswaram he visited Madurai; from there, to Kanyakumari, the last of India's land; then travelling northwards and sideways, visiting Ramnad and Pondicherry, he arrived in Madras. That was in the beginning of 1893. Invited to visit Hyderabad, he arrived there on 10 February and stayed there till 17 February. When he arrived, about five hundred persons of rank had assembled at the railway station to receive him; when he left, more than a thousand had come to see him off.[45] The numbers meant little to him; what touched him was the sadness which the family with whom he stayed felt on his leaving, as if someone very dear was going away for a long time.

He returned to Madras. Within the next few months, with the name Swami Vivekananda, Narendranath the chosen apostle of Sri Ramakrishna, would set out on another long pilgrimage—to the West, to America, destination Chicago.

* * *

From July 1890, when he left the Baranagore monastery with a resolve never to return there, to the day on which

---

[43] *Reminiscences*, pp. 22–51; p. 38.
[44] See K. Sundararama Iyer's reminiscence of Swami Vivekananda, *Reminiscences*, p. 57.
[45] See *The Life*, p. 274, and p. 276.

he left Bombay for America, 31 May 1893, a period of less than three years, Swami Vivekananda had come to know India intimately. That knowledge had been as exhilarating to his imaginative mind as it had been disturbing to his feeling heart. In these contradictory feelings, each with an intensity that distinguished him from other sannyasins, already lay one source of his self-division. He began to understand, more clearly than ever before, his own nature. What he saw of the place and people where he had been last, he spoke about to the people he met next—now in a distant, dreamy voice, and then in a voice touched with fire.

'Self-division' is generally understood in psychoanalytical literature as schizophrenia or split personality, regarded a pathological condition. That is *not* the meaning of Swami Vivekananda being self-divided, of which he was speaking in the plainest words, almost always words of anguish, in his letters.[46] He was self-divided because, in the first place, his inheritance from the dust of India was sharply divided—India's glorious past and its miserable reality as he saw it. He carried both within himself. He could not talk of the one without truthfully talking of the other, and talked of both with passion.

Walking along the course of the river Ganga, the most sacred of the sacred rivers, Swami Vivekananda walked with intense emotion of wonder and pride through the history of the civilization that grew as the Ganga flowed, never merely a physical river but also a metaphor for seeking the divine. In the forests of the Himalayas he heard, as it

---

[46] *Letters of Swami Vivekananda* (Advaita Ashrama, Calcutta, 4th ed, 1976). Hereafter, *SV Letters*. The dates and the emphasis upon certain words are as in the original, *in italics*. Where I have added emphasis, it is indicated.

were, the chants of the Upanishads and their teaching as to the relation of man with the universe. In Lucknow, Agra and Delhi, he saw with the same intense emotion of wonder and pride what the Muslim part of India's history had gifted. The Swami was not just *seeing* dead stones of forts and tombs but *feeling* the surge of vitality and beauty of the inheritance the Muslim rulers of the past ages had bequeathed. He was moved to tears on seeing the Taj Mahal, which he saw from many angles, physically and metaphorically. He felt the same emotions in his travels through what are now Gujarat and Maharashtra, standing, for example, in the vast courtyard of the mosque at Ahmedabad. What he would feel at the sacred Dwaraka and Prabhasapatnam a little later, he felt no less in the mosque at Ahmedabad, and he talked about it. The climax was reached in his feelings at the temple of Rameswaram, and even more at the temple of the Mother Goddess at Kanyakumari.[47] Vivekananda's travels to the sacred places were not just a pilgrimage, tirtha-yatra, in its conventional meaning, to 'earn merit' for prosperity in this life and improving one's prospects in the next. Vivekananda was no ordinary pilgrim, nor was he one of those countless itinerant sadhus.

What Swami Vivekananda also saw at close quarters in villages and towns was the dark world of poverty of the masses, their ignorance deliberately created, and their exploitation by the greedy priests and the cynical rich alike. He saw the pain and suffering of hunger he had himself known after his father's death and during his travels in the Himalayas, too. He even saw the darker world of women

---

[47] For details, read *The Life*, pp. 193–285.

kept in ignorance on purpose. In the eyes of children, behind their look of fun and merriment, he saw the menacing shadows of fear. And he wept hot tears. The inheritance of India and the condition of its inheritors were distinctly different: Swami Vivekananda, who took intense pride in the one and felt the pain and the shame of the other, could only be self-divided likewise.

He did not accept the contention that religion in India was the cause of the degradation of the masses. This had happened because the teachings of the Upanishads, of the Samkhya and Yoga and the Vedanta, of the Buddha and of the poet–saints had been sullied by the pundits and priests who knew little of love and even less of the divine. They practised and preached not religion but, in his devastating phrase, 'don't-touchism', which was atheism, he said, not religion. What was needed, therefore, was to bring to the masses in simple language the teachings of the ancients, all leading to the awareness of the oneness of life and that all life is the manifestation of the Divine. He spoke of the earlier part of Indian inheritance with passion and with authority even more.[48]

In religion lies the vitality of India, and so long as the Hindu race do not forget the great inheritance of their forefathers, there is no power on earth to destroy them.

Nowadays everybody blames those who constantly look back to their past. It is said that so much looking back to the past is the cause of all India's woes. To me, on the contrary, it seems that the opposite is true. So long as they forgot the past, the Hindu nation remained in a state of stupor; and as soon as they have

---

[48] For that refer CWSV, already cited.

begun to look into their past, there is on every side a fresh manifestation of life. It is out of this past that the future has to be moulded, this past will become the future.

The more, therefore, the Hindus study the past, the more glorious will be their future, and whoever tries to bring the past to the door of every one is a great benefactor to his nation. The degeneration of India came not because the laws and customs of the ancients were bad, but because they were not allowed to be carried to their legitimate conclusions.[49]

Separating this strand of his thought from the rest of what he was saying, and quoting him selectively, he was then, as even now, quickly portrayed as a Hindu revivalist, the patron saint of renascent Hinduism.

But with equal passion, Swami Vivekananda had spoken of the poverty of the Indian masses, of their ignorance and of their exploitation.[50] He spoke of them with the authenticity of one who had in his travels seen with his own eyes and had heard with his own ears the accounts of the pain of their degradation as human beings. It is in the poor masses of India that Swami Vivekananda had found the Shiva he was to serve for the rest of his life. That was 'the work' to which Sri Ramakrishna had yoked him. Nothing roused the Swami's anger more, and nothing his greater contempt, than the cynical misuse of the theory of karma which the orthodox upper classes put forward as an explanation for the degraded condition of the lower classes; they called this 'their just desert'. When, with even greater cynicism, their degradation was

---

[49] In his reply to the address by Raja Ajit Singh of Khetri. *SV Letters*, pp. 231-32. Read the whole letter, pp. 229–37.
[50] Study *CWSV*, particularly Vols. III, IV, V and VII, and the *SV Letters*.

sought to be justified by quoting some Western theories of heredity, Vivekananda would explode, his eyes flashing fire:

...all sorts of most demoniacal and brutal arguments, culled from the crude ideas of hereditary transmission and other such gibberish from the Western world, are brought forward in order to brutalise and tyrannise over the poor all the more.[51]

Ay, in this country of ours, the very birthplace of the Vedanta, our masses have been hypnotised (into slavery and weakness) for ages. To touch them is pollution, to sit with them is pollution! Hopeless they were born, hopeless must they remain! And the result is that they have been sinking, sinking, sinking, and have come to the last stage to which a human being can come. For what country is there in the world where man has to sleep with the cattle? And for this, blame nobody else, do not commit the mistake of the ignorant. The effect is here and the cause is here too. We are to blame. Stand up, be bold, and take the blame on your own shoulders. Do not go about throwing mud at others: for all the faults you suffer from, you are the sole and the only cause.[52]

The one thing that is at the root of all evils in India is the condition of the poor...The only service to be done for our lower class is to give them education, *to develop their lost individuality*. That is the great task between our people and princes. Up to now nothing has been done in that direction. Priest-power and foreign conquest have trodden them down for centuries, and at last the poor of India have forgotten that they are human beings.[53]

---

[51] *CWSV*, Vol. III, p. 192. At a lecture he gave at Kumbakonam, 'The Mission of the Vedanta', after his return in 1897 from America, but the date is not mentioned.

[52] Ibid., Vol. III, p. 429; at a lecture he delivered on 'The Vedanta', at Lahore, 12 November 1897.

[53] His letter dated 23 June 1894 from Chicago to the Raja of Khetri, Raja Ajit Singh. *SV Letters*, pp. 117-18. *Read the whole letter*. Hereafter, this suggestion to be added to every letter of SV quoted in this book.

Then, in the tone of apostolic anger, this:

...So long as the millions live in hunger and ignorance, I hold every man a traitor who, having been educated at their expense, pays not the least heed to them! I call those men who strut about in their finery, having got all their money by grinding the poor, wretches, so long as they do not do anything for those two hundred millions who are now no better than hungry savages.[54]

Separating his concern with the poverty-stricken masses of India from the rest of what he was saying, and then quoting him selectively, Swami Vivekananda now came to be portrayed as a socialist in ochre robe.[55] Being a 'socialist' presupposed adherence to the fundamentals of 'socialism' and its political philosophy, with the word 'masses' as its central mantra. It was quickly concluded that, because he was talking so strongly about the Indian masses, Vivekananda had adopted also the theoretical apparatus of Western 'socialism', which he had not. His concern with the condition of the Indian masses, and his action in that regard, were not the products of Western socialism or of any other *ism*.

On the other hand, it has been suggested (at least in one study[56]) that:

---

[54] His undated letter from Chicago to Alasinga Perumal. *SV Letters*, p. 147.
[55] Dr Bhupendranath Datta, Swamiji's youngest brother (who took his PhD from Hamburg University), an avowed socialist in the later part of his life, brought together at one place, from *CWSV*, Vivekananda's thoughts relating to the Indian masses. See his *Swami Vivekananda Patriot-Prophet—A Study* (already cited), pp.241–79.
[56] Dietmar Rothermund, *The Phases of Indian Nationalism* (Nachiketa Publications, Bombay, 1970), 'Traditionalism and Socialism in Vivekananda's Thought', pp. 57–64.

The traditionalist element of his (Vivekananda's) thought with its urge for harmony and solidarity was stronger than the socialist and egalitarian aspirations which he asserted occasionally, in very forceful terms, setting the style for that verbal radicalism which characterized the speeches of Indian leaders for many years to come.[57]

As far as this relates to Swami Vivekananda, nothing could be more mistaken. In the enormous mass of written evidence we have of the countless people who knew him, both in India and the West, many of them intimately, one recognition is common: his deep sincerity. With Vivekananda nothing was ever just *verbal*, nothing an affectation.

If there was a divide between the glorious inheritance and the miserable condition of its inheritors, the divide between what that inheritance truly was and what it was made out to be by its dispensers was no less. Both disturbed Swami Vivekananda greatly. Talking of the immeasurably rich inheritance of India, he could not but truthfully also talk of the wretchedness of many Hindu customs and practices that had grown. He did both with his characteristic passion. Pointing to Narendra, Sri Ramakrishna had once said, 'He seems to be walking with an unsheathed sword in his hand.'[58]

Narendra as Swami Vivekananda never ceased to ask, 'Why should the Hindu nation with all its wonderful intelligence and other things have gone to pieces?'[59] He attributed it to a variety of causes, all of them interrelated. In the first place, as mentioned above, he traced it to that Hindu disease he called *don't-touchism*.

---

[57] Ibid., p. 64.
[58] M—*The Gospel*, entry dated Thursday, 22 April 1886, p. 964.
[59] His letter dated 29 January 1894 to the Dewan of Junagad. *SV Letters*, p. 67.

How many people really weep for the sorrows and sufferings of the millions of poor in India? Are we *men*? What are we doing for their livelihood, for their improvement? We do not touch them, we avoid their company. Are we men? Those thousands of Brahmanas—what are they doing for the low, downtrodden masses of India? 'Don't touch', 'Don't touch', is the only phrase that plays upon their lips! How mean and degraded has our eternal religion become at their hands! Wherein does our religion lie now? In 'Don't-touchism' alone, and nowhere else![60]

To his brother-monk Rakhal (Brahmananda), he wrote at great length:[61]

…The whole truth about austerities and spiritual exercises is, in a nutshell, that I am pure and all the rest are impure! A beastly, demoniac, hellish religion this![62]

…Monks and Sannyasins and Brahmins of a certain type have thrown the country into ruin. Intent all the while on theft and wickedness, these pose as preachers of religion! They will take gifts from the people and at the same time cry, 'Don't touch me!' And what great things they have been doing!—'If a potato happens to touch a brinjal, how long will the universe last before it is deluged?' 'If they do not apply earth a dozen times to clean their hands, will fourteen generations of ancestors go to hell, or twenty-four?'—For intricate problems like these they have been finding out scientific explanations for the last two thousand years—while one-fourth of the people are starving.[63]

---

[60] In a letter dated 28 December 1893 to Haripada Mitra. Ibid., pp. 61-62.
[61] Written in the year 1895, but without any date. Ibid., pp. 251–56.
[62] Ibid., p. 254.
[63] Ibid.

...A dreadful slough is in front of you—take care; many fall into it and die. The slough is this, that the present religion of the Hindus is not in the Vedas, nor in the Puranas, nor in Bhakti, nor in Mukti—religion has entered into the cooking pot. The present religion of the Hindus is neither the path of knowledge, nor that of reason—it is 'Don't-touchism'. 'Don't touch me!', 'Don't touch me!'—that exhausts its description. See that you do not lose your lives in this dire irreligion of 'Don't-touchism'. Must the teaching *atmavat sarvabhuteshu* [in the original letter, in Sanskrit script]—'Looking upon all beings as your own self'—be confined to books alone? How will they grant salvation who cannot feed a hungry mouth with a crumb of bread? How will those who become impure at the mere breath of others purify others? Don't-touchism is a form of mental disease. Beware![64]

...The poor, the downtrodden, the ignorant, let these be your God.[65]

Secondly, he traced the disorder of Indian society largely to the fact that education was wilfully confined to the privileged among the social classes of India.

From the day when education and culture, etc., began to spread gradually from patricians to plebeians, grew the distinction between the modern civilization as of Western countries and the ancient civilization of India, Egypt, Rome, etc. I see it before my eyes, a nation is advanced in proportion as education and intelligence spread among the masses. The chief cause of India's ruin has been the monopolising of the whole education and intelligence

---

[64] Ibid., pp. 255–56.
[65] Ibid., p. 255.

of the land, by dint of pride and royal authority, among a handful of men. If we are to rise again, we shall have to do in the same way, i.e., by spreading education among the masses.[66]

He was convinced, he said, that the regeneration of India would come from the masses of India, among whom education had to be spread first.

Thirdly, he saw in Indian life a visible divide between meaning and form, substance and ritual. He saw it everywhere, most markedly in the religious life of India and, by some transformation, in other areas of Indian society as well. He noticed it even among his brother-monks, the children of Sri Ramakrishna, which at once saddened and angered him. In a scourging letter to them,[67] he spoke fire:

There is no hope for our nation. Not one original idea crosses anyone's brains, all fighting over the same old, threadbare rug— that Ramakrishna Paramahamsa was such and such and cock-and-bull stories—stories having neither head nor tail...Those whose heads have a tendency to be troubled day and night over such questions as whether the bell should ring on the right or on the left; whether the sandal-paste mark should be put on the head or anywhere else; whether the light should be waved twice or four times—simply deserve the name of wretches, and it is due to that sort of notion that we are the outcasts of Fortune...There is an ocean of difference between idleness and renunciation.[68]

---

[66] Vivekananda to Sarala Ghoshal, an educationist, letter dated 24 April 1897, from Darjeeling. *SV Letters*, p. 328.
[67] Ibid., pp. 108–12.
[68] Ibid., p. 109.

If you want any good to come, just throw your ceremonials overboard and worship the Living God, the Man-God—every being that wears a human form—God in His universal as well as individual aspect. The universal aspect of God means this world, and worshipping it means serving it—this indeed is work, not indulging in ceremonials. Neither is it work to cogitate as to whether the rice-plate should be placed in front of the God for ten minutes or for half an hour—that is called lunacy. Millions of rupees have been spent only that the temple-doors at Varanasi or Vrindaban may play at opening and shutting all day long! Now the Lord is having his toilet, now He is taking His meals, now He is busy on something else we know not what…And all this, while the Living God is dying for want of food, for want of education![69]

…Spread ideas—go from village to village, from door to door—then only there will be real work.

…It is only by doing good to others that one attains to one's own good, and it is by leading others to Bhakti and Mukti that one attains them oneself. Take that up, forget your own self for it, be mad over the idea. As Shri Ramakrishna used to love you, as I love you, come, love the world like that. Bring all together.[70]

Bring all together: in these three words Swami Vivekananda had summed up the substance of his mission and its direction.

Swami Vivekananda saw clearly, and talked about it truthfully, that it was from the divide, established quite early in Indian history, between meaning and form, substance and ritual, that the Hindu divide between ideal and practice arose. Feeling the pain and the hurt of it, he said:

---

[69] Ibid., pp. 109-10.
[70] Ibid., p. 111.

No religion on earth preaches the dignity of humanity in such a lofty strain as Hinduism, and no religion on earth treads upon the necks of the poor and the low in such a fashion as Hinduism.[71]

We have brains, but no hands. We have the doctrine of Vedanta, but we have not the power to reduce it into practice. In our books there is the doctrine of universal equality, but in work we make great distinctions. It was in India that unselfish and disinterested work of the most exalted type was preached, but in practice we are awfully cruel, awfully heartless—unable to think of anything besides our own mass-of-flesh bodies.[72]

Nobody ever understood the inner suffering of the man who had set out to open to the world the Indian riches of 'unselfish and disinterested work of the most exalted type', but also had to hold the mirror to the Hindus that in practice they were 'awfully cruel, awfully heartless'.

There were in the times of Swami Vivekananda not a few, the traditionalists, who talked only of the prevalent Hindu customs deriving their sanctity from the sacred traditions of the past without concerning themselves with the condition of the masses and the disturbing questions it gave rise to. They had frozen the Hindu past in their own limited notions of it and, furthermore, fancied it as providing sanctity for customs and usage that were the very negation of ancient teachings. And there were reformers who talked only of the urgent need to discard many of the customs considered inviolable but harmful,

---

[71] Vivekananda to Alasinga Perumal, letter dated 20 August 1893. *SV Letters*, p. 41.
[72] Vivekananda to Sarala Ghoshal, letter dated 6 April 1897. *SV Letters*, p. 324.

without showing the slightest concern with the poverty and ignorance among the masses. Drawn generally from the middle class, both the groups were fragmenting social reality in seemingly two neat but conflicting parts. What was happening in the late nineteenth century, in which Swami Vivekananda's work came to be, was actually far more complex. The victims of the oppressive customs and practices were also their ardent adherents. The language of the reformers from 1885 onwards was insincere at its worst and confused at its best.[73] Besides, the conduct of the leading reformers in their personal lives seemed no different from that of the traditionalists.[74]

On 24 January 1894, from Chicago, Swami Vivkananda wrote to his followers in Madras:

Remember that the nation lives in the cottage. But, alas! nobody ever did anything for them. Our modern reformers are very busy about widow remarriage. Of course, I am a sympathizer in every reform, but the fate of a nation does not depend upon the number of husbands their widows get, but upon the *condition of the masses*. Can you raise them? Can you give them back their lost

---

[73] For a brief analysis of the language of social reform, the reader may want to have a look at my *Dharma, India and the World Order. Twenty-one Essays* (Saint Andrew Press, Edinburgh, and Pahl-Rugenstein, Bonn, 1993), Chapter 21, 'Modern Indian Perceptions of India and the West', section (vii), 'Social Reform: Underlying Assumptions', pp. 185–201.

[74] When the wife of Mahadev Govind Ranade (1841–1901) died and he married again, he, a champion of widow remarriage and a fighter against child-marriage, not only did *not* marry a widow, but also married a girl who was barely ten years old. When publicly criticized, he explained it away by attributing it to his father's wish which he said he could not disobey. The explanation, from a serving judge, was as astonishing as was the conduct.

individuality without making them lose their innate spiritual strength? Can you become an occidental of occidentals in your spirit of equality, freedom, work, and energy, and at the same time a Hindu to the very backbone in religious culture and instincts? This is to be done, and *we will do it*.[75]

Although the thoughts of Swami Vivekananda cited above belong to a later period in their actual expression, both in his public lectures and letters, he was expressing them already in informal talks with those who came to see him during his journeys in India. In some of his extant letters of that period (written in Bengali), we hear him, for example, asking a Vedic scholar of Varanasi to show him *where* in the Veda and the Upanishad is there a sanction for declaring caste to be hereditary?[76] It is right, therefore, to bring some of those thoughts of his here so as to indicate the historical source of his self-division. His perceptions of the past, the present and the future of India were not only radically different from those of the traditional pundits and the social reformers alike,[77] he was also showing how the pundits had corrupted the pure teachings of the Upanishads and how the reformers were mistaken in their assumptions; 'in order to cure the boil', as he said in another context, they were 'amputating the arm'. When neither of these two groups could meet his intellectual challenge honestly, some among them would later heap calumny upon him.

---

[75] *SV Letters*, p. 64.
[76] Vivekananda to Pramadadas Mitra, letters dated 7 and 17 August 1889, from Baranagore Math. *SV Letters*, pp. 6–11.
[77] Chaturvedi Badrinath, *Dharma, India and the World Order*, section (viii) 'Vivekananda: Vedanta and the Masses', pp. 201–10.

Orthodox Hindus would listen with bowed heads and a surge of spiritual pride when Swami Vivekananda spoke of the ancient Hindu heritage, but question the ways in which he showed complete freedom from the narrow, sectarian Hindu prejudices. For example, an orthodox Hindu of those days, and in most cases even now, would in normal circumstances not stay with a Muslim, described as *mlechchha*, or take the food offered by him. Swami Vivekananda did both. During his stay of some seven weeks at Alwar in Rajasthan, February–March 1891, a beautiful relationship grew between him and a Maulvi Saheb, a Muslim teacher of Urdu and Persian, and many other Muslims of Alwar. They invited him to their homes with great affection, and he shared with them a modest meal.[78] To the orthodox Hindu, it was pollution; to Swami Vivekananda, whatever was offered with love and grace by whoever was blessed. He despised the word mleccha and the attitudes it signified, and said, 'India's doom was sealed the very day they invented the word MLECHCHHA and stopped from communion with others.'[79]

At Mt Abu, he stayed with a Muslim lawyer who had invited him, saying, 'If you would condescend to come and live with me, I shall feel myself greatly blessed. But I am a Mussalman. I shall, of course, make separate arrangements for your food.' Swami Vivekananda didn't hear a word of *that*. On being asked by a visitor, 'Well, Swamiji, you are a Hindu monk. How is it that you are living with a Mussalman? Your food might, now and then, be touched by him,' this Hindu monk replied:

---

[78] For details, see *The Life*, pp. 207–10.
[79] Vivekananda to Alasinga Perumal, letter dated 27 October 1894. *SV Letters*, p. 171.

Sir, what do you mean? I am a Sannyasin. I am above all your social conventions. I can dine even with a Bhangi.[80] I am not afraid of God, because He sanctions it. I am not afraid of the scriptures, because they allow it. But I am afraid of you people and your society. You know nothing of God and the scriptures. I see Brahman everywhere manifested through even the meanest creature. For me there is nothing high or low. Shiva, Shiva![81]

Swami Vivekananda was confronted with something else besides. From 1813 onwards, when the East India Company had opened India to Christian missionaries, though reluctantly, the latter began their labours in India by attacking Hinduism, or what they understood of it, in a language that was not only un-Christian but also foul. Because India was non-Christian, they had assumed that it was for that reason also uncivilized. To these missionaries, Christianity was the answer to a false religion as well as the means to civilizing an innately depraved people. That phase of abusive evangelicalism, lasting for a hundred years, had reached its climax when Alexander Duff (1806–78) declared with supreme confidence that 'Of all the systems of false religion ever fabricated by the perverse ingenuity of fallen man, Hinduism is surely the most stupendous.'[82] The Protestant missionaries of that period saw themselves

---

[80] A sweeper, a scavenger, considered 'untouchable'.
[81] *The Life*, which describes this incident, p. 218.
[82] Alexander Duff, *India, and Indian Missions: Including Sketches of the Gigantic System of Hinduism etc.* (Edinburgh, 1839), p. 179. For a history of the encounter of Western Christianity with Indian civilization, the reader may have a look at my *Finding Jesus in Dharma. Christianity in India* (Indian Society for Promoting Christian Knowledge, ISPCK, Delhi, 2000). Hereafter, *Jesus in Dharma*. For the phase of the abusive Christianity in India, see Chapter 4 therein, pp. 20–34.

as missionaries not only of Christ but also of civilization, to a people to be saved by the two redeeming lights of Christianity and Western civilization.[83] Swami Vivekananda, who carried with him the *Imitation of Christ* along with the *Bhagvad-Gita* during his parivrajaka days, had to show the truth that the Christian missionaries of those times understood little of Christ and nothing of the depths of Indian culture. Neither did they know that Christianity had flourished as a respected faith in a southern part of India at least four centuries before Europe and England came to be Christianized. Monier Williams (1819–99), a British Orientalist, was telling them, 'We can avoid denouncing in strong language what we have never thoroughly investigated, and do not thoroughly understand.' That was in 1877.[84] Alone and defenceless, Jesus Christ had taught that it is love that redeems, and was nailed to the Cross: the missionaries who came to India in His name, secure under British rule, were spreading hatred. Swami Vivekananda had to teach the Christian West that 'love is life, hatred is death', the essence of the Vedanta, and that no one religion can claim for itself absolute truth.

We are fortunate in having in Haripada Mitra's reminiscences of October 1892 a narration of the Swami's ideas on the many questions concerning life and truth many people ask, as Haripada did and did most intelligently. The question about Christian missionaries also came up between them. Haripada remarked, 'They had done, and had been doing, a great deal of good to our country.' At this, Swami Vivekananda said:

---

[83] Chaturvedi Badrinath, *Jesus in Dharma*, p. 20.
[84] Ibid., p. 22. See also pp. 19–23.

But the amount of evil they have done is no less. They have done all in their power to throw to the winds the little faith that our people had in themselves and their own culture. Loss of faith means disintegration of personality itself. Does anybody understand that? How can the missionaries prove the superiority of their own religion without decrying our deities, without condemning our religion? There is another point to consider. If anyone has to preach a particular religion, he must not only believe in it fully, but also practise it in life with full faith and sincerity. Most of the missionaries say one thing and do something else. I can never tolerate dishonesty.[85]

Furthermore, he suffered at the sight of his motherland under foreign domination. He had to fight the untruth of the British rulers; for, in search of a moral justification for British rule in India, a resolute effort was being made to show it as a mission of civilization to barbarians. It was being argued that Indians had no political philosophy, had never had any self-governing institutions, had no idea of civic liberty and freedom; steeped in darkness, they had only a long history of one tyranny replacing the other. The racial arrogance of the imperialists showed in their behaviour towards Indians. During a journey by train, two Englishmen, travelling in the same coach as Vivekananda, began between themselves to use the rich vocabulary of denigration of everything that was Indian. The Swami listened, seemingly unconcerned. At a particular station, somebody came with whom he spoke

---

[85] *Reminiscences*, pp. 42-43. For the response of Indian Christians themselves to missionary Christianity, see again Chaturvedi Badrinath, *Jesus in Dharma*, pp. 76–98: for the concerns and the direction of Indian Christian thought, pp. 99–138.

in English. Afterwards, those two asked him why he didn't tell them that he knew English. The Swami answered, in English, 'It is not for the first time that I am seeing fools!'

Sri Ramakrishna had once said: 'There are two characteristics of knowledge: a peaceful nature and absence of pride.'[86] These were the two innate characteristics also of Swami Vivekananda, to which all those who met him and heard him during his parivrajaka days bore witness. Haripada Mitra, with whom he stayed at Belgaum in October 1892, later recalled:

He would be merry, full of gaiety, fun, and laughter, just like a boy, even when imparting the highest instruction. He laughed and made others laugh with him. Then, suddenly, he would start explaining an intricate point with such seriousness that people wondered at his mastery over the subject and over himself.[87]

His easy sense of fun and laughter, which he would retain as long as he lived, came from the deep peace within him, and was reflected in his eyes. There are numerous accounts of how somebody agitated and disturbed would feel within himself the miracle of peace in his even fleeting nearness with Vivekananda. As regards his own self, there was in Swami Vivekananda not a trace of pride. Nor a trace of arrogance in the replies he would give to the questions people asked, even though the questions were often silly, and as often asked only to test his knowledge of the subject. A pundit from the south would discover not before long that Vivekananda knew Sanskrit grammar and the meaning of a philosophical text better than he did. A teacher of science

---

[86] M—The Gospel, entry dated 2 September 1885, p. 831.
[87] Reminiscences, p. 30.

would quickly discover that this itinerant sadhu knew his
Darwin better than he did, and he could take lessons from
him in the fundamentals of science. But, through all these,
there would be playing on Vivekananda's lips a smile of
great amusement; that is, when he saw why the question
was asked.

Yet, when Swami Vivekananda walked, there was a
grandeur of pride about him that nobody could miss. It
was his pride in the inheritance bequeathed to him; not all the
riches of the world could ever equal this. For that very reason,
inner peace he did not have. When he spoke, it was a mixture
of anger and sadness at what India had reduced itself to,
never for anything concerning himself. Nobody could miss
that either. Many were amazed at his easy transition from
the Upanishads to Kant and Hegel and back again, which
was never with a view to showing off his knowledge of
Western philosophy, but because an intricate argument
was involved concerning, for example, the concepts of 'space'
and 'time'. But they were perplexed even more that the face
they earlier saw radiating peace and tranquillity was now
suddenly flushed with tears of anger and sadness. At one
moment, he was speaking, in his deep melodious voice, of
the riches of Indian spiritual perspectives; in the next, of the
Indian masses and the causes of their degradation. Nobody
understood that Swami Vivekananda was caught in the net
of history when his deepest nature was to float in the vastness
of transcendence. All his writings, like the person, are
clearly divided between these two.

In his parivrajaka years, Vivekananda was forming
relationships that would endure as long as he lived and,
with humility, was learning from them. In that, he had
the example of Sri Ramakrishna; except that whereas
Sri Ramakrishna mostly remained at Dakshineswar, apart

from his pilgrimage to Vrindavan and Varanasi and Vaidyanath where Mathur Babu took him, his apostle Narendranath had known many more roads. Vivekananda's life was distinguished by the *quality* of his relationships, touching so many lives almost always at the core. Nor was it ever a case of only giving. He was receiving no less; for such was the quality of his giving. If we are to *meet* Swami Vivekananda at all, and not kill him in advance by confining him to a few images of him, we have to meet also those with whom he had relationships of great emotional and spiritual depths. It is in them that he *lived* Vedanta, not as some self-conscious programme, but as something that was as natural to him as breathing.

It is a strange but hardy notion both of 'spirituality' and 'greatness' that the spiritually great only dispense *to* ordinary mortals—blessing, benediction, enlightenment— and themselves do not need any of these *from* others. Swami Vivekananda entertained no such notion of self-importance. One should be careful then, in narrating the import of Swami Vivekananda to our times, not to fall in with the prevalent tendency of chanting how he had transformed so many lives in India and the West, without saying that his life was enriched, too, by those who loved him. The first, he was not aware of, and not once did he claim that he had 'transformed' anybody's life; the second, he acknowledged *always*—another distinctive mark of his spiritual greatness. One never tires of hearing how, wherever he went, even before he had spoken a word people felt greatly drawn towards his magnetic personality. But we hardly ever hear that there were not a few towards whom Swami Vivekananda felt greatly drawn too. He said, in words most touching, that he *did*.

Swami Vivekananda never entertained the widespread notion that it would lessen the sainthood of a saint if he were to say to another, 'I miss you'.

Pramadadas Mitra, a renowned Vedic scholar of Varanasi, was one of those whom he missed. He had met him during his second journey to Varanasi sometime in 1888; a deep friendship of spirit and intellect blossomed between them. In his letter (written in Bengali) of 4 July 1889 from the Baranagore Math, Vivekananda, more accurately Narendranath, or 'Vividishananda',[88] wrote to him:

Words fail to describe how strong is the desire in my mind to go to Varanasi and have my soul blessed by meeting you and sojourning with you in good converse, but everything depends on His will! I wonder what linking of heart existed between us, sir, from some previous incarnation that…only through one day's interview, my heart felt charmed enough to accept you as a near relative and friend in spiritual life![89]

And the following, on 3 March 1890 from Ghazipur: 'Is it a mere idle fancy of mine that between us there is some connection from previous birth? Just see how one letter from you sweeps away all my resolution, and I bend my steps towards Varanasi leaving all matters behind!'[90]

In his letters to Pramadadas Mitra, Narendranath was raising some challenging questions concerning, for example, the philosophical positions of Shankara, and was

---

[88] In the *Letters of Swami Vivekananda*, he is shown signing his letters even of those days as 'Vivekananda etc.', which is manifestly wrong, 'etc.' or not; for 'Vivekananda' would be born only four years later, at Khetri.

[89] *SV Letters*, p. 4.

[90] Ibid., p. 22.

seeking answers to them. But he was also confiding in him his inner anguish in leaving, for a life of renunciation, his mother and two very young brothers in their poor financial circumstances, living in the same city as them, Calcutta, all the time aware of the unhappy situation of those he dearly loved.[91]

From Ghazipur again, he was writing to Pramadadas Mitra all about Pavahari Baba and the complex developments that had taken place between them. The Swami had felt greatly drawn towards this saint.[92] Yearning for a life of complete withdrawal from the outside world in the fashion of Pavahari Baba, he visited him every day for many days, but the saint seemed in no hurry to gift Vivekananda anything from his spiritual treasury of Yoga, only two words 'stay on'. 'So I wait in hope.'[93] He felt even more troubled for many days by the thought that Sri Ramakrishna, who had shown that true worship of God is in the service of man, was being replaced in his devotion to Pavahari Baba. But that was not the only thing: Swami Vivekananda was suffering from lumbago, and was in great physical pain. Besides, the news reached him that Kali (Abhedananda) was ill at Hrishikesh, and he would have to go to him if required. His relationship with Pavahari Baba was coming to a curious end. On 3 March, he wrote to Pramadadas:

...The lumbago obstinately refuses to leave me, and the pain is very great. For the last few days I haven't been able to go to see

---

[91] Vivekananda to Pramadadas Mitra, letters dated 4 July, 7 and 17 August 1889, from Baranagore Math. *SV Letters*, pp. 3–5, 6-7 and 7–11 respectively.
[92] For Vivekananda's description of Pavahari Baba, see his letter dated 7 February 1890. *SV Letters*, pp. 12-13.
[93] In the same letter as above, p. 13.

Pavahariji, but out of his kindness he sends every day for my report. But now I see the whole matter is inverted in its bearings! While I myself have come, a beggar, at his door, he turns round and wants to learn of me! This saint is perhaps not yet perfected—too much of practices, vows, observances, and too much of self-concealment...So it is not good, I have decided, to disturb this Sadhu for nothing, and very soon I shall ask leave of him to go.[94]

So, most likely in late March or early April 1890, Vivekananda left Ghazipur and headed straight to Varanasi, to his loved friend of the spirit and intellect—Pramadadas Mitra, and to the river Ganga. But his joy in the nearness of both was short-lived. There he heard the news that Balaram Bose had died on 13 April and Surendranath Mitra was seriously ill. And he felt deeply grieved. On Pramadadas expressing surprise that a sannyasin and a Vedantin should be assailed by ordinary human emotions, Narendranath said to him: 'Please do not talk that way. We are not dry monks. What! Do you think that because a man is Sannyasin he has no heart!'[95]

Vivekananda rushed back to Calcutta. Surendranath Mitra,[96] the provider of the Baranagore Math, died on 25 May that year. These two deaths in quick succession greatly saddened him.

Meanwhile, Pavahari Baba was in no hurry to let him go. The brother-monks of Vivekananda had come to know of his attachment to Pavahari Baba at Ghazipur and feared that, in this new love of his, Sri Ramakrishna was being

---

[94] SV Letters, p. 21.
[95] The Life, p. 189.
[96] See page 82-83 of this chapter.

replaced.[97] We learn from *The Life* that 'Premananda was one of those who had mistaken Naren's devotion to Pavahari Baba for disloyalty to Sri Ramakrishna, and he had come to Ghazipur to persuade Naren to go to Varanasi. Naren was very harsh with him and sent him away'.[98] Their attitude irritated him. There was a world of difference between *his* fear and theirs. What he had feared, if only for a few days, was that he was now on the road, not of service to man Sri Ramakrishna had put him on but of the bliss of divine solitude which Pavahari Baba could take him into. Vivekananda had recognized in himself two equally powerful but opposite forces at work, one demanding energetic action on behalf of the downtrodden masses of India, and the other seeking that state of being in which there is the limitless joy of floating in *sat-chit-ananda*—alone. Self-divided thus, he saw that the one could be achieved only at the expense of the other.[99] But his brother-monks seemed to think that the devotion to Sri Ramakrishna should exclude even an acknowledgement that spiritual greatness exists elsewhere too. It was no different from the demand commonly heard among ordinary men and women: 'If you love me, you must not love anyone else.' He had to cure them of that limited thinking. His own attitude did not confine greatness, and had a wider sweep: 'I make no distinction as to householder or Sannyasin in

---

[97] Sri Ramakrishna had heard of Pavahari Baba when, returning from their visit to Ghazipur, some Brahmos had told him about the great Yogi. See M–*The Gospel*, entry dated 27 October 1882, p. 62.
[98] *The Life*, p. 188.
[99] *The Life* clearly speaks of this self-division in Vivekananda and shows a deep understanding of what it was; p. 185.

this, that for all time my head should bend low in reverence wherever I see greatness, broadness of heart, and holiness.'[100]

And these he saw as much in Pavahari Baba as in Pramadadas, in Balaram Bose and in Surendranath Mitra. As long as Swami Vivekananda lived, he would find greatness, broadness of heart and holiness, in many other men and women. And his head never failed to bow.

He later wrote about Pavahari Baba as, 'a man of wonderful humility and self-realization', and ended by saying that he 'owes a deep debt of gratitude to the departed saint and dedicates these lines, however unworthy, to the memory of one of the greatest Masters he has loved and served.'[101]

Many persons would speak of Swami Vivekananda in the same words. Some would write him into the lines of their lives. Sharat Chandra Gupta, the stationmaster of the Hathras railway station, was one of them. The story of their relationship is fascinating; which is true about every single relationship in Vivekananda's life.

To condense *any* relationship is to do injury to it; for *every* relationship has so many levels and so many colours, even more so when it is with a man like Swami Vivekananda. And every relationship is the lived story of two persons, each having others too in their respective lives. That was true, as we saw in the previous chapter, about Narendranath's own relationship with Sri Ramakrishna. Therefore, every relationship has to be narrated fully; that

---

[100] Vivekananda to Pramadadas Mitra, letter dated 17 August 1889. *SV Letters*, p. 8.
[101] *CWSV*, Vol. IV, p. 295. His 'Sketch of the Life of Pavahari Baba' is to be found at pp. 283–95.

is, as much of it as is accessible, though much of it remains inaccessible even to the two persons concerned, unfolding only gradually.[102]

The story of Sharat Chandra Gupta (later Swami Sadananda) and his guru Vivekananda requires a fuller narration than what exists now. But here it will have to be condensed even more than elsewhere.[103] It was sometime in 1888, perhaps in September of that year, that the two met. Vivekananda was on his way to Haridwar from Vrindavan and decided to take a train from Hathras. While he was waiting for the train, the stationmaster noticed him, came up to him, asked him if he was hungry, and when the monk said that he was, Sharat took him to his quarters. After the Swami had been fed, they plunged into poetry and philosophy; but the stationmaster had to return to minding the trains. The Swami stayed in Hathras for several days, during which Sharat Gupta invited his friends to meet him. Many evenings of stirring conversations followed, as they did whenever Vivekananda discovered an old friend and moved to his house. Sharat, himself a Bengali, had grown up in Jaunpur in an environment of Muslim culture and manners, full of Urdu poetry and literature. Very perceptive as a result, one day he noticed the Swami looking sad and asked him why. The Swami said that it was the poverty and ignorance of the Indian masses, to whose service he had dedicated himself, that had made him sad. Sharat

---

[102] It is in recognition of this that Pravrajika Atmaprana wrote the life story of Margaret Noble (Sister Nivedita), and Pravrajika Prabuddhaprana of Josephine MacLeod and of Sara Chapman Bull, the strong life currents of their subjects mixing with other lives, never weakly, although Swami Vivekananda remained the dominant flow.
[103] See *The Life*, pp. 175–78.

Gupta asked if he could be of any service. Vivekananda said, 'Yes, take up the kamandalu and go begging.' Sharat, never a literal-minded person, quickly understood the metaphorical meaning of both. 'Renounce the limited interests of your life and work for the good of many.' And that is what he promptly did. Later he would say, in a poet's language, 'I followed those devilish eyes.'

After making satisfactory arrangements for someone to replace him, Sharat gave up his career. The two left Hathras, by train, for Haridwar, and from there, on foot, for Hrishikesh. There they felt the inexpressible inner joy of being in the forests and the nearness of the Ganga. For centuries, the forests and the Ganga had their own poetry, and Swami Vivekananda loved being with someone with whom he could *feel* that poetry, which he never could, and never did, with any of his brother-monks. He initiated Sharat Gupta into a life of renunciation with a new name for him—Swami Sadananda, his first direct monastic disciple. Not used to the rigours of an itinerant monk, Sharat one day felt exhausted and collapsed in a forest in Hrishikesh. His guru literally carried his disciple on his back, and his shoes on his head. Sharat being ill, both of them returned to Hathras. There, Vivekananda himself was struck with malaria. On recovering from it, he returned to the Baranagore Math. Sadananda came there later, and the direct disciples of Sri Ramakrishna had with them the first monastic disciple of Naren. Sadananda remained attached to his guru with the bonds of love till the latter's last day. Feeling forlorn one day, Sadananda expressed his fear that his guru might give him up, and Vivekananda said to him: 'You fool, do you not remember that I even carried your shoes on my head?'[104] 'How can I describe him, friends,' Swami Sadananda later said, 'except by the word Love, Love, Love.'

In the years to follow, it is by that word—'love'—that many of those who would come to know him would best describe Swami Vivekananda; and it is by that word, 'love', that he would best describe the Vedanta, the *living* Vedanta.

Another important relationship Swami Vivekananda formed during his parivrajaka days was with Raja Ajit Singh of Khetri. They met at Mt Abu on 4 June 1891.[105] After many intense conversations with him, seeking spiritual knowledge, Ajit Singh felt so greatly drawn towards the Swami that he entreated him to come with him to Khetri and be his guest. The invitation pressed lovingly, the Swami agreed. They arrived at Khetri on 7 August. The Swami stayed with him for several weeks, during which time Ajit Singh came to look upon him as his spiritual mentor, having for him profound reverence, feeling blessed in serving him. The Swami in turn developed feelings of deep love and affection for the Raja. It was Raja Ajit Singh who would meet the cost of his travel to America. On his part, it was to Raja Ajit Singh, and to no one else, that Vivekananda would turn, as one would to a close relative, to seek financial help for his mother, Bhubaneswari Devi, who lived in Calcutta in a wretched, poor condition. He was among those to whom he would write from America some of his most stirring

---

[104] *The Life*, p. 177.

[105] This, and some other dates concerning the Swami's connection with Khetri, not to be found in any other biography of Vivekananda, are provided by Gautam Ghosh, *The Prophet of Modern India. A Biography of Swami Vivekananda* (Rupa & Co., 2003), p. 38. As the source for this date, Ghosh quotes the state diary.

letters. When the Raja died in 1901 at Agra in a freak accident, the Swami was very sad. The name of Raja Ajit Singh of Khetri will remain inseparable from the life story of Swami Vivekananda.

The number of people whose lives Vivekananda impacted while he was touching the dust of India was incredibly large. Many of them were highly educated people, lawyers, doctors, administrators and were men of means but quite as many were illiterate and poor. We know the names of many of them, but quite as many remain nameless, Hindus and Muslims alike. At many places, he met eminent Sanskrit grammarians, from whom he sought to learn, and with whom he spent much time. In big towns and cities, his perceptive eyes also saw the harmful effects of English education, because that education carried with it cultural presuppositions which were uncritically accepted though they were not true. Among the people he met in the villages, he saw not only the tyranny of priest craft, but also a quest for higher truths, simple faith, and goodness of heart. With all of them he forged bonds, into which he poured his immense spiritual energy and love. That was Swami Vivekananda's *living* Vedanta.

Among the numerous people whose lives the Swami touched in different degrees, several were Maharajas and their Dewans: of Alwar, Khetri, Junagad, Kutch, Kolhapur, Baroda, Mysore, Travancore, Ramnad. He never sought their company but, when invited respectfully, he never refused to meet them either. Rather, in his conversations with them, he stressed that the Indian rulers change their perceptions and employ their resources in the service of the masses, in the area of education most of all. Which Maharaja was not struck by the amazing sweep and depth of his knowledge and the illumination of his spirit, and did not bow? And which Maharaja was not struck by the easy grace of his kingly manners? With this difference, though, that this kingly sannyasin was as happy in spending a night at the house of a scavenger.

There was another difference which became a subject of some astonishment. This sannyasin spoke English with a remarkable command over that language. That is how the word would spread in the town he was visiting. But the greatest difference, people quickly found, was that every word he spoke quivered with deep *feeling*, changing thereby the familiar spiritual stuff from a sannyasin into a vibrant experience. On hearing Swami Vivekananda on the Vedanta or on the depressing condition of the Indian masses, people felt related to *him* in the first place and only then to the other two. The result was that on his leaving, they felt an inexpressible loss. At Alwar, many young people insisted on walking with him as far as he would let them as their personal farewell, and he felt deeply touched. It turned into a happy caravan, singing, dancing, sitting under a tree listening to his words—not empty words but words burnished gold in the fire of his self-realization. K. Sundararama Iyer, with whom Vivekananda would stay at Trivandrum for nine days in December 1892, wrote in his reminiscences of him:

...I must not fail to mention the fact that during all the time he stayed, he took captive every heart within the home. To everyone of us he was all sweetness, all tenderness, all grace...It hardly seemed as if there was a stranger moving in our midst. When he left, it seemed for a time as if the light had gone out of our home.[106]

---

[106] K. Sundararama Iyer in *Reminiscences*, p. 69.

Not all relationships are spectacular or even outwardly lasting; often they arise from a gesture, from a look and then pass, but actually remain somewhere in one's consciousness throughout one's life. The following are only two of the many such instances relating to Vivekananda.

When he was leaving Mysore, the Maharaja, Chamaraja Wodeyar,[107] entreated him to accept from him some gifts and so did the Dewan of the Mysore State. Vivekananda would not hear of it. But not wanting to hurt their feelings when the gifts were being pressed on him reverentially, he said to the Maharaja that, maybe, he could give him a pipe and the Dewan could give him a cigar. The Maharaja gifted him a beautifully carved pipe, which he enjoyed smoking on his subsequent journeys. When he arrived in Madras towards the end of December 1892, and was staying with an old friend of his Calcutta days, Manmatha Nath Bhattacharya, one day he saw his cook looking admiringly at that carved pipe of his. Noticing that look, the Swami asked him if he would like to have it. Not believing what he had heard, the cook remained speechless, still looking longingly at the pipe. The Swami put it into his hands: 'Here, it is yours.' That too was a relationship, of a moment, but complete in itself which the cook would have carried in his heart all his life.[108]

Of equal importance in knowing Swami Vivekananda, is another such relationship Manmatha Nath Ganguli (not Bhattacharya) witnessed at the Belur Math and narrated in his memories of him:

---

[107] This is how the name is spelled in *The Life*, 'Wadiyar', p. 241; elsewhere, in *Vivekananda. A Biography in Pictures* (Advaita Ashrama, Kolkata; 5th ed., 2003), as 'Wodeyar', p. 36.
[108] This incident is described in *The Life*, see p. 270.

…That afternoon some young men had come to see Swamiji. They were about ten or twelve and most of them might be college students. They had assembled on the veranda facing the Ganga on the first floor before Swamiji's room. Swamiji came out after a short time and talked with them very freely. He was so jovial that he himself looked like them—quite young and enthusiastic.

…There was a solid gold chain, around his neck, attached to a gold watch in his pocket…One of the young men touched the chain with his fingers and said, 'It is very beautiful.' At once Swamiji took the watch out of his pocket and put the chain with the gold watch in the hand of that youth who in amazement had then cupped his palms. He said, 'You like it! Then it is yours. But my boy, do not sell it. Keep it with you as a souvenir.' Needless to say the young man was extremely happy. I marvelled at the ease with which Swamiji could part with such a valuable thing; not only for its cost but the present was also invaluable for its association.[109]

That gold watch with the gold chain had belonged to Vivekananda's father. Nobody knows who that young man was, for Ganguli does not seem to have asked him his name. When one is witnessing an act of such spontaneous selfless giving, one's thoughts are on the giver and not on the receiver. It could have been *any* young man. Neither do we know what that young man did with that gold watch and chain or whether, in later years, anybody claimed being given by the Swami Vivekananda what had been on his person once.

None of Vivekananda's relationships during his parivrajaka days, of whom a few have been described briefly in the foregoing pages, nor any of those he would form in the West, was the portrait of a man self-divided. The truth

---

[109] Manmatha Nath Ganguli, in the *Reminiscences*, pp. 347-48.

about Vivekananda is that when someone gave something
to him, he gave it away to others; and, then, not only
material *things*. What he received as spiritual inheritance,
he was at all times restless to give to others. It can truthfully
be said that there was perhaps no other man with a richer
inheritance and driven more to share all of it with the
whole world, and no other man more torn apart as a
consequence. The story of Swami Vivekananda's life is a
puzzling, often incomprehensible, story of one of the great
men of all times, integrated within and yet so self-divided;
floating in the ecstasy of divine love, taking others into
it, and yet so painfully tormented. A tempest on a tranquil
sea.

4

Towards the New World

Swamiji, I am afraid you cannot do much in this country. Few will appreciate you here. You ought to go to the West where people will understand you and your worth. Surely you can throw a great light upon Western culture by preaching the Sanatana Dharma!
—Pandit Shankar Pandurang,
Vedic scholar, to Swami Vivekananda[1]

It is profoundly ironical that it was at Porbandar, where Mahatma Gandhi was born twenty-two years earlier, in 1869, Swami Vivekananda seriously began to think of going to the West to seek help for the regeneration of the masses of India. From 1908, when Gandhi first wrote his *Hind Swaraj* in his mother tongue Gujarati,[2] to the end of his days in January 1948, he remained steadfast in his complete rejection of Western civilization with its institutions as embodying violence. (Ironically, it is now the people in the West, whose civilization he had rejected, who are upholding and advocating him and his philosophy of life.) With a deep knowledge of Western thought, which Gandhi never had, Vivekananda was correcting *in advance*, as it were,

---

[1] *The Life*, pp. 226-27.
[2] Translated into English and published as *Hind Swaraj* the following year, 1909.

Gandhi's one-sided view of Western civilization, of its disorders without seeing the richness of what it had bequeathed to mankind. It was so one-sided that it was violence no less, and amounted to untruth besides.[3] The great son of Porbandar had always had a limited understanding of Indian civilization too, having little knowledge of the development of Indian thought beyond Vaishnavism and some aspects of Jaina ethics. Misconceptions of Hinduism were quite as Hindu as they were Western.[4] It was at Porbandar, by thinking of going to the West, that Swami Vivekananda was correcting in advance the Hindu misconceptions of Hinduism as well. That juxtaposition between Swami Vivekananda and Gandhi, unknown to each other, might have had some unseen mystic irony. In 1891, Gandhi had returned to India from England, was in Bombay, and had learnt of his mother's death; it is most unlikely that he did not visit Porbandar, where Vivekananda was staying with Pandit Shankar Pandurang, a great Vedic scholar. There is nothing to suggest that the future 'Mahatma' and the Swami met then or ever. Yet, they did—*via* irony. It is *via* the irony of Porbandar that the two very different perceptions of Indian and Western civilizations met, in the persons of two among the greatest men of India.

---

[3] On this, Rajmohan Gandhi, a grandson of the Mahatma, says: '*Hind Swaraj* is a text for its times, not for all time. I for one am unable to accept the sweeping statement: "The tendency of the Indian civilization is to elevate the moral being; that of the Western civilization is to propagate immorality. The latter is godless, the former is based on a belief in God."' See his *The Good Boatman* (Viking, Penguin Books India, 1995), p. 139.

[4] See Chaturvedi Badrinath, *Dharma, India and the World Order*, already cited; Chapter 21, 'Modern Indian Perceptions of India and the West', pp. 151–328.

Pandit Shankar Pandurang was not only a Vedic scholar but also the Dewan of the princely state of Porbandar. When Swami Vivekananda met him, he was translating the Vedas. A great friendship developed between the two. The shastri quickly discovered that this itinerant monk was himself a scholar, with deep insights into the meanings embedded in a text, and could help him through several obscure passages in the Vedas. He requested him to stay as long as he possibly could. But what the shastri said to the monk, reproduced at the beginning of the chapter, was the first unfolding of the latter's invisible destiny. During the eleven months that they were together, Shankar Pandurang made yet another suggestion—to learn French: 'It will be of use to you, Swamiji!'[5] Together with exploring further the depths of Patanjali's *Mahabhashya* and the Vedas, Swami Vivekananda began to learn French, and must have felt the thrill of learning a new language not only as something 'of use', but as a door to another sensibility. As we shall see later,[6] this too was a preparation for a destiny yet unknown.

But preaching to the West was not what was on Swami Vivekananda's mind. The regeneration of India was his main passion.

...I am thoroughly convinced that no individual or nation can live by holding itself apart from the community of others, and whenever such an attempt has been made under false ideas of greatness, policy, or holiness—the result has always been disastrous to the secluding one.

To my mind, the one great cause of the downfall and the degradation of India was the building of a wall of custom—whose

---

[5] Ibid., p. 226.
[6] In Chapter 10.

foundation was hatred of others—round the nation, and the real aim of which in ancient times was to prevent the Hindus from coming in contact with the surrounding Buddhistic nations.

Whatever cloak ancient or modern sophistry may try to throw over it, the inevitable result—the vindication of the moral law, that none can hate others without degenerating himself—is that the race that was foremost amongst the ancient races is now a byword, and a scorn among nations. We are object lessons of the violation of that law which our ancestors were the first to discover and discriminate.

Give and take is the law, and if India wants to raise herself once more, it is absolutely necessary that she brings out her treasures and throws them broadcast among the nations of the earth, and in return be ready to receive what others have to give her. Expansion is life, contraction is death. Love is life and hatred is death. We commenced to die the day we began to hate other races, and nothing can prevent our death unless we come back to expansion, which is life.

We must mix, therefore, with all the races of the earth. And every Hindu that goes out to travel in foreign parts renders more benefit to his country than hundreds of men who are bundles of superstitions and selfishness and whose one aim in life seems to be like that of the dog in the manger...[7]

It was at Kathiawar, and later at Khandwa, that the Swami had first heard of a Parliament of Religions to be held at Chicago in 1893. He spoke about it definitely to his host, Haripada Mitra, at Belgaum in October 1892: 'I shall go there if I get an opportunity.' 'When I proposed to raise money by subscription,' Haripada later recalled,

---

[7] Vivekananda to Raja Pyari Mohan Mukherjee of Calcutta, letter dated 18 November 1894, from New York. *SV Letters*, pp. 171-72.

'he refused it for some reason best known to himself.'[8] The Swami had spoken generally of his feeling about a mission to the West also to the Maharaja of Mysore, Chamaraja Wodeyar, who offered to meet all expenses for his journey to the West; but that offer, too, was politely declined.[9]

That was because he was not yet certain. It was only after his visit to Kanyakumari, praying at the shrine of the Virgin Goddess, after his now well-known experience there, that he was convinced of a mission beckoning him from faraway. It was a vision of Sri Ramakrishna, telling him 'Go', and he was certain of his destiny. Yet, he seemed to alternate between certainty and doubt, but not out of confusion or out of weakness. It only showed another trait of his character. Everyone who met Swami Vivekananda, or saw him even from a distance, was struck by his grandeur; but Vivekananda had no grandiose ideas about himself. Not even after what Sri Ramakrishna Paramahamsa had told him *who* he was. Visiting Rameswaram, Ramnad, Madurai and Pondicherry, when the Swami arrived in Madras in early January 1893, he was charged with an even more intense energy that glowed on his face, as if he were on fire. At the same time there was around him a sea of tranquillity, without a ripple. Those who knew him at that time, saw both.

Madras was to play a central part in the story of 'the work', in the service to man, about which Vivekananda was always restless. Without knowing its exact form, he was now burning with the certainty of the first steps towards its fulfilment. The story of his days in Madras at

---

[8] Haripada Mitra, in *Reminiscences*, p. 32.
[9] *The Life*, p. 243.

the beginning of 1893 was in most respects a replay of what was by then a pattern of response to him elsewhere. Although true, this is not so simple. For it is also true that, *to* Vivekananda, nothing, no person, was ever 'as of a pattern', he least of all. What was different was that, in Madras, a group of young men gathered round him, some of them householders, with a far more resolute dedication than he had found elsewhere. Alasinga Perumal was the most prominent among them.

Once it became known that the Swami wanted to go to the Parliament of Religions in America, there were many offers of financial help, some from the rich bankers of Madras. But he was clear in his mind where the money was to come from—from the ordinary people, on whose behalf he was going to the West. Himself charged with spiritual energy, Alasinga Perumal went with others from door to door, to raise the required money. A close bond that was not of this world was established between him and Swami Vivekananda. Many of the most important letters the Swami wrote from America were addressed to Alasinga Perumal. The Swami loved him, cared for him, guided him in his spiritual journey, in a fleeting mood of despair wrote to him angrily, scolded him, gave him his blessings and, above all, expressed his gratitude to him for what he had done for him.

Beyond the fact that Alasinga Perumal was the headmaster of a high school attached to the Pachaiyappa's College, and a Vaishnava and a householder, we know practically nothing about him. The Indian biographers of Swami Vivekananda had evidently no interest in Alasinga Perumal apart from mentioning that he had begged from door to door and collected the major part of the money.[10] This is *not* an insignificant omission. It shows an attitude, which has a pattern throughout. Whereas Swami Vivekananda never drowned anyone who came into his life in the sea of his greatness, never dissolved the *other*, his Indian biographers tend to do mostly that.

Swami Vivekananda commands, as it were, that before a word more is said about *him*, what K. Sundararama Iyer had said about Alasinga Perumal should be recounted. In the previous chapter, Sundararama Iyer was mentioned as the Swami's host in Trivandrum. His second reminiscence relating to Vivekananda's stay in Madras on his return from America opens with Alasinga Perumal.

I must first mention the name of Mr. M.C. Alasinga Perumal, late headmaster of the High School attached to Pacheyappa's College. From the time when the Swami first came to Madras in December 1892 after his visit to Kanyakumari and Rameswaram, he attached himself with adoring love and never-failing enthusiasm to the Swami's person and to his ministry in the world in all its phases and details—an adhesion and service to the Great Master which, to me at least, has always seemed a thing of beauty and brought to me a consolation and joy in many a dark hour of my heart's sinkings. That our degenerate Hindu society could still produce one who had in his nature so pure and perfect a passion for reverence and tender affection towards the Swami's prophetic soul was to me a discovery; and I have seen nothing like it in this southern peninsula at least of the Indian continent. He was the life and soul of the work of all kinds done in South India in support

---

[10] That is all that the 'Eastern and Western Disciples' who wrote *The Life of Swami Vivekananda* have to tell us about Alasinga Perumal; see p. 278. Swami Nikhilananda, in his biography of Vivekananda, does not even mention him.

of the Swami's ministry, or by his direction and suggestion. 'Achinga'—as we familiarly used to call him—was hard at work and ever vigilant.[11]

It is a common experience that, floating on love, one is hardly aware of the practical questions of life. Floating on divine love, one is even less so. Not surprisingly, therefore, neither to Shrimat Swami Vivekananda nor to his 'Madras boys', as he called them, did it occur to first find out when exactly the Parliament of Religions was to be held, and what were the requirements for being a delegate to it, and also, equally important, what the daily cost of living in a big American city might probably be. Thoroughly oblivious about such things, they didn't. As it turned out, each one of these three acts of oversight brought into Vivekananda's life men and women whose lives would merge with each other and whose names would remain inseparable from the story of his life. It is not entirely improbable that there was a mystic *reason* in those as well, although that is no recommendation for being unmindful.

While Alasinga Perumal and the other 'boys' were collecting funds for the Swami's journey to America, the Swami approached Colonel (Henry Steel) Olcott (1832–1907),[12] the leading theosophist, whether he would write a letter introducing him to his friends in America, as this could be helpful. Vivekananda knew all about theosophy and the theosophists; his serious disagreements with them, known to the theosophists in Calcutta, were on philosophical grounds. In Madras, he was on their home turf, for Adyar,

---

[11] K. Sundararama Iyer, in *Reminiscences*, p. 71.
[12] Born, 1 August 1832, in New Jersey, USA; died, 17 February 1907, in Adyar, Madras.

Madras, was the headquarters of the Theosophical Society. Olcott refused to write any such letter. The more the American men and women opened their hearts and minds to Swami Vivekananda and to his *living* Vedanta, the greater was the calumny that American theosophists heaped upon him. But they were not the only ones; there were others, too. A more detailed account of that painful episode had better be reserved for a later chapter.[13] However, it is right that Olcott's own denial of the accusation against him be set down here, even though it belongs to 1897. In a long letter to the *Indian Mirror*, published in that newspaper on 12 March 1897,[14] he said, concerning his alleged refusal to introduce Vivekananda to the American Theosophists:

...He (Vivekananda) has, through lapse of memory or artificially excited present nervous excitement, perhaps, misreported the conversation between us at Adyar before his departure for America. I never uttered one word, capable of being understood, as he explained my reply to his alleged demand for a circular letter and introduction for America, nor have I the least recollection of his having asked me for any such letter. I am so convinced of this that nothing short of documentary evidence in my own handwriting would make me alter my belief. The Swami was hostile to our Society in Calcutta before coming here, and his tone, when speaking about Madame Blavatsky, our Theosophical ideas, and our revered, personally known *Gurudevas*, was so cold and unsympathetic as to give me the impression of his being our enemy.

What should also be set down here is the response to Colonel Olcott that followed. Somebody with the initials 'S.S.S.'

<hr />

[13] See Chapter 10.
[14] See Sankari Prasad Basu and Sunil Bihari Ghosh, *Vivekananda in Indian Newspapers 1893–1902*, pp. 182-83.

wrote in the same newspaper an even longer letter, dated 19 March 1897:

...So far as the conversation that took place in Madras between the Swami and the Colonel before departure of the former for America is concerned, the allegation is that the latter refused to help the Swami unless he joined the Theosophical movement. He (Olcott) virtually admits this, though it is cleverly put forward as a possibility.

It is, perhaps, useless to offer the corroborative testimony of those that were actually present on the occasion to one, who has made up his mind not to accept anything short of a written admission...I have been assured that the Swami's version of the conversation is quite true. And it will gladden the heart of many an honest Theosophist, who is not too much of a partisan, to know that there were present at that interview two European Theosophists, one of whom thoroughly disapproved of the Colonel's attitude and tried to make amends for it by himself giving introductions to his friends in England. Certainly, no one expects and the Swami does not pretend to give us the very words that passed between them. Who that has known or heard the Swami even for a day has not been impressed with his extraordinary memory, his great earnestness, and absolute truthfulness?[15]

Could there have been some meaning in the irony, that in the same city, Madras, where the foundations were being laid for Swami Vivekananda's work of bringing the world together in the oneness of all life, were the seeds of calumny to tarnish his personal character being sown? Irony carries within its womb a certain future, even as it explains the past in a way no theory does or can. Along with the irony

---

[15] Ibid., pp. 185-86.

of Porbandar, there was the irony of Madras even before Swami Vivekananda embarked on his journey to America.

Even as the arrangements were being made for the Swami's departure for America from Madras, Munshi Jagmohanlal, private secretary to the Raja of Khetri, arrived, carrying a letter from Raja Ajit Singh, entreating the Swami to visit him soon. During his long stay with Ajit Singh earlier, the Raja had sought the Swami's blessings to have a son who would be heir to the kingdom. A son was born and the Raja was most desirous that the Swami bless the child. Ajit Singh had this faith that the Swami, for whom he had the reverence of a disciple, would not turn down his request. Jagmohanlal was sent to escort him to Khetri. The Swami put aside for a moment all thoughts of his *mission* to the West and decided to share the joy of Ajit Singh and his wife[16] on having a son—through his blessings as they believed; and he knew how very happy his going there would make them.[17] That it most certainly did; but to Swami Satchidananda, the name under which Narendranath had been travelling in the south and also earlier, that visit to Khetri would be of even greater historic significance. He and Jagmohanlal left Madras for Bombay, where they stayed for a few days, and reached Khetri in the middle of April 1893.

It might appear not a little astonishing, perhaps even strange and irrational, that in the midst of all those earnest preparations for his voyage to America, the Swami himself

---

[16] The name of Ajit Singh's wife, the Rani, is not mentioned anywhere in the Indian biographies of Vivekananda.

[17] The introduction of '*them*' is wholly mine; for Ajit Singh's wife remains totally invisible in the story of the Raja of Khetri–Vivekananda relationship.

should suddenly take a train to Khetri—only to bless the newborn son of a Raja. But in this, the Swami was showing another trait of his character that would astonish, delight, sometimes irritate, his women friends and supporters in America. *Swami Vivekananda was never in a hurry.* He walked at a lordly pace and talked as if time had stopped for him and for his audience. Just before it would be time for him to leave for his lecture, his audience waiting with great expectations, a small girl or a woman in the home where he was staying would ask him how he wound his turban which looked so very magnificent. And to make *this* audience happy, he would start to give a practical demonstration. Hearing a mild protest from Josephine MacLeod that he was definitely getting late for the lecture, Mrs Roxie Blodgett would say to him:

Swami, don't hurry. You are like the man on his way to be hanged. The crowd was jostling each other to reach the place of execution, when he called out, '*Don't* hurry. There will be nothing interesting until I get there.' I assure you, Swami, there will be nothing interesting until you get there. This so pleased him that often afterwards he would say, 'There will be nothing interesting "till I get there",' and laugh like a boy.[18]

Nobody ever said that *nothing* interesting happened at the Parliament of Religions at Chicago in September 1893 until Swami Vivekananda reached there; but everybody unanimously said that *the most interesting* things happened there because he was there.

However, the Swami himself explained the reasons for his sudden visit to Khetri. In his letter, written from Khetri,

[18] In *Reminiscences*, p.359.

dated only as 'May, 1893', to Haridas Viharidas Desai, Dewan of Junagad, he said:

...The fact is this. You may remember that I had from before a desire to go to Chicago. When at Madras, the people there of their own accord, in conjunction with H.H. of Mysore and Ramnad, made every arrangement to send me up. And you may also remember that between H.H. of Khetri and myself there are the closest ties of love. Well, I, as a matter of course, wrote to him that I was going to America. Now the Raja of Khetri thought in his love that I was bound to see him once before I departed, especially as the Lord has given him an heir to the throne and great rejoicings were going on here; and to make sure of my coming he sent his Private Secretary all the way to Madras to fetch me, and of course I was bound to come.[19]

Swami Satchidananda stayed with Raja Ajit Singh for three weeks, and the plans concerning his voyage to America were evidently changed. He would now sail from Bombay, not from Madras. But the momentous event that took place at Khetri was that Raja Ajit Singh gave the Swami the name 'Vivekananda'. Swami Satchidananda was respectfully laid to rest; *Swami Vivekananda* was born—at Khetri, in May 1893.

On leaving Khetri on 10 May 1893 for Bombay, the Swami was escorted by Ajit Singh up to Jaipur, and by Jagmohanlal up to Bombay to see to the Swami's comfort there and put him on the boat. The party must have stayed

---

[19] *SV Letters*, p. 29. This letter to 'Dewanji Saheb' was written to explain why he could not go to see him and his brother at Nadiad, the ancestral palace of Dewan Haridas Viharidas Desai. The rest of the letter is concerned with that: 'Let me not be haunted with the impression that I was ever ungrateful to one who was so good to me.'

at Jaipur for a couple of days, maybe a little longer. It was there that Swami Vivekananda met another teacher of his, a dancing girl, he never forgot for the rest of his days. The Raja had arranged an evening of entertainment which, the Swami probably thought, was to be an evening of classical music. When a young dancing girl, a nautch girl as they were called in nineteenth-century India, especially in Bengal and the princely states, appeared and began her dance, the monk got up to leave. Deeply hurt, she began to sing a song by the famous blind poet–singer Suradas of Mathura (1483–1563). As if addressed to this young monk, its substance was a philosophical reproach against the arrogance of virtue. 'Even God does not make a distinction between a sinner and a saint. Why do *you*? Do not look at my evil qualities, Lord, but at the purity of my heart.' Hardly had she sung the first notes of the song with pain in her heart than the sannyasin sat down in an attitude of respect. [20] She sang and danced with deep feelings, and he was deeply moved. The look of hurt in that girl's eyes, on being despised and insulted, haunted the young monk Vivekananda for many years. She led him to serious self-reflection.

Swami Vivekananda, accompanied by Munshi Jagmohanlal, now took a train to Bombay. At Abu Road

---

[20] There are two versions of this incident. The one, given in *The Life*, pp. 280-81, is that the Swami was in his room when the Raja sent a message requesting him to join the party, but he had refused to come, saying that he was a sannyasin; whereupon, deeply hurt, she sang that song as *her* reply to the monk. The other is that he was present and got up to leave when she began to dance. Most probably that is what happened. Leave alone a sannyasin, anyone is free not to watch a dance if one doesn't want to, and that would in itself be no insult to the dancer. But it *would be* an insult to her if, being there, one leaves no sooner than she began to dance.

railway station on the way, unexpectedly he again met Rakhal (Brahmananda) and Hari (Turiyananda). Later, Turiyananda spoke of what happened:

I vividly remember some remarks made by Swamiji at that time. The exact words and accents, and the deep pathos with which they were uttered still ring in my ears. He said, 'Haribhai, I am still unable to understand anything of your so-called religion.' Then with an expression of deep sorrow in his countenance and an intense emotion shaking his body, he placed his hand on his heart and added, 'But my heart has expanded very much, and I have learnt to feel. Believe me I feel intensely indeed.'

Turiyananda narrated how Vivekananda's voice choked with feeling, tears rolling down his cheeks, and he could say no more.

Can you imagine what passed through my mind on hearing the Swami speak thus? 'Are not these,' I thought, 'the very words and feelings of Buddha?'...I could clearly perceive that the sufferings of humanity were pulsating in the heart of Swamiji—his heart was a huge cauldron in which the sufferings of mankind were being made into a healing balm.[21]

The Swami stayed in Bombay for a little more than two weeks, during which time, on the instructions of Raja Ajit Singh, Jagmohanlal bought him a first-class ticket on S.S. *Peninsular*, and presented him a new silk ochre robe and a handsome purse. Alasinga Perumal had come from Madras to bid farewell and give him the money that was collected there.

---

[21] *The Life*, p. 282.

The Swami wrote to Haridas Viharidas Desai, 'You
are at liberty, my friend, to think that I am a dreamer, a
visionary; but believe at least that I am sincere to the
backbone, and my greatest fault is that I love my country
only too, too well.'[22] It is with that 'greatest fault' of his
that Swami Vivekananda boarded the ship *Peninsular* on
31 May 1893, carrying with him also his staff, his
kamandalu and his coarse woollen rug—his intimate
companions for two-and-a-half years of his life traversing
the dust of India. They were with him on his journey now
across the seas.

'I have launched my boat in the waves, come what
may.'[23] And he launched his boat with his abiding faith:
'It is the Lord who protects His children in the depths of
the sea.'[24]

---

[22] Letter dated 20 June 1894. *SV Letters*, p. 116.
[23] 28 June 1894. *SV Letters*, p. 124.
[24] In a letter dated 27 October 1894, to Alasinga Perumal. *SV Letters*,
pp. 169-70.

5

The Web of Love and Its Maya

*Providence has dealt me my death to make me so
tender!*

—Swami Vivekananda[1]

The truth is that Providence had ensured for Swami
Vivekananda a deathless life by making him 'so
tender' as he complained. He would teach Vedanta as a
living reality, not through dry intellect but through his
infinite capacity to love whereby he would show that
human suffering is not just a metaphysical concept and
religion, joyless.

The earliest *written* expressions of his complaint that
his tenderness was another 'greatest fault' are to be found
in his letters, from Ghazipur. He was expecting
Gangadhar (Akhandananda) to visit him there, but
Gangadhar was still in Tibet and therefore could not
come. In his letter of February 1890, Vivekananda wrote
to him: '…I am sorry to learn that you will not be able to
come, for I had a great longing to see you. It seems that I
love you more than all others. However, I shall try to get
rid of this Maya too.'[2]

---

[1] Vivekananda to Pramadadas Mitra, letter dated 3 March 1890. *SV
Letters*, p. 21.
[2] *SVLetters*, p. 17.

Still in Ghazipur, on 19 February 1890, he wrote to Pramadadas Mitra of Varanasi, whom we met in the previous chapter:

...Brother Kali (Abhedananda) is having repeated attacks of fever at Hrishikesh. I have sent him a wire from this place. So if from the reply I find I am wanted by him, I shall be obliged to start direct for Hrishikesh from this place, otherwise I am coming to you in a day or two. Well, you may smile, sir, to see me weaving all this web of Maya—and that is no doubt the fact. But then there is the chain of iron, and there is the chain of gold. Much good comes of the latter; and it drops off by itself when all the good is reaped. The sons of my Master are indeed the great objects of my service, and here alone I feel I have some duty left for me.[3]

On 3 March 1890, Vivekananda wrote to Pramadadas again:

You know not, sir, I am a very soft-natured man in spite of the stern Vedantic views I hold. And this proves to be my undoing. At the slightest touch I give myself away; for howsoever I may try to think only of my own good, I slip off in spite of myself to think of other peoples' interests. This time it was with a very stern resolve that I set out to pursue my own good, but I had to run off at the news of the illness of a brother (Yogananda) at Allahabad! And now comes this news from Hrishikesh, and my mind has run off with me there.[4]

During his parivrajaka days in the Himalayas, Gangadhar had fallen ill, and Vivekananda had tended to him like a mother. He had brought him down to Dehradun for medical

---

[3] Ibid., p. 16.
[4] Ibid., p. 21.

attention, and had gone around from house to house, saying 'My brother is ill. Can you give us some help?' But, thinking that that too was a web of love and its maya, sometime afterwards Vivekananda said to him, 'If you fall ill, I have to look after you; if I fall ill, you have to look after me. Let us go alone.' We saw in a previous chapter how Sharat Chandra Gupta fell seriously ill in Hrishikesh and how, with the same motherly love, Vivekananda tended to him, putting aside *sat-chit*, 'Being-Consciousness', and its *ananda*, 'Bliss'. Then he would float alone. In northern India, when he remained out of sight for a somewhat long time, two or three of his brother-monks would follow him and find him, or just meet him accidentally, for example, in the latter part of January 1891 in Delhi. When he looked at them sternly, they said, quite truthfully, 'We heard of an English-speaking sadhu, Swami Vividishananda, and we came to see him.' One part of Vividishananda was happy to see them; another part, their Narendra, said to them even more sternly, '*Don't follow me, I asked you not to follow me, I will break all connections with you if you do.*' [5] This would happen repeatedly; and Swami Vivekananda, fighting within himself, as it were, his two opposite natures, would repeatedly break clear from his brother-monks, and walk alone, his mind humming the words of the Buddha:

> Go forward without a path!
> Fearing nothing, caring for nothing,
> Wander alone, like the rhinoceros!
> Even as the lion, not trembling at noises,
> Even as the wind, not caught in the net,

---

[5] *The Life*, p. 206.

> Even as the lotus leaf, unstained by the water,
> Do thou wander alone, like the rhinoceros![6]

Vivekananda was the wind caught in the net. As Swami
Vivekananda it would soon become impossible for him
to wander alone, without a path.

It was at Almora, in the Himalayas, in the latter part
of 1890, perhaps, that Vivekananda's tender heart
received a grievous hurt. He got the news that one of his
sisters had committed suicide. As if there was a mystical
inner connection between the two, that news came soon
after he had, sitting under a tree, discovered the oneness
of the microcosm, the individual, the specific, and the
macrocosm, the *virat*.[7] It is most instructive how the
authors, monastic and lay, of *The Life of Vivekananda:
By His Eastern and Western Disciples* tell us of that event:

Terrible news reached the Swami here. A telegram came from
the brother telling of the suicide of one of his sisters. A letter which
followed gave details. This caused the Swami great anguish of
heart; and yet even in this grief he saw other realities. Through
this perspective of personal woe he seemed to have been rudely
awakened to the great problems of Indian womanhood. He now
decided to travel into the wilder mountains. The situation was a
peculiar one, a mingling of the domestic and monastic consciousness;
but the balance of thought and determination swung with power
in the latter direction.[8]

---

[6] See *The Life*, p. 206.
[7] He spoke about that discovery to Gangadhar who recorded it. See
The Life, p. 197.
[8] *The Life*, p. 198.

The last sentence was written a little too easily and misrepresents Swami Vivekananda. The immense evidence on record, including what he was saying about himself in the clearest of words, shows that his 'monastic consciousness' *never* excluded 'domestic consciousness'. Neither in his conduct nor in his teachings was there that duality. Even the words and the states of the mind they denote are not his. They only seem to reflect the 'monastic consciousness' of his monastic followers. This, I believe, is of the utmost importance in understanding Vivekananda. He cautioned his brother-monk Shashi (Ramakrishnananda) that 'A besetting sin with Sannyasins is the taking pride in their monastic order. That may have its utility during the first stages, but when they are full grown, they need it no more. One must make no distinction between householders and Sannyasins— then only one is a true Sannyasin.'[9] During his second visit to America, at a lecture he gave, 'My Life and Mission', at the Shakespeare Club of Pasadena, California, on 27 January 1900, he said, 'Well, I must tell you, that I am not a very great believer in monastic systems. They have great merits, and also great defects. There should be a perfect balance between the monastics and the householders.'[10]

Furthermore, the quickness with which that grievous event of his sister committing suicide is passed over is astonishing. 'A telegram came from the brother'—*which* 'brother'? The Swami had two younger brothers, Mahendranath and Bhupendranath. Was the telegram from one of them? Or was it from one of his monastic-

---

[9] *SV Letters*, p. 86.
[10] See *CWSV*, Vol. VIII, p. 89.

brothers? 'A letter which followed gave details'; since
that much was definitely known to the writers of *The
Life*, why should those details have been withheld,
especially when the suicide of the Swami's sister was an
instance of the oppressive condition of Indian women?

It was left to Sister Nivedita to describe some twenty
years later, in 1910, how deeply his sister's suicide had
affected Vivekananda, and which he must have discussed
with her.

It had been at Almora, as we now know, that news reached him, of
the death in pitiful extremity, of the favourite sister of his childhood,
and he had fled into the wilder mountains, leaving no clue. To
one who, years after, saw deep into his personal experience, it
seemed that this death had inflicted on the Swami's heart a wound,
whose quivering pain had never for one moment ceased. And we
may, perhaps, venture to trace some part at least of his burning
desire for the education and development of Indian women to
this sorrow.[11]

What is equally instructive is the fact that nobody tells
us *who*, of the four sisters of Vivekananda, Haramoni,
Swarnamayee, Kiranbala and Jogendrabala, had
committed suicide. Nor *why*. Nor *when*. One would expect
the three brothers of 'the dearly loved' but tragic sister,
Narendranath, Mahendranath and Bhupendranath, to tell
us at least her name. None of them does. Bhupendranath
does not mention the suicide at all;[12] and Mahendranath
has only this to say: 'Probably in the month of Baisakh on

[11] Sister Nivedita, *The Master As I Saw Him* (Udbodhan Office,
Baghbazar, Calcutta, 1910; 9th edition, 1962), p. 62.
[12] Bhupendranath Datta, *Swami Vivekananda: Patriot-Prophet*.

a Sunday morning in the year 1891 a letter came from Shimla hills that a younger sister of Narendranath had committed suicide there.'[13] We can guess it was either Kiranbala or Jogendrabala, the two younger sisters of Vivekananda.

In *Saint Sara*,[14] Pravrajika Prabhuddhaprana tells us something altogether startling about that suicide: that it was sati. That information is apparently attributed to Vivekananda himself, but not quite clearly. He had taken Mrs Sara Bull, Josephine MacLeod and Nivedita[15] on a trip to Kashmir in August–September 1898. On the basis of what Sara had perhaps recorded, Prabuddhaprana tells us of a conversation Vivekananda had with them in Srinagar on 22 September. It was about Hindu widowhood, and the Swami talked of his mother.

…His mother fainted when she heard that her widowed daughter resolved to commit herself to the flames of her husband's funeral pyre. Then he (Vivekananda) talked for a half-hour or more on legal questions involved in the position of women in Hindu law. The Swami was a law-student, so every point he brought up was detailed and supported by anecdotes and examples.

Perhaps remembering the tragedy of his dearly loved sister and the sad plight of Hindu widows, he wanted to be alone. He had received the news of his sister's suicide (i.e., *sati*) years ago during his practice of intense austerities in the Kasar Devi cave at Almora. Then he was torn from his resolve to immerse his mind

---

[13] See his *Shrimat Vivekananda Swamijir Jibaner Ghatanabali* (Events in the Life of Swami Vivekananda), (written in Bengali; Mahendra Publishing Committee, Calcutta), Vol. I, p. 212.
[14] Already cited.
[15] We will meet them later in this book.

in meditation, never to return. When the news reached him, his heart filled with rage against the wrong done to women and he was determined to do something for them.[16]

Even in this, however, the name of the dead sister is missing. Besides, since Nivedita was present at the conversation cited above by Prabuddhaprana, why did she, in *her* mention of the suicide, not say that it was not suicide but sati? Though sati is technically suicide, the two are entirely different. The silence on this sister's death is baffling.

Swami Vivekananda, a monastic sannyasin, remained attached to his mother, Bhubaneswari Devi, till the end of his life. On 29 January 1894, from Chicago, he wrote to Haridas Viharidas Desai, who on a visit to Calcutta had gone to see Bhubaneswari Devi:

I am glad you did. But you have touched the only soft place in my heart. You ought to know, Dewanji, that I am no hardhearted brute. If there is any being I love in the whole world, it is my mother. Yet I believed and still believe that without my giving up the world, the great mission which Ramakrishna Paramahamsa, my great Master, came to preach would not see the light...So on the one hand, my vision of the future of Indian religion and that of whole world, my love for the millions of beings sinking down and down for ages with nobody to help them, nay, nobody with even a thought for them; on the other hand, making those who are nearest and dearest to me miserable; I choose the former. Lord will do the rest. He is with me, I am sure of that if of anything.[17]

In her reminiscences of Swami Vivekananda, Sister Christine recorded:

---

[16] Prabuddhaprana, *Saint Sara*, p. 308.
[17] *SV Letters*, p. 65.

How he loved his mother! Sometimes when he was in other parts of India the fear would come that something had happened to her, and he would send to inquire. Or perhaps he was in the monastery in Belur, in which case he would send a messenger post-haste. To the very end her comfort and her care was one of his chief considerations.[18]

Many were the stories he told of his mother—the proud, little woman who tried so hard to hide her emotions and her pride in him. How she was torn between disapproval of the life he had chosen and her pride in the name he had made for himself. In the beginning she would have chosen a conventional life for him, perhaps marriage and worldly success, but she lived to see the beggar exalted and princes bowing before him. But in the meantime, hers was not an easy task.[19]

The story of his abiding concern for his mother unfolded even as the immensity of his work in America and England was unfolding. One may wonder, though, why Vivekananda's attachment to his mother is significant. There are countless people in the world, even among the poorest, who remain attached to their mothers as long as they live, and consider their comfort and well-being as their primary duty as son or daughter. Why does then *his* love for his mother require any special attention? It does, I believe, for the following reason most of all.

In the first place, Swami Vivekananda had from the very beginning stepped out of the traditional *pauranic* notion of a sannyasin. In his teachings, but in his life and relationships even more, he had shown, as the Mahabharata

---

[18] Sister Christine, in *Reminiscences*, p. 175.
[19] Ibid., p. 174.

had three millennia earlier, that true renunciation, *tyaga*, lies not in outward giving up of *things* or *persons* but in lighting one's consciousness with a new fire.[20] The fire in which all petty, limited, self-interests are burned, because, there is no real joy in being limited; what arises in their place is the joy of the limitless, of uniting one's good, *sva-hita*, with the good of many, *para-hita*. In that, the ordinary bonds of human love and affection are not repudiated, only more heightened, but now from a different perspective.

'I am not a pauranic sannyasin,' he declared with authority. 'Was I ever an orthodox Pauranika Hindu, an adherent of social usages? I do not pose as one.'[21] Then, with even greater authority, he declared: 'You do not know the sannyasin, he stands on the head of the Vedas!'[22] That authority he attributed to the Vedas themselves. But the authority he felt within himself, walking in its freedom even more than a king could, did not come to him from scriptures, but from that very thing that he had complained of: his tenderness, his heightened capacity to feel for others. The pauranic idea of sannyasa, renunciation, which concentrated only on one's self while depending all the time upon others for something or the other, had become so selfish that it was no less a web of maya. With this difference, though, that in the maya of renunciation, there is not even the redeeming love.

---

[20] Discussed in the author's *The Mahabharata—An Inquiry into the Human Condition*, awaiting publication.
[21] In his letter, which does not mention the date, only the year 1895; from Reading, England, to Rakhal (Brahmananda). *SV Letters*, p. 262.
[22] Vivekananda to Mary Hale, letter dated 1 February 1898. *SV Letters*, p. 212.

Vivekananda's abiding love for his mother was a manifestation of his radically changed perception of sannyasa. Swami Vivekananda had thought that the one must be renounced for the sake of the world; Vivekananda began to assert that that was a mistaken notion. His dedication to restore to the masses of India their lost individuality and his deeply felt concern for them, were even greater repudiation of the narrow, limited, mistaken notions of sannyasa. Under the influence of the notion of vairagya as renunciation, love was seen as bondage. The whole life of Vivekananda is a proof of the truth that, on the contrary, love is the very foundation of renunciation.

And yet, he tried hard to free himself from the web of love and its maya even as he was teaching the incontestable truth that the *living* Vedanta could be found in that web also.[23] It was from the maya of love that Swami Vivekananda touched at their deepest core so many lives in India and the West alike. 'Madness of love, and yet in it no bondage. Why, this is the very essence of our Vedanta,' he said.

Such was the man who was on board S.S. *Peninsular*, heading for the New World, to teach that *all love is freedom and life, all hatred is bondage and death*, and to learn from what the West had to give him in return.

---

[23] This is discussed fully in Chapter 11.

6

Swami Vivekananda Reaches America

*I am here amongst the children of the Son of Mary,
and the Lord Jesus will help me.*
                                    —Swami Vivekananda[1]

S wami Vivekananda arrived in Chicago an hour before
midnight on Sunday, 30 July 1893. He had travelled
by train from Vancouver, Canada, where his ship, the
Empress of India from Yokohama had docked on
Tuesday, 25 July, at seven in the evening. He had to
spend the night at Vancouver for the train eastwards,
the 'Atlantic Express', had left hours earlier. Next
morning, travelling second class, he took a train to
Winnipeg, reaching there Friday night. Taking another
train that would bring him to the United States, through
the lake-splashed hills and farms of Minnesota, he reached
St. Paul. From there, a third train would carry him some
400 miles farther east to Chicago. It is with these details—
date, day, time and *place*—that Marie Louise Burke ushers
us into the life of Swami Vivekananda in America during
his first visit to the West that began on 30 July 1893 in

---

[1] Vivekananda to Alasinga Perumal, letter dated 20 August 1893. *SV Letters*, p. 39.

Chicago.[2] She enables us to visualize and feel him contemporaneously. In his very long letter of 20 August 1893 to Alasinga Perumal,[3] the Swami himself enables us to do so.

Marie Burke's detailed research on Vivekananda in the West, spanning a little more than half a century, enables us to know him even more vividly by feeling those who came into his life and whose lives he entered. If they were men, and had a family, the names of the wives and the children are given, and then not just as names. If they were women, married or unmarried, they are introduced to us with a description of their family background and their past. Because their photographs are included, we know what those men and women in Vivekananda's life looked like, indeed, we can almost touch them. The photographs of their houses where Vivekananda stayed, often for long, are also given, with the names of the streets on which they stood. Looking at them, one may easily press the calling bell and, if answered, ask if one could see the Swami. The dates of his travels in America, England and on the Continent are provided, so that we know where he was and when and for how long. In most cases, the dates of his lectures and the names of the places where he spoke are given. In some cases, if only a few, Marie Louise Burke would caution that the address given on a letter by the Swami did not necessarily mean that it was from there that he was writing. The letter might have

---

[2] Marie Louise Burke, see SV New Discoveries, 'Introduction', p.5. The details given above are to be found in SV New Discoveries, Vol. 1, p. 16.
[3] SV Letters, pp. 38–45.

been written on the stationery of his previous host or hostess, of which he might have carried a sheet or two where he went next. If someone recalled many years later that the Swami had stayed with her for, say, fifteen days, Burke would correct it to *eleven* days (or some such), suggesting probable reasons why it could not have been fifteen days. She corrects *The Life*, and does so throughout, on details that are *not* unimportant. Most of all, she ushers us into the numerous relationships Swami Vivekananda was forming, each one of them a fascinating story of the riches of being human, and all of them together the immeasurable measure of the man.

An Indian mind would wonder what have all those details got to do with 'spirituality', or with 'the innate divinity of man', Swami Vivekananda was talking about. To Marie Burke, a *brahmacharini* in the Ramakrishna Order but a westerner, spirituality did not dissolve historical facts, the *desha*, the *kala* and the *patra*, 'the place', 'the time' and 'the person(s) concerned'. To her, scrupulous care about their accuracy as far as humanly possible was also a matter of truth, as it was with Swami Vivekananda. To the Mahabharata, the deepest inquiry into the human condition, *history* always was a settled method of knowing what *being* is. But that method began to be buried deeper as the Indian litany of spirituality began to be sung louder. Carelessness about facts, seemingly on principle, is no indicator of spirituality. Facts by themselves are no indicators of truth either. But to dissolve persons, contexts and times in carefully selected images and legends is the surest path to untruth about them.

The three acts of oversight on the part of the Swami and his 'Madras boys', mentioned in Chapter 4 (page 138), seemed for a while to turn his divine dreams into ashes. He learnt that, in order to be a delegate to the Parliament, he had to have specific authority from those of his religious faith whom he represented; and he had brought with him no credentials. In any case, even if he had, it was too late for him to be included. Furthermore, he had arrived in Chicago some six weeks before the Parliament of Religions was to begin on 11 September. The daily cost of living in Chicago was high—'The expense I am bound to run into here is awful'—and the money he was provided with when he left India, hardly sumptuous,[4] was dwindling fast. He wrote to Alasinga Perumal:

All those rosy ideas we had before starting have melted, and I have now to fight against impossibilities. A hundred times I had a mind to go out of the country and go back to India. But I am determined, and I have a call from Above. I see no way, but His eyes see.

...I am here among the children of the Son of Mary, and the Lord Jesus will help me. They like much the broad views of Hinduism and my love for the Prophet of Nazareth.[5]

The Prophet of Nazareth knew that this young Hindu dreamer, dreaming great dreams of *bringing all together*, in the unity of all religions, in the oneness of all life, had in his wanderings as a monk carried with him *The Imitation of Christ* along with the *Bhagvad-Gita*. His dreams were not to turn into ashes just because, in certain essential respects, he and his Indian supporters had been thoroughly impractical. Great dreams, if they are selfless, do not

---

[4] 'You remember, you gave me £178 in notes and £9 in cash.' Vivekananda to Alasinga Perumal, letter dated 20 August 1893. *SV Letters*, p. 38.

[5] Ibid., p. 39.

vanish. The Prophet of Nazareth made someone suggest to him, as it were, that it was much cheaper to live in Boston. So, Vivekananda took a train to Boston. The grace of Jesus of Nazareth, in whom he had great faith, was to be with him thereafter.

Even as Sri Ramakrishna had abdicated his self at the feet of a woman, the very first person to help his chosen apostle Narendranath, now in an unknown land as Swami Vivekananda, was a woman. Travelling with him on the same train, Katherine Sanborn began a conversation with him, at the end of which she was so impressed that she invited the Hindu monk to be her guest at her farmhouse in Metcalf, Massachusetts, not too far from Boston, and he gratefully accepted. Here is her account, perhaps the very first in America, of the man himself. Kate Sanborn wrote:

A magnificent specimen of manhood, as handsome as Salivini at his best, with a lordly, imposing stride, as if he ruled the universe, and soft dark eyes that could flash fire if roused or dance with merriment if the conversation amused him...He wore a bright yellow turban many yards in length, a red ochre robe, the badge of his calling; this was tied with a pink sash, broad and heavily befringed. Snuff-brown trousers and russet shoes completed the outfit...He spoke better English than I did, was conversant with ancient and modern literature...could repeat pages of our Bible...He was an education, an illumination, a revelation.[6]

Miss Katherine Sanborn was a known author, had taught at Smith College, and the name of her farmhouse, 'Breezy Meadows', reflected much of her own personality.[7] It was

---

[6] SV *New Discoveries*, Vol. 1.
[7] For Marie Burke's portrait of Kate Sanborn, see SV *New Discoveries*, Vol. 1, pp. 23-24.

from 'Breezy Meadows' that Vivekananda wrote his letter of 20 August to Alasinga:

Just now I am living as the guest of an old lady[8] in a village near Boston. I accidentally made her acquaintance in the railway train, and she invited me to come over and live with her. I have an advantage in living with her, in saving for some time my expenditure of £1 per day, and she has the advantage of inviting her friends over here and showing them a curio from India. And all this must be borne![9]

In certain biographies of Swami Vivekananda, much has been made of that remark, indeed, it was made the basis of a sweeping statement that Swamiji wanted to rid himself of the patronage of his rich women friends in America, who were showing him off as a 'curio'.[10] That was not true and this is of sufficient importance to be said straightaway. No rich woman friend, American or English, of Swami Vivekananda ever tried even remotely to *patronize* him, as if anyone could 'patronize' a Vivekananda, or present him as a 'curio'. It is true that Kate Sanborn took her royal-looking monk, 'Rajah, Swami Vivekananda', for a drive to Hunnewell's, a public park, behind a pair of trotting horses, a liveryman in attendance, and all eyes were upon them.[11] That was two

---

[8] Marie Louise Burke promptly corrects this description of Kate Sanborn. 'Although Swamiji referred to her as "an old lady", she was, by American standards, not old when he first knew her. She was fifty-four and very energetic.' Ibid., Vol. 1, p. 23.

[9] *SV Letters*, p. 39.

[10] As, for example, in Swami Nikhilananda's biography of Vivekananda, in exactly these words; p. 169.

[11] *SV New Discoveries*, Vol. 1, pp. 22-23.

days before he wrote to Alasinga. But if Kate Sanborn, given her lively nature, enjoyed that grand spectacle, Swami Vivekananda, with his unfailing capacity of seeing the funny side of situations, saw it as an exchange of mutual advantage, as he wrote to Alasinga. He was saving his fast-dwindling money by staying with her; and she was showing him off to her friends! His words, 'as a curio', are not to be taken literally, nor the following sentence in his letter, 'And all this must be borne', to be heard as a lament. If we are to understand Vivekananda, we should not take words literally.

Kate Sanborn was far too intelligent a woman to revel only in showing off her 'Rajah' monk. She did something that was to open the second door to Swami Vivekananda's mission to the West, she being the first that was opened to him, as he said 'accidentally'. But nothing in his life ever happened 'accidentally'. She invited Professor John Henry Wright, Professor of Greek Studies at Harvard University, to meet the man she thought was 'an education', 'an illumination', 'a revelation'. For some reason, the meeting between them could not take place there. So, John Wright invited the Swami to spend the weekend with the Wright family, spending the summer at Annisquam, a seaside resort. It did not take him long to recognize what Vivekananda was. After several conversations with him, Professor Wright wrote to a director of the Parliament of Religions about Vivekananda not being included as a delegate because he had brought with him no formal credentials. 'He is more learned than all our learned professors put together,' Professor John Wright said. Moreover, he said, to insist on such a man producing formal credentials would be like asking the sun for the right with which it shines. These words coming from so eminent a scholar as

Professor John Wright, Swami Vivekananda was promptly included as a delegate to the Parliament of Religions, representing Hinduism. That big door was now opened to him, for which he had launched his boat on the waves, as he said on leaving Bombay.

But it was not at the Parliament of Religions that the Swami spoke first. It was at the Boston Ramabai Circle that he addressed his first gathering in America, where he probably gave a true picture of the Hindu widows in contrast to what Pandita Ramabai (1858–1922), a Brahmin woman converted to Christianity, had been painting in America. More importantly, he spoke to a gathering at Annisquam village, of which Mrs Mary Tappan Wright, Professor Wright's wife, left a vivid account.[12] Even more importantly, it was there that he developed the idea of the 'Vengeance of History'. 'If man cannot believe in the Vengeance of God, he certainly cannot deny the Vengeance of History,' he said.[13] He spoke of the degradation of India caused by British imperialism and he spoke fire against the English, as Mary Wright recorded. But, in his characteristic intellectual and moral honesty, he spoke, as he would write in many of his letters to India, also of the degradation of India caused by Indians themselves for centuries.

If you grind down the people, you will suffer. We in India are suffering the vengeance of God. Look upon these things. They ground down those poor people for their own wealth, they heard not the voice of distress, they ate from gold and silver when the people cried for bread, and the Mohammedans came upon them slaughtering and killing: slaughtering and killing they overran

[12] Ibid., pp. 31–35.
[13] Ibid., p. 33.

them. India has been conquered again and again for years, and last and worst of all came the Englishman.[14]

...And God has had no mercy upon my people because they had no mercy. By their cruelty they degraded the populace, and when they needed them the common people had no strength to give for their aid. If man cannot believe in the Vengeance of God, he certainly cannot deny the Vengeance of History. And it will come upon the English; they have their heels on our necks, they have sucked the last drop of our blood for their own pleasures, they have carried away with them millions of our money, while our people have starved by villages and provinces. And now the Chinaman is the vengeance that will fall upon them; if the Chinese rose today and swept the English into the sea, *as they well deserve*, it would be no more than justice.[15]

If Swami Vivekananda's 'Vengeance of History', which he said 'you cannot deny', sounded biblical, it was only a restatement of the theory of karma, in which the inner logic of one's acts, individual or collective, must work itself out in history. No one can hurt and degrade another without at the same time hurting and degrading one's self. But whereas this sounds plainly scientific, without passion or anger, his '*Vengeance of History*' had in it both: '...Occasionally he cast his eyes up to the roof and repeated softly, "Shiva! Shiva!" and the little company, shaken and disturbed by the current of powerful feelings and vindictive passion which seemed to be flowing like molten lava beneath the silent surface of this strange being, broke up, perturbed.'[16]

---

[14] Ibid., p. 32.
[15] Ibid., pp. 32-33.
[16] Ibid., p.33.

In the next moment, so to say, forgetting 'the Vengeance of God or of History', Vivekananda, 'this strange being', would be seen playing happily with the three Wright children: Elizabeth, then thirteen; Austin, who had turned ten; and John, who was only two years old. Their mother wrote of Vivekananda in her diary: 'He was wonderfully unspoiled and simple, claiming nothing for himself, playing with the children, twirling a stick between his fingers with laughing skill and glee at their inability to equal him.'[17]

On 29 August 1893, Mary Wright wrote to her mother:

Kate Sanborn had a Hindu monk in tow as I believe I mentioned in my last letter. John went down to meet him in Boston and missing him, invited him up here. He came Friday! In a long saffron robe that caused universal amazement. He was a most gorgeous vision. He had a superb carriage of the head, was very handsome in an oriental way, about thirty years old in time, ages in civilization. He stayed until Monday and was one of the most interesting people I have yet come across. We talked all day all night and began again with interest the next morning. The town was in a fume to see him...Chiefly we talked religion. It was a kind of revival, I have not felt so wrought up for a long time myself! Then on Sunday John had him invited to speak in the church and they took up a collection for a Heathen college to be carried on strictly heathen principles—whereupon I retired to my corner and laughed until I cried.[18]

Swami Vivekananda would always have deep gratitude for Professor John Wright for securing a place for him in the Parliament of Religions, saving him thereby from what

---

[17] Ibid., p. 36.
[18] Ibid., p. 28.

had threatened to be a disastrous result of his forgetfulness.
But he would feel also a bond of love for him and his family.
'You and your noble wife and sweet children have made
an impression in my brain which is simply indelible, and
I thought myself so much near to heaven when living with
you. May He, the giver of all gifts, shower on your head
His choicest blessings.'[19] Meanwhile, in the same letter,
the Swami showered on the head of the Professor of Greek
Studies his own 'few lines written as an attempt at poetry'.
The long poem[20] was a condensed autobiography, his
restless search for God, and finding Him 'not in temple,
church, or mosque' but in love. The song the Swami
Vivekananda would sing a week later at the Parliament
of Religions, touching the hearts of thousands, was being
sung already in that 'attempt at poetry'.

> ...Thou wert my God with prophets old,
>   All creeds do come from Thee;
>   The Vedas, Bible, and Koran bold
>   Sing Thee in harmony.[21]

The Swami left Annisquam on 28 August and went to
Salem, Massachusetts, fifteen miles southwest, where he
was invited by Mrs Kate Tannatt Woods (1838–1910) to
be her guest. She had met him at Kate Sanborn's house,
had decided that he was somebody very special, and had
even drawn some plans for him in Salem, apart from having

---

[19] Vivekananda to Prof. John Henry Wright, letter dated 4 September
1893. *SV Letters*, p. 45. In *SV New Discoveries*, Vol. 1, p. 53, the letter
is shown having the date as 'Sept.2, 1893'.
[20] *SV Letters*, pp. 46–48.
[21] Ibid., p. 48.

the blessedness of his presence near her, of which she must have felt the first stirrings. She was fifty-eight years old, a widow, and her only son, Prince Woods, was studying medicine. Like Kate Sanborn, an author, a tireless lecturer, she was moreover one of the founders of the Thought and Work Club in 1891, the first literary group of women in that town, and was particularly interested in children. Her invitation to Swami Vivekananda must have had in it such quiet lovingness that it was happily accepted. He stayed with Kate Woods from 29 August to 4 September.[22]

The two events that took place during that week and soon thereafter, apart from his lecture at Thought and Work Club held in Wesley Church on 28 August 1893, should be mentioned here. One, he addressed a group of children whom Kate Woods had specially invited to meet him in the garden of her house. On the previous day, the Swami had been heard, questioned and was met by some prominent church ministers in the spirit of open hostility; for what he had said about the people of India was the very opposite of what Christian missionaries to India had been telling them. In that, however, as in a slow unfolding of a grand story, Swami Vivekananda had a glimpse of missionary hostility that would follow him to Detroit some months later. But at 'Breezy Meadows' and Annisquam, he had already experienced, as another part of that unfolding, that selfless love and friendship he would receive in America in all the days to follow. He was happy with children and they with him. He once said that he could make

---

[22] For the details of his lectures, its reports in the local newspapers, and his other experiences in Salem, turn to Marie Louise Burke, *SV New Discoveries*, Vol. 1, pp. 41–52.

even a child understand the Vedanta in its essence. And *that* Vedanta, the manifest oneness of all life, he conveyed to the children gathered in Kate Wood's garden by narrating in his musical voice the stories of the colourful Indian animals and, even more vividly, of the children in Indian villages and the games they play. Two, on 5 September, the Swami was addressing scholars at the American Social Science Association at Saratoga Springs. The juxtaposition of these two events might appear as somewhat contrived. But here it was happening in actual reality, as if designed to show Swami Vivekananda's easy and natural transition from being a happy child with children to being a formidable scholar among scholars, with not a trace of self-consciousness in either.

Another event relating to Mrs Woods and the Swami was as metaphorical in its meaning as it was moving in its simple beauty. On his second visit, he gave to her son, Prince, his monk's staff, and to her, his woollen blanket and his trunk, saying to them: 'Only my most precious possessions should I give to my friends who have made me at home in this great country.'[23] That staff and that blanket had been his intimate companions during his wandering days from 1890 to the time he boarded the ship to the New World in May 1893. Both were witnesses, as it were, to his intense feelings of exaltation and of sadness during his journeys through the whole of India. They were not inanimate objects; they were parts of his spiritual history. In giving them to Mrs Kate Tannatt Woods and her son Dr Prince Woods, he was sharing with them in a

---

[23] For the full story, turn to Marie Louise Burke, *SV New Discoveries*, Vol. 1, pp. 41-42.

visible, symbolic way that history. They would be preserved in the Woods family as relics, and Prince Woods would not part with them even when the British Museum wanted to acquire them and had offered a certain price. He would not have parted with them for all the gold in the world. This tells us something of the *living* Swami Vivekananda, but it tells us no less about the beauty and greatness of the mother and her son.

In the meantime, still at Salem at the Woods's homestead, the Swami was informed that his name *was* included among the delegates to the Parliament of Religions that was to open on the morning of 11 September 1893 in Chicago. He was provided with an address at which he had to present himself a day before, to meet other delegates. Now happy in the same proportion as he had felt despondent when he reached Chicago weeks earlier, he was, however, not astonished. He quietly saw in that news the unfolding of the same divine power that had guided and protected him so far. But divine power mostly acts through human agency. The Swami promptly wrote to his 'Adhyapakji' ('professor', 'teacher'), as he addressed Professor Wright, expressing his 'heartfelt gratitude' to him for his letters of introduction that had made it possible for him to speak at the Parliament at all.

Swami Vivekananda arrived in Chicago by train from Saratoga Springs most probably on 9 September sometime in the afternoon. What happened next demonstrates, first of all, how once a myth is formed, contrary to the known facts, it remains in the popular mind either because it is comfortable or because it is greatly romantic. *Floating in the Absolute the Swami had lost the address of the Parliament of Religion offices he was to go to.* We read in

The Life that, because it was mostly the foreign immigrants around the railway station he must have approached, nobody could understand what he was saying when he tried to explain where he wanted to go. Even this part of the story can be read as a metaphor for the lost soul knowing neither its destination nor the path to it. However, this is not to say that Swami Vivekananda was a lost soul. *The Life* tells us:

Night was coming on. He could not even make anyone understand that he wanted to learn at least the whereabouts of a hotel. He was lost and knew not what to do. At length, he lay down to sleep in a huge empty box in the railroad freightyards, and trusting to the guidance of the Lord he soon freed himself of all anxieties and fell asleep.[24]

Marie Louise Burke questions the myth of Swami Vivekananda sleeping in a huge empty box; for it does not 'stand up under a close examination', being the product of the confusion in the minds of the authors of *The Life* between a 'box' and a 'boxcar'.[25] A 'boxcar' in the American idiom is what in India would be called a 'goods wagon'—'a traditional American shelter for the homeless and penniless wanderer'. The authors of *The Life* turned it into 'a huge empty box'. 'This box has become legendary,' Marie Burke says, 'even in stories of Swamiji's life written for children, one finds drawings of it with him curled up most uncomfortably and implausibly inside. There is, I believe, no way to get rid of this box; engraved now on the minds of innumerable children, it is with us for all time.'[26]

---

[24] *The Life*, p. 298.
[25] *SV New Discoveries*, Vol. 1, p. 59.
[26] Ibid.

There is no doubt, though, that the image of the man who would be heralded by thousands of men and women with their deafening applause as a great spiritual force, sleeping just two nights earlier in a huge empty box in a railway yard, is hugely romantic.

If what happened the next morning had not actually happened, its account would seem like an amateur attempt at fiction. The first part of the account, identical in *The Life* and Marie Burke's *SV New Discoveries* is, however, most baffling. It is said that next morning Swami Vivekananda, hungry and weary, started walking. He walked a long distance and given his instincts of a sannyasin, began to beg for food from door to door. 'Dark-skinned, unshaven, wearing what must have been by now a very crumpled orange robe and a strange-looking turban, Swamiji was a matter for alarm. Housewives turned away; servants slammed doors in his face; some verbally insulted him.'[27] During his wanderings in India for two-and-a-half years as a sannyasin, he had hardly ever begged at any door for food, much less from door to door. He ate when someone gave him food, but he would not ask; the result being that if nobody asked whether he was hungry and gave him something to eat, he remained hungry, once for a stretch of five days as he recalled. Therefore, it is unbelievable that as a sannyasin in Chicago, however hungry and tired, he would have begged for food from door to door. Nor is it likely that when he left Annisquam and Saratoga Springs he was penniless and therefore could not have gone to an eating place to have something to eat.

---

[27] Ibid., pp. 59-60; *The Life*, pp. 298-99.

The Swami continued to walk and came into a street where there were elegant homes on both sides. Hungrier and even more tired, he could no longer walk and sat down on the curbside of the street, re-enacting what he had experienced many times during his wandering days in India. What was enacted *now* was a miracle and every miracle is always a story of love coming *unasked*. A woman emerged from a house opposite, walked up to him and asked him, 'Sir, are you a delegate to the Parliament of Religions?' On learning that he indeed was, she took him, this strangest of all strangers, inside her home, gave him breakfast, attended to his other needs and sent for his luggage from the railway station. Thereafter, she took the Swami to the offices of the Parliament where he was, of course, awaited. She was Mrs Ellen George W. Hale, of 541 Dearborn Avenue, Chicago. That address would become a familiar one to those to whom Swami Vivekananda would write many of his greatest letters. Of all the families he would know in the West, the Hale family would remain the dearest to him always.

Soon after reaching America, when Vivekananda stayed in the vicinity of Boston with Kate Sanborn, he did not know that there lived in Boston another woman, Mrs Sara Chapman Bull, who would become one of the greatest supporters of his work, his guide in practical matters and his emotional anchor. That unseen juxtaposition, seen in retrospect, was another element in the divine plan for his life. 'Divine plan' is an overworked, even suspicious, supposition, but in the life of Swami Vivekananda that seems to be literally true, in which every happening was meant to happen exactly in the way it happened.

And in that divine plan for Swami Vivekananda, if that it was, women were destined to be central.

7

At the Parliament of Religions

Sisters and Brothers of America...
> —Swami Vivekananda

...upon the banner of every religion will soon be written, in spite of resistance: 'Help and not Fight', 'Assimilation and not Destruction', 'Harmony and Peace and not Dissension'.
> —Swami Vivekananda

Chicago. 11 September 1893. It was a most solemn occasion, perhaps the first in the history of the world—a coming together of all the major religions. The setting in which it was taking place gave its own message; a World Fair displaying the products of the industrializing West. Since no religion has ever been wholly separate from the material conditions of the society that professed it, the superiority of American industry and the riches it brought was a display of the superiority of Christianity as well. Some decades later, a German sociologist, Max Weber (1864–1920), would demonstrate a direct connection between Protestant ethics and the spirit of capitalism, the material prosperity of the West, the Christian nations; and, still later, trace the backwardness of the Hindus to their 'world-denying and otherworldly' religion, Hinduism.[1] The assembly of religious dignitaries, representing their respective religions, was literally as colourful as it was solemn in its purpose. In their midst was seated Swami Vivekananda, formally representing Hinduism. The audience, several thousands that filled the huge Columbus Hall where the Parliament was taking place, was charged with inexpressible expectations. But the thirty-year-old representative of a religion that was at least thirty centuries old was nervous, for he had never spoken before such a large and august gathering, and let his turn to speak pass many times.

Let us hear the Swami himself describe in three of his letters the scene at the Parliament, quoting from the newspapers that had described his impact upon it.[2] His very first letter, of 2 October 1893, was to his Adhyapakji, Professor Henry Wright.

I do not know what you are thinking of my long silence. In the first place I dropped in on the Congress in the eleventh hour, and quite unprepared, and that kept me very very busy for sometime. Secondly, I was speaking almost every day in the Congress, and had no time to write; and last and greatest of all—my kind friend, I owe so much to you that it would have been an insult to your *ahetuka*

---

[1] On this, see the author's 'Max Weber's Wrong Understanding of Indian Civilization', published in *Recent Research on Max Weber's Studies of Hinduism and Buddhism*; ed. Detlef Kantowsky (Munich; Weltforum Verlag, 1986), being a collection of some of the papers, including the author's, presented at the seminar 'Max Weber's Study of Hinduism and Buddhism', New Delhi, 1–3 March 1984; pp. 45–58. And reproduced in the author's *Dharma, India and the World Order*, pp. 108–28.

[2] For the text of Swami Vivekananda's famous speech at the Parliament of Religions, see *CWSV*, Vol. I, pp. 3-4.

(unselfish) friendship to have written to you business-like letters in a hurry. The Congress is now over.

Dear brother, I was so, so afraid to stand before that great assembly of fine speakers and thinkers from all over the world and speak; but the Lord gave me strength, and I almost every day heroically (?) faced the platform and the audience. If I have done well, He gave me the strength for it; if I have miserably failed—I knew that beforehand—for I am hopelessly ignorant.[3]

The Adhyapakji must have chuckled at the 'I am hopelessly ignorant' coming from a man whom he had described as 'more learned than all our learned professors put together'. But few know the Vivekananda who, famous all over America at the time of his writing that letter, was addressing a part of it to the Wright children, especially to the ten-year-old Austin. What he was saying to these children was no less important than what he had said at the Parliament of Religions. Quoting from Upanishad, he said to them:

The four Vedas, sciences, language, philosophy, and all other learnings are only ornamental. The real learning, the true knowledge, is that which enables us to reach Him who is unchangeable in His love.

How real, how tangible, how visible is He through whom the skin touches, the eyes see, and the world gets its reality!

Hearing Him nothing remains to be heard.

Seeing Him nothing remains to be seen.

Attaining him nothing remains to be attained.

He is the eye of our eyes, the ear of our ears, the Soul of our souls.

---

[3] *SV Letters*, p. 49.

He is nearer to you, my dears, than even your father and mother. You are innocent and pure as flowers. Remain so, and He will reveal Himself unto you. Dear Austin, when you are playing, there is another playmate playing with you who loves you more than anybody else: and Oh, He is so full of fun. He is always playing—sometimes with great big balls which we call the sun and the earth, sometimes with little children like you and laughing and playing with you.

How funny it would be to see Him and play with Him! My dear, think of it.[4]

God as a child's playmate—this was Swami Vivekananda's *living* Vedanta.

His second letter, a long one he wrote on 2 November 1893,[5] was to Alasinga Perumal, in which he gave many more details about that great event.

...Men from all nations were there. From India were Mazoomdar of the Brahmo Samaj, and Nagarkar of Bombay, Mr. Gandhi representing the Jains, and Mr. Chakravarti representing Theosophy with Mrs. Annie Besant. Of these, Mazoomdar and I were, of course, old friends, and Chakravarti knew me by name. There was a grand procession, and we were all marshalled on to the platform. Imagine a hall below and a huge gallery above, packed with six or seven thousand men and women representing the best culture of the country, and on the platform learned men of all the nations of this earth. And I, who never spoke in public in my life, to address this august assemblage!! ...Of course my heart was fluttering and my tongue nearly dried up; I was so nervous and could not venture to speak in the morning...They were all prepared

---

[4] Ibid., pp. 50-51.
[5] Ibid., pp. 53–57.

and came with ready-made speeches. I was a fool and had none, but bowed down to Devi Sarasvati[6] and stepped up, and Dr. Barrows introduced me. I made a short speech. I addressed the assembly as 'Sisters and brothers of America', a deafening applause of two minutes followed, and then I proceeded, and when it was finished, I sat down, almost exhausted with emotion. The next day all the papers announced that my speech was the hit of the day, and I became known to the whole of America.

Continuing, he quoted from one or two newspapers.

'Ladies, ladies, ladies, packing every place—filling every corner, they patiently waited and waited while the papers that separated them from Vivekananda were read', etc. You would be astonished if I sent over to you the newspaper cuttings, but you already know that I am a hater of celebrity. Suffice it to say, that whenever I went on the platform a deafening applause would be raised for me. Nearly all the papers paid high tributes to me, and even the most bigoted had to admit that 'This man with his handsome face and magnetic presence and wonderful oratory is the most prominent figure in the Parliament', etc. etc. Sufficient for you to know that never before did an Oriental make such an impression on American society.[7]

In his letter of 15 November 1893,[8] to the Dewan of Junagad, Haridas Viharidas Desai, the Swami sent him a few lines from the *New York Critique* and from the *Herald*. The latter had said, 'Vivekananda is undoubtedly the greatest figure in the Parliament of Religions. After hearing him, we feel how foolish it is to send missionaries

---

[6] The Goddess of Learning.
[7] *SV Letters*, p. 54.
[8] Ibid., pp. 57–60.

to this learned nation.'[9] He asked the Dewan if, after reading the reports in American newspapers about the impact he had made by giving what the *Critique* had described as '*a new idea of Hindu civilization*', he thought that 'it was worthwhile to send a Sannyasin to America?'

You may not understand why a Sannyasin should be in America. But it was necessary, because the only claim you have to be recognized by the world is your religion, and good specimens of our religious men are required to be sent abroad to give other nations an idea that India is not dead.[10]

On the concluding day of the Parliament of Religions, 27 September 1893, Swami Vivekananda said:

If the Parliament of Religions has shown anything to the world, it is this: It has proved to the world that holiness, purity and charity are not the exclusive possessions of any church in the world, and that every system has produced men and women of the most exalted character. In the face of this evidence, if anybody dreams of the exclusive survival of his own religion and the destruction of the others, I pity him from the bottom of my heart, and point out to him that upon the banner of every religion will soon be written, in spite of resistance: 'Help and not fight', 'Assimilation and not Destruction', 'Harmony and Peace and not Dissension'.[11]

Today one may wonder what was so extraordinary in those five words, 'Sisters and Brothers of America', with which the young Hindu monk had greeted his largely Christian audience, that they were responded to by 'a deafening applause of two minutes'. In putting the

---

[9] Ibid., p. 59.
[10] Ibid., p. 58.
[11] *CWSV*, Vol. 1, p. 24.

womankind first, Swami Vivekananda was paying his tribute to the two women, Kate Sanborn and Mrs Ellen George W. Hale, the very first to help him. Deep within him, he was saluting his mother, Bhubaneswari Devi, and Sri Sarada Devi. But the audience would have known none of that, and this does not explain its extraordinary response. As all the newspapers reported, the audience consisted mostly of women. The customary way of addressing a mixed audience, 'Ladies and Gentlemen', also puts the womankind first, but that too had rarely, if ever, evoked the response 'Sisters and Brothers of America' did. By all accounts it was not even these five words, but the man who spoke, that drew that kind of response. It was something very deep in the people that he had touched, some unspoken aspiration, unfulfilled search. The man, his opening words, the people who had assembled, and their response, all were charged with an upsurge of energy that would always remain inexplicable.

Swami Vivekananda had lifted, as much for India as for the West, the prevalent notion of 'religion' itself to a much higher plane. He put forth the substance of his teachings about what religion truly is, as follows. And that, not just in his lectures but, by all accounts, in his life and relationships most of all. That was the secret, if it was a secret at all, of his immense appeal.

Religion is not an outgrowth of fear; religion is joyous. It is the spontaneous outburst of the songs of birds and the beautiful sight of the morning. It is an expression of the spirit. It is from within an expression of the free and noble spirit.

If misery is religion, what is hell? No man has a right to make himself miserable. To do so is a mistake; it is a sin. Every peal of laughter is a prayer sent to God.

To go back, what I have learned is this: Religion is not in books, not in forms, not in sects, not in nations: religion is in the human heart. It is engrafted here. The proof of it is in ourselves. …It is love alone that can conquer hatred. If there is power in hate, there is infinitely more power in love.[12]

On 27 October 1894, he wrote to Alasinga Perumal:

I do not believe in a God or religion which cannot wipe the widow's tears or bring a piece of bread to the orphan's mouth. However sublime be the theories, however well-spun may be the philosophy—I do not call it religion so long as it is confined to books and dogmas. The eye is in the forehead and not in the back. Move onward and carry into practice that which you are very proud to call your religion, and God bless you![13]

…Love never fails, my son; today or tomorrow or ages after, truth will conquer. Love shall win the victory. Do you love your fellow men? Where should you go to seek for God—are not all the poor, the miserable, the weak, gods? Why not worship them first?

…Have you love?—You are omnipotent. Are you perfectly unselfish?—you are irresistible. It is character that pays everywhere.[14]

---

[12] In a talk he gave at the People's Church, Washington, D.C. on 28 October 1894, and reported on the following day in the *Washington D.C. Times*. *SV New Discoveries*, Vol. 2, Appendix B, p. 404.
[13] *SV Letters*, pp. 169-70.
[14] In the same letter, Ibid., p. 170.

8

After the Parliament of Religions: Swami Vivekananda's Temptation and 'The Work'

My mission in America was not to the Parliament of Religions.

—Swami Vivekananda

I had had the greatest temptation of my life in America.
—Swami Vivekananda to Mrs Emily Lyon

The Parliament of Religions came to a close after seventeen days, on 27 September 1893. To Swami Vivekananda, who would draw from the audience a cheerful applause should he as much as cross the platform, that was, however, only 'a first step'. On his return to India after three-and-a-half years in the West, in what is now his famous speech, 'My Plan of Campaign', delivered in Madras, he said:

I did not go to America, as most of you know, for the Parliament of Religions, but this demon of a feeling was in me and within my soul. I travelled twelve years[1] all over India, finding no way to work for my countrymen, and that is why I went to America. Most

---

[1] At other times also, he spoke of 'twelve years'. This is puzzling. The period was just a quarter that much, actually even less. See Chapter 3.

of you know that, who knew me then. Who cared about this Parliament of Religions? Here was my own flesh and blood sinking every day, and who cared for them? This was my first step.[2]

Later, in Calcutta, in his reply to the public address given to him,[3] he said:

The Parliament of Religions was a great affair, no doubt. From various cities of this land we have thanked the gentlemen who organised the meeting, and they deserved all our thanks for the kindness that has been shown to us...[4]

On the other hand, my mission in America was not to the Parliament of Religions. That was only something by the way, it was only an opening, an opportunity...[5]

Brothers, you have touched another chord in my heart, the deepest of all, and that is the mention of my teacher, my master, my hero, my ideal, my God in life—Shri Ramakrishna Paramahamsa.[6]

...Ay, long before ideas of universal religion and brotherly feelings between different sects were mooted and discussed in any country in the world, here, in sight of this city, had been living a man whose whole life was a Parliament of Religions as it should be.[7]

That was no hyperbole but literally true, as we saw in a previous chapter.[8] The truth was even greater than the

---

[2] That whole speech is to be found in the *CWSV*, Vol. III, pp. 207–27. This particular passage, on p. 226.

[3] Both the Calcutta public address and the Swami's reply to it are to be found in the *CWSV*, Vol. III, pp. 306–21.

[4] Ibid., p. 309.

[5] Ibid., p. 310.

[6] Ibid., p. 312.

[7] Ibid., p. 315.

[8] Chapter 2.

Swami had stated. Whereas Sri Ramakrishna had personally experienced all different strivings towards God in their *substance* having an inner unity, the underlying spirit, even if not the aim, of the Parliament of Religions, organized by the Catholics, was to demonstrate the superiority of Christianity over other religious faiths. In his letter of 11 January 1895 to Narasimhachariar ('G.G.'), Swami Vivekananda said: 'The Parliament of Religions was organized with the intention of proving the superiority of the Christian religion over other forms of faith, but the philosophic religion of Hinduism was able to maintain its position notwithstanding.'[9] He thought it was meant to be 'a heathen show': '...allow me to construe for you the history of the Parliament of Religions. They wanted a horse, and they wanted to ride it. There were people there who wanted to make it a heathen show, but it was ordained otherwise, it could not help being so.'

By examining the background literature concerning the Parliament and some of the speeches in the Parliament itself, Marie Louise Burke showed that to be indeed the case.[10] It was known even at that time that the Archbishop of Canterbury had refused to send anyone to represent the Church of England. He thought it simply inconceivable that Christianity could sit on the same platform with other religions as its equal; for it was only in Christianity that God had fully revealed His plan for man and it could not be equated with other faiths.

It would, therefore, be a mistake to think that the organizers of the Parliament of Religions really believed in the inner unity of all religions. But it would be a greater

---

[9] *SV Letters*, p. 194.
[10] For details, see *SV New Discoveries*, Vol. 1, pp. 67–74.

mistake to think that the only motive behind the Parliament was to show the divine superiority of Christianity. That Swami Vivekananda thought it to be 'a heathen show' is *not* to be interpreted as his outright dismissal of that great effort. On the contrary, in his letter to Raja Ajit Singh of Khetri he said:

What a wonderful achievement was that World's Fair at Chicago! And that wonderful Parliament of Religions where voices from every corner of the earth expressed their religious ideas! I was also allowed to present my own ideas through the kindness of Dr. Barrows and Mr. Bonney. Mr. Bonney is such a wonderful man! Think of that mind that planned and carried out with great success that gigantic undertaking, and he no clergyman, a lawyer presiding over the dignitaries of all the churches—the sweet, learned, patient Mr. Bonney with all his soul speaking through his bright eyes...[11]

While Swami Vivekananda was always perceptive of what spoke through one's eyes, the American newspapers almost always mentioned *his* eyes and their astonishing effect upon the audience, especially upon the women who constituted the larger part of his audiences anyway. It was sometimes reported, with a touch of mirth, that 'listening to him the women hardly ever looked below his eyes!'

It is undeniable that he remained personally untouched by that immense chorus of attention in the Parliament and praise in the newspapers. But not long thereafter, Swami Vivekananda had the greatest temptation of his young life—and he succumbed to it. In the story of his life, that

---

[11] This letter is undated, giving only the year, '1894'. *SV Letters*, p. 77.

temptation, and his 'fall', make in many ways *a*, indeed *the*, central piece. A six-year-old girl heard his 'confession' and told the world about it sixty years later. It is best to hear the young witness, Cornelia Conger, describe the temptation and the fall of 'someone I have loved for all these 62 years', as she said.

Before the Congress [or Parliament] of Religions met in Chicago at the time of the Columbian Exposition in 1893, members of various churches volunteered to ask into their homes as guests delegates to it. My grandmother, Mrs. John B. Lyon, was one of these, requesting, if possible, that a delegate who was broad-minded be sent to us, as my grandfather was much interested in philosophy but heartily disliked bigots...We had been given no idea who he would be, nor even what religion he was representing. A message came that a member of our Church—the First Presbyterian— would bring him after midnight...When she answered the door- bell, there stood Swami Vivekananda in a long yellow robe, a red sash, and a red turban—a very startling sight to her, because she had probably never seen an East Indian before. She welcomed him warmly and showed him to his room.

...He seemed to feel especially close to my grandmother, who reminded him of his own mother. She was short and very erect, with quiet dignity and assurance, excellent common sense, and a dry humour that he enjoyed. My mother, who was a pretty and charming young widow, and I—who was only six years old— lived with them. My grandmother and my mother attended most of the meetings of the Congress of Religions and heard Swamiji speak there and later at lectures he gave. I know he helped my sad young mother who missed her young husband so much.

Once he [the Swami] said to my grandmother that he had had the greatest temptation of his life in America. She liked to tease him a bit and said, 'Who is she, Swami?' He burst out laughing and said, 'Oh, it is not a lady. It is Organisation!'[12]

It was this *Temptation of Swami Vivekananda* that disturbed his brother-monks greatly. On his return, early in 1897, from his first visit to the West, Swami Vivekananda had established, on 1 May 1897, the Ramakrishna Mission Association, saying, 'From my travels in various countries I have come to the conclusion that without organisation nothing great and permanent can be done.' Soon thereafter, one of his brother-monks (Yogananda) reproached him for introducing into Ramakrishna's teachings the Western ideas of social action, public good, and organization. He was expressing what others thought as well. On their journey to the blissful heights of bhakti and mukti, how did 'social action' and 'organization' creep in? That touched him to the quick, and he spoke to them harshly; for, when roused, he could breathe fire.

You are Bhaktas, or in other words, sentimental fools. What do you understand of religion? You are babies. You are only good at praying with folded hands: 'O Lord! How beautiful is Your nose, how sweet are Your eyes,' and all such nonsense; and you think that your salvation is secured, that Shri Ramakrishna will come at the final hour and take you up by the hand to the highest heaven! Study, public preaching, and doing humanitarian works are, according to you, Maya because Shri Ramakrishna did not do them himself! Because he said to someone, 'Seek and find God first; doing good to the world is a presumption!' As if God-realisation is such an easy thing to be achieved! As if He is such a fool as to make Himself a plaything in the hands of the imbecile!

---

[12] Cornelia Conger in *Reminiscences*, pp. 130-31, 133.

You think you understand Shri Ramakrishna better than myself! You think Jnana is dry knowledge to be attained by a desert path, killing out the tenderest faculties of the heart. Your Bhakti is sentimental nonsense, which makes one impotent. You want to preach Ramakrishna as you have understood him which is mighty little! Hands off! Who cares for *your* Ramakrishna? Who cares for your Bhakti and Mukti? Who cares for what the scriptures say? I will go to hell cheerfully a thousand times, if I can rouse my countrymen immersed in Tamas, and make them stand on their own feet and be Men, inspired with the spirit of Karma-Yoga. I am not a follower of Ramakrishna or any one. I am a follower of him only who carries out my plans! I am not a servant of Ramakrishna or any one, but of him only who serves and helps others, without caring for his own Mukti.

His face flushed, his voice choked, his body shaking and trembling, he suddenly fled to his own room. Overwhelmed, all were moved to silence. After a few minutes, some of his gurubhais went and looked in his room, and found him in deep meditation. After he had returned, he said to them softly:

When one attains Bhakti one's heart and nerves become so soft and delicate that they cannot bear even the touch of a flower! Do you know that I cannot even read a novel nowadays! I cannot think or talk of Shri Ramakrishna long, without being overwhelmed. So I am trying and trying always to keep down the welling rush of Bhakti within me. I am trying to bind and bind myself with the iron chains of Jnana, for still my work to my motherland is unfinished, and my message to the world not yet fully delivered. So, as soon as I find that Bhakti feelings are trying to come up to sweep me off my feet, I give a hard knock to them and make myself adamant by bringing up austere Jnana.

Oh, I have work to do! I am a slave of Ramakrishna, who left his work to be done by me and will not give me rest till I have finished it! And, oh, how shall I speak of him! Oh, his love for me![13]

Here we see a divided self, but a divided self of an entirely different kind.

The authors of *The Life* observed:

Of the Swami's numerous triumphs one of the greatest was the conversion of his Gurubhais from individualistic to the universal idea of religious life in which public spirit and service to fellow-men occupied a prominent place. Up to this time the ideal of the monks of the Math was, to strive for personal Mukti and realisation of the Supreme Atman by severe penance and meditation, remaining as much as possible aloof from the world and its cares and sorrows, according to the prevailing Hindu idea, sanctified by tradition, and sanctioned by the sages and the seers from the Vedic period down to the present day. But with the appearance of the Swami among them a new order of things was inaugurated...The age demanded, he said, that they should carry the new light unto others, that they themselves should show by their example how to serve the poor, the helpless, and the diseased, seeing God in them, and that they should inspire others to do the same. The mission of his life, he said, was to create a new order of Sannyasins in India who would dedicate their lives to help and save others.

The proposition, though grand and inspiring, was to them too revolutionary and staggering. How could they suddenly change at another's bidding their precious religious ideal to which

---

[13] *The Life*, pp. 507-08. This and the previous passage are narrated also in Romain Rolland's *The Life of Vivekananda and the Universal Gospel*, pp. 124–26.

they had given their lives, for one which apparently went against their whole nature and training? With them the struggle was hard and long. But who could resist the Swami?[14]

It was most ironical that 'converting' his own brother-monks to the Vedanta as a *feeling* of oneness with all living beings, and hence to the realization that true renunciation was not a selfish seeking of one's own salvation but involved a passionate concern with their suffering, should have been considered as one of Swami Vivekananda's 'greatest triumphs'. That he had to first remove from *their* minds the limited notions of the great concepts of Indian philosophy and their application to life was ironical no less.

The authors of *The Life* themselves seemed to be of the view that whereas the religious ideals to which the other monks of Sri Ramakrishna had dedicated their lives had the sanction of the sages from the Vedic times, it was the Swami who was bringing into them the Western ideas of social action and organization. On the contrary, he had been showing, both in the West and in India, that this was so limited a view of Indian spiritual traditions, so as to be almost a caricature. And, in that context, he repeatedly talked of the Buddha who had dedicated his life to the good of all and let his own nirvana pass by many a time.

After the incident mentioned above, it is true, there were no longer reproaches from the Swami's brother-monks. They loved him, as he loved them, and they submitted, for they saw more clearly than ever before that their Master, Sri Ramakrishna, was working through his anointed Narendra. Yet they did not understand him. Love

---

[14] *The Life*, p. 494.

and submission do not necessarily mean understanding. From what we know of them, they were one-dimensional men. How could they understand a man as multifaceted as Vivekananda, each facet demanding its fulfilment, a man of incredibly varied potential but all subordinated to that one dominating demand from the poor, the oppressed and the miserable? It is easy to understand, to follow, even worship, a one-dimensional man, or a one-dimensional woman, and this may be the reason why we mostly tend to confine our great men and great women to that one dimension of theirs which appeals to us most and to dissolve the rest. Swami Vivekananda was showing that bhakti alone is one-dimensional, and so is jnana alone, and mukti likewise; and what is one-dimensional, does violence to one's self and therefore to the *other*. Hence the Upanishad's cry: *neti neti*, 'it is not this *alone*', 'it is not this *alone*'.

Swami Vivekananda wrote to Haripada Mitra from Chicago, 'I came to this country not to satisfy my curiosity, nor for name or fame, but to see if I could find any means for the support of the poor in India.'[15] Swami Vivekananda went to America to earn money for the regeneration of the poor, the miserable, the ignorant, the oppressed masses of India. Saying to him, '*you have work to do*', Sri Ramakrishna had yoked him to the service of man, pulling him away from absorption in the bliss of the Absolute. It was only after closely watching Sri Ramakrishna *living* what he was teaching, and thereafter seeing the lives of the toiling masses of India and their sufferings, that the phrase 'service to man' became something concrete and living to Narendranath. He was called to dedicate his life to it.

---

[15] Letter dated 28 December 1893. *SV Letters*, p. 60.

Deeply conscious of the pain he was causing to his mother by doing so, Narendra took to the ochre robe—if only to change the prevalent notions of 'the ochre robe' first.

In his letter of 20 August 1893, from 'Breezy Meadows', to Alasinga Perumal, Swami Vivekananda wrote as regards 'the work':

...A hundred thousand men and women, fired with the zeal of holiness, fortified with eternal faith in the Lord, and nerved to lion's courage by their sympathy for the poor and the fallen and the downtrodden, will go over the length and breadth of the land, preaching the gospel of salvation, the gospel of help, the gospel of social raising-up—the gospel of equality.[16]

To Swami Vivekananda, the gospel of salvation was not something apart from the gospel of equality. To the lines quoted above, he quickly added: 'No religion on earth preaches the dignity of humanity in such a lofty strain as Hinduism, and no religion on earth treads upon the necks of the poor and the low in such a fashion as Hinduism.'[17]

To his 'Madras boys', he wrote on 24 January 1894 from Chicago:

My whole ambition in life is to set in motion a machinery which will bring noble ideas to the door of everybody, and then let men and women settle their own fate. Let them know what our forefathers as well as other nations have thought on the most momentous questions of life. Let them see specially what others are doing now, and then decide. We are to put the chemicals together, the crystallization will be done by nature according to her laws.[18]

---

[16] Ibid., p. 41.
[17] Ibid., p. 41.
[18] Ibid., pp. 63-64.

To his noble friend, the Dewan of Junagad, he wrote on 29 January 1894:

...But appreciation or no appreciation, I am born to organize these young men; nay, hundreds more in every city are ready to join me; and I want to send them rolling like irresistible waves over India bringing comfort, morality, religion, education to the doors of the meanest and the most downtrodden. And this I will do or die.[19]

In his long letter of 19 March 1894 to Shashi (Ramakrishnananda), written from Chicago,[20] the first to his brother-monks since his coming to America, he wrote:

A country where millions of people live on flowers of the Mohua plant—and a million or two of Sadhus and a hundred million or so of Brahmins suck the blood out of these poor people, without even the least effort for their amelioration—is that a country or hell? Is that a religion, or the devil's dance?

...My brother, in view of all this, specially of the poverty and ignorance, I had no sleep. At Cape Comorin sitting in Mother Kumari's temple, sitting on the last bit of Indian rock—I hit upon a plan: We are so many Sannyasins wandering about and teaching the people metaphysics—it is all madness. Did not our Gurudeva use to say, 'An empty stomach is no good for religion'? That those poor people are leading the life of brutes is simply due to ignorance. We have for all ages been sucking their blood and trampling them under foot.

...Suppose some disinterested Sannyasins, bent on doing good to others, go from village to village, disseminating education

[19] Ibid., pp. 65-66.
[20] Ibid., pp. 78–83.

and seeking in various ways to better the condition of all down to the Chandala, through oral teaching, and by means of maps, cameras, globes, and such other accessories—can't that bring forth good in time? ...We as a nation have lost our individuality, and that is the cause of all mischief in India. We have to give back to the nation its lost individuality and *raise the masses*.

...To effect this, the first thing we need is men, and the next is funds.[21]

...You may perhaps think what Utopian nonsense all this is! You little know what is in me. If any of you help me in my plans, all right, or Gurudeva will show me the way out.[22]

Swami Vivekananda's concern for women was equally intense. 'The work' consisted also of restoring to them *their* lost individuality, *their innate dignity as women*. In that same letter to his brother-monk, he compared the state of women in America with that of women in India, and then denounced the Hindu denigration of woman.

Nowhere in the world are women like those of this country. How pure, independent, self-relying, and kind-hearted! It is the women who are the life and soul of this country. All learning and culture are centred in them. The saying [here in Sanskrit a line from *Chandi*] 'Who is the Goddess of Fortune Herself in the families of the meritorious'—holds good in this country, while that other [another line in Sanskrit] 'The Goddess of ill luck in the homes of the sinful'—applies to ours. Just think on this...And look at our girls, becoming mothers below their teens! Good Lord! I now see it all. Brother, [a quotation in Sanskrit, from Manu] 'The gods are pleased where women are held in esteem'—says the old Manu.

---

[21] Ibid., pp. 81-82.
[22] Ibid., p. 83.

We are horrible sinners, and our degradation is due to our calling women 'despicable worms', 'gateway to hell', and so forth. Goodness gracious! There is all the difference between heaven and hell![23]

In another very long letter to Ramakrishnananda,[24] in which he gave him fourteen instructions, which were actually principles upon which the 'work' and the 'organization' were to be based, he wrote:

11. There is no chance for the welfare of the world unless the condition of women is improved. It is not possible for a bird to fly on only one wing.

12. Hence, in the Ramakrishna Incarnation, the acceptance of a woman as the Guru; hence His practising in the woman's garb and *frame of mind* (emphasis mine); hence too His preaching the motherhood of women as representations of the Divine Mother.

13. Hence it is that my first endeavour is to start a Math for women. This Math shall be the origin of Gargis and Maitreyis, and women of even higher attainments than these...[25]

    ...In India there are two great evils. Trampling on the women, and grinding the poor through caste restrictions.[26]

Starting a math for women did not mean that 'the work' included monasticism for women. It meant education of women, as it meant the education of masses.

---

[23] Ibid., p. 80.
[24] His undated letter, only saying 'U.S.A, 1895'. *SV Letters*, pp. 200–08.
[25] Ibid., pp. 201-02.
[26] Ibid., p. 207.

But the same work I want to do, on parallel lines, for women. And my principle is: each one helps himself...No man shall dictate to a woman; nor a woman to a man. Each one is independent. What bondage there may be is only that of love. Women will work out their own destinies—much better, too, than man can ever do for them. All the mischief to women has come because men undertook to shape the destinies of women.[27]

With perfect consistency of attitude and thought, he simultaneously said: 'My help is from a distance. There are Indian women, English women, and I hope American women will come to take up the task. As soon as they have begun, I wash my hands off it!'

It may appear strange that Swami Vivekananda's work for the masses of India was being done in America! Not many understood why, in the first place, should a sannyasin who had renounced the world feel so intensely as he did about the condition of the poor, the oppressed, and the miserable of India? What did *that* have to do with spirituality and salvation, the two primary objects of a sannyasin? A few did understand, but his brother-monks of Sri Ramakrishna were not among them, at the beginning at any rate. That the Swami believed the funds required for the work were to be raised in America, and not in India, seems even more puzzling. As regards the first, one of his greatest contributions has been to remove the false but deep-rooted notions of renunciation and spirituality. As for the second, he explained it in his letter to Ramakrishnananda and to others in India.

---

[27] At a lecture he gave, during his second visit to America, in California, on 27 January 1900, 'My Life and Mission'. See *CWSV*, Vol. VIII, p. 91.

...the first thing we need is men, and the next is funds. Through the grace of our Guru I was sure to get from ten to fifteen men in every town. I next travelled in search of funds, but do you think that the people of India were going to spend money?...Selfishness personified—are they to spend anything? Therefore I have come to America, to earn money myself, and then return to my country and devote the rest of my days to the realization of this one aim of my life.

As our country is poor in social virtues, so this country is lacking in spirituality. I give them spirituality, and they give me money.[28]

A perfect exchange! However, one must not read the last two lines above too literally. If one does not see Swami Vivekananda's sense of humour and laughter amidst the most serious utterances, one understands him little. He saw the deep currents of spirituality flowing in the West not only in those who came in close contact with him but also in many among his varied audiences. Were that not so, he would never have had the response to him and to his teachings that he did. And he always acknowledged it. Swami Vivekananda *never* said that 'the materialist West' was a spiritual desert, and 'the spiritual India' free from the ugly expressions of acquisitive materialism.

Swami Vivekananda made a sharp distinction between 'religion' and 'society', and spoke of it throughout, contrasting India with the West mainly in the terms that distinction suggested. It is a theme that came up repeatedly in his earlier letters from America to India.

Liberty is the first condition of growth. Your ancestors gave every liberty to the soul, and religion grew. They put the body under

---

[28] Ibid., p. 82.

every bondage and society did not grow. The opposite is the case in the West—every liberty to society, none to religion. Now are falling off the shackles from the feet of Eastern society as from those of Western religion.[29]

To this he added as a postscript:

The present Hindu society is organized only for spiritual men, and hopelessly crushes out everybody else. Why? Where shall they go who want to enjoy the world a little with its frivolities? Just as our religion takes in all, so should our society. This is to be worked out by first understanding the true principles of our religion, and then applying them to society. This is the slow but sure work to be done.[30]

Now the question before us is this. There cannot be any growth without liberty. Our ancestors freed religious thought, and we have a wonderful religion. But they put a heavy chain on the feet of society, and our society is, in a word, *horrid*, *diabolical*. In the West, society always had freedom, and look at them. On the other hand, look at their religion.

Liberty is the first condition of growth. Just as man must have liberty to think and speak, so he must have liberty in food, dress, and marriage and in every other thing, so long as he does not injure others.[31]

In India religion was never shackled. No man was ever challenged in the selection of his Ishta-Devata, or his sect, or his preceptor, and religion grew, as it grew nowhere else. On the other hand, a fixed point was necessary to allow this infinite

[29] Vivekananda to Alasinga Perumal, letter dated 29 September 1894. *SV Letters*, p. 149.
[30] Ibid., p. 150.
[31] Vivekananda to Alasinga Perumal, letter dated 19 November 1894, from New York. *SV Letters*, p. 173.

variation to religion, and society was chosen as that point in India. As a result, society became rigid and almost immovable. For liberty is the only condition of growth.

On the other hand, in the West, the field of variation was society, and the constant point was religion. Conformity was the watchword, and even now is the watchword, of European religion, and each new departure had to gain the least advantage only by wading through a river of blood. The result is a splendid social organization, with a religion that never rose beyond the grossest materialistic conceptions.

Today the West is awakening to its wants; and the 'true self of man and spirit' is the watchword of the advanced school of Western theologians.[32]

These being Swami Vivekananda's perceptions, they formed the first fundamental presuppositions of his work. The Indian masses had to be liberated from the degeneration of Indian *society*, and that is what he meant by restoring to them their lost individuality: 'No priestcraft, no social tyranny! ...None deserves liberty who is not ready to give liberty. Suppose the English give over to you all the power. Why, the powers that be, then, will hold the people down, and let them not have it. Slaves want power to make slaves.'[33]

The work consisted in, '...insisting on our religion and giving liberty to society. Root up priestcraft from the old religion, and you get the best religion in the world. Do

[32] Vivekananda to the Hindus of Madras, in his very elaborate reply, September 1894, to their appreciation of his work in America. *SV Letters*, pp. 150–69. This passage, on p. 163.
[33] In the same letter, dated 19 November 1894 to Alasinga, quoted above. *SV Letters*, p. 174.

you understand me? Can you make a European society with India's religion? I believe it is possible and must be.'[34]

However, Swami Vivekananda was mistaken in posing such absolute distinction between *society* and *religion*, even though what he was pointing *to* was, in a sense, undoubtedly true. A profound student both of Western philosophy and of the history of Western nations, he must have known that as late as the nineteenth century, even in the times he was living, the social laws in the West were for the most part ecclesiastical laws dictated by the Church. Nor did the people of the West have the liberty of thought and action the Swami attributed to them; at any rate, not until the authority the Church claimed over even their secular affairs was repudiated decisively. Furthermore, the use of the word 'religion' applied to the Indian context had been misleading from the start. The centre of Indian thought and life has been dharma, and dharma is not 'religion'.[35] Dharma, of which we have the clearest exposition in the Mahabharata but completely obscured, is the universal foundation of life.[36] There had been thus a double error of identity in using the word 'Hinduism' denoting a 'religion', the creation of the Portuguese missionaries in the sixteenth century. In his reply to the Madras Address, a part of which was cited above, Swami Vivekananda also said:

---

[34] Ibid., p. 174.
[35] This is discussed in detail in the author's *Dharma, India and the World Order* and in his *Finding Jesus in Dharma: Christianity in India.* Both cited earlier in this book.
[36] This subject is taken up in the greatest detail, as in the Mahabharata so in the author's *The Mahabharata—An Inquiry into the Human Condition*, awaiting publication.

A friend criticized the use of European terms of philosophy and religion in my addresses. I would have been very glad to use Sanskrit terms; it would have been much more easy, as being the only perfect vehicle of religious thought. But the friend forgot that I was addressing an audience of Western people...[37]

Nevertheless, the misconception has remained.[38] It has had the consequence of obscuring the plainly universal meaning of dharma and the Swami being caught in the muddle created by applying the word 'religion' to Indian thought. The irony is that when he talked of the Vedanta as the future religion, he was not talking of 'religion' at all. The Vedanta is not 'religion' in the sense the word 'religion' is generally understood. It is a *feeling* of oneness with all beings; it is *love*. It is in that feeling, of love, that the metaphysics of the Vedanta becomes the *living* Vedanta. And in everything that he was, Swami Vivekananda was its embodiment.

It is manifest in what may be called *Swami Vivekananda's Testament*, addressed to one of his 'Madras boys',[39] on 3 March 1894, from Chicago, but actually his guiding philosophy of sane life everywhere.

...I agree with you so far that faith is a wonderful insight and that it alone can save; but there is the danger in it of breeding fanaticism barring further progress. Jnana is all right; but there is the danger of its becoming dry intellectualism. Love is great and noble; but it may die away in meaningless sentimentalism. A harmony of

[37] *SV Letters*, p. 161.
[38] The Swami was perfectly aware of the confusion created by the use of the words 'Hindu' and 'Hinduism'. In his lecture 'Vedanta in its Application to Indian Life', he dwelt upon it. See *CWSV*, Vol. III, pp. 228-29.
[39] Vivekananda To 'Kidi' (Singaravelu Mudaliar), Ibid., pp. 68–71.

all these is the thing required. Ramakrishna was such a harmony...And if amongst us, each one may not individually attain to that perfection, still we may get it collectively by counteracting, equipoising, adjusting, and fulfilling one another. This would be *harmony* by a number of persons, and a decided advance on all other forms and creeds.

For a religion to be effective, enthusiasm is necessary. At the same time we must try to avoid the danger of multiplying creeds.

God, though everywhere, can be known to us in and through human character.

We preach neither social equality nor inequality, but that every being has the same rights, and insist upon freedom of thought and action in every way.

We reject none, neither theist, nor pantheist, monist, polytheist, agnostic, nor atheist; the only condition of being a disciple is modelling a character at once the broadest and the most intense.

Nor do we insist upon particular codes of morality as to conduct, or character, or eating or drinking, except so far as it injures others.

Whatever retards the onward progress or helps the downward fall is vice; whatever helps in coming up and becoming harmonized is *virtue*.

We leave everybody free to know, select, and follow whatever suits and helps him. Thus, for example, eating meat may help one, eating fruit another. Each is welcome to his own peculiarity; but he has no right to criticize the conduct of others, because that would, if followed by him, injure him, much less insist that others should follow his way. A wife may help some people in this progress, to others she may be a positive injury. But the unmarried man has no right to say that the married disciple is wrong, much less to force his own ideal of morality upon his brother.

We believe that every being is divine, is God. Every soul is a sun covered over with clouds of ignorance, the difference between soul and soul is due to the difference in density of these layers of clouds. We believe that this is the conscious or unconscious basis of all religions, and that this is the explanation of the whole history of human progress either in the material, intellectual, or spiritual plane—the same spirit in manifesting through different planes.

We believe that it is the duty of every *soul* to treat, think of, and behave to other *souls* as such, i.e. as *Gods*, and not hate or despise, or vilify, or try to injure them by any manner or means. This is the duty not only of the Sannyasin but of all men and women.

The soul has neither sex, nor caste, nor imperfection.

We believe that nowhere throughout the Vedas, Darshanas, or Puranas, or Tantras, it is ever said that the soul has any sex, creed, or caste. Therefore, we agree with those who say, 'What has religion to do with social reforms?' But they must also agree with us when we tell them that religion has no business to formulate social laws and insist on the difference between beings. Because its aim and end is to obliterate all such fictions and monstrosities.

If it be pleaded that through this difference we would reach the final equality and unity, we answer that the same religion has said over and over again, that mud cannot be washed with mud.

As if a man can be moral by being immoral!

Social laws were created by economic conditions under the sanction of religion. The terrible mistake of religion was to interfere in social matters. But how hypocritically it says and thereby contradicts itself—'Social reform is not the business of religion!' True, what we want is that religion should not be a social reformer, but we insist at the same time that religion has no right to become a social law-giver. Hands off! Keep yourself to your own bounds and everything would come right.

1. Education is the manifestation of the perfection already in man.

2. Religion is the manifestation of the Divinity already in man. Therefore the only duty of the teacher in both cases is to remove all obstructions from the way. Hands off! as I always say, and everything will be right. That is, our duty is to clear the way. The Lord does the rest.

...only take care that no form becomes necessary—unity in variety—see that universality be not hampered in the least. Everything must be sacrificed, if necessary, for that one sentiment, *universality*...remember this specially, that universality—perfect acceptance, not tolerance only—we preach and perform, take care how you trample on the least right of others. Many a huge ship has floundered in that whirlpool. Remember, perfect devotion minus its bigotry—this is what we have got to show.[40]

...To advance oneself towards freedom—physical, mental, and spiritual—and help others to do so, is the supreme prize of man. Those social rules which stand in the way of the unfoldment of this freedom are injurious, and steps should be taken to destroy them speedily. Those institutions should be encouraged by which men advance in the path of freedom.[41]

There was another dimension to Swami Vivekananda's mission both for India and for the West, manifest throughout, but unnamed until decades later—*dialogue*. He had opened a dialogue with those, no matter of which religion, who thought that in their religion alone is the light of God and Truth and in all others, darkness. He was calling on them to rethink their suppositions that had until then only spread fear and hatred among the followers of diverse faiths. That was the significance of his address

---

[40] Vivekananda to Ramakrishnananda, from Chicago. *SV Letters*, p. 85.
[41] Vivekananda to Mrs Mrinalini Bose, letter dated 3 January 1899. *SV Letters*, p. 386.

at the 1893 Parliament of Religions. The indisputable fact
is that what has been in the air for several decades now,
interfaith dialogue, has its genesis in Swami
Vivekananda.[42] Even more importantly, he showed
authentic dialogue to be not only between the self and
the *other*, but also between the self and the self within the
self, collectively and interpersonally. Dialogue with one's
self is the first condition of the dialogue with the *other*:
when there is no dialogue with the self, there is no dialogue
with the *other* either. Therefore, much before that famous
event took place in Chicago, he had opened an intense
dialogue first with his own society, and continued to engage
in it till his dying day. At the same time as he was calling
on the Christians to rethink their suppositions about
Christianity and its relation to Hinduism and other
religions, he was calling on the Hindus to ask: 'with their
richest inheritance, whence their wretched degradation?'
Just as he was asking the social reformers to rethink their
suppositions about social reform in India, he was calling
on his brother-monks to rethink their suppositions about
spirituality and renunciation. Thus, dialogue with the self,
even more than dialogue with the *other*, was an essential
part of Swami Vivekananda's 'work'. This dimension
ignored, he is almost always presented as the strongest
challenge of Hinduism to Christianity, and because British
rulers were Christians, to their self-professed moral
justification of British rule in India. What ought to be
stated also, but seldom is, is the truth that Swami
Vivekananda was the strongest Hindu challenge to what

[42] This itself will require a separate study. See the author's *Finding Jesus in Dharma*, Chapter 8, 'The Dialogue: Promise & Problems', pp. 139–64.

the Hindus had turned religion into. All his observations, in his letters and lectures, about the Hindus and the Hindu society were clearly in that light and are to be read again today as such—dialogue of the self with the self. And he conducted that dialogue from the ground of the Vedanta; for, he said, 'The only way is love and sympathy. The only worship is love.'[43] That is the *living* Vedanta.

It will, however, be a great mistake to see Swami Vivekananda's mission as only that of calling on others to rethink their suppositions about themselves and others. His mission was one of demonstrating how very limited the 'self' is; that there *is* a state of being, accessible to all, in which miseries created by distinctions of every kind are dissolved, and one lives in the joy of feeling the oneness of all that exists, transcending all limitations. But this, too, is only incompletely stated—*neti*.

It needed a French novelist and thinker, Romain Rolland, to say: 'Every mission is dramatic, for it is accomplished at the expense of him who receives it, at the expense of one part of his nature, of his rest, of his health, often of his deepest aspirations.'[44] It may not be too rewarding, from the standpoint of history seen in a chosen framework, to study them if they were confined merely to outward sacrifices such as health or rest. Their study becomes eminently instructive when a mission is achieved by a great figure in history by suppressing one

---

[43] Vivekananda to Haridas Viharidas Desai, undated letter from Chicago, showing only the year '1894'. *SV Letters*, p. 96.
[44] Romain Rolland, *The Life of Vivekananda and the Gospel*, pp. 126–27.

or several aspects of his, or her, personality; each of them not only demanding its own fulfilment, but being such that, given a chance, each could lead to other extraordinary results.

If the brother-monks of Swami Vivekananda were disturbed by his *American temptation*, Vivekananda tired of it even more as its inherent logic unfolded, which it quickly did. He gradually refused to be limited to 'the work' and to 'organization' which that work required. Yet he saw that he had to limit himself thus and, self-divided, he suffered greatly. He was a wind caught in the net.

9

The *Prakriti* and the Swami: The Climate, Clothes, and the Diet

It was very cold and I suffered much for want of warm clothing.
—Swami Vivekananda to Alasinga Perumal
(On ship from Yokohama to Vancouver, July 1893)

I have eaten a good slice of meat—just now because in the evening I am going to speak in a vegetarian dinner!
—Vivekananda to Isabelle McKindley, 1 May 1894.

People in spiritual India seem to float on the Brahman of the Upanishads, the 'Absolute', or on the Purusha of the Samkhya metaphysics, so did Swami Vivekananda. It occurred neither to him nor to those who had urged him to go to America and take it by storm with the resounding sound of the Brahman, to ask what the climate there would be like and what kind of clothes he might need for it. A favourite phrase of the Swami was, 'Hands off! And everything will be right.' Filled with an inner power, he seemed to be saying to Prakriti or 'Nature': 'Hands off! I am the Brahman, the Purusha, you have no power over me. I am free, ever free!' The Prakriti whispered into his ears, 'Even so, dear son, go and get some warm clothes for your physical body. Your magnificent ochre silk robe alone will not do in the American climate. It is cold, and will become freezing cold as the winter approaches.' And the Nature's dear son, too, thought that to be a most sensible thing to do.

In his long letter of 20 August 1893 to Alasinga Perumal, the Swami had also said that on his voyage in July from Yokohama to Vancouver, it was very cold and that he suffered much for want of warm clothing: 'Winter is approaching, and I shall have to get all sorts of warm clothing, and we require more warm clothing than the natives.'[1] The urgency of equipping himself with warm clothing apart, the Swami told Alasinga:

I must first go and buy some clothing in Boston. If I am to live longer here, my quaint dress will not do. People gather by hundreds in the streets to see me. So what I want is to dress myself in a long black coat, and keep a red robe and turban to wear when I lecture. This is what the ladies advise me to do, and they are the rulers here, and I must have their sympathy.[2]

That he would have in abundance in the days to come.

In the meantime, what the Swami needed to have was some more money to supplement what was left out of the sum given him at the time of his leaving Bombay. Some three weeks *before* the Parliament of Religions he was to write to Alasinga Perumal:[3]

---

[1] *SV Letters*, p. 39.
[2] Ibid., p. 43.
[3] On his return to India, in his first public speech in Madras, the city where his vision of going to the West had begun to take definite shape, he recalled those early difficult days in America. See *CWSV*, Vol. III, p. 209. See also *SV New Discoveries*, Vol. 1, pp. 20-21.

Before you get this letter my money would come down to somewhat about £70 or £60. So try your best to send some money. It is necessary to remain here for some time to have any influence here...Gradually, I can make my way: but that means a longer residence in this horribly expensive country...Just now I have been to the tailor and ordered some winter clothings, and that would cost at least Rs. 800 and up. And still it would not be good clothes, only decent.[4]...If you fail in keeping me here, send some money to get me out of the country.[5]...With a bleeding heart I have crossed half the world to this strange land, seeking for help. The Lord is great. I know He will help me. I may perish of cold or hunger in this land, but I bequeath to you, young men, this sympathy, this struggle for the poor, the ignorant, the oppressed.[6] ...After such a struggle I am not going to give up easily. Only try your best to help me as much as you can, and even if you cannot, I must try to the end, and even if I die of cold or disease or hunger here, you take up the task. Holiness, sincerity, and faith!...If you can keep me here for six months at least, I hope everything will come right. In the meantime I am trying my best to find any plank I can float upon. And if I find out any means to support myself, I shall wire to you immediately.[7]

Months later, in his letter of 19 March 1894 to Shashi (Ramakrishnananda) in which he had given a clear outline of what 'the work' was to be, he also described the climate in America, the hot and the cold and the snowfall, especially the cold.

---

[4] *SV Letters*, p. 44.
[5] Ibid., p. 45.
[6] Ibid., p. 42.
[7] Ibid., p. 44.

Extreme cold produces a sort of intoxication…I was mortally afraid that my nose and ears would fall off, but to this day they are all right. I have to go out, however, dressed in a heap of warm clothing surmounted by a fur-coat, with boots encased in a woollen jacket, and so on. No sooner do you breathe out than the breath freezes among the beard and moustache![8]

Two days earlier, making fun of himself, from Detroit he had written to his 'Dear Sister' Harriet McKindley, who had sent him some stockings: 'Got your package yesterday. Sorry that you sent those stockings—I could have got some myself here. Glad that it shows your love. After all, the satchel has become more than a thoroughly stuffed sausage. I do not know how to carry it along.'[9] Protected from the Prakriti of the dreadful American cold, the Swami was now laughing at himself for looking like a stuffed sausage!

A great many Indians eat meat; to an equally large number, eating meat is inconceivable. Those who do and those who don't are divided mostly on caste lines. The brahmins, who consider themselves the highest born, pure, spiritual, given to cultivating the energy of *sattva*, not only do not eat meat but look down upon those 'lower castes' who do. There are exceptions of course. The pandits of Kashmir traditionally eat meat because of the cold climate there; and the brahmins of Bengal cannot do without their hilsa fish, persuading themselves that fish is not meat. The sannyasins of course do not eat meat and if anyone among them does, it is considered his 'fall'. The

---

[8] *SV Letters*, pp. 78-79.
[9] Vivekananda to Harriet McKindley, letter dated 17 March 1894. *SV Letters*, p. 73.

orthodox Hindus began attacking Swami Vivekananda for his eating meat during his days in the West. That was evidently conveyed to him by Alasinga and drew a very reasonable response: 'If the people in India want me to keep strictly to my Hindu diet, please tell them to send me a cook and money enough to keep him. This silly *bossism* without a mite of real help makes me laugh...As for me, mind you, I stand at nobody's dictation.'[10]

Meanwhile he was reporting to his brother-monks what one could have to eat in America:

...By the bye, nowadays we have plenty of Hilsa fish here. Eat your fill, but everything digests. There are many kinds of fruits; plantain, lemon, guava, apple, almond, raisin, and grape are in abundance, besides, many other fruits come from California. There are plenty of pineapples, but there are no mangoes or lichis, or things of that sort.

There is a kind of spinach, which, when cooked, tastes just like our Note of Bengal, and another class, which they call asparagus, tastes exactly like the tender Dengo herb, but you can't have our Charchari made of it here. There is no Kalai or any other pulse; they do not even know of them. There is rice, and bread, and numerous varieties of fish and meat, of all description. Their menu is like that of the French. There is your milk, rarely curd, but plenty of whey. Cream is an article of everyday use.[11]

For the rest, he ate what those with whom he stayed ate, meat and fish. Cornelia Conger, the granddaughter of John B. and Emily Lyon of Chicago, recalled:

---

[10] Vivekananda to Alasinga Perumal, letter dated 9 September 1895, from Paris. *SV Letters*, p. 257.
[11] *SV Letters*, p. 100.

As our American food is less highly seasoned than Indian, my grandmother was afraid he might find it flat. He told us, on arrival, that he had been told to conform to all the customs and the food of his hosts, so he ate as we did. My grandmother used to make a little ceremony of making salad dressing at the table, and one of the condiments she used was Tabasco Sauce, put up by some friends of hers, the Mrs. Ilhennys, in Louisiana. She handed him the bottle and said, 'You might like a drop or two of this on your meat, Swami.' He sprinkled it on with such a lavish hand that we all gasped and said, 'But you can't do that! It is terribly hot!' He laughed and ate it with such enjoyment that a special bottle of the sauce was always put at his place after that.[12]

The Swami had an eye always on cream. 'I can renounce every thing, except this,' he once said. His fondness for ice cream was altogether endearing, and it did not in the least detract from his spiritual greatness in the eyes of those who knew him well. Of the days when he stayed with his dearly loved friends Francis and Betty Leggett, at their country home called Ridgely Manor[13] in the Hudson River Valley, some eighty miles north of New York City, there is a charming story about the Swami at dinner.

Swamiji, sitting always on Mrs. Leggett's right, was perfectly at liberty to excuse himself for a smoke or for a walk. There was, however, a way to hold him. A very quick word from Lady Betty (how many times! Miss Stumm recalled) that she believed there was to be ice cream would turn him back instantly, and he would sink into his place with a smile of expectancy and pure delight

---

[12] Cornelia Conger, *Reminiscences*, pp. 132-33.
[13] Some ten weeks in August–October of 1899 during the Swami's second visit to the West.

seldom seen on the face of anybody over sixteen. He just loved it, and he had all he wanted, too.[14]

It would be foolish to think that Swami Vivekananda's love for ice cream was all that there was to him at Ridgely Manor. Drawing on what was being said at that time, and on the later recollections of the people who were there, Marie Louise Burke concludes: '...the group of people that centered around a saint and prophet of the highest magnitude formed a house party such as the world had probably never known before and very likely will not know soon again.'[15]

As to the criticism of the orthodox Brahmins that in the West the Swami, a Kshatriya, was eating meat, he sent a devastating response:[16]

You speak of the meat-eating Kshatriya: meat or no meat, it is they who are the fathers of all that is noble and beautiful in Hinduism. Who wrote the Upanishads? Who was Rama? Who was Krishna? Who was Buddha? Who were the Tirthankaras of the Jains? Whenever the Kshatriyas have preached religion, they have given it to everybody; and whenever the Brahmins wrote anything, they would deny all right to others.

...*Is God a nervous fool like you that the flow of His river of mercy would be dammed up by a piece of meat? If such be He, His value is not a pie!* [17]

---

[14] *SV New Discoveries*, Vol. 5, p. 124.
[15] Ibid., p. 111.
[16] In the same letter to 'Kidi' in which he wrote what I have described as *Swami Vivekananda's Testament*, mentioned in the previous chapter.
[17] The liberty that I have taken with this part of the Swami's letter to 'Kidi' (*SV Letters*, p. 70) is that whereas in the original what is cited here makes one paragraph, here I have broken it into two. The two separate things he was saying stand out even more clearly thereby.

It should promptly be added that the Swami was *not*
saying that the Tirthankaras of Jains, all Kshatriyas, also
ate meat. He was saying that—and this is historically
true—the philosophical thoughts concerning man and the
world which the Kshatriyas had put down, they shared
with everybody. In contrast, whenever the Brahmins
wrote deep philosophical thoughts, they denied all rights
to others. And he traced historically the degeneration of
Hindu society to the fact that the masses were kept
ignorant, while education and knowledge remained
confined to the higher castes. Above all, he was showing
the error of correlating spirituality and the lack of it with
not eating or eating meat. *God is not a fool!*

The joys of *Prakriti* are no less than the joys of *sat* and
chit, 'being' and 'consciousness'. Prakriti unfolds itself in
the amazing diversity of forms, colours, sounds, and of
feelings arising from the diverse states of the body at
different times and different places. In none of his
teachings did Swami Vivekananda ever say that the great
diversity of Prakriti ought to be dissolved in the thick
broth of the Brahman, the 'Absolute'. The joys of diversity
are not a negation of the inner unity of all life. Along
with the joys of poetry and music, of words and sounds
and feelings, Swami Vivekananda's father had also
bequeathed to his son the joy of cooking. The Swami
hugely enjoyed it, and there are numerous stories of his
cooking, with diverse effects of what was produced on
the palate of his Western friends. After giving a soul-
stirring lecture on the Vedanta, or some other subject,
Mrs Blodgett recalled:

The emphasis in the second is mine. Also I have left out the contrast he
made between Krishna and Vyasa.

He would come home from a lecture where he was compelled to break away from his audience, so eagerly would they gather around him—come rushing into the kitchen like a boy released from school, with, 'Now we will cook.' The prophet and sage would disappear, to reveal the child side or simplicity of character.[18]

Josephine MacLeod, one of Swami Vivekananda's closest friends and an abiding supporter of his work, later narrated an incident that amazed her for what she thought to be his utter lack of self-consciousness and self-importance. After giving a lecture on 'Jesus of Nazareth', which she considered to be the most outstanding lecture she ever heard, 'when he seemed to radiate a white light from head to foot, so lost was he in the wonder and the power of Christ', they were returning home.

I was so impressed with this obvious halo that I did not speak to him on the way back for fear of interrupting, as I thought, the great thoughts that were still in his mind. Suddenly he said to me, 'I know how it is done.' I said, 'How what is done?' 'How they make mulligatawny soup. They put a bay leaf in it,' he told me. That utter lack of self-consciousness, of self-importance, was perhaps one of his outstanding characteristics.[19]

---

[18] Mrs Roxie Blodgett in *Reminiscences*, pp. 358-59.
[19] Josephine MacLeod in *Reminiscences*, p. 240.

10

Simultaneity in the Life of
Swami Vivekananda

I have been driven and worshipped by princes. I have been slandered by priests and laymen alike. But what of it? Bless them all. They are my very Self.
—Swami Vivekananda[1]

There is a simultaneity in incidents as they unfold in our lives, each related with much of the past, not all of which is known, and with what is happening far beyond itself in the present, of which much remains unseen. There is thus a synchronization not only between what is happening *here* and *elsewhere*, but also between what has happened *before* and *somewhere else*. The *before* is simultaneously present with the *now* and so is the *future*. Furthermore, what is happening is not only outside one's self; much is happening within as well and there is simultaneity between the two. There are, moreover, different levels in both. No language so far has been able to describe happenings as they progress, both outside and within at different levels, in their related simultaneity. Language by its very nature can describe them only in sequence and then too in the measure of known time.

---

[1] To E.T. Sturdy, letter dated 9 August 1895, from New York. *SV Letters*, p. 248.

Despite the qualifying clause beginning with the word 'however' or 'nevertheless', language is one-dimensional, whereas nothing in life it seeks to describe is ever one-dimensional.

All this is true to a most marked degree in the case of someone like Swami Vivekananda, in whose life so many different things of different dimensions were happening simultaneously, and who was living with them simultaneously, at so many different levels of consciousness within: one, intense feeling and equally intense engagement; the other, complete detachment but still with intense feeling, in itself a puzzling combination; and a great many others in between. Above all, his *before*, not limited to this life alone, which Ramakrishna Paramahamsa had seen with clarity and he himself began to see gradually, was present with what he was *now*. And there was within him an increasing conflict between the two. This chapter is about the interconnected *simultaneity* in the happenings in the life of Swami Vivekananda, both external and internal, as far as language still enables one to speak in that way.

The Parliament of Religions over, and now famous all over America, Swami Vivekananda was travelling in the Midwest and the East Coast with a view to earning money for his Indian work by giving lectures on the Indian philosophical heritage and what religion and spirituality might mean to the modern age. The American newspapers were reporting in great detail, often sensational, the personality and the sayings of Swami Vivekananda, and the editors were writings editorials on both, mostly in high praise. He was being described in various picturesque phrases, some quite imaginative, such as 'the cyclonic monk', which amused him greatly. 'I am not "cyclonic" at all,' he said.

He had signed up with a lecture bureau, the Slayton Lyceum Bureau of Chicago. With his dignified good looks, and words that touched the depths of one's soul with the beatitude of love at one moment and with the fire of truth in the next, he was an excellent money earner for that agency. With a further advantage that he had the innocence of a child and could easily be exploited or plainly speaking, cheated. The Swami was travelling long distances by train at all odd hours, the lecture bureau grinding him and defrauding him, giving him only a fraction of the money each lecture of his was actually earning. On 11 July 1894, he wrote to Alasinga: 'In the Detroit lecture I got $900, i.e. Rs 2700. In other lectures, I earned in one $2500, i.e. Rs 7500 in one hour, but got only 200 dollars! I was cheated by a roguish Lecture Bureau. I have given them up.'[2] The Honorable Thomas Witherell Palmer of Detroit, an admirer and friend of the Swami, managed to free him from the clutches of the Slayton Bureau by proving the contract the agency had drawn up to have been fraudulent to start with.

At Dakshineswar, Narendranath used to sing whenever he went to meet Sri Ramakrishna. On hearing Narendra sing, the Saint of Dakshineswar would go into a trance and float in the ecstasy of the love of God, and those present would feel the magic both of Narendra's voice and the words of the songs he sang. Since coming to America as Swami Vivekananda, he had not sung even once and never would, except occasionally humming to himself some Sanskrit hymns. Many songs were welling up in his heart, but now he was singing them in ways very different from that at Dakshineswar. Alongside the sound of those songs, the

---

[2] *SV Letters*, p. 127.

Song of the Bliss of Life, which was deeply stirring thousands of American men and women, also being heard were the menacing howls of calumny against him.

The Christian missionaries were enraged because Swami Vivekananda had proved their accounts of Hinduism and of Indian civilization to be false, and in their untruth unchristian as well. As a result, their funding for evangelical work, in what they had hitherto been portraying as the area of darkness, had already come down very considerably. From the very day of his spectacular impact at the Parliament of Religions, people were astonished to discover how very mistaken their perceptions of India and of Hinduism had been. In his lectures he was not only dispelling, for the most part successfully, the false impressions Americans had hitherto been given of them, but was drawing them closer to Jesus Christ by teaching them what it truly means to be Christian. In their intoxication with material prosperity, the Americans had forgotten Jesus. The hundreds of people who heard him speak at the Unitarian Church in Detroit, on 14 February 1894, had felt an uplifting power of the kind they had not experienced before; and this was being said by many at that time. The newspapers were full of him, writing about his person and his thoughts in words of amazement and genuine respect.

Swami Vivekananda was, therefore, the one enemy the missionaries had to destroy by using whatever weapons they could find, or invent, against him. Since they could no longer smear the beauty of Indian thought, they began to smear the character of the man. He did not represent the Hindus of India; he came without credentials; and even now there was not a word from India recommending him. He was a fraud; and the gullible American women, who constituted the larger part of all his audiences, were misled by his undeniable attractive personality. And since it was mostly women who were upholding him and taking care of him, his enemies found in that the easiest, and the cheapest, ground of attacking him. The Hindu monk was of dubious character, they alleged, and even more shamefully, that Mrs John Judson Bagley, the wife of a former Governor of Michigan, whose guest in Detroit the Swami was, had had to dismiss her maid because of his improper conduct towards her.

Mrs John Judson Bagley, among the most cultured and influential women in Detroit, rose fiercely to the Swami's defence. She and her daughter Helen proclaimed that every word of the calumny against Swami Vivekananda was false. And they still had with them the maid alleged to be dismissed. The substance of the two letters that Mrs Bagley wrote, one on 22 June 1894 and the other on 20 March 1895, was this:

You write of my dear friend, Vivekananda. I am glad of an opportunity to express my admiration of his character and it makes me most indignant that anyone should call him in question. He has given us in America higher ideas of life than we have ever had before. In Detroit, an old conservative city, in all the Clubs he is honoured as no one has ever been, and I only feel that all who say one word against him are jealous of his greatness and his fine spiritual perceptions; and yet how can they be? He does nothing to make them so.

He has been a revelation to Christians...As a religious teacher and an example to all I do not know his equal...He has been a guest in my house more than three weeks...and in my family he will always be honoured and welcomed...He is a strong, noble human being, one who walks with God. He is simple and trustful as a child. In Detroit I gave him an evening reception, inviting ladies and gentlemen, and two weeks afterwards he lectured to invited guests in my parlour...I had included lawyers, judges, ministers, army-officers, physicians and businessmen with their wives and daughters. Vivekananda talked two hours on 'The Ancient Hindu Philosophers and What They Taught'. All listened with intense interest to the end. Wherever he spoke people listened gladly and said, 'I never heard man speak like that.' He does not antagonize, but lifts people up to a higher level—they see something beyond man-made creeds and denominational names, and they feel one with him in their religious beliefs.

Every human being would be made better by knowing him and living in the same house with him...I want everyone in America to know Vivekananda.

...We all know Vivekananda. Who are they that they speak so falsely?[3]

Although her testimony as regards Swami Vivekananda was undoubtedly the most credible, for having had him as a guest in her home she and her family knew the man, it was not Mrs Bagley alone who rose to his defence. Others were also raising their voices in his support and against the bigotry of missionaries. They included a Rabbi and a Christian cleric, Rabbi Grossman and Reverend Reed Stuart. A most animated correspondence was published in the *Free Press* and in other newspapers of Detroit, which was more about Swami Vivekananda's thoughts.[4]

Pratap Chandra Mazoomdar, the leader of Brahmo Samaj, already known in America for a decade, had also spoken at the Parliament of Religions and was now back in Calcutta. Jealous of the great American response to

---

[3] Marie Louise Burke, *SV New Discoveries*, Vol. 1, pp. 452-53.
[4] For details, see *SV New Discoveries*, Vol. 1, Chapter Six.

Vivekananda, Mazoomdar quickly picked up the missionary stories of the Swami's imaginary immoral life, invented some of his own, and told people that, pretending to preach the Vedanta, he was actually living a thoroughly immoral life with white women.

The Theosophists and the people of the Ramabai Circle in America were inventing their own scandalous stories about Swami Vivekananda. In India, the orthodox Brahmins were attacking the Swami because not only was he mixing and staying with the white mlechchhas, but worse, was eating beef and had degenerated morally; for if one ate meat and beef, one must be sexually immoral, too. The main reason why they were incensed was, of course, that the young sannyasin had been saying, in a voice with authority, that Hindu society had degenerated as a result of the tyranny of priests for centuries. With his immense learning of Sanskrit, he had been showing, moreover, that the religion of the Hindus exists not in the rituals and ceremonials on which Brahmin priests thrive, but in the teachings of the Upanishad concerning man and the world.

At the same time as the missionaries and bigoted clerics were heaping calumny upon him, Swami Vivekananda was being invited by a number of liberal clergymen to speak from the pulpit of their churches. The newspapers were reporting, at most times substantially correctly, his teachings and the fervent response of the congregation to them and to the teacher. The Swami was now travelling and lecturing on his own. Public lectures apart, he was holding classes for an ever-increasing number of more earnest seekers, for which he took no fee.

Human energies have human limits, even when divinely inspired. The ceaseless flow of intellectual, emotional and physical energies, with which Swami Vivekananda was sharing with others the rich inheritance given to him, began to adversely affect his health. He was often ill, aggravating 'a hereditary foe' he carried in his body, diabetes, and he suffered also from asthma. He had neither rest nor inner quiet and was 'whirling to and fro' as he wrote in one of his letters. His *giving* was literally endless—in his lectures, letters and relationships, all these *simultaneously*. In all of them flowed the energy of *feeling*, the kind of which, it could be said without the least exaggeration, had been seen neither before nor since. But it was taking its toll upon his health. He was young, thirty-one, but he had a human body, even though his mind and his heart were soaked in the divine, or shall we say in the Absolute?

At the end of Swami Vivekananda's now-famous address at the Parliament of Religions, an elderly lady, Mrs Roxie Blodgett, watched from the rear of the hall the extraordinary scene of several young women, elegantly dressed, jumping over the benches to crowd around him. As if sending a message to him, she said: 'Well, my lad, if you can withstand that onslaught, you are indeed a God.' Even as she was making that witty remark to herself, she never could have imagined that in that moment lay the genesis of a future. Six years later that 'lad' would come to stay with her in Los Angeles, and her main concern would be not the Vedanta but to give him a delicious meal after he returned home from lecturing. But she didn't need to hear a lecture on the Vedanta, even if it were by that magnificent 'lad'. Roxie Blodgett had already within her something of the living Vedanta—her capacity to give love.[5]

---

[5] See her reminiscences of the Swami, *Reminiscences*, pp. 358–61.

Far from being an onslaught, Swami Vivekananda was receiving from many American women (all of them remarkable, each in her own way, and all of them Christians) deep friendship, love, reverence and support for his work. Their homes were being opened to him. To some, he was like a son, a great spiritual force but still like a son; to some others, a brother full of love and fun or a loving friend who had been long in coming.[6] One of them, Mrs Emily Lyon, was showing him how to tell American coins,[7] but was also expressing her motherly apprehension that all those pretty elegant young women swept away by his attractive personality, in seeking to gain his interest might create for him some embarrassing situation. Deeply touched by her concern, he would laugh, and say to her, 'Dear Mrs Lyon, you dear American mother of mine, don't be afraid for me...I am used to temptation, and you need not fear for me!'[8] There was only one temptation he was not used to, and he succumbed to it, as he 'confessed' to Mrs Lyon. That story has been narrated in an earlier chapter.

Mrs Ellen Hale, twenty-six years older than the Swami, who had brought him inside her home when she saw him nearly collapse in the street the day before the Parliament, opened a bank account in which she deposited the money

---

[6] Of each of these, there is an immense volume of written record.

[7] Cornelia Conger, Mrs Emily Lyon's granddaughter, many years later wrote: 'When he began to give lectures, people offered him money for the work he hoped to do in India. He had no purse. So he used to tie it up in a handkerchief and bring it back—like a proud little boy—pour it into my grandmother's lap to keep for him. She made him learn the different coins and to stack them up neatly to count them. She made him write down the amount each time.' *Reminiscences*, p. 133.

[8] Ibid., p. 135.

he was earning. He gave her the authority to operate that account for him. She sent him money when, away from Chicago, he needed it. Her home had become his home—in one of his letters to his brother-monks, he even described it as his 'Math', his domestic monastery, to which he always returned. He loved them as much as they loved him. Of all the families he would know in the West, the Hale family would remain dearest to him always. He addressed them by the names he *decided* for them. Ellen Hale was 'Mother Church', her husband George W. Hale 'Father Pope' and their two young daughters, Mary and Harriet, and two nieces, Isabelle and Harriet McKindley, 'Babies'.[9] He wrote to his 'Mother Church' and to the 'Babies', more especially to Mary Hale, and also to Isabelle McKindley, from wherever he was. In all his letters to them there is an amazing simultaneity of spiritual heights with the bubbling laughter of a child who occasionally teased his yet-spinster 'sisters'. From the earnings of one of his lectures, he bought a meerschaum pipe for $13, and asked Isabelle not to tell 'Father Pope'; nor did he tell her that it was going to be a surprise gift he sent to him by post. When the Swami was at his 'domestic monastery', 541 Dearborn Avenue, Chicago, he and George W. Hale, puffing at their pipes, had long conversations that filled the elderly man with inner peace. And smoking a good pipe always helps that.[10]

Swami Vivekananda was at the same time thinking of his 'Madras boys' and was writing long letters, mostly to Alasinga Perumal. He was beckoning them to great

---

[9] For details about the Hale and McKindley girls, see *SV New Discoveries*, Vol. 1, pp. 278–84, and p. 286.

[10] As this author knows from personal experience!

selfless work in the service of the poor, the downtrodden, and the ignorant. He was inspiring them to move forward on that path, one of true spirituality, with 'indomitable energy', with no weakness of any kind.

Push on with the organization. At any cost, we must succeed, we must. No nay in this case. Nothing else is necessary but these— *Love*, *Sincerity*, and *Patience*. What is life but growth, i.e. expansion, i.e. *love*? Therefore all love is life, it is the only law of life, all selfishness is *death*, and this is true here or hereafter. Even if there is no hereafter, it is life to do good; it is death not to do good to others. Ninety per cent of human brutes you see are dead, are *ghosts*—for none lives, my boys, but he who loves. Feel, my children, feel; feel for the poor, the ignorant, the downtrodden; feel till the heart stops and the brain reels and you think you will go mad—then pour the soul out at the feet of the Lord and then will come power, help and indomitable energy.[11]

It was in this letter that he was telling them that 'Liberty is the first condition of growth'. He was calling them to the spiritual riches that are human inheritance. At the same time he was teaching them that spirituality is not opposed to the material part of life.

...We talk foolishly against material civilization. The grapes are sour. Even taking all that foolishness for granted, in all India there are, say, a hundred thousand really spiritual men and women. Now, for the spiritualization of these, must three hundred millions be sunk in savagery and starvation? Why should any starve? ...Material civilization, nay, even luxury, is necessary to create work for the

---

[11] Vivekananda to his 'Brave Boys' in Madras, through Alasinga Perumal; letter dated 19 November 1894, from New York. *SV Letters*, p. 173.

poor. Bread! Bread! I do not believe in a God who cannot give me bread here, giving me eternal bliss in heaven! Pooh! India is to be raised, the poor are to be fed, education is to be spread, and the evil of priestcraft is to be removed. No priestcraft, no social tyranny! More bread, more opportunity for everybody![12]

...No shilly-shally, no *esoteric blackguardism*, no secret humbug, nothing should be done in a corner. No special favouritism of the Master, no Master at that even. Onwards my brave boys—money or no money—men or no men! Have you love? Have you God? Onward, and forward to the breach, you are irresistible.

...Take care! Beware of anything that is untrue, stick to truth, and we shall succeed, slowly but surely.[13]

The Swami was asking Alasinga to take care of yet another thing. 'Do not try to "boss" others, as the Yankees say. Because I always direct my letters to you, you need not try to show your consequence over my other friends. I know you never can be such a fool, but still I think it is my duty to warn you.'[14]

He was scolding them in words that would make weaker minds and hearts move away; and then, as quickly, he was pouring out his love and gratitude to them. And he was not above showing contriteness for his harshness, pleading with Alasinga:

So far you have done wonderfully, my boy. Do not mind what I write in some moments of nervousness. One gets nervous sometimes alone in a country 15,000 miles from home, having to fight every

[12] Ibid., p. 174.
[13] Ibid., p. 175.
[14] Ibid.

inch of ground with orthodox inimical Christians. You must take those into consideration, my brave boy, and work right along.[15]

He was thinking of his brother-monks, and wrote long letters to one or two of them, to Shashi (Ramakrishnananda) mostly, if only infrequently and very different in tone from his letters to Alasinga.

In each one of Swami Vivekananda's letters to his 'Madras boys' and to Ramakrishnananda or to Brahmananda, there is evident simultaneity of thought and feeling on different questions with which he was greatly concerned. Those questions apparently belonged to different domains but had an inner coherence and unity, *all in the same letter*. To his brother-monks he was writing that while meditating on the Brahman and the Atman, they must also boil and filter the water before drinking it, for water is the source of all kinds of diseases, and pay attention to their health first.[16] He was equally, probably more concerned that they should filter out from their minds that dangerous impurity to which, he repeatedly said, the Hindu character was most prone: *jealousy*.[17] In saying

---

[15] Vivekananda to Alasinga Perumal, letter dated 31 August 1894. *SV Letters*, p. 133.

[16] Vivekananda to Shashi, letter dated 11 April 1895. *SV Letters*, p. 220.

[17] He speaks about it in many of his letters to India. In his letter dated 29 January 1894, from Chicago, to his Dewanji Saheb, he wrote simultaneously with other things, 'Why should the Hindu nation with all its wonderful intelligence and other things have gone to pieces? I would answer you, *jealousy*. Never were there people more wretchedly jealous of one another's fame and name than this wretched Hindu race...Three men cannot act in concert together in India for five minutes. Each one struggles for power and in the long run the whole organisation comes to grief. Lord! Lord! When will we learn not to be jealous!' To 'Kidi' (Singaravaelu Mudaliar), he wrote, 'Jealousy is

this, he used the phrase 'among *us*', the children of Sri Ramakrishna, expressing both a fear and a fervent hope 'may that never happen among us.'[18]

There was in the life of Swami Vivekananda the play of another simultaneity, a cause of his inner torment. This was his deep love and concern for some people along with his very poor estimate of their character; his renouncing everything in the service of those from whom he knew he could expect little.

To silence the missionary slander that had reached its climax in 1894 in Detroit, he had asked Alasinga Perumal and other 'Madras boys' to organize a public meeting and pass a resolution commending his services and thanking the American people for the support they had given him. Nothing came for months and he felt tormented. On 28 June 1894,[19] he wrote a long letter, not to Alasinga but to someone whose identity is concealed (not by the Swami). Among other things, he wrote:

…Your letters say again and again how I am being praised in India. But that is between you and me, for I never saw a single Indian paper writing about me, except the three square inches sent to me by Alasinga. On the other hand everything that is said by Christians in India is sedulously gathered by the missionaries and regularly published, and they go from door to door to make my friends give me up. They have succeeded only too well, for there is not one word for me from India. Indian Hindu papers may laud me to the skies, but not a word of that ever came to America,

---

the bane of our national character, natural to slaves.' Letter dated 3 March 1894, from Chicago. *SV Letters*, pp. 67 and 71 respectively.

[18] Vivekananda to Shashi, letter bearing no date, only the year '1894'. *SV Letters*, pp. 85-86.

[19] Ibid., pp. 121–24.

so that many people in this country think me a fraud. In the face of the missionaries and with the jealousy of the Hindus here to back them I have not a word to say...I came here without credentials. How else to show that I am not a fraud in the face of the missionaries and the Brahmo Samaj? Now, I thought nothing so easy as to spend a few words: I thought nothing would be so easy as to hold a meeting of some respectable persons in Madras and Calcutta and pass a resolution thanking me and the American people for being kind to me and sending it over officially, i.e. through the Secretary of the function, to America, for instance, sending one to Dr. Barrows and asking him to publish it in the papers and so on, to different papers of Boston, New York, and Chicago. Now after all I found that it is too terrible a task for India to undertake. There has not been one voice for me in one year and every one against me, for whatever you may say of me in your homes, who knows anything of it here? ...Oh! If only I had one man of some true abilities and brains to back me in India! But His will be done. I stand a fraud in this country. It was my foolishness to go to the Parliament (of Religions) without any credentials, hoping that there would be many for me. I have got to work it out slowly.

On the whole the Americans are a million times nobler than the Hindus, and I can work more good here than in the country of the ingrate and heartless.

...Good-bye, I have had enough of the Hindus. Now His will be done. I obey and bow down to my Karma. However, do not think me ungrateful...The Madras people have done for me more than I deserved and more than was in their power. It was my foolishness—the forgetting for a moment that we Hindus have not yet become human beings, and giving up for a moment my self-reliance and relying upon the Hindus—that I came to grief. Every moment I expected something from India. No, it never came. Last two months especially I was in torture at every moment. No, not even a newspaper from India! My friends waited—waited month after month; nothing came, not a voice. Many consequently grew cold and at last gave me up. But it is the punishment of relying upon man and brutes, for our countrymen are not men as yet. They are ready to be praised, but when their turn comes even to say a word, they are nowhere.[20]

Even as the Swami was writing this anguished letter, a public meeting *had* been held in Madras two months earlier, 28 April 1894, but he did not know about it. Neither did he know about the public meeting in Bangalore that followed on 26 August, the Dewan of Mysore presiding over it.[21] The proceedings of the famous Madras public meeting sent to the Swami by Alasinga, did not reach him until the early part of July because he had addressed his letter wrongly. And it was not until September that those proceedings reached the persons the Swami had specified that they should be sent to, primarily to Professor John Wright, Mrs Bagley, Mrs Hale and to Senator Palmer.[22] Meanwhile the Swami suffered the torment of anxiety—not for *his* sake, but for the sake of his closest friends, to whom he owed total assurance that his voice was the voice of authentic Hinduism. And *this* assurance could be obtained only by a public Indian acclaim of his work. Marie Louise Burke, along with her passion for accuracy of facts in the minutest detail, was deeply sensitive to the Swami's state of mind during those months when she said:

---

[20] *SV Letters*, pp. 121–23.
[21] Reported in the *Indian Mirror*; see *Vivekananda in Indian Newspapers 1893–1902*, already cited, pp. 45–48.
[22] For full details, the reader should turn to Marie Louise Burke, *SV New Discoveries*, Vol. 2, pp. 93–121.

I do not believe that his trial in this respect has been fully appreciated. Some hitherto unpublished letters which he wrote to Professor John Henry Wright reveal how deeply disturbed he was by the slander of his enemies and by the ever-present possibility that his friends would consider themselves to have been duped.[23]

Some American newspapers published the proceedings of the Madras meeting, as they did the acclaim accorded to the Swami in the Calcutta public meeting, held at the Town Hall on 5 September 1894, in which 'enthusiasm reached a pitch of frenzy'. Many prominent Indian newspapers published, almost in full, the Resolutions passed at the Calcutta meeting.[24] None of these public meetings to honour Swami Vivekananda was a formal affair. Their proceedings contained some of the main teachings of the Swami on Hinduism both as religion and philosophy. The Indian newspapers were reporting them correctly and with pride and enthusiasm.[25] Burke is right in saying that the Calcutta meeting carried a greater weight and that was because of three reasons: Calcutta was the Swami's birthplace where his life and character were well known; it was the home of Mazoomdar's Brahmo Samaj opposition to him; and many renowned orthodox Brahmin pundits were present, which silenced the criticism that the Hinduism Swami Vivekananda was advocating in America was not the orthodox Hinduism.[26]

But this last point involves a continuing confusion created by the use of the words 'orthodox' and 'Hinduism'.

[23] SV New Discoveries, Vol. 2, p. 93.
[24] For example, see the Indian Mirror of 16 September 1894, at SV in Indian Newspapers, pp. 55–60.
[25] The reader should study SV in Indian Newspapers.
[26] SV New Discoveries, Vol. 2, p. 112.

In his own words, repeated with varying degrees of emphasis, Swami Vivekananda was saying that the Hinduism he was talking about was *not* the brahmanical Hinduism of priests and pundits, the Hinduism of ceremonials and rituals and of caste restrictions, if that is what was meant by 'orthodox Hinduism'. 'Was I ever an orthodox, Pauranika Hindu, an adherent of social usages? I do not pose as one.'[27] He was preaching the Hinduism the essence of which is to be found in the Upanishads. His message was the message of the Vedanta and the Vedanta is not 'Hinduism'; it is the universal foundation of what *religion* truly is, beyond its Semitic meanings. Even his Vedanta was not the Vedanta confined to some ontological theory of man and the universe; it was the *living* Vedanta, to be realized in the *oneness of all life*, not in theory alone but in daily practice, in the living of relationships. Swami Vivekananda was no salesman of 'Hinduism'; indeed, he was a salesman of no *ism*. Rather, living in Truth and in God, he was a scourge of all *ism*s.

However, that whole episode showed, as similar episodes in his life would again, Swami Vivekananda as being human enough to feel disturbed by what was untrue and hurtful, a fact *he did not conceal* and yet rose above. After the American newspapers had published the acclaim accorded to him at the Calcutta meeting, he wrote to his 'sisters' at 541, Dearborn Avenue, Chicago, one of his most moving letters:

Glory unto Jagadamba (Mother of the Universe)! I have gained beyond expectations. The prophet has been honoured and with a *vengeance*. I am weeping like a child at His mercy—He never

---

[27] In his letter to Shashi; year 1895, from Reading, England. *SV Letters*, p. 262.

leaves His servants, sisters. The letter I send you will explain all, and the printed things are coming to the American people. The names there are the very flower of our country. The President was the chief *nobleman* of Calcutta, and the other man Mahesh Chandra Nyayaratna is the principal of the Sanskrit College and the chief Brahmin in all India and recognized by the Government as such. The letter will tell you all. O Sisters! What a rogue am I that in the face of such mercies sometimes the faith totters—seeing every moment that I am in His hands. Still the mind sometimes gets despondent. Sisters, there is a *God*—a Father—a *Mother* who never leaves His children, never, never, never. Put uncanny theories aside and becoming children take refuge in Him. I cannot write more—I am weeping like a woman.[28]

His other self, Vivekananda, was at the same time feeling disgusted and pained that the Swami Vivekananda should ever require any public acclaim, even if it were only to vindicate himself in the eyes of his closest friends who had supported him throughout in the face of slander and calumny. He expressed that disgust and pain in his letters to Mrs Hale and Sara Bull. But that is best discussed in the next chapter.

***

Mrs Sara Ole Bull (1850–1911), born Chapman, came into the life of Swami Vivekananda. She was seventeen years old when she fell in love with the famous Norwegian violinist Ole Bull and married him. They lived in Norway for a while, and then set up home at Cambridge, Massachusetts. Sara always accompanied her husband on his concert tours,

---

[28] *SV Letters*, p. 126.

and took care of him and his finances with great skill and devotion; for, though a great musician, Ole Bull was untutored in practical matters. Their home became a centre of sparkling intellectual conversations, to which came some well-known philosophers of Harvard University: William James (1842–1910), George Santayana (1863–1952), Josiah Royce (1855–1916) and others, all of them Sara's friends. Their home was a centre, too, of much musical activity. Then Ole Bull, famous and absolutely lovable, died. A widow for fourteen years, who had read the *Bhagvad Gita* translated by Mohini Mohan Chatterji, whom she also knew as a friend, Sara had come to hear Swami Vivekananda. It was the spring of 1894. She was in her early forties, 'a delicate, sweet voiced woman with a tender dreamy face and masses of dark hair'. A deeply spiritual person, Sara Bull recognized straightaway the depths of the Swami. In the following winter she invited him to be her guest at Cambridge. She invited Professor William James, her friend, to meet the young monk who would, before long, be her 'son' and guru, a combination that would trouble her increasingly. She soon discovered that the 'son' was as untutored in the ways of the world, as innocent, as her husband had been, and required guidance in practical matters. But could one presume to guide, even scold should that be necessary, he who was also one's spiritual mentor, or, say, one's guru?

The Professor and the Swami had a long conversation when they met first; and they met often, having longer conversations. William James had come to the conclusion that the traditional distinction that Western philosophy made between mind and matter, subject and object, is baseless and is to be discarded; as a logical consequence, the classical notions of 'truth' are to be reconsidered. That was the view also of the Vedanta which the Swami was putting forth in his lectures. Of William James, it is said: 'His warm-heartedness and his delightful humour caused him to be almost universally beloved.'[29] That was being said, in many newspapers, of Swami Vivekananda too. In the case of William James, there was only one known exception—Santayana. In the case of the Swami, the known exceptions were many and that was because he had challenged far too many and much more deeply. William James's *The Varieties of Religious Experience*, published in 1901, and *The Psychology of Religion*, published in 1902, undoubtedly reflected much of the conversations the two of them had. However, since, as far as we know (I am tempted to say 'as far as Marie Louise Burke knows'), there is no written record of those conversations, we cannot say with any definiteness how much William James owed to Swami Vivekananda.

What we do know is that the philosopher known for his 'radical empiricism' was not above taking a good-natured shot at the 'Absolute' of the Swami, which now and then he did. The Swami himself was doing that, now and then. In the August–September of the same year, 1894, he was at Annisquam, a guest of Mrs John J. Bagley, and was hugely enjoying going into the sea on a small boat, which overturned and the Swami had a thorough drenching. A few days later, now in Boston, he was writing to Mary

[29] Bertrand Russell (1872–1970), *A History of Western Philosophy* (Simon and Schuster, New York; fourteenth printing, 1960), p. 811. Russell tells us that there was only one exception, Santayana, whose doctoral thesis William James had described as 'the perfection of rottenness'. Ibid., p. 811.

Hale: '...When I had that drenching at Annisquam I had on that beautiful black suit you appreciate so much, and I do not think it can be damaged in any way; it also has been penetrated with my deep meditation on the Absolute.'[30]

With her whole being, Sara Bull was now interesting herself both in her 'son' Vivekananda and in the American work of her spiritual guru Swami Vivekananda, which would soon include her deepest engagement with his work in India. She had an unwavering place both in the life of the Swami and the progress of the Sri Ramakrishna Mission he would establish on his return to India in 1897. She donated liberally to the establishment of Vedanta Societies in America, and would donate more than one hundred thousand rupees to building the Belur Math.[31] Important though it was, that was the least part of what she gave to Swami Vivekananda. She gave him her unlimited love and care, but more than that, a sensitive understanding of his inner sufferings as well. It is to her that he turned, not only in matters pertaining to 'the organization' that was growing, but also for rest and peace.

In his established custom, he gave Sara Bull a Sanskrit name, *Dhira-mata*, the 'Steady Mother'. Their long, occasionally stormy, relationship is best understood in the simultaneity of their relationships with others that were often tangled. We find that *simultaneity* described in Pravrajika Prabuddhaprana's very detailed biography of her. From that we learn many facts about Swami Vivekananda hitherto unknown but exceedingly significant.

---

[30] Letter dated 17 September 1894. *CWSV*, Vol. VIII, p. 321. See also Marie Louise Burke, *SV New Discoveries*, Vol. 2, p. 165.

[31] Pravrajika Prabuddhaprana, *Saint Sara*, pp. 269-70.

The Swami was not the only person in Sara Bull's life, nor were the concerns of propagating Vedanta in America her only concern. She was living with her other relationships, some of them difficult and painful—with her married daughter Olea Vaughan above all, towards whom Sara felt at once a strong binding obligation and an increasing emotional distance. She was exceedingly sad when her first granddaughter, Edwina Vaughn, died. Between Sara Bull and Swami Saradananda (Sharat), called to America in 1896 to help Swami Vivekananda's work, developed a relationship of tenderness and great trust. Prabuddhaprana tells us: 'Swami Saradananda was gentle and receptive, whereas Vivekananda was either in a lofty mood or full of some new idea or plan. She could easily express to Saradananda her feelings and problems, which it had been difficult to do with Vivekananda.'[32]

When Saradananda wrote to Sara Bull about his first lecture in New York on 6 January 1897 on the principles of Vedanta, and also described his lodgings in New York, she cautioned him (Vedanta is very good *but*) 'to keep a window open when he slept with gas stove on'.[33] And it is in her that he confided without reserve his serious problems with Swami Vivekananda that were making him tense and miserable. In some of his letters to Sara, which he asked her to destroy after reading, Saradananda spoke of what he perceived as the Swami's 'inherent suspicious nature'. Both he and Brahmananda seemed to have misinterpreted the Swami's insistence that they send accurate accounts of the money received for the work, to Sara Bull, as his lack of trust in them.

---

[32] Ibid., p. 235.
[33] Ibid., p. 234.

Sara's sense of motherhood being a great part of her own nature, and because she had the financial resources, she undertook to finance the education of Swami Saradananda's two brothers.[34] From some of Swami Vivekananda's letters to her, on his return from his first visit to the West, we learn that she was sending money to help a cousin of his.[35] Even more touching and far-reaching in its significance, Sara sent to the monastic disciples of Sri Ramakrishna who had served his mother, Chandradevi, till the last day of her life, a donation to provide a home for their mothers visiting the Math. In her letter written on Christmas Day of 1896, she wrote:

Giving on your part to these, your mothers, the spiritual bread of life, as faithfully as they cherished your helpless infancy and childhood that you should become men and Sons of God, makes the bond of Motherhood the world over Divine. Like your Sankara Acharya, you will never fail to hear the call of your mothers, through whom all women are blessed by your labours. Their gift of their sons to homelessness and service makes the record of Mary of more effect to us at this Christmas time.[36]

...The ideal of Divine motherhood made luminous by Ram Krishna while sending your Sannyasis across the earth if needs be, not withholding in cloistered retirement or forest life your message of light and love, has indeed brought to Western mothers the consolation of timely help.

No sweeter or nobler message than that of Vivekananda's mother, blessing the work of her son in our midst, has come to

---

[34] The names of the brothers are not given.

[35] Who this cousin was, most probably the daughter of one of his (unnamed!) surviving sisters, we are not told; the Swami referred to her as only 'my cousin'.

[36] Pravrajika Prabuddhaprana, *Saint Sara*, p. 233.

us. The human weakness of a mother's heart received strength in wishing that her function be fulfilled to him in homes his message has entered. Such mothers are indeed worthy to bear and cherish children fit to become the Sons of a Ram Krishna.[37]

In her relationships even with those that would first support and then seek to destroy the Swami's work and turn upon him, as in the case of Kripananda (Landsberg) and E.T. Sturdy, it was unwavering *giving* on the part of Sara Bull. But when she felt she was being made use of, as by Kripananda, and she was no fool, she would explode—but enclose a cheque nonetheless.

Supporting in every way the work of Swami Vivekananda, and those devoted to it, Sara Bull gave at the same time her emotional support to Jagadis Chandra Bose,[38] struggling against the hostile British trying to put him down, indeed crush him, as a scientist.[39] When he was operated for the treatment of a serious illness in London on 12 December 1900, she gave him a mother's caring and, with Sister Nivedita, attended upon him day and night. Feeling the injustice of the English scientists trying to belittle an Indian scientist of very great achievements, Sara Bull gave Jagadis Bose $ 4000 to set up his botanical research laboratory he desperately needed. Worried that he would have to spend the rest of his life paying back the debt, Sara assured him that she was giving that money as a mother to a son. Of that noble and loving act, we hear only from Prabuddhaprana's *Saint Sara*. In his public address at the opening of the Bose

[37] Ibid.
[38] Born, 30 November 1858; died, 23 November 1937.
[39] For details, see Pravrajika Prabuddhaprana, *Saint Sara*, especially pp. 390–92.

Research Institute in Calcutta, in 1917, mostly financed by Sara Bull, Jagadis Chandra Bose did not even mention her name, let alone acknowledge his indebtedness to her.[40] Neither did he publicly acknowledge how much he owed to Sister Nivedita, which was very considerable, even in his scientific work.[41] The truth is that these two women, Sara Bull and Nivedita, through their loving support to Jagadis Bose, did more for the development of scientific research in India at that time than anyone else.

At the height of his fame, if Swami Vivekananda wept for the poor of his country whom he had known and seen during his parivrajaka days, he felt no less concern for his mother, Bhubaneswari Devi. In his lecture on 17 December 1894, on 'The Women of India',[42] he was speaking also of her.

...The love which my mother gave to me has made me what I am and I owe a debt to her that I can never repay.

...I know that before I was born my mother would fast and pray and do hundreds of things which I could not do for five minutes even. She did that for two years. I believe whatever religious culture I have I owe to that. It was consciously that my mother brought me into the world to be what I am. Whatever little good impulse I have was given to me by my mother, and consciously, not unconsciously.[43]

---

[40] Ibid., p. 392.
[41] For the details of what Nivedita did for Jagadis Chandra Bose, see Pravrajika Atmaprana's *Sister Nivedita*, pp. 239–43. Rabindranath Tagore was among those few who acknowledged it. Addressing his students at Santiniketan in 1937, he said: 'In the day of his success, Jagadis gained an invaluable energiser and helper in Sister Nivedita and in any record of his life's work, her name must be given a place of honour.' Cited in Atmaprana, p. 243.
[42] *SV New Discoveries*, Vol. 2, p. 407.
[43] Ibid., p. 239, repeated on p. 417.

It was not about himself that the Swami was worried at the nasty scandals the Christian missionaries, the Theosophists, and P.C. Mazoomdar were inventing and circulating, sometimes anonymously, in order to discredit him and his work. The Swami was worried about the effect those scandalous stories would have upon his mother. On 26 April 1894, he wrote to Isabelle McKindley:

...Now I do not care what they, even my own people, say about me—except for one thing. I have an old mother. She has suffered much all her life, and in the midst of all, she could bear to give me up for the service of God and man; but to have given up the most beloved of her children—her hope—to live a beastly immoral life in a far distant country—as Mazoomdar was telling in Calcutta, would have simply killed her. But the Lord is great, none can injure His children.

...Poor Mazoomdar—he has injured his cause by telling lies through jealousy. Lord knows I never attempted any defence.[44]

A fortnight earlier he had written to Alasinga Perumal:

...Of course, the orthodox clergymen are against me; and seeing that it is not easy to grapple with me, they try to hinder, abuse, and vilify me in every way; and Mazoomdar has come to their help. He must have gone mad with jealousy. He has told them that I was a big fraud and a rogue! And again in Calcutta he is telling them that I am leading a most sinful life in America, specially unchaste! Lord bless him! My brother, no good thing can be done without obstruction.[45]

---

[44] SV Letters, pp. 91-92.
[45] Letter dated 9 April, 1894. SV Letters, pp. 89-90.

And a few months later, he wrote to Alasinga again: '...Tell my friends that a uniform silence is all my answer to my detractors. If I give them tit for tat, it would bring us down to a level with them. Tell them that truth will take care of itself, and that they are not to fight anybody for me.'[46]

As a sannyasin, Swami Vivekananda had taken two vows: of poverty and chastity; and these two vows he never broke. Having made this limited statement about him—in the genre 'he never did *this*, he never did *that*'—it must be said that Swami Vivekananda was far too great a person to be measured by the yardstick of sexual chastity alone. One day, I hope, some student of human psyche will devote his, or her, attention to the question: why is it that, to the Hindu mind, sexual chastity confers such an extraordinary value (even upon a fool)? That Swami Vivekananda remained sexually chaste, and there is no evidence that he did not, is by no means central to his personality and its meaning to our times. What is important about him is the fact that, although he put distinct emphasis on the need to transmute sexual energy into spiritual force, and praised chastity highly, he did not reduce spirituality to sexual chastity. As if one could, by walking the path only of sexual chastity, see God. Swami Vivekananda kept saying, '*God is no fool!*' Selflessness, concern for the happiness of the *other*, freedom and liberty to others, trust, childlike simplicity, honesty to himself and to others, and the power to awaken the deeper self of another by his love—manifest in *every* relationship of Swami Vivekananda—were infinitely more worthy of respect and example.

On 6 July 1896, from London, he wrote to Francis Leggett:

---

[46] Letter dated 27 September 1894. *SV Letters*, p. 148.

...I think I am slowly approaching to that state when I should be able to love the very 'Devil' himself, if there were any.

At twenty years of age I was the most unsympathetic, uncompromising fanatic; I would not walk on the footpath on the theatre side of the streets in Calcutta. At thirty-three, I can live in the same house with prostitutes and never would think of saying a word of reproach to them. Is it degenerate? Or is it that I am broadening out into the Universal Love which is the Lord Himself? Again, I have heard that if one does not see the evil round him, he cannot do good work—he lapses into a sort of fatalism. I do not see that. On the other hand, my power of work is immensely increasing and becoming immensely effective. Some days I get into a sort of ecstasy. I feel that I must bless every one, everything, love and embrace everything, and I do see that evil is a delusion.

...I have learnt a thing or two: Beyond, beyond reason and learning and talking is the feeling, the 'Love', 'the Beloved'. Ay, Sake, fill up the cup and we will be mad.[47]

He signed this letter 'Yours ever in madness—Vivekananda'.

His feelings, not 'compassion', for the degraded and the wretched were not an occasional exaltation of spirit. He put them into social practice. Somebody wrote to him that because many public women (meaning prostitutes) attended the anniversary festival of Sri Ramakrishna at Dakshineswar, persons from decent families were less inclined to go there. Swami Vivekananda gave his decision on this point as follows. In his letter from Lake Lucerne, Switzerland, on 23 August 1896, he wrote to Shashi (Ramakrishnananda):

---

[47] Letter dated 6 July 1896. *SV Letters*, pp. 296-97.

1.   If public women are not allowed to go to such a great place
     of pilgrimage as Dakshineswar, where else shall they go to?
     It is for the sinful that the Lord manifests Himself specially, not
     so much for the virtuous.

2.   Let distinctions of sex, caste, wealth, learning and the whole
     host of them, which are so many gateways to hell, be confined
     to the world alone. If such distinctions persist in holy places
     of pilgrimage, where then lies the difference between them
     and hell itself?

3.   Ours is a gigantic City of Jagannath, where those who have
     sinned and those who have not, the saintly and the vicious,
     men and women and children irrespective of age, all have
     equal rights. That for one day at least in the year thousands
     of men and women get rid of the sense of sin and ideas of
     distinction and sing and hear the name of the Lord is in
     itself a supreme good.

4.   If even in a place of pilgrimage people's tendency to evil be
     not curbed for one day, the fault lies with you, not them.
     Create such a huge tidal wave of spirituality that whatever
     people come near will be swept away.

5.   Those who, even in a chapel, would think this is a public
     woman, that man is of a low caste, a third is poor, and yet
     another belongs to the masses—the less be the number of
     such people (whom you call gentlemen, that is), the better.
     Will they who look to the caste, sex, or profession of Bhaktas
     appreciate our Lord? *I pray to the Lord that hundreds of
     public women may come and bow their heads at His feet; it
     does not matter if not one gentleman comes. Come public
     women, come drunkards, come thieves and all—His gate is
     open to all.* [48]

---

[48] *SV Letters*, pp. 302-03. Here the added emphasis is mine; but it is that
of SV throughout.

This is the living Vedanta.

One may say that written in an exalted state in a letter, those were still *words*. A perfect illustration of them in practice was provided by an episode that took place in Cairo some four years later, at the end of Swami Vivekananda's second visit to the West. Although it was still in the future, it was present at the time of his writing the above letter; and therefore it is best narrated here, as recorded by Madame Emma Calve in her journal and also narrated by her to her friend Mme Paul Verdier:

One day we lost our way in Cairo. I suppose we had been talking too intently. At any rate, we found ourselves in a squalid, ill-smelling street, where half-clad women lolled from windows and sprawled on doorsteps.

The Swami noticed nothing until a particularly noisy group of women on a bench in the shadow of a dilapidated building began laughing and calling to him. One of the ladies of our party tried to hurry us along, but the swami detached himself gently from our group and approached the women on the bench.

'Poor children!' he said. 'Poor creatures! They have put their divinity in their beauty. Look at them now!' (According to Mme Calve's account of this incident to her friend Mme Paul Verdier, Swamiji's words were: 'Poor child, she has forgotten who she is and has put her divinity in her body.')

He began to weep, as Jesus might have done before the woman taken in adultery. The women were silenced and abashed. One of them leaned forward and kissed the hem of his robe, murmuring brokenly in Spanish '*Hombre de Dios, hombre de Dios*!' (Man of God!) Another, with a sudden gesture of modesty and fear, threw her arm in front of her face as though she would screen her shrinking soul from those pure eyes.[49]

Swami Vivekananda's spiritual daughter, Nivedita, has left for us a similar lesson. In her letter of 14 April 1904 to Joe, she reported how, on the suggestion of Girish Chandra Ghosh, she entertained at her house in Bagh Bazar, Calcutta, 'two ladies of un-virtue' (meaning prostitutes), and expressed her belief, 'One who has *given*, however mistakenly, has *not* fallen, never—never—never. He who *takes*, has. Selfishness is the only sin.' Continuing with this thought, she said:

Of course I am also beginning to see that many respectable householders are also courtesans. If my appetite leads me to confine my ravages to one human being instead of a thousand, I am a cannibal just the same. Sex is the faculty of gobbling up human beings, just as hunger is of food, and thirst, of drink; it is moral cannibalism.

...only Jesus could understand Mary Magdalene. Remember that. He alone. There was no other great enough for that.[50]

I know of no other man in modern Indian history who, remaining sexually aloof (meaning 'chaste'), gave to women so much as Swami Vivekananda did. Nor do I know of another man who owed to women as much as he did. At the same time as he was acknowledging his debt to his mother, he was acknowledging his debt to American

---

[49] Reminiscences of Madame Emma Calve, in *Reminiscences*, pp. 260–61. But here the narration is as given at *SV New Discoveries*, Vol. 6, p. 396, and first published in the *Saturday Evening Post* of 9 September 1922.

[50] *Nivedita Letters*, Vol. II, p. 644. Read the whole letter.

women. John Stuart Mill, in his *Autobiography*, had acknowledged his intellectual and emotional debt to Mrs Harriet Taylor (1807–1858), who had liberated him from his father's soul-less utilitarianism, and later (in 1851) became his wife. John Stuart Mill was the Swami's favourite English philosopher.[51] The editor who wrote the introduction to Mill's *Autobiography* expressed his, unwritten but visible, astonishment bordering on disbelief, not that so great a mind as John Stuart Mill should have owed so much to another, but that so great a mind should have owed so much to a *woman*![52] Mill must have been applauding, from heavens above, another great mind acknowledging his debt to *women*. Swami Vivekananda was expressing his gratitude to women, not only to *them* but was also conveying it to his countrymen first of all.

In one of his earliest letters to India, dated 28 December 1893 from Chicago, Swami Vivekananda was writing to Haripada Mitra:

...I have seen thousands of women here whose hearts are as pure and stainless as snow. Oh, how free they are! It is they who control social and civic duties. Schools and colleges are full of women,

---

[51] Swami Vivekananda never mentioned what in Mill's philosophy attracted him so much. But from his own thoughts we can rightly infer that it was Mill's avowal of equality and liberty and his upholding the women's innate right to equality. Later he would show that the ideas of equality and liberty were inherent in the Vedanta as oneness of all life.
[52] See Jack Stillinger's 'Introduction' to Mill's *Autobiography* (Oxford University Press; 1971), pp. xvii-xviii. Deeply troubled by Mill's acknowledgement of his intellectual and emotional debt to Harriet, the editor observes: 'It is unfortunate that Mill did not simply thank his wife for encouragement, perhaps also for transcribing a manuscript or making an index, and let it go at that.' p. xix.

and in our country women cannot be safely allowed to walk on the streets! Their kindness to me is immeasurable. Since I came here, I have been welcomed by them to their houses. They are providing me with food, arranging for my lectures, taking me to market, and doing everything for my comfort and convenience. I shall never be able to repay in the least the deep debt of gratitude I owe to them.[53]

A few weeks later, in his letter of 24 January 1894, he told his 'Madras boys', 'About the women of America, I cannot express my gratitude to them for their kindness. Lord Bless them.'[54]

Next he was writing to Raja Ajit Singh:

...American women! A hundred lives would not be sufficient to pay my deep debt of gratitude to you! I have not words enough to express my gratitude to you! 'The Oriental hyperbole' alone expresses the depth of Oriental gratitude—'If the Indian Ocean were an inkstand, the highest mountain of the Himalayas, the pen, the earth, the scroll and time itself, the writer, still it will not express my gratitude to you!'

Last year I came to this country in summer, a wandering preacher of a far distant country, without name, fame, wealth, or learning to recommend me—friendless, helpless, almost in a state of destitution—and American women befriended me, gave me shelter and food, took me to their homes and treated me as their own son, their own brother. They stood my friends even when their own priests were trying to persuade them to give up the 'dangerous heathen'—even when day after day their best friends had told them not to stand by this 'unknown foreigner,

---

[53] *SV Letters*, p. 60.
[54] Ibid., p. 63.

may be, of dangerous character'. But they are better judges of character and soul—for it is the pure mirror that catches the reflection.[55]

To that 'Oriental hyperbole', through which Swami Vivekananda was expressing his debt of gratitude to American women, not a word need have been added. But he never ceased to add to it, both in words and conduct. And not to women alone, but to men as well. In practically every letter he was writing to Professor John Henry Wright, to Haridas Viharidas Desai, to his 'Madras boys', and to many others, he was expressing with the same depth of feeling his gratitude to them. This was an integral part of Swami Vivekananda, and is not to be passed over as something expected of any decent human being anyway and therefore requiring no special attention. In his case it *does* for it demonstrates several other things simultaneously and has a deeper meaning that goes far beyond.

First, the attitude commonly seen among the spiritually great and those believed to be enlightened souls is that *they* owe nothing to ordinary mortals, and none among the latter will ever presume that they do. The ordinary mortal is conditioned to think that, should no more than even their fleeting glance float towards him or her, it is *he*, or *she*, who would owe a deep debt of gratitude to *them*. This is the result of the theory of *anugraha* or 'grace'. And grace in spiritual India is always a one-way street. Sri Ramakrishna, among the greatest of mystic saints, was singularly free from that attitude. And so was Narendra,

---

[55] Ibid., p. 76. This letter bears no date, only the year '1894', nor any address, just 'America'.

now Swami Vivekananda, whom he had pronounced not only as a nitya-siddha, 'ever perfect', 'ever free', but also an incarnation of Narayana, 'God', who had come to serve the wretched and the miserable. Despite the spectacular impression he had made upon the men and the women of America, he had not put himself on a high pedestal. Even a small act of kindness to him he did not forget, and never ceased to express his gratitude for the grace of love and friendship he was receiving in abundance. To Swami Vivekananda, grace was not a one-way street.

Secondly, if the debt of gratitude is great, it becomes oppressive. Under its burden most people compromise truth above all; they tend to become false to themselves, and thereby false to the *other*. Swami Vivekananda did not for a moment entertain the wrong notion that being true to one's self lessened one's gratitude to others. There was in him not even a suspicion that there might be at times a conflict between the two. Thus, if a suggestion Mrs Sara Bull made seemed to him to be wrong in *his* context, he told her so in plain words, and did what he knew to be right. He gave hard raps to Mary Hale and even harder raps to Alasinga Perumal. The next moment nobody could be more loving.

A friend, Ruth Ellis, wrote to Sara that she had heard the Swami say many times, 'Mrs Bull is the very best friend I have in America. She understands my thought and appreciates all that is good and true in me.'[56] Sara, however, wanted the Swami to appreciate, among other things, that the 'right kind of people' should come to hear him.[57] In the winter of 1895, he was in New York, giving

[56] Pravrajika Prabuddhaprana, *Saint Sara*, pp. 146-47.
[57] Ibid., p. 145.

lectures and holding classes. For the latter purpose he had rented rooms that were in a poor district of the City, 54 West 33rd Street, where 'right kind of people' might not want to come, so said Miss Hamlin. Elizabeth Hamlin, Sara's secretary and housekeeper in whose judgement Sara had much faith, was helping the Swami in New York, and strongly advising him to take the rooms in a better area. When this 'right kind of people' business became too much for him, on 11 April 1895 he wrote to Sara Bull, the person to whom he kept expressing his 'eternal gratitude':[58]

...Miss Hamlin[59] has been helping me a good deal. I am very grateful to her. She is very kind and, I hope, sincere. She wants me to be introduced to the 'right kind of people'. This is the second edition of the 'Hold yourself steady' business, I am afraid. The only 'right sort of people' are those whom the Lord sends—that is what I understand in my life's experience. They alone can and will help me. As for the rest, Lord help them in a mass and save me from them.

Every one of my friends thought it would end in nothing, this my getting up quarters all by myself, and that *no ladies would ever come there*. Miss Hamlin especially thought that 'she' or 'her right sort of people' were *way up* from such things as to go and listen to a man who lives by himself in a poor lodging. But the 'right kind' came for all that, day and night, and she too. Lord!

---

[58] As another example, see his letter dated 14 February 1895 to her. *SV Letters*, p. 215.

[59] 'Miss Hamlen, whose name Swamiji spelled Hamlin', Marie Louise Burke corrects the spelling. However, Pravrajika Prabuddhaprana in her *Saint Sara* consistently spells it as 'Hamlin'. So, let Miss Hamlen remain Miss Hamlin. To a Hindu, it would not matter in the least if Hamlet were spelled as 'Hamlit'; his tragedy would remain nonetheless!

How hard it is for man to believe in Thee and Thy mercies. Shiva! Shiva! Where is the right kind and where is the bad, mother? It is all *He*! In the tiger and in the lamb, in the saint and the sinner all *He*!

...Truce to this 'right sort of presentation'. Thou art my right, thou my wrong, my Shiva. Lord, since a child I have taken refuge in Thee. Thou wilt be with me in the tropics or at the poles, on the tops of the mountains or in the depths of oceans. My stay— my guide in life—my refuge—my friend—my teacher—my God— my real Self. Thou wilt never leave me, *never*, I know it for sure. Sometimes I become weak, being alone and struggling against odds, my God; and I think of human help. Save Thou me for ever from these weaknesses, and may I never, never seek for help from any being but Thee.[60]

Pravrajika Prabuddhaprana, Sara Bull's biographer, tells us:

Sara's and Miss Hamlin's efforts were defeated when they tried to impress Swami Vivekananda with the idea that he should meet 'the right sort of people,' (meaning people with money and position). The Swami did not want to make a cult among the elite and exclusive. As much as they hoped to have classes in 'good' neighbourhoods, he insisted upon living in a flat in the poorer section of New York. Vivekananda protested, saying that the 'best people' were the people whom the Lord sent him. He was yearning to teach a group of sincere intimate students, not those interested in spiritual materialism, in gaining psychic powers, in having a 'spiritual' thrill, or using his teaching to cure diseases, physical or mental.[61]

He had signed his letter to Sara Bull as 'Your ever obedient son, Vivekananda'. But the 'obedient son' refused to be

---

[60] *SV Letters*, pp. 219-20.
[61] Prabuddhaprana, *Saint Sara*, p. 145.

obedient when 'mother' advised him not to be so uncompromisingly forthright with truth, nor quarrel when he heard untruth and plain lies about India and Hindu society, for that would affect his work adversely. The 'son' would have none of that, and would not compromise with truth, come what may. That was the inheritance he had received from his mother, Bhubaneswari Devi.

Still in New York, the Swami had a fight with a Presbyterian at the house of Emma Thursby, a celebrated concert singer, a close friend of Sara Bull, deeply drawn to the teachings of the Swami, whom she had invited for a parlour-lecture, and who became his friend. The Presbyterian would have, one may reasonably presume, spread out the usual Christian missionary fare of the Hindu mothers throwing their newborn babies to a crocodile in the river, the widows being burnt, and so forth. Reprimanded by Sara for his conduct, he wrote a long letter on 1 February 1895 to Mary Hale:

...The other day at Miss Thursby's I had an excited argument with a Presbyterian gentleman, who, as usual, got very hot, angry, and abusive. However, I was afterwards severely reprimanded by Mrs. Bull for this, as such things hinder my work. So, it seems, is your opinion.

I am glad you write about it just now, because I have been giving a good deal of thought to it. In the first place, I am not at all sorry for these things—perhaps that may disgust you—it may. I know full well how good it is for one's worldly prospects to be *sweet*. I do everything to be *sweet*, but when it comes to a horrible compromise with the truth within, then I stop. I do not believe in *humility*. I believe in *Samadarshitva*—same state of mind with regard to all. The duty of the ordinary man is to obey the commands of his 'God', society; but the children of light never do so. This is an eternal law. One accommodates himself to surroundings and social opinion and gets all good things from society, the giver of all good to such. The other stands alone and draws society up towards him. The accommodating man finds a path of roses; the non-accommodating, one of thorns. But the worshippers of 'Vox populi' go to annihilation in a moment; the children of truth *live for ever*.

...I am so, so sorry, Sister, that I cannot make myself sweet and accommodating to every black falsehood. But I cannot. I have suffered for it all my life. But I cannot. I have essayed and essayed. But I cannot. At last I have given it up. The Lord is great. He will not allow me to become a hypocrite. Now let what is in come out. I have not found a way that will please all, and I cannot but be what I am, true to my own self. 'Youth and beauty vanish, life and wealth vanish, name and fame vanish, even the mountains crumble into dust. Friendship and love vanish. Truth alone abides.' God of Truth, be Thou alone my guide! I am too old to change now in milk and honey. Allow me to remain as I am...I have no desire for wealth or name or fame or enjoyments, Sister—they are dust unto me. I wanted to help my brethren. I have not the *tact to earn money*, bless the Lord. What reason is there for me to conform to the vagaries of the world around me and not obey the voice of Truth within? The mind is still weak, Sister, it sometimes mechanically clutches at earthly help. But I am not afraid. Fear is the greatest sin my religion teaches.

...The last fight with the Presbyterian priest and the long fight afterwards with Mrs. Bull showed me in a clear light what Manu says to the Sannyasin. 'Live alone, walk alone.' All friendship, all love, is only limitation. There never was a friendship, especially of women, which was not exacting. O great sages! You were right. One cannot serve the God of Truth who leans upon somebody. Be still, my soul! Be alone! And the Lord is with you...Sister, the way is long, the time is short, evening is approaching. I have to go home soon. I have no time to give my manners a finish. I cannot find time to deliver my message. You are good, you are so kind, I will do anything for you; and do not be angry, I see you all are mere children.

Dream no more! Oh, dream no more, my soul! In one word, I have a message to give. I have no time to be sweet to the world, and every attempt at sweetness makes me a hypocrite. I will die a thousand deaths rather than lead a jelly-fish existence and yield to every requirement of this foolish world, no matter whether it be my own country or a foreign country. You are mistaken, utterly mistaken, if you think I have a *work*, as Mrs. Bull thinks; I have no *work* under or beyond the sun. I have a message, and I will give it after my own fashion. I will neither Hinduise my message, nor Christianise it, nor make it any 'ise' in the world. I will only my-ise it and that is all. *Liberty, Mukti*, is all my religion, and everything that tries to curb it, I will avoid by fight or flight. Pooh! I try to pacify the priests!!

...Sister, do not take this amiss. But you are babies and babies must submit to be taught. You have not yet drunk of that fountain which makes 'reason, unreason, mortal, immortal, this world a zero and of man a God'. Come out, if you can, of this network of foolishness they call this *world*. Then I will call you indeed brave and free. If you cannot, cheer those that dare dash this false God, society, to the ground and trample on its unmitigated hypocrisy; if you cannot cheer them pray, be silent, but do not try to drag them down again into the mire with such false nonsense as *compromise* and becoming nice and sweet.[62]

...I hate this world, this dream, this horrible nightmare, with its churches and chicaneries, its books and black-guardisms, its

---

[62] *SV Letters*, pp. 210–12.

fair faces and false hearts, its howling righteousness on the surface and utter hollowness beneath, and, above all, its sanctified shopkeeping. What! Measure my soul according to what the bond-slaves of the world say?—Pooh! Sister you do not know the Sannyasin. 'He stands on the heads of the Vedas!' say the Vedas, because he is free from churches and sects and religions and prophets and books and all of that ilk.[63]

The storm involved, at its heart, the question of truth. From the Buddha onwards, through Socrates, Jesus Christ, the Sufi saints of Islam, the Bhakti saints, modern science, and in all personal relationships, the question of truth had always been stormy. Sara Bull and Mary Hale, anxious that the Swami's forthright speech not hurt him and the prospects of his work in America, were sincerely advising him to be more compromising in dealing with his opponents. But one can be sincere and yet mistaken. Moreover, it is a common human tendency that, in reading a letter, as in reading a book, one's eyes fall on a particular cluster of sentences, even on a particular word, and people respond mostly to *that*, fragmenting it from the rest. It is likely that Mary's eyes fell on 'I hate this world' 'with its fair faces and false hearts'; and it is equally likely that she thought the Swami was including in that her as well, which he most certainly was *not*. Not understanding the main point of what her 'brother' Vivekananda was saying, but stunned by his letter, Mary Hale wrote to him:

I did not intend answering your first letter. I thought best to let the matter drop and have no more words on the subject but now that the second one has come, beginning with the same story,

---

[63] Ibid., p. 212.

full of the same spirit, not of love but of hate—of revilings, of bitterness and rancor, I cannot but express myself. I confess dear Brother, to a feeling of terrible disappointment—a year ago such a letter from your pen would have been an utter impossibility. I am glad to have that time to look back upon! Where is the great and glorious soul that came to the Parliament of Religions, so full of love of God that his face shone with divine light, whose words were fire, whose very presence created an atmosphere of harmony and purity, thereby drawing all souls to himself? It is our turn to cry 'My!!!' Where now is your illustration of the light in the lamp? The force of the Lord reflected in all his creation?[64]

Feeling that he had been perhaps harsh on Mary Hale, the Swami followed his letter of 1 February with another, of 15 February, this time writing to her not in prose but in verse. We learn that there were in his letter-in-verse fourteen stanzas, of which the first was as follows:

> Now Sister Mary,
> You need not be sorry
> For the hard raps I gave you,
> You know full well,
> Though you like me to tell,
> With my whole heart I love you.[65]

Marie Louise Burke provides us with a few lines of Mary's response in verse:

> One day he sat and mused alone—

---

[64] Marie Louise Burke discovered this fragment of what was probably a longer letter. *SV New Discoveries*, Vol. 3, pp. 33-34. See also her 'Note' on this, pp. 98-100.

[65] *SV New Discoveries*, Vol. 3, p. 36.

Sudden a light around him shone,
The 'still small voice' his thoughts inspire
And his words glow like coals of fire
And coals of fire they proved to be,
Heaped on the head of contrite me—
My scolding letter I deplore
And beg forgiveness o'er and o'er.[66]

While writing to Sara Bull and Mary Hale that he would not sacrifice truth to make others and himself comfortable, the Swami was teaching at his 'poor lodgings' in New York that: '"Comfort" is no test of truth; on the contrary, truth is often far from being "comfortable". If one intends to really find truth, one must not cling to comfort. It is hard to let all go, but the Jnani *must* do it.'[67]

The aim of life is not to seek comfort, but to free ourselves from the demands of our lower nature, and 'it is truth alone that makes us free'.[68] 'Ask not for healing, or longevity, or prosperity, ask only to be free.'[69]

Swami Vivekananda was teaching that much has to be thrown away: the superstition of one being only the body or the mind; the superstition of '*me*' and '*mine*'; the idea of time fragmented as past, present and future; inherited beliefs; sacred words; notions of heaven and hell; creeds and churches. 'When everything has been thrown away until what cannot be thrown away is reached, that is the Self.'[70] When one has reached the Self, it is all bliss; for

---

[66] Ibid., pp. 36-37.
[67] In his talks on *Jnana-yoga*. CWSV, Vol. VIII, p.1 4.
[68] Ibid., p. 7.
[69] Ibid., p. 11.
[70] Ibid., p. 11.

bliss is the nature of the Self when free from the bondage of what is only limited. The self, with its selfishness, is limited, is bondage. The Self, which is God, has no limits, is love in which the self has been extinguished. 'God is a circle,' he said, 'whose circumference is nowhere and whose centre is everywhere, and when we can get out of the narrow centre of body, we shall realize God—our true Self.'

Furthermore, Swami Vivekananda related truth mostly with joy, and untruth with misery and sorrow.

We must be bright and cheerful, long faces do not make religion. Religion should be the most joyful thing in the world, because it is the best. Asceticism cannot make us holy. Why should a man who loves God and who is pure be sorrowful? He should be like a happy child, be truly a child of God.'[71]

By the same reckoning, a child of God does not fear that, in being truthful, he might hurt his worldly prospects.

Expressing his sincerest gratitude to others, Swami Vivekananda had at the same time the clearest insight that gratitude *can* become another web of untruth, another prison. Through his life he demonstrated that one should be unwavering in the first and be free of the second.

Thirdly, 'giving', 'doing good to others', turn into instruments of power; in many cases expressly, in some imperceptibly but the eyes speak.[72] On the basis of all that

---

[71] Ibid., pp. 7-8.
[72] The Mahabharata examines the difficult relationship between the one who gives and the one who receives. That is discussed in the author's forthcoming *The Mahabharata—An Inquiry into the Human Condition*. In one of his letters to Brahmananda, 17 July 1898, Swami Vivekananda said in a certain context, 'I always lost sight of the demoralising influence of charity on the receiver.' *SV Letters*, p. 381.

is known about him, it can be said that Vivekananda was completely free of that common human failing. It must also be said, on that same basis, that among those very many, mostly women, who were giving to Swami Vivekananda their friendship, their love, devotion, energy, and material help, there was not *one* who for that reason entertained even remotely any feeling of power over him. Someone might caution him, even admonish him, about this or that, which Sara Bull and Mary Hale did, but there was never the attitude that only *because* he or she was doing much for him, *therefore* he had better act according to the suggestions made. In that respect, too, the greatness of their character must be acknowledged, but seldom is.

Swami Vivekananda was acknowledging all the time greatness of character in others. It is said that John B. Lyon, whose guest he was during the days of the Parliament of Religions, felt embarrassed when he heard that the Swami had told some of his friends at the Chicago Club, 'I believe Mr Lyon is the most Christ-like man I ever met!'[73] The reader will recall the Swami telling his brother-monks, 'I make no distinction as to householder or Sannyasin in this, that for all time my head should bend low in reverence wherever I see greatness, broadness of heart, and holiness.'[74]

There were not a few American men who, transcending *history*, were taking him into their hearts, for they instantly saw in him greatness, holiness, and ever expanding love. Dr Egbert Guernsey, in his seventies, an eminent physician of New York, also a writer and editor, and loved for his

[73] Cornelia Conger, *Reminiscences*, p. 131; also *SV New Discoveries*, Vol. 1, p. 152.
[74] See Chapter 3 of this book.

nobility, was one of them. He wrote to Sara Bull that the Swami

...by the kindness of his heart, great intelligence, purity and nobility of character has endeared himself to me almost like a son...The Swami from time to time has formed a part of my family for several months. Always welcome, we have all of us derived both profit and pleasure from the rich stores of a mind full of thought in which he seemed to have been able in his investigations of spiritual matters to have eliminated the discordant elements for the true and the harmonious.[75]

In the *disciple* mentality that has grown among those of Ramakrishna Order, to which the Indian mind is most prone anyway, anyone who loved and helped the Swami has promptly been described as his 'disciple'. The truth is that neither Sri Ramakrishna nor Swami Vivekananda ever entertained this *disciple* business. Neither of them was out to make disciples, but only to open the minds of others to the incalculable treasures of the spirit that lie veiled within each human being, and then let each work out his and her freedom. Neither of them liked labels as descriptions of a person. The reader should recall what Sri Ramakrishna had said when Dr Mahendra Lal Sarkar, his physician, told him that his son Amrit was a disciple of his (Sri Ramakrishna's).[76] '*There is not a fellow under the sun who is my disciple. On the contrary, I'm everybody's disciple. All are the children of God. All are His Servants. I too am a child of God. I too am His servant.*'

---

[75] *SV New Discoveries*, Vol. 3, pp. 21-22.
[76] See Chapter 2.

Disciples become a sect, and Swami Vivekananda was not out to form another *sect*. Fearing that the children of Sri Ramakrishna might begin perceiving themselves as such, he wrote to Shashi (Ramakrishnananda) and through him to all his brother-monks, cautioning them, indeed warning them:

…it is not necessary to preach that Ramakrishna Paramahamsa was an Incarnation, and things of that sort. He came to do good to the world, not to trumpet his own name—you must always remember this. Disciples pay their whole attention to the preservation of their master's name, and throw overboard his teachings; and sectarianism etc., are the result…I have nothing to do with sectarianism, or party-forming and playing the frog-in-the-well, whatever else I may do…It is impossible to preach the catholic ideas of Ramakrishna Paramahamsa and form sects at the same time.[77]

Swami Vivekananda knew the Hindu psyche embedded in the 'Incarnation' idea. He knew, too, that if that web were not cleared, what would remain would be the 'Ramakrishna-Paramahamsa-is-God' litany, and his essential message to our troubled times drowned in the ringing of bells and the waving of lamps, morning and noon and evening, in front of his photograph. Immediately after saying to his brother-monks that he was ready to lay down his life to help Sri Ramakrishna's message spread all over the world, he said:

What I am most afraid of is the worship-room. It is not bad in itself, but there is a tendency in some to make this all in all and

<hr>

[77] *SV Letters*, p. 249. This letter bears neither address nor date, only the year '1895'. But it was most probably written in June 1895 from 54 West 33rd Street, New York.

set up that old-fashioned nonsense over again—this is what makes me nervous. I know why they busy themselves with those old, effete ceremonials. Their spirit craves for work, but having no outlet they waste their energy in ringing bells and all that.[78]

Swami Vivekananda could never have imagined that in less than a decade he himself would be placed in 'the worship-room'!

On 14 April 1896, from New York, he wrote to Sarada (Trigunatitananda):

...That Ramakrishna Paramahamsa was God, and all that sort of thing, has no go in countries like this. M——[79]has a tendency to put that stuff down everybody's throat, but that will make our movement a little sect. You keep aloof from such attempts; at the same time, if people worship him as God, no harm. Neither encourage nor discourage. The masses will always have the *person*, the higher ones the principle. We want both. But principles are universal, *not* persons. Therefore stick to the principles he taught, let people think whatever they like of his person.[80]

The distinction Swami Vivekananda drew in this respect between 'the masses' and 'the higher ones' was, however, more conceptual than real. 'The higher ones' in India are occupied with the *person* no less than 'the masses' are, and no more mindful of the principles. Indeed, if there is mindfulness to principles, it is more visible among the masses than among the higher ones.

---

[78] Vivekananda to his brother-monks, in a letter simply dated '1894'. *SV Letters*, p. 98.

[79] Identity concealed (but not by the Swami).

[80] *SV Letters*, pp. 286-87. See also his letter dated 27 April 1896, from Reading, England, pp. 287-93, in which he drew a very detailed scheme of the Rules for the Math, especially p. 291.

Furthermore, the 'miracle' idea is quickly attached to the 'Incarnation' idea. An incarnation is expected to perform miracles. Aware of this ever-present danger, Swami Vivekananda was now warning against it. On 30 November 1894, he wrote to Alasinga Perumal:

What nonsense about the miracle of Ramakrishna!...Miracles I do not know nor understand. Had Ramakrishna nothing to do in the world but turning wine into the Gupta's medicine? Lord save me from such Calcutta people! What materials to work with! If they can write a real life of Shri Ramakrishna with the idea of showing what he came to do and teach, let them do it, otherwise let them not distort his life and sayings. These people want to know God who see in Shri Ramakrishna nothing but jugglery!...Now let Kidi translate his love, his knowledge, his teachings, his eclecticism, etc. This is the theme. The life of Shri Ramakrishna was an extraordinary searchlight under whose illumination one is able really to understand the whole scope of Hindu religion...This man had in fifty-one years lived the five thousand years of national spiritual life, and so raised himself to be an object-lesson for future generations.[81]

* * *

There was simultaneity in Swami Vivekananda's reverence for Jesus Christ with his strong criticism of historical Christianity; in this respect he and Kierkegaard, that most authentic of all Christians, were alike. Kierkegaard had uttered a devastating truth when he said, 'Christendom has done away with Christianity, without being quite aware of it. The consequence is that, if anything is to be done, one

---

[81] *SV Letters*, pp. 184-85.

must try again to introduce Christianity into Christendom.'[82]
He argued that the Christianity in the nineteenth-century
West bore little resemblance to the life and the teachings
of Jesus. He was expelled from the Christian Church.
The Swami's deep reverence for Jesus Christ did not touch
Christian missionaries and clerics; the truth of his criticism
of historical Christianity roused their hatred.

Likewise, there was simultaneity in the Swami's
reverence for the Buddha with his strong criticism of
historical Buddhism. Some of his lectures in America on
the Buddha were in such eloquent and feeling terms that
many newspapers mistook him to be a Buddhist monk.
At the end of one such lecture, a woman, unable to
pronounce correctly the word 'Buddhist', asked him,
'Swami, are you a Bud-ist?' To that, the Swami replied—
'wickedly but with a grave face' as Sister Christine
recalled—'No, madam, I am a florist.'[83] But Dharmapala
from Ceylon, who had represented Buddhism at the
Parliament of Religions, was so greatly upset by the truth
of Swami's criticism of historical Buddhism that he wrote
a letter against him, which, in its malice and calumny,
far surpassed anything that Christian missionaries ever
wrote against the Swami. And the Swami had nothing
but praise and much affection, too, for Dharmapala.

As we saw in the earlier pages of this book, there was
simultaneity in Swami Vivekananda's reverence for
ancient Hindu philosophic and religious thought with his
devastating criticism of what 'religion' had become in the

---

[82] Kierkegaard, *Training in Christianity*, p. 39. Also see Chaturvedi
Badrinath, *Jesus in Dharma*, pp. 150-51.
[83] Sister Christine in her reminiscences of Swami Vivekananda;
Reminiscences, p. 172.

Hindu society and of certain aspects of the Hindu character. In his letter of 20 August 1893 to Alasinga Perumal, while saying that the gospel of salvation was not separate from the gospel of equality, he said: 'The Lord has shown me that religion is not in fault, but it is the Pharisees and Sadducees in Hinduism, hypocrites, who invent all sorts of engines of tyranny...'[84]

It is noteworthy that he was criticizing historical Christianity to the Christians in the West, of which he hardly spoke a word in India, and was criticizing to the face of the Hindus what they had turned religion into, of which he mentioned not a word in the West.

The Swami wanted the two philosophies of religion in India, Hinduism and Buddhism, reconciled as guides to living one's life. But his vision of future India had a much greater daring sweep. In his letter of 10 June 1898 to Mohammed Sarfaraz Hussain of Nainital, Swami Vivekananda said:

Whether we call it Vedantism or any *ism*, the truth is that Advaitism is the last word of religion and thought and the only position from which one can look upon all religions and sects with love. I believe it is the religion of the future enlightened humanity. The Hindus may get the credit of arriving at it earlier than other races, they being an older race than either the Hebrew or the Arab; yet practical Advaitism, which looks upon and behaves to all mankind as one's own soul, was never developed among the Hindus.

On the other hand, my experience is that if ever any religion approached to this equality in an appreciable manner, it is Islam and Islam alone.

---

[84] *SV Letters*, p. 41.

Therefore, I am firmly persuaded that without the help of practical Islam, theories of Vedantism, however fine and wonderful they may be, are entirely valueless to the vast mass of mankind. We want to lead mankind to the place where there is neither the Vedas, nor the Bible, nor the Koran; yet this has to be by harmonizing the Vedas, the Bible, and the Koran. Mankind ought to be taught that religions are the varied expressions of THE RELIGION, which is Oneness, so that each may choose the path that suits him best.

For our motherland a junction of the two great systems, Hinduism and Islam—Vedanta brain and Islam body—is the only hope.

I see in my mind's eye the future perfect India rising out of this chaos and strife, glorious and invincible, with Vedanta brain and Islam body.[85]

This strong faith, expressed in even a stronger voice, of the man looked upon as the dominant voice of renascent Hinduism, is muted, ignored and forgotten by those who call themselves his disciples and followers. But, then, this is not the only teaching of Swami Vivekananda that is now muted, ignored and forgotten.

Swami Vivekananda's conception of the work that required to be done, not only for the regeneration of the Indian masses, but also to bring the East and the West together with their respective inheritances for the good of mankind, revolved around a proper understanding of the Vedanta. On 17 February 1896, he wrote to Alasinga Perumal:

---

[85] *SV Letters*, pp. 379-80. Cited in the author's *Dharma, India and the World Order. Twenty-one Essays*, Chapter 21, 'Modern Indian Perceptions of India and the West', the section on 'Vivekananda: Vedanta and the Masses', pp. 209-10.

...The dry Advaita must become living—poetic—in everyday life; out of hopelessly intricate mythology must come concrete moral forms; and out of bewildering Yogi-ism must come the most scientific and practical psychology—and all this must be put in a form so that a child may grasp it. That is my life's work.[86]

On 7 June 1896, he wrote to Margaret Noble (not yet 'Sister Nivedita'):

My ideal indeed can be put into a few words and that is: to preach unto mankind their divinity, and how to make it manifest in every movement of life.

This world is in chains of superstition. I pity the oppressed, whether man or woman, and I pity more the oppressors.

...Religions of the world have become lifeless mockeries. What the world wants is character. The world is in need for those whose life is one burning love, selfless. That love will make every word tell like thunderbolt.[87]

In May 1896, from London, he had written to Mary Hale:

...I have become horribly radical. I am just going to India to see what I can do in that awful mass of conservative jelly-fish, and start a new thing, entirely new—simple, strong, new, and fresh as the first born baby. The eternal, the infinite, the omnipresent, the omniscient is a principle, not a person. You, I, and everyone are but embodiments of that principle: and the more of this infinite principle is embodied in a person, the greater is he, and all in the end will be the perfect embodiment of that, and thus all will be

---

[86] *SV Letters*, p. 284.
[87] Ibid., pp. 294-95.

one, as they are now essentially. This is all there is of religion, and the practice is through this feeling of oneness that is love.[88]

A year earlier, in New York, in his talks on *Jnana-Yoga*, the Path of Knowledge, he was saying:

The essence of the Vedanta is that there is but one Being and that every soul is that Being in full, not a part of that Being. *All* the sun is reflected in each dew-drop...We are not drops to fall into the ocean and be lost; each one is the *whole*, infinite ocean, and will know it when released from the fetters of illusion. Infinity cannot be divided, the 'One without a second' can have no second, all *is* that One. This knowledge will come to all, but we should struggle to attain it now, because until we have it, we cannot really give mankind the best help.[89]

...If a thing happens once, it can happen again. If any human being has ever realised perfection, we too can do so. If we cannot become perfect here and now, we never can in any state or heaven or condition we may imagine. If Jesus Christ was not perfect, then the religion bearing his name falls to the ground. If he was perfect, then we too can become perfect...For the man who has become perfect, nothing remains but to apply his understanding. He lives only to help the world, desiring nothing for himself. What distinguishes is negative—the positive is ever wider and wider. What we have in common is the widest of all, and that is 'Being'.[90]

...We should never try to be guardians of mankind, or to stand on a pedestal as saints reforming sinners. Let us rather purify ourselves, and the result must be that in so doing we shall help others.[91]

---

[88] Ibid., p. 294.
[89] From *Discourses on Jnana-Yoga*, CWSV, VIII, pp. 6-7.
[90] Ibid., pp. 17-18.
[91] Ibid., p. 20.

***

Let us now return to 54 West 33rd Street, New York, the poor lodgings of the Swami. Beginning with 'only three or four persons',[92] among the large number of people who were now coming there to hear the Swami, was Sarah Ellen Waldo (1845–1926). Leon Landsberg was already there. Miss Waldo, as she was generally spoken of, was a distant relative of the famous Ralph Waldo Emerson. She knew well not only the tenets of Emerson's Transcendental school of philosophy but had studied also the works of Max Mueller and, through him, had become interested in the Vedanta. She had heard the Swami's lecture at the Brooklyn Ethical Association on 30 December 1894, and was deeply stirred by it at many levels. She had come to hear him again and to stay. She soon became a familiar figure around the Swami. With her notebook on her lap, she took down, in longhand, what he taught on *Jnana-yoga* at 54 West 33rd Street in New York. It is to her that we owe what would later be published as *Inspired Talks*. She began also to cook for him, not every day though. And she was protecting him in many practical ways. Miss Hamlin did not particularly like her, but was appreciative of what she was doing for the Swami. Leon Landsberg liked her even less and showed it. But Miss Waldo understood the Swami's thoughts better than most others did and on reading her transcripts of his talks, he said to her: 'How could you have caught my thoughts and words so perfectly? It was as if I heard myself speaking!' He gave her a name, Haridasi, meaning 'Servant

---

[92] Sarah Ellen Waldo in *Reminiscences*, p. 115.

of the Lord'. One day he found the 'Servant of the Lord' in tears. 'What is the matter, Ellen? Has anything happened?' the Swami asked her. She answered, probably with some more tears in her eyes, that when others annoyed him he scolded *her*, which (she did not say this) was not fair. With utmost gentleness, the Swami said that he did not know the others well enough to scold them, and so he came to her: 'Whom else can I scold if not those who are my very own?' It is recorded that, on hearing him say that, Miss Waldo's tears vanished forthwith. In her reminiscences of him, first published in the *Prabuddha Bharata* in 1906, Sarah Ellen Waldo completely effaces herself with not a word of what she selflessly did for the Swami, which was considerable.[93] In her devotion there is greatness, too.

Leon Landsberg, a Russian Jew and by citizenship American, on the staff of the *New York Tribune*, had been seeking the deeper truths of human existence, the light of the spirit. At the same time he had longed for simple human love and affection, which his nature made it difficult to get. He had first met the Swami in May 1894 at a parlour-lecture the Swami gave in New York, and soon thereafter formally became his *brahmacharin* disciple, dedicating himself to the Vedanta work, the Swami his object of worship. He started living with him at 54 West 33rd Street, and the two, the guru and the disciple, also did the cooking. But not long thereafter, in one of his letters to Sara Bull, Landsberg wrote:

...I stand alone in the world. Father and mother are long dead. No wife or child that make life worth living and spurs us to restless action! Money, name, and fame, no more entice and

---

[93] See *Reminiscences*, pp. 113–20.

snare my soul with vain visions…But it is in our nature to love something, and so, when I met the Swami…he became to me the object of divine worship. My whole being was absorbed in his personality and work: no thought but for his happiness, no aspiration but for his grandeur, no effort but for his cause…[94]

There is always a hidden violence in one's worshipful adoration of the *other*. There is between the two an unseen *simultaneity*. It is common experience that, just a small twist, just a disappointment in the expectations from the *other*, and the worshipful adoration, quickly formed, turns just as quickly into enmity, or into any one of the varied emotions of that description. That is what now predictably happened to Leon Landsberg in relation to the Swami. In that same letter to Sara Bull, he wrote:

As to the little 'family brawls' we had with regard to the cooking, I lost my patience not on account of the work which I had to perform, but because I regarded it as unworthy of men of spiritual aspirations to waste the greatest part of their time with thinking and speaking of eating, preparing and cooking the food, and washing dishes, while the frugal meals required by a Yogi could be had quicker and cheaper in any restaurant.[95]

…As to myself I have now determined to break once for all my relations to him. Not that I bear any grudge to him, but in the interest of the peace of our souls, in the interest of the cause it is necessary that I keep away from him. Though loving him, I shall flee his presence as if he were my greatest enemy. From today I am non-existent for him or his friends.[96]

---

[94] *SV New Discoveries*, Vol. 3, p. 68.
[95] Ibid., pp. 66-67.
[96] Ibid., p. 70. Read the whole letter as reproduced, pp. 66–70.

Swami Vivekananda had never sought worshipful adoration from anyone; therefore, he was not affected by its reversal either. This is not a mere biographical detail about *him*, but points to something else as well. About anyone adored and worshipped it is generally also true, and commonly seen, that the slightest note of un-acceptance of his or her views, or even a little criticism of his or her conduct, and the *other* is expelled from the Garden of Adoration. That *never* happened in Swami Vivekananda's relationships with others. No one was ever expelled from his company for being critical of him. This has to be related with all that he had been saying. He bound no one and he accepted no bonds. Furthermore, in the Garden of Adoration, only those can enter who share the worship of a common idol; those who come with respect, even love, but with their minds open, do not *belong* and thus have no place. Swami Vivekananda was not out to set up a community of worshippers either of Sri Ramakrishna or of him. He had not come into this world to found a sect.

He had seen the innermost of Leon Landsberg the man, an honest, earnest seeker, having genuine feelings for the poor but starved for love and affection himself. Even though Landsberg had offended and antagonized almost everybody there thanks to his violent temper, and was now turning upon the Swami, the Swami did not abandon him and still gave him his love and spiritual care. He did something more which startled everybody, Sara Bull most of all. At Thousand Island Park, during June–July 1895, he initiated Leon Landsberg into sannyasa, gave him a monastic name, Swami Kripananda, and authorized him to teach. The new Swami deserted his guru and turned against him. But Swami Vivekananda's grace and love for him never diminished.

On 29 January 1895, two sisters, Josephine MacLeod and Betty MacLeod Sturges, the latter a widow having two children, Alberta, eighteen, and Hollister, sixteen, came to 54 West 33rd Street, New York, to hear a lecture by the Swami. They had come with Mrs Dora Roethlesberger, their intimate friend, who had spoken to them about him. Josephine, tall, very attractive, wealthy and, like her sister Betty, dressed in clothes made in Paris, in the latest fashion, had an imperious air about her. The three had come to 'the poor lodgings' of the Swami. He was going to speak 'in his sitting room where were assembled fifteen or twenty ladies and two or three gentlemen'. Even as the Swami was concluding his talk, Josephine was concluding that she had never before heard truth as she heard from him.

He said something, the particular words of which I do not remember, but instantly to me that was truth, and the second sentence he spoke was truth, and the third sentence was truth. And I listened to him for seven years and whatever he uttered was to me truth. From that moment life had a different import. It was as if he made you realize that you were in eternity. It never altered. It never grew. It was like the sun that you will never forget once you have seen.[97]

Born in 1858, Josephine, variously called Joe, Jo-Jo, Yum, or Tantine, had just turned thirty-seven when she first heard Swami Vivekananda. In her later years, she would reckon her age from that day, 29 January 1895. 'It is the Truth that I saw in Swamiji that has set me free'; 'It was

---

[97] Josephine MacLeod, in *Reminiscences*, p. 228. See also Pravrajika Prabuddhaprana, *Tantine*, p. 11.

to set me free that Swamiji came.'[98] To hear him, with the two sisters came Francis Leggett, a very rich businessman of New York, who was courting Betty Sturges and some months later would marry her. Greatly drawn towards the Swami, he invited him, and of course invited Betty and Josephine, to his opulent home 'Ridgely Manor'. Swami Vivekananda came into their lives, and they, more notably Josephine MacLeod, into his. With her nearness to him and his teachings, and seeing him at every turn, in every situation, in every relationship, *living* the Vedanta as love and not just preaching it, she believed Swami Vivekananda to be 'the New Buddha'. She told him so and he looked at her questioningly. When talking about him, she referred to him simply as 'our Prophet'. However, once when someone introduced Josephine as the Swami's disciple, she sprang up and said, 'I am not Swami's disciple. I am his friend.' To that, her niece Alberta, later Lady Sandwich, added: 'She is not Swami's friend. She is *Him*.' Although not a disciple in the sense in which this word is used in the monastic orders of India, Josephine, with that royal freedom a queen would give herself, often signed her name as 'Jayananda'. Swami Vivekananda would love Josephine, his 'Joe', as long as he lived. She was one of those few to whom he wrote about what was taking place in his inner being simultaneously with the great events unfolding outwardly in his life, which he did neither to his brother-monks nor to his 'Madras boys'. In one of his many letters to her, he wrote, 'I can't even in imagination pay the immense debt of gratitude I owe you. Wherever you are you never forget my welfare; and, there, you are

---

[98] Josephine to Alberta, in a letter.

the only one who bears all my burdens, all my brutal outbursts.'[99] 'All blessings attend you, Joe,' he wrote in another letter, 'you have been a good angel to me.'[100] And Josephine's 'New Buddha' remained in her an abiding inner presence, a light of love, as long as she lived, and she lived long. But the welfare of her sister Betty and her family also remained a paramount concern of hers, and there was no conflict between the two. Neither was there any conflict between her love for the Swami, her rational reverence for 'the New Buddha', and her own independent character.

Josephine MacLeod met Mrs Sara Bull and there grew between them a bond of unwavering love for each other, of their shared love for 'our Prophet', and of the togetherness of making his message of Vedanta known even more widely. Independent of their respective relationships with the Swami, these two women understood each other's feelings, joys and sorrows. To this duo was added a third, Margaret Noble; with a twinkle in his eyes, the Swami would often refer to them as the 'Trinity'. The names of these three, Josephine MacLeod, Sara Bull, and Margaret Noble as Nivedita, will ever remain intimately connected with the name of Swami Vivekananda.

***

Not seeking disciples, nor about to start a new sect in the name of Sri Ramakrishna, Swami Vivekananda had not come to the West to *raise funds* either. He had come to

---

[99] *CWSV*, V, p. 164; written from the Belur Math, this letter bears no date, only '1901'.
[100] Ibid., p. 180. This letter is not included in *SV Letters*.

earn money, with which he would establish a centre in India from which, having first liberated themselves, thousands of selfless workers would go to the remotest village, educate, restore to the masses their lost individuality, make them aware of the divinity within them. That was the 'work', for which funds were of course needed. But he was not soliciting funds, he never would—not even from those that were closest to him and were rich. He refused to take money when it was being offered to him but with strings attached which he could clearly see. He once wrote to his 'Mother Church', Mrs Hale, that he had refused to accept money a certain rich woman had offered, for she seemed to be greatly interested in *him*. He offered to return the money some good people in Detroit gave him, saying he was no longer certain of establishing a centre, and he had no right to keep what they so generously gave for that purpose. And they said to him, with unaffected humility, that he could throw that money into the sea if he so liked but they would not take it back. Even in the earliest days of their meeting, when Mrs Sara Bull offered some money for his work, the Swami suggested to her to give it to Mrs Sarah Farmer instead, to support her Greenacre Conferences on the inner unity of all religions he had earlier attended.[101]

...How can I express my gratitude to you for what you have already done for me and my work, and my eternal gratitude to you for your offering to do something more this year. But I sincerely believe that you ought to turn all your help to Miss

---

[101] For Vivekananda's own description of Greenacre conference, from there, read his letter, dated 31 July 1894, to the Hale sisters. *SV Letters*, pp. 130–33.

Farmer's Greenacre work this year. India can wait as she is waiting centuries, and an immediate work at hand should always have the preference.[102]

On 29 December 1895, he would write to Sarah Farmer:

In the universe where nothing is lost, where we live in the midst of death *in life*, every thought that is thought, in public or in private, in crowded thoroughfares or in the deep recesses of primeval forests, lives. They are continually trying to become self-embodied, and until they have embodied themselves, they will struggle for expression, and any amount of repression cannot kill them.

...the kingdom of heaven is already in existence, if we will have it, that perfection is already in man if he will see it.

The Greenacre meetings last summer were so wonderful, simply because you opened yourself fully to that thought which has found in you so competent a medium of expression, and because you took your stand on the highest teaching of this thought that the kingdom of heaven already exists.

You have been consecrated and chosen by the Lord as a channel for converting this thought into life, and everyone that helps you in this wonderful work is serving the Lord.[103]

As mentioned earlier, Swami Vivekananda was not charging any fee for his classes, whereas his public lectures were to be paid. Once, when there was no money even to pay the rent and Josephine MacLeod announced to the class, 'Everyone is going to pay ten cents,' he stopped her and announced, 'Religion is not for sale.'[104]

---

[102] Vivekananda to Sara Bull, letter dated 14 February 1895, from New York. *SV Letters*, p. 215.
[103] Ibid., pp. 275–76.
[104] See Prabuddhaprana, *Saint Sara*, p. 223.

It was the summer of 1895 and Swami Vivekananda was at Thousand Island Park, at a retreat Miss Mary Elizabeth Dutcher had organized for a select few. Here the Swami learnt of the passing away of his 'Dewanji', the Dewan of Junagad, who had given him during his parivrajaka days his love and care and had shown in every way his faith in the Swami's great destiny. On 30 July 1895, he wrote to Mrs Ellen Hale, 'Oh Mother my heart is so so sad the letters bring the news of the death of Dewanji. Haridas Viharidas has left the body. He was as a father to me...My heart is too full to write more.'[105] Through these words one can sense the Swami's inexpressible sadness in the midst of his own spiritual exaltation and of those who had gathered round him.

Sad at heart and yet saying, 'I am enjoying this place immensely,' he wrote to Mary Hale from Thousand Island Park:

...A wonderful calmness is coming over my soul. Everyday I feel I have no duty to do; I am always in eternal rest and peace. It is He that works. We are only the instruments. Blessed be His name! The threefold bondage of lust and gold and fame is as it were fallen from me for the time being, and once more, even here, I feel what sometimes I felt in India, 'From me all difference has fallen, all right or wrong, all delusion and ignorance have vanished. I am walking in the path beyond the qualities.' What law I obey, what disobey? From that height the universe looks like a mud-puddle. Hari Om Tat Sat. He exists: nothing else does. I in Thee and Thou in me. Be Thou Lord my eternal refuge! Peace, Peace, Peace.[106]

---

[105] SV New Discoveries, Vol. 3, pp. 167-68.
[106] This letter bears no date, only the address 'C/o Miss Dutcher, Thousand Island Park, N.Y.' SV Letters, p. 241.

On 7 July 1895, at Thousand Island Park, the Swami initiated into sannyasa another person, this time a woman, a Frenchwoman, Madame Marie Louise,[107] and gave her the monastic name Swami Abhayananda. She too turned against him but the Swami did not expel her either from his grace.[108] However, those two initiations frankly left many bewildered. Some, Sara Bull among them, even questioned Vivekananda's judgement, *viveka*, as to who is worthy, and who is not, of receiving monastic vows. In the opinion of many, neither Leon Landsberg nor Mme. Marie Louise was, and they were puzzled that the Swami did not see that. Exercising the privilege of a mother, Sara Bull expressed her strong disapproval of his initiating into sannyasa those two. [109] His answer was that he does not *choose*, does not *judge*, does not *evaluate*, in the scale of worthiness or unworthiness; if anyone earnestly wanted to travel the path of monastic renunciation, he put him or her on that path. And he would close the discussion by saying, as in everything concerning himself, so in everything concerning others, 'The Lord does the rest.'

Marie Louise, now Swami Abhayananda, sternly insisted that she be addressed as 'Swami', which she considered as a kind of status. She felt offended when Miss Hamlin didn't, not out of any disrespect though, and complained

---

[107] Marie Louise Burke tells us much about her. See *SV New Discoveries*, Vol. 3, pp. 125–28.
[108] For the full story of these two American Swamis, the one a man and the other a woman, the reader should turn to Marie Louise Burke and, even more especially, to Pravrajika Prabuddhaprana's *Saint Sara*.
[109] See *Saint Sara*, p. 152.

to Sara Bull.[110] In a letter to her, Sara still addressed her simply as 'Marie Louise' and suggested to her that she renounce her ego, for that is what sannyasa means in the very first place:

The experience of my life has taught me that back of all differences of thought, of ideals, of individual conceptions of duty and morals, there was something, for me, divine in each sincere human soul with whom I came in contact, if I held to the high purpose of its discovery.

...Whatever stage of development your work as an anarchist led you to, the Vedanta principle of overcoming law by choosing the good and holy things of life for their own sake, and that true freedom devoid of all fear and compulsion, you are necessarily now to illustrate as the Sannyasin.[111]

In the letter that followed, Sara addressed her as 'Swami Abhayananda' and told her:

Please understand that I do not question your right by initiation to the title of Swami or your power to confer it upon others. That Vivekananda honoured his American students by a rapid conferring of the same is, in part, a promise that the end will justify him...

...Your face indicated suffering and made me desire to know you and give you the tenderness of a woman's regard...

...As a matter of politeness I am personally pleased to address you as Swami, as it seems, you exact it...Personally I hardly know which of two men I should most honour—he who honours his title when thrust upon him by inheritance or others, or he whose name is too great to be honoured by any title...

---

[110] Sara had meanwhile sent Abhayananda, through Miss Hamlin, $10 to help her get some undergarments, which the new Swami confided in Miss Hamlin she badly needed but was too poor to buy.
[111] Ibid., p. 148.

I can understand the essential reverence due from the student to the guru. But the man who will not hold his student as any other than a fellow student is to my mind the guru whom we can never outgrow. This giving up of authority, permitting no claim to be made for him, even by his most beloved children, is the power and beauty, to my mind, of Ram Krishna Paramhamsa's life. The rare generosity, the nobility of Vivekananda, whose distinction his friends are likely to make by the prefix of 'The Swami'...the title associated with his name, his scholarship and simplicity combined, have made him loved among us.

This rare generosity, which permits any student to take what they like or to reject what they count unessential to philosophy, makes him worthy of his Master.

Wishing you most sincerely the full attainment of the ideal Swami, I must deny myself the pleasure of your company in my home, since you would insist upon the presentation of your title first and foremost, rather than win for yourself, independently, the interest in your studies and work which would incline people to desire to confer it upon you because of your qualities.[112]

Now, at Thousand Island Park, to the simultaneity of the Swami being sad at heart on receiving the news of the passing away of Dewan Haridas Viharidas; his initiating Swami Kripananda and Swami Abhayananda and the varied feelings generated thereby; an atmosphere of exalted spiritual emotions—was added another event. On 6 July, two women arrived, one of whom, Christine Greenstidel,[113] said to Swami Vivekananda, 'We have come, just as we would go to Jesus if he were still on earth and ask him to

---

[112] Ibid., pp. 149–51. Read the whole letter.
[113] Later called Sister Christine (1866–1930); born, at Nuremberg, of German parents who migrated to America and had settled in Detroit.

teach us.' The Swami looked at them and said, 'If only I possessed the power of the Christ to set you free now.' The other woman was Mrs Mary C. Funke. They had heard the Swami for the first time in Detroit at the Unitarian Church on 14 February 1894. Afterwards, recalling that day, Christine would say: 'Surely never in our countless incarnations had we taken a step so momentous! For before we had listened five minutes we knew that we had found the touchstone for which we had searched so long. In one breath, we exclaimed—"if we had missed this...!"'[114]

But they did not meet him then. Now they had travelled hundreds of miles, in the night and in the rain, to be with him at Miss Dutcher's cottage. Both of them have left their reminiscences of the days at Thousand Island Park and of Swami Vivekananda, which, in their tone and content, are as different as they were from each other.

We come to see Swami Vivekananda still more clearly if we see the two radically different responses to him at the same time, one of Miss Dutcher and the other of Mrs Mary C. Funke. They represent two radically different responses to life. But first let us quickly hear from Sister Christine about a standard association most people made in the West:

To those who have heard much of the personal appearance of the Swami Vivekananda, it may seem strange that it was not this which made the first outstanding impression. The forceful virile figure which stepped upon the platform was unlike the emaciated, ascetic type which is generally associated with spirituality in the

---

[114] Her reminiscences 'Swami Vivekananda as I Saw Him', in *Reminiscences*, pp. 126-227. This particular passage at p. 148.

West. A sickly saint everyone understands, but who ever heard of a powerful saint?[115]

Miss Dutcher was a devout Methodist; but on hearing Swami Vivekananda's talks in the classes at her cottage, all her perceptions and beliefs and prejudices were shaken to their roots. She was so overwhelmed that for two or three days she was not seen. The Swami sensed and understood her inner turmoil: 'Don't you see, this is not an ordinary illness? It is the reaction of the body against the chaos that is going on in her mind. She cannot bear it.'[116] Christine recalled, 'The power that emanated from this mysterious being was so great that one but all shrank from it. It was overwhelming. It threatened to sweep everything before it.'[117] The very opposite was simultaneously true about Swami Vivekananda. By all other accounts, what emanated from him were vibrations of love—and joyful laughter.

To Mary Funke, Swami Vivekananda appeared very differently from what he appeared to Miss Dutcher; and that is because what she saw in him was in her as well. This is *not* to be interpreted: to each, his or her Vivekananda. Let us hear *her* experience of the days with the Swami at Thousand Island Park.

We were nearly frightened to death when we finally reached the cottage, for neither the Swami nor his followers at Thousand Island Park had the remotest idea of our existence and it seemed rather an impertinent thing for us to do, to travel seven hundred

---

[115] Ibid., p. 148.
[116] Ibid., p. 165.
[117] Ibid., p. 148.

miles, follow him up, as it were, and ask him to accept us. But he did accept us—he did—the Blessed one![118]

With many other such happenings, this too is promptly added to the Eulogy of Swami Vivekananda, to show how extraordinarily great he was to have made such an impact on two more women that they would eagerly travel seven hundred miles to hear his teachings and be near him. What is left out, which is no service to Swami Vivekananda, is the truth that these two women, Christine Greenstidel and Mary Funke, had within them greatness, too, to respond in that way. One cannot respond unless there is already life within.

So here we are—in the very house with *Vivekananda*, listening to him from 8 o'clock in the morning until late at night. Even in my wildest dreams I could not imagine anything so wonderful, so perfect! To be with Vivekananda! To be accepted by him!

...Oh, the sublime teaching of Vivekananda! No nonsense, no talk of 'astrals', 'imps', etc., but God, Jesus, Buddha. I feel that I shall never be quite the same again for I have caught a glimpse of the Real.

...In the afternoon, we take long walks and the Swami literally, and so simply, finds 'books in the running brooks, sermons in stones, and good (God) in everything'.

...We are taught to see God in *everything* from the blade of grass to man—'even in diabolical man'.[119]

Equally important, simple merriment and happy laughter were included in 'the glimpse of the Real' Mary Funke

---

[118] *Reminiscences*, p. 251.
[119] Ibid., p. 252.

had caught. The Swami was teaching that they are inseparable from true religion and spirituality.

...And this same Swami is so merry and fun-loving. We just go *mad* at times.

...Swamiji's fun-making is of the merry type. Sometimes he will say, 'Now I am going to cook for you!' He is a wonderful cook and delights in serving the 'brithrin'. The food he prepares is delicious but for 'yours truly' too hot with various spices; but I made up my mind to eat it if it strangled me, which it nearly did. If a *Vivekananda* can cook for me, I guess the least I can do is to eat it. Bless him!

At such times we have whirlwind of fun. Swamiji will stand on the floor with a white napkin draped over his arm, *a la* the waiters on the dining cars, and will intone in perfect imitation their call for dinner—'Last call fo' the dining cah. Dinner served.'—Irresistibly funny! And then, at table, such gales of laughter over some quip or jest, for he unfailingly discovers the little idiosyncrasies of each one—but never sarcasm or malice—just fun.[120]

Just as fun and joyous laughter were not excluded from Swami Vivekananda's teaching on the unity of the microcosm and the macrocosm, an occasional laughing shot at the Brahman, the Absolute, was not excluded either, as it was not from the conversations between William James and the Swami at Boston. Mary Funke tells us:

...One, a Dr. Wright of Cambridge (not John Henry, the 'Adhyapakji'), a very cultured man, creates much merriment at times. He becomes so absorbed in the teaching that he, invariably, at the end of each discourse ends up with asking Swamiji, 'Well,

---

[120] Ibid., p. 253.

Swami, it all amounts to this in the end, doesn't it? I *am* Brahman,
I *am* the Absolute.' If you could only see Swami's indulgent smile
and hear him answer so gently, 'Yes, Dokie, you are Brahman,
you are the Absolute, in the real essence of your being.' Later,
when the learned doctor comes to the table a trifle late, Swami,
with the utmost gravity but with a merry twinkle in his eyes,
will say, 'Here comes Brahman' or 'Here is the Absolute.'[121]

...Sometimes I ask him rather daring questions, for I am so
anxious to know just how he would react under certain conditions.
He takes it so kindly when I in my impulsive way sometimes
'rush in where angels fear to tread'. Once he said to someone,
'Mrs. Funke rests me, she is so naïve.' Wasn't that dear of him?[122]

***

Even if one studies a life from a distance, one cannot but
be amazed at the range of Swami Vivekananda's *giving*, his
spiritual and emotional energies flowing in so many different
channels *simultaneously*. But in that giving, and in that
flow, he was as caring of the individual person as he was
of the Brahman, of the Absolute. From Thousand Island
Park, he was writing to Mary Hale, to Sara Bull, to
Alasinga Perumal, and to his brother-monks Shashi
(Ramakrishnananda) and Rakhal (Brahmananda). Even
today, one cannot read those letters without *feeling* the charge
of uplifting energy in them. There is in them as deep a

---

[121] Ibid., p. 253. Reporting to Brahmananda, from Srinagar in 1898,
that his health was all right, Swami Vivekananda had added playfully,
'Medicine is useless—it has no action on the system of a knower of
Brahman! Everything will be digested—don't be afraid.' *SV Letters*, p.
381.
[122] Mary C. Funke, in *Reminiscences*, p. 254.

caring for 'the person' as for 'the work' and 'the organization', both in India and the West.

For the time being, what was coming from India, from different people, was the question: when was he returning home? Simultaneously with giving those inspired talks, he was answering that question and from his answers we can discern one of the causes of his inner torment. As early as 27 October 1894, he had written to Alasinga:

...Everybody wants me to come over to India. They think we shall be able to do more if I come over. They are mistaken, my friend. The present enthusiasm is only a little patriotism, it means nothing. If it is true and genuine you will find in a short time hundreds of heroes coming forward and carrying on the work. Therefore know that you have really done all, and go on. Look not for me...Here is a great field. What have I to do with this 'ism' or that 'ism'? I am the servant of the Lord, and where on earth is a better field than here for propagating all high ideas? Here, if one man is against me, a hundred hands are ready to help me; here, where man feels for man, weeps for his fellow men, and women are goddesses! ...My son, I believe in God and I believe in man. I believe in helping the miserable, I believe in going even to hell to save others. Talk of the Westerners? They have given me food, shelter, friendship, protection, even the most orthodox Christians! What do our people do when any of their priests go to India? You do not touch them even, they are MLECHCHHAS. No man, no nation, my son, can hate others and live. [123] ...It is good to talk glibly about the Vedanta, but how hard to carry out even its least precepts!...[124]

---

[123] Here follows his thundering judgement, quoted earlier in this book, about India's doom being sealed the day they invented the word mlechchha and stopped communion with others.
[124] SV Letters, pp. 170-71.

On 9 July 1895, now from Thousand Island Park, he was writing to Raja Ajit Singh:

...About my coming to India, the matter stands thus. I am, as your Highness well know, a man of dogged perseverance. I have planted a seed in this country; it is already a plant, and I expect it to be a tree very soon. I have got a few hundred followers. I shall make several Sannyasins, and then I go to India, leaving the work to them. The more the Christian priests oppose me, the more I am determined to leave a permanent mark on their country...[125]

Still at Thousand Island Park, he was again writing to Alasinga: 'You have remarked well: my ideas are going to work in the West better than in India...I have done more for India than India ever did for me...Truth is my God, universe my country.[126]

And to Shashi (Ramakrishnananda), this:

I can say nothing as to whether I shall go back to India and when. There also I shall have to lead a wandering life as I do here; but here thousands of people listen to and understand my lectures, and these thousands are benefited. But can you say the same thing about India?[127]

He followed this by a long letter to Rakhal (Brahmananda),[128] in which, while writing on a variety of subjects, he wrote:

...There is no certainty about my going back to India. I shall have to lead a wandering life there also, as I am doing here. But

---

[125] Ibid., p. 243.
[126] Ibid., p. 244. This letter is dated simply as August, 1895.
[127] Ibid., p. 250. This letter bears no date, beyond '1895'; but in all likelihood, it was from Thousand Island Park.
[128] Ibid., pp. 251–56.

here one lives in the company of scholars, and there one must live among fools—there is this difference as of the poles. People of this country organize and work, while *our* undertakings all come to dust clashing against laziness—miscalled 'renunciation'—and jealousy etc.[129]

At the same time his caring for the individual person, protecting him or her from a decision taken in momentary enthusiasm, or from wrong notions of spirituality, is again reflected in the continuing narration of Mary Funke.

The Swami has accepted C. (Christine) as one fitted for his work in India. She is so happy. I was very disappointed, because he would not encourage me to go to India. I had a vague idea that to live in a cave and wear a yellow robe would be the proper thing to do if one wished to develop spiritually. How foolish of me and how wise Swamiji was! He said, 'You are a householder. Go back to Detroit, find God in your husband and family. *That* is your path at present.'[130]

On 14 August 1895, from New York the Swami sailed for Europe, landing at Le Havre on 24 August, to be present at the wedding of his friends Francis Leggett and Betty Sturges, who decided that it was *Paris* where they would get married. They wanted him to be with them on that occasion of great importance to their lives. They loved him and he loved them, and so he decided to go with them to Paris as their guest. Betty's sister, Josephine MacLeod, and Betty's two children, Alberta and Hollister, would be there too. The wedding took place on 9 September at the Episcopal Church of the Holy Trinity, and Swami

---

[129] Ibid., p. 252.
[130] *Reminiscences*, p. 255.

Vivekananda was a witness.[131] An extraordinary event, because of an extraordinary witness in ochre robe—a *sannyasin* who had renounced all family bonds was now blessing these two he affectionately called 'Turtle Doves', binding themselves with those very bonds. In being a witness to this marriage, Swami Vivekananda was signing a message as well—that true sannyasa is to live for others, in the bonds of love.

A few months earlier, on 2 May 1895, the Swami had written to a young man[132] who had decided to renounce the world:

So you have made up your mind to renounce the world. I have sympathy with your desire. There is nothing so high as renunciation of self. But you must not forget that to forego your own favourite desire for the welfare of those that depend upon you is no small sacrifice. Follow the spotless life and teachings of Shri Ramakrishna and look after the comforts of your family. You do your own duty, and leave the rest to Him.

Love makes no distinction between man and man, between an Aryan and a Mlechchha, a Brahmana and a Pariah, nor even between a man and a woman. Love makes the whole universe as one's own home.[133]

Thus, his high respect for marriage stood alongside his high praise for renunciation. In all his teachings, Swami Vivekananda was teaching the renunciation of *self*, not of *things*, as the highest renunciation. He knew only too well that many of those who had renounced the world,

---

[131] See Prabuddhaprana, *Tantine*, p. 18.
[132] His name has been edited and concealed, just 'S—'.
[133] *SV Letters*, p. 224.

and had taken to ochre robe as a declaration thereof, were also among the most egoistic and selfish; for they had not yet renounced *self*. On the other hand, he had intimately known many married men and women in whom he had seen true holiness because, through marriage, they had renounced *self*. Marriage implies in the very first place the renunciation of *self*.

Swami Vivekananda its witness in the present, a future was simultaneously present as the unseen witness of that marriage in Paris. Betty and Frank emotionally drifted apart, although they never separated. [134] Betty never cultivated renunciation of self, and continued her courting of kings and queens and other royalty, sparkling as a beautiful hostess in Paris and London, neglecting the emotional bonds of marriage. But their love for the Swami, and their financial support for his Vedanta work in the West and in India, never diminished, and Francis Leggett[135] always held him to be the greatest man he had ever met. The Swami's love and concern for them was abiding.

From Paris, the Swami arrived in London, his first visit to England, which lasted from 10 September to 27 November 1895. His fame as a great spiritual teacher had reached England long before he did. Josephine MacLeod was with him, and Betty and Frank joined them after their honeymoon trip. London was an altogether different scene for Swami Vivekananda. He was in the land of the British rulers of India; he belonged to the subject race, crushed and humiliated. But it was also the land of John Stuart Mill and Herbert Spencer, whose thoughts had influenced

---

[134] Prabuddhaprana, *Tantine*, p. 18.
[135] Francis Leggett died in September 1909.

his young mind greatly. Both in emotional and intellectual terms, it was predicted to be an experience wholly unlike that of America. On 22 October, when he began to speak at the Prince's Hall, so deep was the silence that, it was reported, the people gathered there to hear him could hear their heartbeats.

The day after his public lecture at the Prince's Hall, *The Westminster Gazette* (23 October) published an interview with him, describing him as 'an exponent entirely novel to Western people'. Swami Vivekananda was no sectarian monk, nor a missionary of Hinduism. He was touching English minds and hearts with truths that were universal. He mentioned Sri Ramakrishna in whom, he said, he had found his highest ideal realized.

'Then did he found a sect, which you now represent?'

'No,' replied the Swami quickly. 'No, his whole life was spent in breaking down the barriers of sectarianism and dogma. He found no sect. Quite the reverse. He advocated and strove to establish absolute freedom of thought. He was a great Yogi.'

'Then you are connected with no society or sect in this country? Neither Theosophical nor Christian Scientist, nor any other?'

'None whatever!' said the Swami in clear and impressive tones. (His face lights up like that of a child, it is so simple, straightforward and honest.) 'My teaching is my own interpretation of our ancient books, in the light which my Master shed upon them. I claim no supernatural authority. Whatever in my teaching may appeal to the highest intelligence and be accepted by thinking men, the adoption of that will be my reward.'[136]

---

[136] See *CWSV*, Vol. V, p. 186.

The thinking minds in London had opened first to the Raja, Raja Rammohan Roy (1774–1833), and now to the Monk. There were many now opening to the Monk their hearts as well. Miss Margaret Noble was one of them. Of Swami Vivekananda's two visits to England, the second from 20 April to 16 December 1896, she was one of the greatest gains to India. Born on 28 October 1867, Margaret Noble was Irish, and carried within her two inherited Irish passions—for justice and freedom. To these, she added another passion—for truth. These three would ever remain the dominant themes of Margaret's life, justice and freedom subsumed in truth. 'When I was quite young—growing out of childhood—I thought, and I think, I still think, that the only *passion* I would ever know would be the passion for Truth.'[137]

In her late twenties, Margaret Noble met Swami Vivekananda first on 10 November 1895 at the house of her friend, Lady Isabel Margesson, sister of the seventh earl of Buckinghamshire. Lady Henrietta Ripon, wife of Lord George Ripon who was formerly the Viceroy of India (1880–84), was among those select few Lady Isabel had invited to hear the Swami.[138] In her search of truth, at once compelling and agonizing, Margaret Noble had moved from one faith to another, her soul thirsty still. She loved Jesus with her whole heart, but found the Christian doctrines 'incompatible with Truth', as she said. At the same time as her faith in Christianity tottered, and she was very unhappy, she would rush into church 'to feel

---

[137] Nivedita to Josephine MacLeod, letter dated 6 December 1905. *Nivedita Letters*, Vol. II, p. 767.
[138] For details, see Marie Louise Burke, *SV New Discoveries*, Vol. 3, pp. 282–85.

peace within'. But, as she would recall years later, 'No peace, no rest was there for my troubled soul all eager to know the Truth.'[139] That took her to the study of the natural sciences, in which, she had hoped, she would discover the Laws of Nature. Meanwhile, she had read the life of the Buddha and, as she said, 'became more and more convinced that the salvation he preached was decidedly more consistent with the Truth than the preachings of Christian religion'. A founding member of the Sesame Club, she had met George Bernard Shaw, Patrick Geddes and William Butler Yeats. It is in that searching, for truth, that she met Swami Vivekananda. At the end of each talk by him, there was from her always a *but* and a *why*. When these had ended, and before the Swami left London and returned to America, Margaret Noble had called him 'Master'. He unfolded to her his vision, still in general terms but with an intensity she knew well in her own nature. She simply said to him, 'I will help you.' With equal simplicity, he said: 'I know it.' He said this with as deep a conviction as hers when she had said what she did. The vision that he unfolded to her was that of education for the women of India, upon which he had been laying great emphasis.

At the same time as he was lecturing on *the Changeless*, Swami Vivekananda was *changing* his earlier perceptions of the English people. Although he would give the clearest expression to it on his return to India, in 1897, at the huge public meeting in Calcutta to welcome back the conquering hero, that change had already taken place in his mind in 1895 and 1896 while in London.

---

[139] The reader should turn to Pravrajika Atmaprana's biography of Margaret Noble, *Sister Nivedita*.

No one ever landed on English soil with more hatred in his heart for a race than I did for the English, and on this platform are present English friends who can bear witness to the fact; but the more I lived among them and saw how the machine was working—the English national life—and mixed with them, I found where the heartbeat of the nation was, and the more I loved them. There is none among you here present, my brothers, who loves the English people more than I do now.[140]

...My work in England has been more satisfactory to me than in America. The bold, brave, and steady Englishman, if I may use the expression, with his skull a little thicker than those of other people—if he has once an idea put into his brain, it never comes out; and the immense practicality and energy of the race makes it sprout up and immediately bear fruit. It is not so in any other country. That immense practicality, that immense vitality of the race, you do not see anywhere else. There is less of imagination, but more of work, and who knows the well-spring, the mainspring of the English heart? How much of imagination and of feeling is there![141]

On 28 November 1896, from London, he had written to Mary and Harriet Hale:

My ideas about the English have been revolutionised. I now understand why the Lord has blessed them above all other races. They are steady, sincere to the backbone, with great depths of feeling—only with a crust of stoicism on the surface; if that is broken, you have your man.[142]

In a lecture in England, on 'Reason and Religion', Swami Vivekananda was teaching:

---

[140] *CWSV*, Vol. III, p. 310.
[141] Ibid., pp. 311-12.
[142] *SV Letters*, p. 319.

When I say I am separate from you, it is a lie, a terrible lie. I am one with this universe, born one. It is self-evident to my senses that I am one with the universe. I am one with the air that surrounds me, one with heat, one with light, eternally one with the whole Universal Being, who is called this universe, who is mistaken for the universe, for it is He and nothing else, the eternal subject in the heart who says, 'I am,' in every heart—the deathless one, the sleepless one, ever awake, the immortal, whose glory never dies, whose powers never fail. I am one with That.

This is all the worship of the Impersonal, and what is the result? The whole life of man will be changed. Strength, strength it is that we want so much in this life, for what we call sin and sorrow have all one cause, and that is our weakness. With weakness comes ignorance, and with ignorance comes misery. It will make us strong. Then miseries will be laughed at, then the violence of the vile will be smiled at, and the ferocious tiger will reveal, behind its tiger's nature, my own Self. That will be the result. That soul is strong that has become one with the Lord; none else is strong.[143]

However, from the worship of the Impersonal, a concern for the *person*, hence for the *personal* in the ordinary meaning of this word, was never excluded in Vivekananda's thought or life. If it were, the Vedanta would have remained only a cluster of high-sounding slogans, or, to use one of his phrases, 'metaphysical nonsense'. It is only that the very limited notions we have of *person* and *personal* have to be transcended; and of that, we have him as one of the most authentic examples.

---

[143] *CWSV*, I, p. 381.

Talking of 'the worship of the Impersonal',[144] Swami Vivekananda was simultaneously feeling concerned with the future, as regards the marriage of his four 'sisters' whom he dearly loved—Mary and Harriet Hale and Isabelle and Harriet McKindley. In talking about him, the two are to be stated together. During his second visit to England, on hearing from Harriet Hale that she was going to get married, he wrote from Wimbledon both to her and to Mary.

To Harriet, in his letter of 17 September 1896, he wrote:

Your very welcome news reached me just now, on my return here from Switzerland. I am very, very happy to learn that at last you have thought it better to change your mind about the felicity of 'Old Maid's Home'.

...Believe me, dear Harriet, perfect life is a contradiction in terms. Therefore we must always expect to find things not up to our highest ideal. Knowing this, we are bound to make the best of everything. From what I know of you, you have the calm power which bears and forbears to a great degree, and therefore I am safe to prophesy that your married life will be very happy.

All blessings attend you and your *fiance*, and may the Lord make him always remember what good fortune was his in getting such a wife as you—good, intelligent, loving, and beautiful. I am afraid it is impossible for me to cross the Atlanatic so soon. I wish I could to see your marriage.[145]

But he sends her a prayer: 'May you be like Uma, chaste and pure throughout life—may your husband be like Shiva,

---

[144] As we will see in the next chapter, the tension between *personal* and *impersonal* will begin to trouble Margaret Noble, to be known two years later, in 1898, as Sister Nivedita.

[145] *SV Letters*, p. 307.

whose life was in Uma!'[146] On the same day he wrote a long letter to Mary Hale:

Today I reached London, after my two months of climbing and walking and glacier seeing in Switzerland.

...It is impossible to express my joy in words at the good news contained in Harriet's letter. I have written to her today. I am sorry I cannot come over to see her married, but I will be present in 'fine body' with all good wishes and blessings. Well, I am expecting such news from you and the other sisters to make my joy complete. Now, my dear Mary, I will tell you a great lesson I have learnt in this life. It is this: 'The higher is your ideal, the more miserable you are'; for such a thing as an ideal *cannot* be attained *in the world*, or in this life even. He who wants perfection in the world is a madman, for it cannot be.

How can you find the infinite in the finite? Therefore I tell you, Harriet will have a most blessed and happy life, because she is not so imaginative and sentimental as to make a fool of herself. She has enough of sentiment as to make life sweet, and enough of common sense and gentleness as to soften the hard points in life which must come to everyone. So has Harriet McKindley in a still higher degree. She is just the girl to make the best of wives, only this world is so full of idiots that very few can penetrate beyond the flesh! As for you and Isabelle, I will tell you the truth, and my 'language is plain'.

You, Mary, are like a mettlesome Arab—grand, splendid. You will make a splendid queen—physically, mentally. You will shine alongside of a dashing, bold, adventurous heroic husband; but, my dear sister, you will make one of the worst of wives. You will take the life out of our easy-going, practical, plodding husbands

146 Ibid., p. 308.

of the everyday world. Mind, my sister, although it is true that there is more romance in actual life than in any novel, yet it is few and far between. Therefore my advice to you is that until you bring down your ideals to a more practical level, you ought not to marry. If you do, the result will be misery for both of you. In a few months you will lose all regard for a commonplace, good, nice, young man, and then life will become insipid. As to sister Isabelle, she has the same temperament as you; only this kindergarten has taught her a good lesson of patience and forbearance. Perhaps she will make a good wife.[147]

Then the Swami talked of two kinds of persons, of which he said he was one and Mary the other, in the classic divide of *either/or*:

There are two sorts of persons in the world. The one—strong-nerved, quiet, yielding to nature, not given to much imagination, yet good, kind, sweet, etc. For such is this world; they alone are born to be happy. There are others again with high-strung nerves, tremendously imaginative, with intense feeling, always going high one moment and coming down the next. For them there is no happiness. The first class will have almost an even tenor of happiness; the last will have to run between ecstasy and misery. But of these alone what we call geniuses are made. There is some truth in the recent theory that 'genius is a sort of madness'.

Now persons of this class, if they want to be great, must fight to finish—clear out the deck for battle. No encumbrance—no marriage, no children, no undue attachment to anything except the one *idea*, and live and die for that. I am a person of this sort. I have taken up the one idea of 'Vedanta' and I have 'cleared the

---

[147] Ibid., pp. 308-09.

deck for action'. You and Isabelle are made of this metal; but let me tell you, though it is hard, *you are spoiling your lives in vain.* Either, take up one *idea*, clear the deck, and to it dedicate the life; or be contented and practical; lower the ideal, marry, and have *a happy life.* Either 'Bhoga' or 'Yoga'—either enjoy this life, or give up and be a Yogi; *none can have both in one.* Now or never, select quick. 'He who is very particular gets nothing,' says the proverb. Now sincerely and really and for ever determine to 'clear the deck for fight'; take up anything, philosophy or science or religion or literature, and let that be your God for the rest of your life. Achieve happiness or achieve greatness. I have no sympathy with you and Isabelle; you are neither for this nor for that. I wish to see you happy, as Harriet has well chosen, or *great.* Eating, drinking, dressing, and society nonsense are not things to throw a life upon—especially for you, Mary. You are rusting away a splendid brain and abilities, for which there is not the least excuse. You must have ambition to be great. I know you will take these rather harsh remarks from me in the right spirit knowing I like you really as much or more than what I call you, my sisters. I had long had a mind to tell you this, and as experience is gathering, I feel like telling you. The joyful news from Harriet urged me to tell you this. I will be overjoyed to hear that you are married also and happy, so far as happiness can be had here, or would like to hear of you as doing great deeds.[148]

Independent of what he was telling Mary about her, and his personal loving concern for her, there are many things in this letter that call for a discussion. I cannot go into them here beyond saying that the neat *either/or* Swami Vivekananda had posed between *bhoga* or *yoga,* and

---

[148] Ibid., pp. 309-10.

between happiness *or* greatness, was not only un-Vedantic but also uncharacteristic of his own teachings generally. The question here is whether in his descriptions of himself and of Mary he was being just to himself and to her. The portrait of one 'clearing the deck for fight' for *one idea* and devoting everything to that, is the portrait of a fanatic, which everything about him was saying he was *not*.

Moreover, the married life of Harriet Hale as Mrs Clarence Woolley did not turn out to be 'blessed and most happy', as he had prophesied. The marriage ended in divorce.[149] Neither did Mary Hale 'make the worst of wives', as her 'loving brother Vivekananda' thought she would. Her marriage to a rich Italian businessman, Carlo Guiseppe Matteini, much older than her, was by all accounts a happy one and she remained devoted to her husband till his last days, when he died at the age of eighty-nine. Many years later, in a letter Josephine MacLeod would write to Alberta, her niece, she would mention Mary's devotion to her husband: 'She is an angel, protecting, loving, honouring him always.'[150]

It is most puzzling that while Swami Vivekananda felt concerned as to what kind of future his four American 'sisters' would have in marriage, we do not find, even once, at any time, his concern about his own surviving three sisters. He never mentioned them.

* * *

Speaking on the Vedanta as the universal basis of life, Swami Vivekananda was saying:

---

[149] Harriet Hale Woolley died in 1929, in Florence.
[150] *SV New Discoveries*, Vol. 6, p. 263.

...Behind everything the same divinity is existing, and out of this comes the basis of morality. Do not injure another. Love everyone as your own self, because the whole universe is one. In injuring another, I am injuring myself; in loving another, I am loving myself. From this also springs that principle of Advaita morality which has been summed up in one word—self-abnegation. The Advaitist says, this little personalised self is the cause of all my misery. This individualised self, which makes me different from all other beings, brings hatred and jealousy and misery, struggle and all other evils. And when this idea has been got rid of, all struggle will cease, all misery vanish.[151]

While it is undeniable that in injuring another one injures oneself, and in loving another one loves oneself, it does not follow that 'this little personalized self' is the cause of *all* misery. Nor must this individualized self that makes one different from other beings necessarily bring hatred and jealousy and misery. Each of those who were giving to Swami Vivekananda his or her abiding love and care, the kind of which are only rarely seen, was doing so from his or her individual self, *different but not separate*, feeling oneness in the reality of being the *other*. The 'other-ness' of the *other* is no negation of the oneness of all life.

It was as the personal self of a mother that Bhubaneswari Devi suffered anxiety and pain, this time on account of her second son Mahendranath, 'Mohin', twenty-six, who had landed in London in the summer of 1896, wanting to study law and become a lawyer. His elder brother, the Swami, whom he had last seen perhaps in 1890, was there. Mohin

---

[151] Swami Vivekananda while speaking on the Vedanta Philosophy at the Graduate Philosophical Society of Harvard University, 25 March 1896. *CWSV*, Vol. I, pp. 364-65.

started living with him at 63 St. George's Road, Pimlico, London, where the Swami was then living and also holding his classes. The others living with him were E.T. Sturdy, thirty-six, Henrietta Muller, around forty-five, John Fox, twenty-three, J.J. Goodwin, twenty-five, who had come with the Swami from America, and Swami Saradananda (Sharat), thirty, whom the Swami had called to help his 'work' in the West. In a letter that the Swami wrote to Sara Bull, he now sought her advice on 'a very serious thing'.[152] He did not want Mohin to be a lawyer, although their father had been a lawyer (and the Swami himself had studied law but did not take the final examination, for Sri Ramakrishna had appeared in his life meanwhile). Instead, he wanted him to study the science of electricity, and wanted him to go to America for that purpose. But Mahendra had *his* ideas of what he wanted to do. For the time being, he was attracted to the famous Reading Room of the British Museum and it is there that he wanted to spend his time, studying books on law. Also, the little 'household' that had gathered around Swami Vivekananda at 63 St. George's Road was far from being a harmonious, happy household. It was a little theatre of the petty workings of the petty self [153] even as the Swami was giving those soul-stirring talks on *raja-yoga*, in one of which he was saying, the theme of all his teachings *and* of his life: 'The last and highest manifestation of Prana (life force) is love. The moment you have succeeded in manufacturing love out of Prana, you are free. It is the hardest and the greatest thing to gain.'

---

[152] Cited in *SV New Discoveries*, Vol. 4, pp. 179-80.
[153] For details, Ibid., pp. 177–79.

Neither Sturdy nor Miss Muller, 'who dislike each other very much indeed',[154] was greatly interested in manufacturing love out of life force, prana. She had taken a great dislike to Mahendra besides, and was being very rude to him, the Swami did not fail to notice; nor did she particularly love Goodwin or Fox. Sturdy, whom the Swami in some of his letters addressed as 'Blessed and Beloved', would soon turn insolent to the Swami himself. As mentioned earlier, Sturdy, having practised asceticism in the Himalayas, equated asceticism with spirituality and accused the Swami of showing no signs of it. In the eyes of Sturdy, the Swami, after the exhaustion of holding classes and giving lectures, happily drawing on his pipe with some good tobacco in it, was no symbol of 'spirituality' either. Although it would be in the November of 1899 that Josephine MacLeod would write to Nivedita about Sturdy, her perceptions of him were already in the *now* of 1896: 'Poor Sturdy! You have tried to limit the Limitless by your little yard measure— & you couldn't even come up to the knee!'[155] Henrietta Muller had made the air so unpleasant that the Swami sent Mahendra away, and John Fox left too. Simultaneously with these happenings at 63 St. George's Road, the Rev. Hugh Reginald Haweis, Curate of St. James's Church at Marylebone, London, was giving two sermons at his church on the importance of Swami Vivekananda's teachings. He sent to him a collection of his own sermons at his church, inscribing the book with the words: 'To the Master Vivekananda from one who both reverences and admires his teachings, H.R. Haweis.'[156]

---

[154] John Fox reported to Sara Bull; Ibid., Vol. 4, p. 179.
[155] Ibid., p. 177.
[156] Ibid., p. 193.

Just as Margaret Noble was the greatest gain of the Master Vivekananda during his previous visit to London, Charlotte Elizabeth Sevier and her husband, Captain James Henry Sevier, a non-commissioned officer in the British army, were those of this second visit. Josephine MacLeod would recall later that Captain Sevier, coming out of the hall after hearing one of the lectures by the Swami, asked her with that characteristic English scepticism: 'Do you know this young man? Is he really what he seems?' Joe's one-word answer 'Yes' carried such conviction and feeling that the Captain made up his mind then and there: 'In that case one must follow him and with him find God.' The husband and wife asked each other's permission to follow Swami Vivekananda. No impulse of the moment, no gushing of a passing emotion, Charlotte and James Sevier knew for sure that India would thenceforth be their destiny.

Charlotte and James Sevier took the Swami to Switzerland where he could recover his health. It was a party of four, Henrietta Muller being the fourth. The Seviers were with him when, on 9 September 1896, at Kiel, the Swami met Professor Paul Deussen,[157] Professor of Philosophy at the University of Kiel, well known for translating the major Upanishads and for his work on the Vedanta. A few months earlier, on 28 May, at Oxford, the Swami had met Professor Max Mueller,[158] already admired in India for his translation of the *Rig Veda* and of other Indian philosophical texts. In the long line of German Indologists, who in the nineteenth century had made Indian philosophical thought available to the West, Max Mueller and Paul

---

[157] Born, 17 January 1845; died, 6 July 1919.
[158] Born, 6 December 1823; died, 28 October 1900.

Deussen were undoubtedly the most outstanding names. Unlike Max Mueller, Deussen spoke Sanskrit fluently and the Swami was delighted to converse with him in Sanskrit, the flow interrupted only when they suddenly remembered that they had with them two persons, the Seviers, who did not know Sanskrit. The story of Professor Deussen taking the Swami on a quick tour of Germany and Holland does not belong to this book.[159] After that tour, Deussen came with the Swami to London on 16 September. They met practically every day and had long conversations.

It was natural that Swami Vivekananda should have wanted to meet Max Mueller and Paul Deussen, and they him. The last two were, for the major part, in the same flow and Max Mueller was collecting, moreover, the sayings of Sri Ramakrishna and writing a book on his life.[160] It is a different story that whereas Max Mueller's and Deussen's understanding of the Vedanta was mostly textual, that of a scholar, the Swami saw it as a *living* reality, to be recognized in the daily transactions of life and relationships. The Swami was no less a scholar than these two and could recite the *bhashyas*, or the commentaries, with ease; but his Vedanta was *not* confined to the commentaries, no matter by whom, Shankara included. What is puzzling is that Swami Vivekananda should not have wanted to meet Herbert Spencer, whose philosophy had attracted him greatly only a few years

---

[159] Swami Vidyatmananda, in his article 'Swami Vivekananda in Switzerland, 1896', published in the *Prabuddha Bharata*, gives us a vivid picture of the Swami in the mountains of Switzerland. Marie Louise Burke's account, with her comments, of the Swami in the Continent, the reader can see in her *SV New Discoveries*, Vol. 4, pp. 247–303.

[160] It was published in 1898 as *Ramakrishna: His Life and Sayings*.

earlier. John Stuart Mill had attracted him even more. Indeed, he had insisted on his brother-monks studying along with their Bhakti saints and Shankara, the history of Western philosophical thought, more especially of Mill and Herbert Spencer.[161] Mill had died long ago, but Herbert Spencer was still alive and was living in London; he died in 1903. It is true that Spencer found human company increasingly intolerable and in 1896, seventy-six years old, had become practically a recluse, meeting only a few intimate friends, often not even them. However, in the Swami's letters during his months in England, one does not find even a passing mention of his wanting to meet Herbert Spencer—if only to pay Narendranath Datta's tribute to a teacher he had greatly admired but had outgrown.

What is far more puzzling is the inclusion of Henrietta Muller in Swami Vivekananda's recuperating trip to Switzerland, even after his experience of her violent temper and overbearing attitude during the days at 63 St. George's Road. It is true she was one of the hosts of the trip; but Captain and Mrs Charlotte Sevier had begun to find her unbearable. After a while, towards the end of August, she withdrew from the party and returned to London. But during the 'while' that she was with them in Switzerland, which was long enough, 'Miss Muller treated Swami like a dog' Goodwin wrote to Mrs Sara Bull, quoting what the Seviers had told him on return.[162] Still more puzzling is that on his return to England, on 16 September, the Swami came to stay with her at Wimbledon. The fact that that arrangement had been made earlier, before they went to the Continent, is not a sufficient explanation. Everybody

---

[161] See Chapter 3.
[162] *SV New Discoveries*, Vol. 4, p. 277.

by now knew that the Swami was no prisoner of arrangements made earlier; he was a willing prisoner only of his love for others, and of their love for him.

What will ordinarily appear to be puzzling manifests, however, Swami Vivekananda's unending love and grace as much towards those who deserted him and turned against him—Sturdy, Henrietta Muller, Kripananda, Abhayananda—as to those who were, and would ever remain, steadfast in their love of him. This was said earlier in this book but must be repeated here; for if we miss *this*, we miss most of Swami Vivekananda. Yet, his unending love and grace would somehow touch less, because no longer human, if they were not in the simultaneity of his feeling also deeply hurt. He rarely talked about it, but those who were perceptive of him could see it in the way in which he would close his eyes when sometimes those names came up in conversation. Feeling hurt and yet not ceasing to love, and then floating above both, the simultaneity of these in Swami Vivekananda is not to be missed either

On 8 August from Switzerland he wrote to Goodwin:

...A few days ago, I felt a sudden irresistible desire to write to Kripananda. Perhaps he was unhappy and thinking of me. So I wrote him a warm letter. Today from the American news, I see why it was so. I sent him flowers gathered near the glaciers. Ask Miss Waldo to send him some money and plenty of love. Love never dies. The love of the father never dies, whatever the children may do or be. He is my child. He has the same or more share in my love and help, now that he is in misery.[163]

---

[163] *SV Letters*, pp. 299 and 302. Read the whole letter, pp. 299–302, which is not about Kripananda alone.

And a few days earlier, this to Kripananda:

...I went to the glacier of Monte Rosa yesterday and gathered a few hardy flowers growing almost in the midst of eternal snow. I send you one in this letter hoping that you will attain to a similar spiritual hardihood amidst all the snow and ice of this earthly life...[164]

For the present, the Swami was happy to see Kali (Abhedananda), who had arrived in response to his call to help him preserve the flame of the Vedanta he had ignited in England, and had somehow managed to reach Miss Muller's house in Wimbledon. The simultaneity of this event with the rest had so many different levels of feelings and thoughts—and of memories. The Swami had now with him two of his brother-monks: Saradananda in America and Abhedananda in England. Reluctant to go to the West, Saradananda came only after a devastating letter to him from the Swami;[165] therefore, when Abhedananda was asked to come to England, he set out straightaway. Indeed, if he had to swim all the seas between India and England, Abhedananda would have done even that.

Rested and refreshed after his vacation on the Continent, Swami Vivekananda devoted the next three months to intense spiritual *giving*, the word 'spiritual' to be understood as only a word denoting what actually was a very wide range of that giving. It was not limited to what he was giving in his classes at 39 Victoria Street, London, to which he had shifted from Henrietta Muller's house in Wimbledon.

---

[164] Ibid., p. 299.
[165] Vivekananda to Sharat (Saradananda), letter dated 23 December, 1895, from New York. *SV Letters*, pp. 273–75.

We have to read his letters of this period to Shashi,
Alasinga Perumal, to Mary Hale, to the other three
'sisters', to Sara Bull, to Josephine MacLeod and to
several others to understand the range of that giving.
Those are letters addressed to us as well.

In his very long letter of 1 November 1896 to Mary
Hale, her 'ever faithful brother, Vivekananda' was saying:

'Gold and silver,' my dear Mary, 'have I none, but what I have
I give to thee' freely, and that is the knowledge that the goldness
of gold, the silverness of silver, the manhood of man, the womanhood
of woman, the reality of everything is the Lord—and that this
Lord we are trying to realize from time without beginning in the
objective, and in the attempt throwing up such 'queer' creatures
of our fancy as man, woman, child, body, mind, the earth, sun,
moon, stars, the world, love, hate, property, wealth, etc.: also
ghosts, devils, angels and gods, God, etc.

The fact being that the Lord is in us, we are He, the eternal
subject, the real ego, never to be objectified, and that all this
objectifying process is a waste of time and talent. When the soul
becomes aware of this, it gives up objectifying and falls back
more and more upon the subjective. This is the evolution, less and
less in the body and more and more in the mind—man in the
highest form, meaning in Sanskrit manas, thought—the animal
that thinks and not the animal that 'senses' only. This is what in
theology [is] called 'renunciation'. The formation of society, the
institution of marriage, the love for children, our good works,
morality, and ethics are all different forms of renunciation. All our
lives in every society are the subjection of the will, the thirst, the
desire. This surrender of the will or the fictitious self—or the
desire to jump out of ourselves, as it were—the struggle still to
objectify the subject—is the one phenomenon in this world of
which all societies and social forms are various modes and stages.

Love is the easiest and smoothest way towards the self-surrender or subjection of the will, and hatred, the opposite.[166]

But neither in this letter to Mary Hale nor in his public teachings did Swami Vivekananda pretend that there could ever be a world in which there would only be subjection of will and not subjecting the *other* to one's will, love and not hatred, only good and no evil. Rather, he talked of their simultaneity in history. Since history is not separate from the subjective, he talked of their simultaneous existence in the self.

...Objective society will always be a mixture of good and evil—objective life will always be followed by its shadow, death: and the longer the life, the longer will also be the shadow. It is only when the sun is on our own head that *there is no shadow*. When God and good and everything else is in us, there is no evil. In objective life, however, every bullet has its billet—evil goes with every good as its shadow. Every improvement is coupled with an equal degradation. The reason being that good and evil are not two things but one, the difference being only in manifestation—one of degree, not kind.[167]

Our very lives depend upon the death of others—plants or animals or bacilli! The other great mistake we often make is that good is taken as an ever-increasing item, whilst evil is a fixed quantity. From this it is argued that evil being diminished every day, there will come a time when good alone will remain. The fallacy lies in the assumption of a false premise. If good is increasing, so is evil. My desires have been much more than the desires of the masses among my race. My joys have been much greater than

---

[166] *SV Letters*, pp. 315-16.
[167] Ibid., p. 316.

theirs—but my miseries a million times more intense. The same constitution that makes you feel the least touch of good makes you feel the least of evil too. The same nerves that carry the sensations of pleasure carry the sensations of pain too—and the same mind feels both.[168]

Familiar with the Western philosophies of 'progress', advocating the new faith in 'unhampered happiness' as the goal of mankind, the Swami said something on that in the same letter to Mary Hale:

The progress of the world means more enjoyment and more misery too. This mixture of life and death, good and evil, knowledge and ignorance is called Maya—or the universal phenomenon. You may go on for eternity inside this net, seeking for happiness—you find much, and much evil too. To have good and no evil is childish nonsense. Two ways are left open—one by giving up all hope to take up the world as it is and bear the pangs and pains in the hope of a crumb of happiness now and then. The other, to give up the search for pleasure, knowing it to be pain in another form and seek for *truth*—and those that dare try for truth succeed in finding that truth as ever present—present in themselves. Then we also discover how the same truth is manifesting itself both in our relative error and knowledge—we find also that the same truth is bliss which again is manifesting itself as good and evil, and with it also we find real existence which is manifesting itself as both death and life.[169]

On the notion of 'progress', a fundamental presupposition in the nineteenth-century West, the Swami was writing

---

[168] Ibid., pp. 316-17.
[169] Ibid., p. 317.

on 8 August 1896, from Switzerland, to Goodwin whom he had left behind in London:

'A good world', 'a happy world', and 'social progress' are all terms equally intelligible with 'hot ice' or 'dark light'. If it were good, it would not be the world. The soul foolishly thinks of manifesting the Infinite in finite matter, Intelligence through gross particles; but at last it finds out its error and tries to escape. This going-back is the beginning of religion, and its method, destruction of self, that is, love. Not love for wife or child or anybody else, but love for everything else except this little self. Never be deluded by the tall talk, of which you will hear so much in America, about 'human progress' and such stuff. There is *no progress* without corresponding digression. In one society there is one set of evils; in another, another. So with periods of history. In the Middle Ages, there were more robbers, now more cheats. At one period there is less idea of married life; at another, more prostitution. In one, more physical agony; in another, a thousand-fold more mental. So with knowledge. Did not gravitation already exist in Nature before it was observed and named? Then what difference does it make to know that it exists? Are you happier than the Red Indians?[170]

To return to what Swami Vivekananda was writing to Mary Hale about the simultaneous existence of happiness and misery, good and evil, knowledge and ignorance, progress and regression:

Thus we realize that all these phenomena are but the reflections, bifurcated or manifolded, of the one existence, truth-bliss-unity— my real Self and the reality of everything else. Then and then only

---

[170] Ibid., pp. 300-01.

is it possible to do good without evil, for such a soul has known and got the control of the material of which both good and evil are manufactured, and he alone can manifest one or the other as he likes, and we know he manifests only good. This is the Jivan-mukta—the living free—the goal of the Vedanta as of all other philosophies.[171]

But the *jivana-mukta* apart, Swami Vivekananda now talked about the simultaneity of the strength and the grave weakness of each of the four main different social callings, the priests (Brahmin), the soldiers (Kshatriya), the traders (Vaishya) and the labourers (Shudra), and unfolded his social vision.

When the priest (Brahmin) rules, there is a tremendous exclusiveness on hereditary grounds; the persons of the priests and their descendants are hemmed in with all sorts of safeguards—none but they have any knowledge—none but they have the right to impart that knowledge. Its glory is, that at this period is laid the foundation of sciences. The priests cultivate the mind, for through the mind they govern.

The military (Kshatriya) rule is tyrannical and cruel, but they are not exclusive; and during that period arts and social culture attain their height.

The commercial (Vaishya) rule comes next. It is awful in its silent crushing and blood-sucking power. Its advantage is, as the trader himself goes everywhere, he is a good disseminator of ideas collected during the two previous states. They are still less exclusive than the military, but culture begins to decay.

Last will come the labourer (Shudra) rule. Its advantages will be the distribution of physical comforts—its disadvantages, (perhaps)

---

[171] Ibid., p. 317.

the lowering of culture. There will be a great distribution of ordinary education, but extraordinary geniuses will be less and less.

If it is possible to form a state in which the knowledge of the priest period, the culture of the military, the distributive spirit of the commercial, and the ideal of equality of the last can all be kept intact, minus their evils, it will be an ideal state. But is it possible?[172]

Yet the first three have their day. Now is the time for the last—they must have it—none can resist it…I am a socialist not because I think it is a perfect system, but half a loaf is better than no loaf.[173]

The other systems have been tried and found wanting. Let this one be tried—if for nothing else, for the novelty of the thing. A redistribution of pain and pleasure is better than always the same persons having pains and pleasures. The sum total of good and evil in the world remains ever the same. The yoke will be lifted from shoulder to shoulder by new systems, that is all.

Let every dog have his day in this miserable world, so that after this experience of so-called happiness they may all come to the Lord and give up this vanity of a world and governments and all other botherations.[174]

Although in point of time some three years later, but actually at the same time as the above letter was written to Mary Hale, Swami Vivekananda was writing to Mrs Mrinalini Bose, on 3 January 1899, from Deoghar:

What, again, is the meaning of liberty?

Liberty does not certainly mean the absence of obstacles in the path of misappropriation of wealth, etc. by you and me, but

---

[172] Ibid., pp. 317-18.
[173] Ibid., p. 318.
[174] Ibid.

it is our natural right to be allowed to use our own body, intelligence, or wealth according to our will, without doing any harm to others; and all the members of a society ought to have the same opportunity for obtaining wealth, education, or knowledge.[175]

...Freedom in all matters, i.e. advance towards Mukti, is the worthiest gain of man. To advance oneself towards freedom— physical, mental, and spiritual—and help others to do so, is the supreme prize of man. Those social rules which stand in the way of the unfoldment of this freedom are injurious and steps should be taken to destroy them speedily. Those institutions should be encouraged by which men advance in the path of freedom.[176]

Beauty and peace are the two characteristics of true freedom. Enchanted by the beauty and peace of the Alps while in Switzerland, the Swami dreamt his Himalayan dream, of which he talked to the Seviers of course. But he shared it with his four Chicago 'sisters' as well. On 28 November 1896, he wrote to them:

I feel impelled to write a few lines to you before my departure for India. The work in London has been a roaring success...Capt. and Mrs. Sevier and Mr. Goodwin are going to India with me to work and spend their own money on it!

...Now I am going to start a centre in Calcutta and another in the Himalayas. The Himalayan one will be an entire hill about 7,000 ft. high—cool in summer, cold in winter. Capt. and Mrs. Sevier will live there, and it will be the centre for European workers, as I do not want to kill them by forcing on them the Indian mode of living and the fiery plains. My plan is to send

---

[175] Ibid., p. 385.
[176] Ibid., p. 386. Included in what I have described as *Swami Vivekananda's Testament*, Chapter 8; and repeated here.

out numbers of Hindu boys to every civilized country to preach—
get men and women from foreign countries to work in India.
This would be a good exchange. After having established the centres,
I go about up and down like the gentlemen in the book of Job.[177]

The Seviers sold whatever property they owned in
England, left everything that had been their life hitherto,
and came to India with Swami Vivekananda to give
practical shape to his Himalayan dream. What is now
famous as the Advaita Ashrama at Mayavati, Almora,
in the Himalayas, we owe to those two, Captain and Mrs
Charlotte Sevier. To Josiah John Goodwin, the professional
stenographer who had decided to dedicate his life to the
Swami and to his work, we owe the preserved lectures of
the Swami in America and England between December
1895 and December 1896. On 16 December 1896, with
the Seviers and Goodwin, Swami Vivekananda set sail for
India. Captain Sevier would never see England again. Nor
would Goodwin. There was another person who came
to India with the Swami—Henrietta Muller.

The Swami reached Colombo on 15 January 1897, where
he stayed for four days and was given 'a most enthusiastic
reception' by the Buddhists and Hindus alike.[178] From
Colombo he travelled to Jaffna and then crossing over to
the mainland of India, to those places which he had walked
during his parivrajaka days—Rameswaram, Ramnad,
Madurai and Kumbakonam. At each of these places he
was shown the greatest honour for his triumphant work

---

[177] SV Letters, p. 319.
[178] The Indian Mirror, 21 January 1897; see SV in Indian Newspapers,
pp. 124–25.

in the West.[179] Finally, he reached Madras where he stayed for nine days, from 6 to 15 February.[180]

Physically exhausted by the emotional upsurge surrounding him, he took a boat rather than the train to Calcutta and arrived there on 19 February. A special train brought him from the Budge Budge landing to the Sealdah railway station next morning to a rapturous welcome, reported in the newspapers in ecstatic words.

In its long editorial, the *Indian Mirror* of 21 January 1897 had written:

...We cannot yet understand the far-reaching consequences of the work, which Vivekananda has achieved. The gift of the Seer has not been vouchsafed to us, and the inspiration of prophecy is not one of our acquirements. But if the present be the best prophet of the future, 'if coming events cast their shadows before', we may take it upon ourselves to say that Vivekananda has forged the chain, which is to bind the East and the West together—the golden chain of a common sympathy, of a common humanity, and a common and universal religion. Vedantism, as preached and inculcated by the Swami, is the bridge of love, which is to extend from the East right away to the West, and make the two nations one in heart, one in spirit and one in faith—a consummation so devoutly to be wished. Can humanity, then, be ever too thankful to Vivekananda? Can his fellow-countrymen be ever too proud of him or be ever too grateful to him?[181]

---

[179] For the details, as reported in the *Indian Mirror* (to take only one newspaper), see Ibid., pp. 128–36.
[180] For a contemporary personal account of these days, see K. Sundararama Iyer, in *Reminiscences*, pp. 71–97.
[181] *SV in Indian Newspapers*, p. 125.

Simultaneously with the euphoric and frenzied jubilation over Swami Vivekananda's return home, words of hatred and strong criticism were being hurled at him, both in Madras and Calcutta. That was partly because of what he had said in his Madras address, about the conduct of the Indian Theosophists joining the American Christian missionaries in spreading the vilest lies about him. He was only stating the truth. But when has truth not invited hatred and calumny at the same time as love and reverence? What was Swami Vivekananda's attitude towards their simultaneity flowing on to him?

The missionary calumny had stopped but P.C. Mazoomdar, the Brahmo leader, was still busy in Calcutta spreading scandalous canards about the Swami. On hearing from Brahmananda (Rakhal) about it, the Swami's response, written from Florence, on 20 December 1896, on his voyage back to India, was brief: 'Take no heed of Mazoomdar's madness. He surely has gone crazy with jealousy. Such foul language as he has used would only make people laugh at him in a civilized country. He has defeated his purpose by the use of such vulgar words.' Totally untroubled by Mazoomdar, the Swami requested Brahmananda: 'If there are oranges in Calcutta send a hundred to Madras care of Alasinga, so that I may have them when I reach Madras.'[182] He meant it literally but I believe that he was saying something metaphorically as well: 'when a victim of calumny, have some fruits—and laugh.'

Next year, on 27 February 1898, Sri Ramakrishna's birthday had to be celebrated not at Dakshineswar but somewhere else because, influenced by the orthodox

<hr>

[182] Ibid., p. 321.

Brahmanical criticism of Swami Vivekananda eating with Europeans, the proprietor of the Kali temple would not permit him even to enter the courtyard of the temple! Like a detached witness, he observed the simultaneity of *this* with the frenzied welcome to him at the Sealdah railway station. Although not in such extreme forms, he had already experienced such simultaneity during his days in the West. As regards his attitude towards it, he once wrote to Sturdy:

...As for me, I am always in the midst of ebbs and flows. I knew it always and preached always that every bit of pleasure will bring its quota of pain, if not with compound interest. I have a good deal of love given to me by the world; I deserve a good deal of hatred therefore. I am glad it is so—as it proved my theory of 'Every wave having its corresponding dip' on my own person.[183]

Also, what the Swami was experiencing on his person was the simultaneity of spiritual exaltation with shattered

---

[183] In a letter dated 14 September 1899, from Ridgely Manor, to E.T. Sturdy, who was now even more aggressively criticizing the Swami for enjoying 'the luxuries given by his Western friends' and pretending to be a sannyasin. *SV Letters*, pp. 393–94. In the same letter to Sturdy, the Swami said furthermore: 'Mrs. Johnson is of opinion that no spiritual person ought to be ill. It also seems to her now that my smoking is sinful etc. etc. That was Miss Muller's reason for leaving me—my illness. They may be perfectly right, for aught I know—and you too, but I am what I am. In India, the same defects plus eating with Europeans have been taken exception to by many. I was driven out of a private temple by the owners for eating with Europeans. I wish I were malleable enough to be moulded into whatever one desired, but unfortunately I never saw a man who could satisfy everyone. Nor can anyone who has to go to different places possibly satisfy all.

'Of course, it is my own Karma and I am glad that it is so. For, though it smarts for the time, it is another great experience of life, which will be useful either in this or in the next...'

health. At the same time as he was working for the regeneration of India, and for keeping the West from hurling itself mindlessly towards materialistic prosperity only, his asthma was making him suffer physically. Since the humid climate of Calcutta worsened his asthma, he was fleeing from the Alambazar Math either to the hills of Darjeeling or of Almora. Meanwhile, plague was devastating Calcutta, and famine, too, in many parts of Bengal. The direct disciples of Sri Ramakrishna, now awakened to the truth that true spirituality is in uniting the self with the *other*, were working day and night in the areas struck with plague and famine, in complete disregard of their own health.

Simultaneously with his own worrisome health, Swami Vivekananda was worrying about the education of Indian women. No Indian woman had responded to his passionate call, not even Sarala Ghoshal, from whom, since she was a highly educated woman, the Swami had expectations. An Irish woman, Margaret Noble of Wimbledon, did. On 29 July 1897, from Almora, the Swami wrote to her:

Let me tell you frankly that I am now convinced that you have a great future in the work for India. What was wanted was not a man, but a woman; a real lioness, to work for the Indians, women specially.

India cannot yet produce great women, she must borrow them from other nations. Your education, sincerity, purity, immense love, determination, and above all, the Celtic blood make you just the woman wanted.

Yet the difficulties are many. You cannot form any idea of the misery, the superstition, and the slavery that are here. You will be in the midst of a mass of half-naked men and women with quaint ideas of caste and isolation, shunning the white skin through fear or hatred and hated by them intensely. On the other hand, you will be looked upon by the white as a crank, and every one of your movements will be watched with suspicion.

Then the climate is fearfully hot: our winter in most places being like your summer, and in the south it is always blazing.

Not one European comfort is to be had in places out of the cities. If, in spite of all this, you dare venture into the work, you are welcome, a hundred times welcome. As for me, I am nobody here as elsewhere, but what little influence I have, shall be devoted to your service.

You must think well before you plunge in, and after work, if you fail in this or get disgusted, on my part I promise you, *I will stand by you unto death* whether you work for India or not, whether you give up Vedanta or remain in it.[184]

Margaret Noble arrived in Calcutta on 28 January 1898. Swami Vivekananda was at the docks to receive her. On 25 March, he initiated her into the life of the Ramakrishna Order he had brought into being a year earlier and gave her the name 'Nivedita' or 'the Dedicated'. The ceremony over, he asked her to offer flowers at the feet of the Buddha, and in a voice choked with emotion said to her: 'Go thou and follow him, who was born and gave His life for others FIVE HUNDRED TIMES before he attained the vision of the Buddha.'

The irony here enables us to understand Swami Vivekananda still more clearly, for there could be no sharper contrast between the Buddha and him than in their respective attitudes to women. In the vision of the Buddha, woman had not only no place, being incapable of 'going-forth', but was also perceived as a potential destroyer of what he had built upon that vision. In initiating a woman

---

[184] Ibid., p. 363.

into the life of the Ramakrishna Order, Swami Vivekananda was making up, as it were, for the Enlightened One's unenlightened view of woman. Lord Buddha had declared woman as a potential destroyer of religious systems; Swami Vivekananda had been declaring woman as the redeemer of civilization. But, then, the Swami had also declared, nearly a decade earlier, 'Lord Buddha is my Ishta—my God. He preached no theory about Godhead—he was himself God, I fully believe it.'[185] In a letter to Sarala Ghoshal, he said, 'By Ishta is meant the object of love and devotion.'[186]

When Gotami Pajapati (also, Gautami Prajapati), foster-mother of the Buddha, asked to be initiated into his dhamma and Sangha, she was refused. On her asking the Lord three times to reconsider his decision, she was refused three times and was sent away. After some months, when the Buddha was at Vaishali, she returned; this time her hair cut, clad in a yellow robe, her feet swollen, because she had walked a long distance from Kapilavasthu. She again asked the Buddha to accept her into his Order as a renouncer of the world and was refused again. At this point, Ananda, his disciple and his intimate personal attendant, interceded; for Gotami was crying, and he felt disturbed by seeing the state she was in. He said to the Buddha: 'Mahapajapati Gotami, the aunt of the Lord, was of great service, she was his nurse and foster-mother, and gave him milk, and when his mother died, fed him from her own breast. It were good, Lord, for women to be allowed to go forth...'[187]

---

[185] See his letter of 'February, 1890', from Ghazipur, to Gangadhar (Akhandananda). *SV Letters*, p. 19.
[186] Ibid., p. 387.
[187] See Edward J. Thomas, *The Life of Buddha as Legend and History*, p. 108, citing *Anguttara-nikaya*, iv 274 and *Vinaya*, ii 253.

The Buddha agreed, but reluctantly. He subjected her ordination, and of women subsequently, to eight conditions, in the Buddhist Cannons called 'Strict Conditions'. Four of them are: a nun even of a hundred years' standing should be the first to salute a monk even if he had been just ordained, and shall be the first to rise as a mark of respect. A nun shall not rebuke a monk, though the monk may rebuke a nun. Every fortnight a nun shall seek instructions from a monk. And no statement (meaning direction) shall issue from a nun to a monk, but it may from a monk to a nun. Pajapati agreed to all the eight conditions and was ordained into the Sangha. But the Buddha did not stop with imposing unequal conditions upon women as nuns. He said to Ananda furthermore:

...if women had not received the going forth in the doctrine and discipline, the religious system (*brahmacariya*) would have lasted long, the good doctrine would have stayed for a thousand years; but as women have gone forth, now the religious system will not last long, now, Ananda, the good doctrine will last only five hundred years. For just as houses, where there are many women and few men, are easily broken into by robbers, even so in the doctrine and discipline in which a woman goes forth the religious system will not last long.[188]

At the First Council, called soon after the *mahaparinirvana* (passing into eternity) of the Buddha, one of the charges brought against Ananda was that he had persuaded the Lord to admit women into the Sangha. Were the First Council to meet again, at the end of the nineteenth century, Swami Vivekananda would be charged with even a greater

---

[188] Ibid., p. 109.

offence. Declaring the Lord Buddha as his Ishta, he had insisted that there *shall* be a Math for women as well, which would in all respects be equal to the Math for male sannyasins and in no way subject to the latter.

That speech by the Enlightened One, that women would blight the Sangha and along with it his dhamma, appears in a great many scholarly works on the Buddha and Buddhism, and is as quickly passed over.[189] It was certainly passed over by Swami Vivekananda. What was also passed over by him is the puzzling simultaneity of a Vedantin, advocating the eternal Self, the atman, having as his Ishta the One who had reasoned that there *is* no permanent entity as the Self and had advocated 'no-Self', *anatta*, instead. This will require a separate discussion. Here it will suffice to say that just as Swami Vivekananda had the courage of truth to say to his brother-monks: 'Who cares for *your* Ramakrishna? You think you understand him, which is mighty little,' he would have said to the First Council, 'Who cares for *your* Buddha? You have reduced him to a set of doctrines. The Buddha is much more than his doctrines.'

What special greatness does his theory of Nirvana confer on him? His greatness lies in his unrivalled sympathy. The high orders of Samadhi etc., that lend gravity to his religion, are almost all there in the Vedas; what are absent there are his intellect and heart,

---

[189] E.J. Thomas points out that while Oldenberg thought the story of Gotami Pajapati to have had indeed a historical basis, another scholar, Miss M.E. Lulius van Goor, rejected the legend entirely. Ibid., p.110. Karen Armstrong, in her *Buddha*, (published by Penguin Books, 2001), does ask the question, 'What are we to make of this misogyny?' but stops short of asking whether the Buddha's fear of women, and hence his dismissal of them as spiritually inferior to men, was compatible with his Enlightenment. See pp. 151–56.

which have never since been paralleled throughout the history of the world.[190]

Swami Vivekananda never seemed to have asked the Buddha, 'Then why did you, the Enlightened One, exclude from your unrivalled sympathy women—excepting that one visit by you to Amrapali, the courtesan of Vaishali?'

A year-and-a half later, Sister Nivedita would write to Josephine MacLeod:

...Oh Yum, what ideals of womanhood Swami holds! Surely no one, not even Shakespeare or Aeschylus when he wrote of Antigone or Sophocles when he created Alcestis had such a *tremendous* conception. As I read over the things he has said to me of them, and as I realise that it is all, every word of it, a trust for the women of the whole world's future—but first and chiefly for them of his own land—it seems a trifle thing whether oneself should ever be worthy or not—and EVERY thing that a heart so great as his should have willed to create.[191]

At the same time as Swami Vivekananda was worrying about his own mother, Bhubaneswari Devi, he was even more concerned about securing a place for Sri Sarada Devi. 'As to money, I have determined first to build some place for Mother, for women require it first,' he wrote to Shivananda (Tarak) from America, in 1894. 'I can send nearly Rs. 7, 000 for a place for Mother. If the place is first secured, then I do not care for anything else.'[192]

---

[190] In his letter to Gangadhar (Akhandananda) cited earlier. *SV Letters*, p. 18.

[191] Her letter dated 18 October 1899, from Ridgely Manor. *Nivedita Letters*, Vol. I, p. 222.

[192] See also Vivekananda to Sanyal, letter dated 14 February 1895, from New York. *SV Letters*, p. 214.

...You have not yet understood the wonderful significance of Mother's life—none of you. But gradually you will know. Without Shakti (Power) there is no regeneration for the world. Why is it that our country is the weakest and the most backward of all countries?— Because Shakti is held in dishonour there. Mother has been born to revive that wonderful Shakti in India; and making her the nucleus, once more will the Gargis and Maitreyis be born into the world...Hence it is her Math that I want first...Without the grace of Shakti nothing is to be accomplished...Hence we must first build a Math for Mother. First Mother (Sri Sarada Devi) and Mother's daughters, then Father (Sri Ramakrishna) and Father's sons— can you understand this?...To me, Mother's grace is a hundred thousand times more valuable than Father's...Please pardon me, I am a little bigoted here as regards Mother.

...Brother, I shall show how to worship the living Durga and then only shall I be worthy of my name.[193]

Swami Vivekananda's *living* Vedanta was inseparable from his passionate concern for the living Durgas, the women of India.[194]

It was not until 2 December 1954 that Sri Sarada Math would come into being, the tangled story of its founding most instructive in many ways.[195]

In her letter of 22 May 1898, from Almora, to her friend Nell Hammond, Nivedita wrote about Sri Sarada Devi whom she had met on 17 March in Calcutta, along with Sara Bull and Josephine. Nivedita's description of her had a different sound:

---

[193] Ibid., p. 182.
[194] See furthermore, for his views on 'Indian Women—Their Past, Present and Future', *The Prabuddha Bharata*, November 1898; see *SV in Indian Newspapers*, pp. 615–17.
[195] But outside the scope of this book.

...She is the very soul of sweetness—*so* gentle and loving and as merry as a girl. You should have heard her laugh the other day when I insisted that the Swami must come up and see us at once, or we would go home. The monk who had brought the message that the Master would delay seeing us was quite alarmed at my moving towards my shoes, and departed post haste to bring him up, and then you should have heard Sarada's laughter! It just pealed out. And she is so tender—'my daughter' she calls me. She has always been terribly orthodox, but all this melted away the instant she saw the first two Westerns—Mrs. Bull and Miss MacLeod, and she tasted food with them! Fruit is always presented to us immediately, and this was naturally offered to her, and she to the surprise of everyone accepted. This gave us all a dignity and made my future work possible in a way nothing else could possibly have done.[196]

...Then you should see the chivalrous feeling that the monks have for her. They always call her 'Mother' and speak of her as 'The Holy Mother'—and she is literally their first thought in every emergency. There are always one or two in attendance on her, and whatever her wish is, it is their command. It is a wonderful relationship to watch. I should love to give her a message from you, if you care to send her one. A monk read the Magnificat in Bengali to her one day for me, and you should have seen how she enjoyed it. She really is, under the simplest, most unassuming guise, one of the strongest and greatest of women.[197]

Some six years later, Nivedita would again write on Sarada Devi, this time to Joe:

...She grows dearer and dearer, so girlish and young and full of life and brightness, and she told me *always* to give you her blessings.

---

[196] *Nivedita Letters*, Vol. I, p. 10.
[197] Ibid., p. 10.

She is always the same. Oh what a comfort, the one person who never changes, ideal Hindu, ideal disciple, ideal *woman* of all place and time.[198]

On 20 June 1899, Swami Vivekananda boarded the S.S. *Golconda* at Calcutta, on his second visit to the West, first to England and then to America, Nivedita and Swami Turiyananda (Hari) with him. Josephine MacLeod had sent the passage money. Nivedita came with him to create among the Western women interest in the education of Indian women and raise funds for the school for girls she had established in Calcutta.

Before leaving, in a talk he gave at the Belur Math on 9 May 1899, the Swami said:

The end should never be lost sight of. For all my respect of the Rishis of yore, I cannot but denounce in the strongest terms their method which they always followed in instructing the people. They always enjoined them to do certain things, but never took care to explain to them why they should do so. This method was pernicious to the very core and instead of enabling men to attain the end, it laid upon their shoulders a mass of meaningless nonsense. They said they kept the end hidden from the view of the people only because they could not understand its real meaning, because they were not worthy recipients of such high instructions. This *adhikarivada*, as they call it, is the result of pure selfishness...Those who were so eager to support the *adhikarivada* ignored the tremendous fact of the infinite possibilities of the human soul...The result is that the grand truths are soon buried under heaps of rubbish and the latter is eagerly held as real truths.[199]

---

[198] Letter dated 'Easter Week 1904', *Nivedita Letters*, Vol. II, p. 646.
[199] Cited in Marie Louise Burke, *SV New Discoveries*, Vol. 5, pp. 13-14.

It was to open every human soul to its infinite possibilities that Swami Vivekananda's work and life were dedicated.

The ship *Golconda* docked at Tilbury Dock on the Thames on 30 July 1899. Sister Christine and Mrs Mary Funke had once travelled hundreds of miles, 'in rain and night', to be with Swami Vivekananda at Thousand Island Park; now they had crossed the Atlantic, to receive him. The simultaneity of *this* with the absence of Sturdy said more than any words could. The Swami stayed in Wimbledon for a fortnight, of which a few days were with Nivedita's mother, sister May and brother Richmond, the whole family receiving him with the utmost love. Simultaneously, the Swami discovered that his London work had virtually collapsed—thanks to Sturdy. He discovered something more: Henrietta Muller, on her return from India, after donating the entire money for purchasing the land for building Belur Math, had been criticizing everything Indian, the Swami and his gurubhais most of all.[200] On 17 August, the two Swamis and the two American women took from Glasgow a boat for New York. The Swami headed towards Ridgely Manor, the country home of the Leggetts, where Josephine and Sara Bull were waiting for him with the utmost eagerness. Nivedita stayed back to

---

[200] On this, Burke says, 'What Miss Muller's grievances were, I do not know, but whatever they may have been, she had returned to England in the early part of 1899 filled with resentment. A stream of criticism (not all of it original) of India, of Swamiji, of his gurubhais, of his work, of the Math, flowed from her lips: the swamis were not ascetic enough; the new Math at Belur had *three* big rooms; Swamiji intervened in the affairs of his family; Hinduism was based on phallic worship, and so on. To Dr . Lewis G. Janes, a staunch and level-headed friend of Swamiji, who was to hear Miss Muller's lecture on India in 1901, it was clear that she was mentally unbalanced.' *SV New Discoveries*, Vol. 5, p. 70.

witness the wedding of her sister May, but soon thereafter joined her Master at Ridgely Manor.

During his second visit to America, if his purpose was still to earn money in the service of India as it was during the first, Swami Vivekananda was reaching out even more to the human universe of self-created pain and suffering—with the message of regeneration and joy. This is not to say that he had not done that earlier. This time he lectured mostly in Northern and Southern California, living at different times in San Francisco, Alameda, Pasadena and Los Angeles. As before, the newspapers were full of him and of his teachings. Many more women were giving him their selfless love, their affectionate care, and devoting their energy to help him deliver his message of the living Vedanta in a fragmented and troubled world.

Of course he visited New York, Detroit and Chicago—the three cities inseparable from the story of his life during his first visit to America. As during his first visit to America, as in all the days in India thereafter, so during this second visit, the Hale family of Chicago remained in the Swami's heart and he in theirs. Meanwhile, time had changed much for them. 'Father Pope' had died in February and the remaining family no longer lived at 541 Dearborn Avenue; indeed, it was scattered. Early in June 1900, the Swami made what he knew would be his last visit to Mary Hale. Of that visit, the only thing that is known is the last scene, recounted by Swami Nikhilananda from what he had heard about it from Josephine MacLeod.

...On the morning of his departure, Mary came to the Swami's room and found him sad. His bed appeared to have been untouched, and on being asked the reason, he confessed that he had spent the whole night without sleep. 'Oh,' he said, almost in a whisper, 'it is so difficult to break human bonds!'[201]

In September 1895, when Swami Vivekananda had come to Paris to witness the marriage of his loving friends Francis Leggett and Betty Sturges,[202] it would be prescient of a future happening which unfolded itself in Paris through August–October 1900. At the time of the Great *Exposition Universelle Internationalle* in Paris, the Sorbonne University had organized a Congress of the History of Religions, to which Max Mueller and Swami Vivekananda were invited. Owing to his poor health, Max Mueller could not come. The Swami gave a talk at the Congress on 7 September. Joe, the Leggetts with their family, Sara Bull, Nivedita, Emma Thursby and Emma Calve—they were all there to hear the Swami. Much was happening to each one of them, independent of their nearness to the Swami; yet all of them were being touched, as always, by the light and grace of that nearness. Much was happening to Nivedita, primarily in relation to the conflict with her Master, and therefore in anguish and suffering. Joe's chief concern was to introduce to Swami Vivekananda many of the great and the grand, including Princess Demidoff, the Duke of Richelieu and Sarah Bernhardt, who had come to Paris for the Great Exposition. To the Swami, the unknown of Paris were of as much interest as the great and the grand, and this he showed during his stay of three months in that centre of European civilization.[203]

---

[201] Swami Nikhilananda, *Vivekananda: A Biography*, pp. 330-31. See also *SV New Discoveries*, Vol. 6, p. 261.
[202] See page 293 of this book.
[203] For details, turn to Marie Louise Burke, *SV New Discoveries*, Vol. 6, Chapter 11.

Emma Calve invited Swami Vivekananda to a tour of Egypt with her and he accepted. Of her, he had said, 'She is a great woman. I wish I saw more of her. It is a grand sight to see a giant pine struggling against a cyclone.' The party consisted of Emma Calve, Josephine MacLeod, the Swami, an occult philosopher called Jules Bois, Pere Hyacinthe, who had given up his monastic vows in a Roman Catholic Order and was called Monsieur Charles Loyson, Mrs Loyson, an American woman he had married (only to regret it)[204] and Hiram Maxim, the inventor of the machine gun. Leaving Paris on 24 October 1900, they travelled by the famous *Orient Express*, breaking the journey in Vienna for three days, through eastern Europe to Constantinople (Istanbul) and then to Cairo. Although her beloved Joe was there, Nivedita did not approve of that strange company and therefore did not go, staying behind with Sara Bull in Brittany.[205] The Swami would himself write, in Bengali, his detailed impressions of that journey, through different histories of different people, which engaged Swami Vivekananda simultaneously with his floating in the region beyond history.

Suddenly ending, in Egypt, his second visit to the West much sooner than his Western friends had expected, Swami Vivekananda set sail for India on 26 November 1900, boarding an Italian ship *Rubattino* at Port Tawfiq, at the south-end of the Suez Canal, reaching Bombay on 6 (or 7) December. Taking a train to Howrah, he arrived,

---

[204] Marie Louise Burke, in her most admirable passion for absolute accuracy of facts, says that the Loysons were actually not members of the party but only co-travellers, they going to Jerusalem. *SV New Discoveries*, Vol. 6, p. 383.
[205] For details, Ibid.

unannounced, at the Belur Math on Sunday, 9 December, to the great delight of everyone.

It is said that one of the reasons for his abruptly ending his days in the West was his premonition that Captain Sevier was dying and he wanted to be with him. Actually, Sevier had died on 28 October 1900 at Almora. Because the Swami was travelling through Europe on his way to Egypt, he could not have known about it. Yet another death, of someone who had given him and to India his selfless love and devotion, deeply saddened the Swami. Not long after his return to the Belur Math, though he himself was in declining health, and the journey was arduous, he set out for Almora, to be with Charlotte Sevier.[206]

Of the Seviers, Swami Vivekananda had said:

...I remember in England Capt. and Mrs. Sevier, who have clad me when I was cold, nursed me better than my own mother would have, borne with me in my weaknesses, my trials; and they have nothing but blessings for me. And that Mrs. Sevier, because she did not care for honour, has the worship of thousands today; and when she is dead, millions will remember her as one of the great benefactresses of the poor Indians.[207]

---

[206] Charlotte Sevier died in England on 20 October 1930, at the age of eighty-three.
[207] In his letter, of *November 1899*, from New York, to E.T. Sturdy. *SV Letters*, p .400.

11

Swami Vivekananda and Vivekananda: The Divided Self

...may I be born again and again, and suffer
thousands of miseries so that I may worship the only
God that exists, the only God I believe in, the sum
total of all souls; and above all, my God the wicked,
my God the miserable, my God the poor of all races,
of all species, is the special object of my worship.
                                    —Swami Vivekananda

Now I am sure my part of the work is done, and I
have no more interest in Vedanta or any philosophy
in the world or the work itself. I am getting ready
to depart to return no more to this hell, this world.
Even its religious utility is beginning to pall me. My
Mother gather me soon to Herself never to come
back any more!
                                    —Vivekananda

Vivekananda appeared within a year of the Swami Vivekananda touching countless hearts and minds of the thinking and the seeking America, many of them deeply. He progressed simultaneously with the Swami Vivekananda rousing, furthermore, the Indian consciousness in a way rarely witnessed before. But, for very valid reasons, Swami Vivekananda kept at least the earliest expressions of it from his brother-monks and from his 'Madras boys'. His letters to them are markedly different in tone and feeling, and consciously so, from those that Vivekananda was writing to his nearest American women friends. In them, we meet two different persons. The Swami Vivekananda, caught in the net of 'work', of 'organization', and their inescapable logic; caught in the web of 'teaching', of 'creating a new order of humanity', as he said, and their inevitable exacting demands upon him— the net of *history*. And his other self, Vivekananda, hearing another call, that of *transcendence*, he could neither ignore nor fulfil, longing for freedom he knew he never would have, tormented mentally and in pain physically, and knowing besides that he did not have much time to live. Their stories, in intimate simultaneity in the same person, are among the most magnificent stories of all times. They have to be *felt* and not simply read.

The key to the conflict lies in the two equally strong but opposite parts of nature dwelling in the same person. The one heard the cries of the poor and the outcasts of society, felt and worked for them so that they regain the human dignity denied to them for centuries. That person wanted to bring back to its spiritual roots a society where the preaching of man's divinity went hand in hand with the acquiescence in his social and moral degradation. He wanted to set up a centre from which would go forth thousands of selfless men and women, sannyasins or householders, first to teach through their own lives that he who is selfish, is dying; he who loves, lives; and then make selfless *men* out of selfish cowards. That required organization, concerted work, funds, money, keeping accurate and scrupulously open accounts, among other things. Organization required strict rules, or *vinaya*, in the terms of the Buddhist Sangha, to which the Buddha was obliged to pay nearly as great attention as to his philosophic teachings. Consisting of human beings, organization inevitably witnesses the power game, one trying to dominate the others, jealousy and resultant schisms. The first schism in the Buddha's Sangha took place in his own lifetime.[1] Being a thorough student of the history of world religions, the Swami Vivekananda was well aware of it, but was caught in a net he had himself woven, a magnificent net but a net nevertheless.

His other self, the other person, Vivekananda, longed for absorption in a state in which all distinctions are dissolved and all human limitations transcended.

But their self-division lies, even more dramatically, in the two events that took place between Narendranath and Sri Ramakrishna before the passing away of the Paramahamsa, narrated in an earlier chapter but to be dwelt on again in the context here. One evening, in fulfilment of his deepest longing to realize from personal experience the meaning of the central utterance of the Upanishads, *aham Brahamasi*, 'I am the *Brahman*, the Absolute', Naren went suddenly into a strangely exalted state, losing all consciousness of his body except his head.[2] Frightened, he cried out to another disciple meditating in the same room, 'Gopalda, Gopalda, where is my body?' When the latter rushed to Sri Ramakrishna for help, the Paramahamsa said with a smile, 'Let him stay in that state for a while. He has teased me long enough for it.' Soon afterwards Naren passed into a deep trance, from which

---

[1] That story is most instructive, but we cannot go into that here.
[2] There is a metaphorical meaning here, that 'he didn't lose his head', as the saying goes.

he emerged only hours later. Thereupon, looking deep into his eyes, Ramakrishna said to Naren, 'Just as a treasure is locked in a box, so will the realization you have just had be locked up and the key shall remain with me. You have work to do. When you will have finished my work, the treasure-box will be unlocked again.' Afterwards the Paramahamsa said to his other disciples, 'The time will come when Naren will shake the world to its foundations.'

The other event took place just four or five days before Sri Ramakrishna died of a cancerous growth in his throat. Always certain of Narendra's own potentialities for great work, the Master called Naren and, looking deep into his eyes, passed into a trance. Precisely at that moment Narendra felt as if a powerful electric shock was going through his body. On coming to, Ramakrishna burst into tears, saying, 'Oh Naren, today I have given you my all and have become a faqir, a penniless beggar.' Thus was transmitted into Narendranath Datta another person who was the very opposite of all that Naren himself was.[3] Narendranath as Swami Vivekananda hardly ever talked about that event; but always felt, and continued to say, in moments of distress most of all, that 'there is a force behind me greater than man, or god, or devil'. Whether or not he believed that any such mystic transmission of one person into another could take place—most probably he didn't— is not of importance. Rather, of great importance is the

---

[3] Frithjof Schuon remarks, 'Each of them was the ideal and the victim of the other.' *Spiritual Perspectives and Human Facts* (Faber and Faber, London; mcmliv), p. 116. The reader may want to have a look at this remarkably profound book and in it, Part Four, on the Vedanta, Chapter 3, pp. 113–25. That contains Schuon's analysis of what he perceives as 'the enigma of Ramakrishna' and of the equally enigmatic 'Ramakrishna–Narendra relationship'.

fact that he passionately believed in the transforming energy of love flowing from one to another, transcending all limitations. And in that he saw the essence of the *living* Vedanta, living himself in that flow.

The Vedanta of Swami Vivekananda acknowledged, as part of Reality, also the energy of hatred born out of fear. The campaign of calumny against him had reached its peak in 1894. But that was not what was primarily disturbing Vivekananda. On 15 March that year, from Detroit, Vivekananda wrote to the Hale and the McKindley girls, the 'Babies':

...So far all is well; but I do not know—I have become very sad in my heart since I am here—do not know why.

I am wearied of lecturing and all that nonsense. This mixing with hundreds of varieties of human animal has disturbed me. I will tell you what is to my taste; I cannot write and I cannot speak, but I can think deeply, and when I am heated, can speak fire. It should be, however, to a select, a very select, few. Let them, if they will, carry and scatter my ideas broadcast—not I. This is only a just division of labour. The same man never succeeded both in thinking and scattering his thoughts. A man should be free to think, especially spiritual thoughts.

I am really not 'cyclonic' at all. Far from it. What I want is not here, nor can I longer bear this 'cyclonic' atmosphere. This is the way to perfection, to strive to be perfect, and to strive to make perfect a few men and women. My idea of doing good is this: to evolve out a few giants, and not to strew pearls before swine, and so lose time, health, and energy.

...Well, I do not care for lecturing anymore. It is too disgusting, this attempt to bring me to suit anybody's or any audience's fads.[4]

---

[4] *SV Letters*, pp. 72-73.

However, two days later, on 17 March, still in Detroit, Vivekananda was happily reporting to Harriet McKindley:

Here is a beautiful young girl. I saw her twice, I do not remember her name. So brainy, so beautiful, so spiritual, so unworldly! Lord Bless her! She came this morning with Mrs. M'cDuvel and talked so beautifully and deep and spiritually—that I was quite astounded. She knows everything about the Yogis and is herself much advanced in Practice!!

'The ways are beyond searching out.' Lord Bless her—so innocent, holy, and pure! This is the grandest recompense in my terribly toilsome, miserable life—the finding of holy, happy faces like you from time to time. The great Buddhist prayer is, 'I bow down to all holy men on earth.' *I feel the real meaning of this prayer whenever I see a face upon which the finger of the Lord has written in unmistakable letters 'mine'.*[5]

On 23 August, Vivekananda wrote to his 'Mother Church', Mrs Hale:

...Every ounce of fame can only be bought at the cost of a pound of peace and holiness. I never thought of that before. I have become entirely disgusted with this blazoning. I am disgusted with myself. Lord will show me the way to peace and purity. Why, Mother, I confess to you—no man can live in an atmosphere of public life even in religion—without the devil of competition now and then thrusting his head into the serenity of his heart. Those who are trained to preach a *doctrine* never feel it for they never knew *religion*. But those that are after God and not after the world—feel at once that every bit of name & fame is at the cost of their purity. It is

[5] Ibid., p. 74. Here, the added emphasis is mine, but it was always Swami Vivekananda's own emphasis.

so much gone from that ideal of perfect unselfishness, perfect disregard of gain, or name and fame. Lord help me—pray for me, Mother. I am very much disgusted with myself. Oh why the world be so that one cannot do anything without putting himself on the front, why cannot one act hidden and unseen and unnoticed. The world has not gone one step beyond idolatry yet. They cannot act from ideas; they cannot be led by ideas, they want the person— the man. And any man that wants to do something must pay the penalty, no hope. This nonsense of the world. Shiva, Shiva, Shiva.[6]

However, in the midst of 'this nonsense of the world', Vivekananda was happy, now for another reason—he had got a beautiful edition of *The Imitation of Christ*. That must have resurrected the memories of Swami Vividishananda and Swami Satchidananda (his two names in those days), who had carried that book along with the *Bhagvad Gita* during his wandering days in India. In the same letter to Mrs Hale, he wrote:

By the by I have got such a beautiful edition of Thomas a Kempis— How I love that old monk. He caught a wonderful glimpse of the [?] behind the veil. Few ever got such. My—that is religion. No humbug of the world. No shilly shallying—tall talk, conjecture—I presume, I believe, I think—How I would like to go out of this piece of painted humbug they call the beautiful world with Thomas a Kempis—beyond beyond—which can only be felt, never expressed. That is religion. Mother, there is God. There all the saints, prophets and incarnations meet. Beyond the Babble of Bibles and Vedas, creeds and crafts, duped and doctrines—where

---

[6] We owe the discovery of this letter to Marie Louise Burke, who cites it in full. *SV New Discoveries*, Vol. 2, pp. 105–06.

is all light, all love—where the miasma of this earth can never reach. Ah! who will take me thither. Do you sympathise with me, Mother?...[7]

About a month later, on 21 September, Vivekananda wrote to Alasinga:

...I hope to return soon to India. I have had enough of this country, and especially as too much work is making me nervous. The giving of too many public lectures and constant hurry have brought on this nervousness. I do not care for this busy, meaningless, money-making life. So you see, I will soon return. Of course, there is a growing section with whom I am very popular, and who will like to have me here all the time. But I think I have had enough of newspaper blazoning, and humbugging of a public life. I do not care the least for it...

There is no hope for money for our project here. It is useless to hope.

...After all, I am getting disgusted with this lecturing business.[8]

On 10 February 1895, from New York, Vivekananda wrote to Mary Hale:

...My health is very much broken down this year by constant work. I am very nervous. I have not slept a single night soundly this winter. I am sure I am working too much, yet a big work awaits me in England.

...Now I am longing for rest. Hope I will get some and the Indian people will give me up. How I would like to become dumb for some years and not talk at all.

---

[7] Ibid., Vol. 2, p. 106.
[8] Ibid., pp. 136-37.

I was not made for these struggles and fights of the world. I am naturally dreamy and restful. I am a born idealist, can only live in a world of dreams; the very touch of fact disturbs my visions and makes me unhappy. Thy will be done!

I am ever, ever grateful to you four sisters; to you I owe everything I have in this country. May you be ever blessed and happy. Wherever I be, you will always be remembered with deepest gratitude and sincerest love. The whole life is a succession of dreams. My ambition is to be a conscious dreamer, that is all.[9]

Vivekananda's letters on this subject became more and more anguished. From Lucerne, Switzerland, on 23 August 1896, he was writing to Mrs Sara Bull:

...I think I have worked enough. I am now going to retire. I have sent for another man from India who will join me next month. I have begun the work, let others work it out. So you see, to set the work going I had to touch money and property for a time. Now I am sure my part of the work *is* done, and I have no more interest in Vedanta or any philosophy in the world or the work itself. I am getting ready to depart to return no more to this hell, this world. Even its religious utility is beginning to pall me. My Mother gather me soon to Herself never to come back any more! These works, and doing good etc. are just a little exercise to cleanse the mind. I had enough of it. This world will be world ever and always. What we are, so we see it. Who works? Whose work? There is no world. It is God Himself. In delusion we call it world. Neither I nor thou nor you—it is all He the Lord, all One. So I do not want anything to do about money matters from this time. It is your money. You spend what comes to you just as you like, and blessings follow you.[10]

---

[9] Ibid., pp. 214-15.
[10] Ibid., p. 304.

Three days after writing to Sara Bull, that he (Vivekananda) had 'no more interest in Vedanta or any philosophy in the world, or in the work itself', Swami Vivekananda was expressing his worry that Indians were wanting in strict business principles, and that was not good for the organization. He wrote to Nanjunda Rao, one of his 'Madras boys':

The work is going on very beautifully, I am very glad to say…I will give you one advice, however. All combined efforts in India sink under the weight of one iniquity—we have not yet developed strict business principles. Business is business, in the highest sense, and no friendship—or as the Hindu proverb says 'eye-shame'—should be there. One should keep the clearest account of everything in one's charge—and never, never apply the funds intended for one thing to any other use whatsoever—even if one starves the next moment. This is business integrity. Next, energy unfailing. Whatever you do let that be your worship for the time…

…Work unto death—I am with you, and when I am gone, my spirit will work with you. This life comes and goes—wealth, fame, enjoyments are only of a few days. It is better, far better to die on the field of duty, preaching the truth, than to die like a worldly worm. Advance![11]

On his return to London from Switzerland, Swami Vivekananda wrote to Alasinga in the same tone:

The Madrasis have more of go and steadiness, but every fool is married. Marriage! Marriage! Marriage!…Then the way our boys are married nowadays!…It is very good to aspire to be a non-attached householder; but what we want in Madras is not that just now—but non-marriage…

---

[11] Ibid., p. 306. Letter dated 26 August 1896.

My child, what I want is muscles of iron and nerves of steel, inside which dwells a mind of the same material as that of which the thunderbolt is made.[12]

Towards the close of his first visit to America, on 24 January 1896, Vivekananda wrote to Sara Bull:

I have worked my best. If there is any seed of truth in it, it will come to life. So I have no anxiety about anything. I am also getting tired of lecturing and having classes. After a few months' work in England I will go to India and hide myself absolutely for some years or for ever. I am satisfied that I did not remain an idle Swami.[13]

On 8 August 1896, from Switzerland, the Swami had written a long letter to J.J. Goodwin in which we hear also Vivekananda: 'I feel as if I had my share of experience, in what they call "work". I am finished. I am longing now to get out.'[14]

Then, from Almora, 15 June 1897, around which time many more things were simultaneously happening in his life, Swami Vivekananda wrote to Akhandananda (Gangadhar):

I am getting detailed reports of you and getting more and more delighted. It is that sort of work which can conquer the world. What do differences of sect and opinion matter? Bravo! Accept a hundred thousand embraces and blessings from me. Work, work, work—I care for nothing else. Work, work, work, even unto death!

I am soon going down to the plains. I am a fighter and shall die in the battlefield.[15]

---

[12] Ibid., p. 311. No date given, only the year '1896'.
[13] Ibid.
[14] Ibid., p. 300.
[15] *SV Letters*, p. 342.

A few days earlier, on 3 June 1897, Vivekananda had written to Margaret Noble:

...As for myself I am quite content. I have roused a good many of our people and that was all I wanted. Let things have their course, and Karma its way. I have no bonds here below. I have seen life, and it is all self—life is for self, love for self, honour for self, everything for self. I look back and scarcely find any action I have done for self—even my wicked deeds were not for self. So I am content; not that I feel I have done anything specially good or great, but the world is so little, life so mean a thing, existence so, so servile— that I wonder and smile that human beings, rational souls, should be running after this self—so mean and detestable a prize.

This is the truth. We are caught in a trap, and the sooner one gets out, the better for one. I have seen the truth—let the body float up and down, who cares?

I was born for the life of a scholar—retired, quiet, poring over my books. But the Mother dispenses otherwise—yet the tendency is there.[16]

On 30 June, Swami Vivekananda was again writing to Akhandananda (Gangadhar):

Monday next, trip to Bareilly, then to Saharanpur, next to Ambala, thence, most probably, to Mussoorie with Captain Sevier, and as soon as it is a little cool, return to the plains and journey to Rajputana etc. Go on working at top speed. Never fear! I, too, have determined to work. The body must go, no mistake about that. Why then let it go in idleness? 'It is better to wear out than rust out'. Don't be anxious even when I die, my very bones will work miracles. We must spread over the whole of India in ten

---

16 Ibid., p. 341.

years, short of this it is no good. To work, like an athlete!—
Victory to the Guru! Money and all will come of themselves, we
want men, not money. It is man that makes everything, what
can money do?[17]

On 9 July 1897, still in Almora, Swami Vivekananda
wrote in a very different tone a long letter to Mary Hale:

...Dear, dear Mary, do not be afraid for me...The world is big,
very big, and there must be some place for me even if the 'Yankees'
(missionaries) rage...Only one thing was burning in my brain—
to start the machine for elevating the Indian masses—and that I
have succeeded in doing to a certain extent.

    ...I had to talk a lot about myself because I owed that to you.
I feel my task is done—at most three or four years more of life
are left. I have lost all wish for my salvation. I never wanted
earthly enjoyments. I must see my machine in strong working
order, and then knowing sure that I have put in a lever for the
good of humanity, in India at least, which no power can drive
back, I will sleep, without caring what will be next; and may I be
born again and again, and suffer thousands of miseries so that I
may worship the only God that exists, the only God I believe in,
the sum total of all souls; and above all, my God the wicked, my
God the miserable, my God the poor of all races, of all species,
is the special object of my worship.[18]

A few days earlier, on 3 July, Swami Vivekananda had
written to Sharatchandra a letter in Sanskrit, stating again
the philosophical premise underlying 'the work': love,
prema, and not compassion, *daya*: 'not to pity but to serve'.

---

[17] Ibid., p. 344.
[18] *SV Letters*, p. 350.

The Lord of all cannot be any particular individual. He must be the sum total. One possessing Vairagya does not understand by Atman the individual ego but the All-pervading Lord, residing as the Self and Internal Ruler in all. He is perceivable by all as the sum total. This being so, as Jiva and Ishvara are in essence the same, serving the Jivas and loving God must mean one and the same thing...Our principle, therefore, should be love, and not compassion. The application of the word compassion even to Jiva seems to me to be rash and vain. For us, it is not to pity but to serve. Ours is not the feeling of compassion but of love, and the feeling of Self in all.[19]

That, and not his trances alone, was the substance of Sri Ramakrishna's life and teachings. But none of his direct disciples understood it at that time, at any rate there is no evidence that any one of them did, except one— Narendranath. Hence, that famous scene between Swami Vivekananda and his brother-monks, described in the previous chapter.

The letter we are reading here was concluded with the Swami saying:

For thy good, O Sharman, may thine be Vairagya, the feeling of which is love, which unifies all inequalities, cures the disease of Samsara, removes the three-fold misery inevitable in this phenomenal world, reveals the true nature of all things, destroys the darkness of Maya, and which brings out the Selfhood of everything from Brahma to the blade of grass![20]

However, the Swami was at the same time aware of the requirements of the phenomenal world as well. They

[19] Ibid., p. 345.
[20] SV Letters, p. 346.

included things like 'proofs' of what was being published and printed, and they had to be free of error. Therefore, simultaneously with writing to Sharatchandra those great thoughts, the Swami was writing to Rakhal (Brahmananda): 'Today I send back the proofs of the Objects of our Association that you sent me, corrected. The rules and regulations portion (which the members of our Association had read) is full of mistakes. Correct it very carefully and reprint it, or people will laugh.'[21]

Just as the 'proofs' were to be corrected with care, Swami Vivekananda was worrying also that the accounts of the money donated to the work were to be maintained accurately.[22] Brahmananda and Saradananda began to resent the Swami's insistence that accurate accounts be produced and sent to Mrs Sara Bull. They felt he distrusted them, which of course he did *not*.[23] It was not about accounts alone; the Swami was anxious that, in the organization he had set up, responsibility be shared by all. On 1 August 1898, from Srinagar, he wrote a sharp letter to Brahmananda:

You are always under a delusion, and it does not leave you because of the strong influence, good or bad, of other brains. It is this: whenever I write to you about accounts, you feel that I have no confidence in you...My great anxiety is this: the work has somehow been started, but it should go on and progress even when we are not here; such thoughts worry me day and night. Any amount of theoretical knowledge one may have; but unless one does the

---

[21] Ibid., p. 346.

[22] For Vivekananda's precise instructions to Brahmananda as regards account-keeping, read his letter dated 12 October 1897, written from Murree; Ibid., pp. 371-72.

[23] Turn again to Chapter10, Saradananda writing to Mrs Sara Bull about what he mistakenly thought to be the Swami's 'inherent suspicious nature'.

thing actually, nothing is learnt. I refer repeatedly to election, accounts, and discussion so that everybody may be prepared to shoulder the work...We Indians suffer from a great defect; viz. We cannot make a permanent organisation—and the reason is we never like to share power with others and never think of what will come after we are gone.[24]

Eight weeks later if counted in days, but in his inwardness simultaneously, Vivekananda went away, alone, to Kshir Bhawani, the temple of Mother Kali, and returned to Srinagar on 6 October. On 13 October (1898), Nivedita was writing about him to someone not identified:

A fortnight ago, he went away alone, and it is about 8 days since he came back, like one transfigured and inspired.

I cannot tell you about it. It is too great for words. My pen would have to learn to whisper.

He simply talks, like a child, of 'the Mother'—but his soul and voice are those of a God.

...To him at this moment 'doing good' seems horrible. 'Only the Mother' does anything. 'Patriotism is a mistake. Everything is a mistake'—he said when he came home. 'It is all Mother...*All* men are good. Only we cannot *reach* all...I am never going to teach any more. Who am I, that I shd. teach anyone?'

Silence and austerity and withdrawal are the keynotes of life to him just now and the withdrawal is too holy for us to touch.

...He is *all* love now. There is not an impatient word, even for the wrongdoer or the oppressor, it is all peace and self-sacrifice and rapture. 'Swamiji is dead and gone' were the last words I heard him say.[25]

---

[24] *SV Letters*, p. 382.
[25] *Nivedita Letters*, Vol. 1, pp. 24-25.

On the same day, she wrote a fuller letter about him to the same unidentified person, in which she said furthermore:

...My own feeling (mind that is all) is that the ascetic impulse has come upon him overwhelmingly and that he may never visit the West or even teach again. Nothing would surprise one less than his taking the vow of silence and withdrawing forever. But perhaps the truth is that in his case this would not be strength, but self indulgence and I can imagine that he will rise even above this mood and become a great spring of healing and knowledge to the world.

...Only all the carelessness and combativeness and pleasure-seeking have gone out of life and he speaks and replies to a question with the greatness and gentleness of a soul as large as the universe, all bruised and anguished, yet all Love. To say anything to him seems sacrilege and curiously enough the only *language* that does not seem unworthy of his Presence is a joke or a witty story—at which we all laugh. For the rest—one's very breath is hushed at the holiness of every moment.

Can I tell you more? The last words I heard him say were 'Swamiji is dead and gone' and again, 'there is bliss in torture'. He has no harsh word for anyone. In such vastness of mood Christ was crucified.[26]

But Swamiji was *not* dead and gone, although that is what Vivekananda had announced to Nivedita, neither jubilantly nor with sadness, just a quiet announcement coming from the silence of his innermost. After announcing firmly '*I* am never going to teach any more. Who am I that I should teach anyone?' and despite Nivedita's fear that he might never visit the West again, Swami Vivekananda was boarding, on 20 June 1899, S.S. *Golconda* on his

---

[26] Ibid., Vol. 1, p. 26.

second voyage to the West, to teach whoever was seeking.
Nivedita and Hari (Turiyananda) were with him.

On 27 December 1899, from Los Angeles, Swami
Vivekananda had written to Sara Bull, 'I am very much
more peaceful, and find that the only way to keep my
peace is to teach others. Work is my only safety valve.'[27]
Divided between the drive for work and longing for inner
peace, on 24 January 1900, from Los Angeles, he now
wrote a brief letter, very different in tone, to Nivedita:

I am afraid the rest and peace I seek for will never come. But Mother
does good to others through me, at least to some in my native
land, and it is easier to be reconciled to one's fate as a sacrifice. We
are all sacrifices—each in his own way. The great worship is going
on—no one can see its meaning except that it is a great sacrifice.
Those that are willing, escape a lot of pain. Those who resist are
broken into submission and suffer more. I am now determined to
be a willing one.[28]

Vivekananda was hearing the chiming of the bells of a greater
worship in which 'country', 'church', 'organization', 'work',
'cause', are only as many limitations and 'sacrifice' perhaps
yet another self-congratulatory illusion. Whatever the heroic
words of Swami Vivekananda, his other self, Vivekananda,
was determined not to be broken into submission. And
he knew he did not have much longer to live.

On 4 March 1900, Vivekananda wrote to Nivedita:

I don't want to work. I want to be quiet, and rest. I know the
time and the place; but the fate or Karma, I think, drives me

---

[27] *SV Letters*, p. 407.
[28] Ibid., pp. 408-09.

on—work, work. We are like cattle driven to the slaughter-house—
hastily nibbling a bite of grass on the roadside as they are driven
along under the whip. And all this is our work, our fear—fear,
the beginning of misery, of disease, etc. By being nervous and
fearful we injure others. By being so fearful to hurt we hurt more.
By trying so much to avoid evil we fall into its jaws.

    ...Oh, to become fearless, to be daring to be careless of
everything![29]

On 12 March, Vivekananda was writing to Rakhal
(Brahmananda):

...Now, brother, all of you are Sadhus and great saints. Kindly pray
to the Mother that I do not have to shoulder all this trouble and
burden any longer. Now I desire a little peace; it seems there is no
more strength left to bear the burden of work and responsibility.
Rest and peace for the few days that I shall yet live...No more
lectures or anything of that sort. Peace!

    As soon as Sharat (Saradananda) sends the trust-deed of the
Math, I shall put my signature to it. You all manage—truly I
require rest.[30]

Towards the close of his second visit to America,
Vivekananda wrote to Mary Hale, on 22 March 1900,
from San Francisco:

You are correct that I have many other thoughts to think besides
Indian people; but they have all to go to the background before
the all-absorbing mission—my Master's work.

    I would that this sacrifice were pleasant. It is not, and naturally
makes one bitter at times; for know, Mary, I am yet a man and
cannot wholly forget myself; hope I shall some time. Pray for me.

---

[29] Ibid., p. 413.
[30] Ibid., p. 414.

...I do not want to work any more. My nature is the retirement of a scholar. I never get it! I pray I will get it now that I am all broken and worked out.[31]

On 17 June, from Los Angeles, he again wrote to Mary Hale:

I am dead tired of the platform work for a living. It does not please me any more. I retire and do some writing if I can do some scholarly work.

I have worked for this world, Mary, all my life and it does not give me a piece of bread without taking a pound of flesh. If I can get a piece of bread a day, I retire entirely, but this is impossible—this is the increasing purpose that is unfolding all the devilish inwardness, as I am growing older!

...P.S. If ever a man found the vanity of things, I have it now. This is the world, hideous, beastly corpse. Who thinks of helping it is a fool! But we have to work out our slavery by doing good or evil; I have worked it out, I hope. May the Lord take me to the other shore! Amen! I have given up all thoughts about India and other land. I am now selfish, want to save myself![32]

Just when Swami Vivekananda had put in working order his machine for India's uplift, and for the spread of the gospel of love in the oneness of all life, he renounced any place in it for himself. *By a legally registered will* he relinquished his power over the property and the organization of the Ramakrishna Math and Mission to Swami Brahmananda (Rakhal) and others in succession, giving Vivekananda the freedom he had wanted for so long. On 25 August 1900, from Paris, where he had the trust deeds executed at the British Consulate, he wrote to Nivedita:

---

[31] Ibid., p. 415.
[32] *SV Letters*, pp. 427-28.

...Now I am free, as I have kept no power or authority or position for me in the work. I also have resigned the Presidentship of the Ramakrishna Mission.

The Math etc. belong now to the immediate disciples of Ramakrishna except myself.

I am so glad a whole load is off me, now I am happy. I have served Ramakrishna through mistakes and success for 20 years[33] now. I retire for good and devote the rest of my life to myself.

I no longer represent anybody, nor am I responsible to anybody. As to my friends, I had a morbid sense of obligation. I have thought well and find I owe nothing to anybody—if anything, I have given my best energies, unto death almost, and received only hectoring and mischief-making and botheration. I am done with everyone here and in India.[34]

A few days later, on 1 September, he wrote to Hari (Turiyananda):

...I am somewhat freed from worries; that is to say, I have signed the trust-deed and other things and sent them to Calcutta. I have not reserved any right or ownership for myself. You now possess everything and will manage all work by the Master's grace.

I have no longer any desire to kill myself by touring. For the present I feel like settling down somewhere and spending my time among books.

...Brother, free me from all work connected with preaching. I am now aloof from all that, you manage it yourselves. It is my firm conviction that Mother will get work done through all of you a hundred times more than through me.[35]

---

[33] 20 years?
[34] *SV Letters*, pp. 431-32.
[35] Vivekananda to Hari (Turiyananda), letter dated 1 September 1900, from Paris. *SV Letters*, p. 434.

About six weeks later, 14 October, still in Paris, he wrote to Sister Christine, writing his letter (most of it) in French which he had learnt quite well but said modestly, 'I have no time any more, nor the power to learn a new language at my age. I am an old man, isn't it?'[36]

...I am sending all the money I earned in America to India. Now I am free, the begging-monk as before. I have also resigned from the presidentship of the Monastery. Thank God, I am free! It is no more for me to carry such a responsibility. I am so nervous and so weak. 'As the birds which have slept in the branches of a tree wake up, singing when the dawn comes, and soar up into the deep blue sky, so is the end of my life.'

I have had many difficulties, and also some very great successes. But all my difficulties and suffering count for nothing, as I have succeeded. I have attained my aim. I have found the pearl for which I dived into the ocean of life. I have been rewarded. I am pleased.

Thus it seems to me that a new chapter of my life is opening. It seems to me that Mother will now lead me slowly and softly. No more effort on roads full of obstacles, now it is the bed prepared with birds' down. Do you understand that? Believe me, I feel quite sure.[37]

---

[36] The Swami had begun to play with, and seemingly enjoy, his notion of being 'an old man'. In the long letter he had written on 25 July 1897 from Almora to Marie Halboister, he had said—at age 34—also this: 'I am glad to find that I am aging fast, my hair is turning grey. "Silver threads among the gold"—I mean black—are coming in fast. It is bad for a preacher to be young, don't you think so? I do, as I did all my life. People have more confidence in an old man, and it looks more venerable. Yet the old rogues are the worst rogues in the world, isn't it? The world has its code of judgement which, alas, is very different from that of truth's...(In three paragraphs in the original letter, here these lines are combined in one.); Ibid., pp. 360-61.

[37] Ibid., pp. 439-40.

In the letter Vivekananda had written on 23 August 1896 from Lucerne, Switzerland, to Sara Bull, he had also said as a postscript: 'I have given up the bondage of iron, the family tie—I am not to take up the golden chain of religious brotherhood. I am free, must always be free. I wish everyone to be free—free as the air.'[38]

It was around this time that, for the first time most expressly, Swami Vivekananda was making his brother-monks aware how tired and exhausted he was physically, although anyone could have seen that. Of the torments and the suffering of his inner being, he spoke to none of them; for there was not one among them who would have understood them, or so he thought. At the same time as he was writing that letter to Nivedita, informing her that he had cut himself off from the 'work' and the 'Organization', he was writing also to Hari (Turiyananda):

My body and mind are broken down; I need rest badly. In addition, there is not a single person on whom I can depend, on the other hand so long as I live, all will become very selfish depending upon me for everything.

...Dealing with people entails constant mental uneasiness...I have cut myself off by a will. Now I am writing to say that nobody will have sole power. All will be done in accordance with the view of the majority...If a trust deed on similar lines can be executed, then I am free...

What you are doing is also Guru Maharaj's work. Continue to do it. Now I have done my part. Don't write to me any more about those things; do not even mention the subject. I have no opinions whatever to give on that subject...[39]

---

[38] Ibid., p. 305.
[39] SV Letters, p. 431.

Swami Vivekananda had been increasingly troubled by the feeling of 'a rankling sin', as he called it, that in order to serve the world he had sadly neglected his mother. On 22 November 1898, he was writing almost a pathetic but deeply moving letter to his devoted friend Raja Ajit Singh of Khetri, asking for financial help for his mother, Bhubaneswari Devi, and his two younger brothers, Mahendranath and Bhupendranath:

...I have one great sin rankling always in my breast and that is to do a service to the world I have sadly neglected my mother. Again since my second brother (Mahendranath) has gone away she has become awfully worn out with grief.[40] Now my last desire is to make seva and serve my mother for some years at least. I want to live with my mother and get my younger brother married to prevent extinction of the family.[41] This will certainly smoothen my last days as well as that of mother. She lives now in a hovel. I want to build a little decent home for her and make some provision for the youngest as there is very little hope of his being a good earning man. Is it too much for a royal descendant of Ramachandra to do for one he loves and calls his friend? I do not know whom-else to appeal to. The money I got from Europe

---

[40] Bhupendranath, in his book already cited, tells us more; p. 60. 'Mahendranath (1869–1956) went in 1896 to England in connection with his studies. From then till 1901 he never wrote a letter to mother. From England he went to North Africa where he travelled extensively. He went on roaming in south-east Europe, south Russia and the Near East. He intended going to Central Asia through Persia. But on not being allowed to do this he came back to India and entered Kashmir. During the years of his hectic sojourn in foreign lands, Bhubaneswari had to pass her days in anxiety on his account. At last after Swamiji's demise in 1902 Mahendranath returned to Calcutta.'

[41] Mahendranath and Bhupendranath remained unmarried; maybe because of the lives they, too, had chosen for themselves.

was for the 'work' and every penny almost has been given over to that work. Nor can I go beg of others for help for my own self. About my family affairs I have exposed myself to your Highness and none else shall know of it. I am tired, heart-sick and dying— do, I pray, this last great work of kindness to me.[42]

A week later, Vivekananda wrote to his friend again:

One thing more will I beg of you—if possible the 100 Rs. a month for my mother be made permanent. So that even after my death it may regularly reach her, or even if your Highness ever gets reasons to stop your love and kindness for me, my poor old mother may be provided, remembering the love you once had for a poor *Sadhu*.[43]

Raja Ajit Singh made certain that Bhubaneswari Devi would get from the Khetri Raj treasury Rs 100 every month, which she did as long as he lived.

During Swami Vivekananda's second voyage to the West, Nivedita with him, Vivekananda talked to her about his mother. In her long letter of 28 June 1899, written from the ship coasting Ceylon (now Sri Lanka), she reported that conversation to Josephine MacLeod, referring to the Swami as 'the King':

...Did I tell you of his exclamation as we came down the Ganges 'Oh what a load of suffering in these 2 ½ years I am leaving behind me now!'? I did not—for I had not strength then to make it sacred enough—tell you how he spoke of his mother and the anguish he had caused her and his determination to come back

---

[42] This letter was discovered by Beni Shankar Sharma, *Swami Vivekananda—A Forgotten Chapter of His Life*, pp. 171-72, cited in Marie Louise Burke, *SV New Discoveries*, Vol. 6, p. 90.

[43] Ibid., pp. 173-74; cited in *SV New Discoveries*, Vol. 6, p. 91.

and devote the rest of his life to her. 'Don't you see?' he cried, 'I have got the true Vairagyam this time! I would undo the past if I could—I would marry—were I 10 years younger—just to make my mother happy—not for any other reason.'[44]

To this, Nivedita replied, 'But I'm awfully glad you're not 10 years younger!' 'And he looked at me and laughed.'[45]

On 17 January 1900, Vivekananda wrote to Sara Bull:

...It is becoming clearer to me that I lay down all the concerns of the Math and for a time go back to my mother. She has suffered much through me. I must try to smooth her last days. Do you know this was just exactly what the great Shankaracharya himself had to do! He had to go back to his mother in the last few days of her life! ...Anyhow, I must try, as I have forebodings that my mother has not many more years to live. Then again, this is coming to me as the greatest of all sacrifices to make, the sacrifice of ambition, of leadership, of fame...But then, it is now shown that— leaving my mother was a great renunciation in 1884—it is *a greater renunciation to go back to my mother now*. Probably Mother wants me to undergo the same that She made the great Acharya undergo in old days. Is it?[46]

And again on 7 March, this:

All my life I have been a torture to my poor mother. Her whole life has been one of continuous misery. If it be possible, my last attempt should be to make her a little happy. I have planned it all out. I have served the *Mother* all my life. It is done; I refuse now to grind her axe. Let Her find other workers—I strike.[47]

---

[44] *Nivedita Letters*, Vol. 1, p. 172.
[45] Ibid., Vol. 1, p. 172.
[46] *CWSV*, Vol. VIII, pp. 489-90.
[47] Ibid., p. 497.

Indeed, Swami Vivekananda worried about his mother greatly. He wanted to buy for her a small house where she could live comfortably. For that purpose, because he had no money of his own, he borrowed from the Math five thousand rupees—borrowing from that which he had earned by driving himself relentlessly! Soon, he was involved in litigation, a second time, forced upon him by an unscrupulous aunt[48] who took the money but did not hand over the house. She had wrongly calculated, as he wrote in one of his letters, that because he was a sannyasin he would be loath to go to a court of law. Finally, however, she compromised in favour of the Swami's family.

Vivekananda's declining health[49] was most probably one of the reasons why he began to resent the very work to which, as Swami Vivekananda, he had devoted every ounce of his stupendous energy, as indeed he was doing even while writing that letter to Brahmananda on 12 March 1900. In that letter he told him, furthermore, of his suffering from neurasthenia, 'a disease of the nerves', which had caught him, he said, during his second visit to America. His asthma was becoming more acute and he often gasped for breath, as if feeling choked. Of all this there was not even the remotest sign when, lecturing to a most eager audience, he floated in the highest regions or dived into the depths of the spirit. According to all contemporary accounts, his face glowed with a divine energy.

---

[48] Predictably, we are not told the name and the background of this aunt either.

[49] The details of which we learn from many of his letters written during 1899 and 1901 to Josephine MacLeod, Nivedita, Sara Bull and Mary Hale.

Another reason was Vivekananda's disappointment, which he did not conceal, with the lack of real response to his work in India. It is true that on his return after his triumph at the Parliament of Religions, the nation had given Swami Vivekananda the welcome of a conquering warrior. A raja and some princes had drawn his carriage. Several thousands of men and women had flung themselves at his feet, people regarding the very dust under his feet as sacred. Wherever he went he created a following. The newspapers apart, Goodwin had seen it all, and he was reporting to Sara Bull what he saw. Deeply touched, even astonished, by India's 'welcome back home', Swami Vivekananda was far too great a man to have been taken in by all this. He did not forget that when something concrete had to be done, his own countrymen were nowhere to be found. The loneliness of working for a people from whom he could expect little, except frothy adoration, was simply killing. And yet, he loved them 'only too, too well'.

Then there were desertions and treachery, as we saw in the previous chapter. Henrietta Muller, who had donated the entire money with which the land for building the Belur Math was purchased, and who in 1897 had followed the Swami to India, turned against him because of his being ill too often which, she imagined, a sannyasi, a yogi, ought never to be.[50]

Swami Vivekananda was upset, moreover, when his brother-monk Swami Abhedananda (Kali), brought over from London to take care of the Vedanta teaching in New York, disrupted the hitherto smooth and harmonious working

---

[50] For a little more about Miss Muller's desertion and nastiness, see Nivedita's letters dated 7 December 1898 and 1 January 1899(?), to Josephine MacLeod. *Nivedita Letters*, Vol. I, pp. 27 and 31-32 respectively.

of the New York Vedanta Society by insisting on being both its spiritual and the organizational head. Abhedananda was exceedingly nasty to Sara Bull, to whom the Swami had entrusted all of the organizational Vedanta work in America. Disgusted with Abhedananda's attitudes, Francis Leggett resigned from the presidentship of the N.Y. Vedanta Society, which he had done so much to nurture. It is from Pravrajika Prabuddhaprana's biography of Sara Bull that we hear about these for the first time.[51] She does not conceal the truth about the Abhedananda episode when it has to be told; for, simultaneously with other events that were taking place, it says much. For that reason, we must study the two letters, one from Abhedananda to Sara and the other on the return journey from Sara, which, with utmost honesty, Prabuddhaprana provides us with. On 12 April 1900, Abhedananda wrote to Sara:

I did not know until this year that you are so unfriendly to me and so much against the Vedanta work in New York. Four years ago, when I came to New York, you had the same quarrel with Miss Phillips as you had with me this year. Then you succeeded in making Swami Saradananda as a tool in your hands. This year you have tried your best to make Swami Turiyananda the same but you have failed. At that time I did not believe in what Miss Phillips, Miss Waldo and others told me about your plans and ideas. But now I can clearly see that you are at the bottom of this quarrel between Mr. Leggett and me... You have tried your best to crush my work and drive me out of New York and to bring a breach between me and my friends.[52]

---

[51] Prabuddhaprana, *Saint Sara*, pp. 369–73.
[52] Ibid., p. 370.

The next day Sara Bull wrote a long reply to Abhedananda:[53]

While your letter in its form of expression would not, of itself, put me under an obligation of courtesy to reply, I recall that I am older, and this hard experience may prove a lesson to help you in the future.

It is easy to tear down in a few hours what it has taken years to construct. I regret that you have done this.

You must recall that I was acquainted with Mr. Leggett before he knew you. And if I were, as you say, your enemy, the opening of my house to give you a Cambridge audience at least gave you the opportunity there to show your ability of head and your warmth of heart ('*and Sara added sarcastically*'—Prabuddhaprana) in whatever degree you possess these.

('Now, Sara lashed out at Abhedananda for his methods as well as his teaching. She wrote in this letter':[54])

Your recent attempts to oppose Mr. Leggett's wishes, and the methods you have employed are open to such grave objection— have been so foolish and childish, (probably because of your inexperience, ignorance and lack of training in organised work)— that they would, from a trained person's view, be counted dishonest, as well as dishonourable.

The address on Sri Ramakrishna that I heard you deliver emphasised his yoga-training and you conveyed by your statement that His disciples had powers, the impression that occult teaching could be given by them. This I regret. In my judgement, if it is proved best that money should be asked for Vedanta teaching, it should not be for Raja-Yoga in its Hatha-yoga form.

---

[53] Most of it to be found in Prabuddhaprana's *Saint Sara*, pp. 370–72. Here, only a part of it can be given.
[54] Ibid., p. 371.

...The good is permanent, and whatever has been, by anyone, contributed to good, stands. Personally, I dare to believe that all touched and awakened by the Swami Vivekananda are serving truly: by the mistakes made, as by the honoured service we all love to acknowledge, nor do I exclude the American Swamis, in saying this.[55]

The Abhedananda episode must have left Swami Vivekananda sad at heart. At the same time he felt detached from it all. 'There is a squabble in New York, I see,' he wrote to Joe on 10 April 1900 from San Francisco. 'I got a letter from A—stating that he was going to leave New York...You tell Mr. Leggett from me to do what is best about the Vedanta Society matter.' On 18 April, from Alameda, California, he again wrote to her:

I am so sorry Mr. Leggett resigned the presidentship.

Well, I keep quiet for fear of making further trouble.

You know my methods are extremely harsh, and once roused I may rattle A—too much for his peace of mind.[56]

I wrote to him only to tell him that his notions about Mrs. Bull are entirely wrong.

---

[55] Ibid., pp. 371-72.

[56] If it were not for Prabuddhaprana's *Saint Sara*, we would not know who 'A—' is. It is not an unimportant detail, to be left unnoticed, that the editor of the *Letters of Swami Vivekananda* conceals the identity of Abhedananda by editing his name simply as 'A—'. The editor of the *Complete Works of Swami Vivekananda*, Vol. VIII, which contains most of the Swami's letters, does the same (see *CWSV*, VIII, pp. 513, 515, 518-19). When, in his three letters to Josephine MacLeod on the subject concerning the events at the New York Vedanta Society, the Swami had mentioned the name of Abhedananda fully and clearly, why this concealing on the part of the editors? From all that we know of him, truth was the very breath of the Swami Vivekananda.

You understand why I do not want to meddle with A—. Who am I to meddle with anyone, Joe? I have long given up my place as a leader—I have no right to raise my voice. Since the beginning of this year, I have not dictated anything in India. You know that. Many thanks for what you and Mrs. Bull have been to me in the past. All blessings follow you ever![57]

The Swami's letter of 18 April to Joe contained much of what his other self, Vivekananda, was saying again. We keep that for the end of this chapter. Meanwhile, on 12 April, he was writing to an unidentified American friend, more or less in the same words of inner withdrawal he had written to Joe two days earlier:

...Work always brings evil with it. I have paid for the accumulated evil with bad health. I am glad. My mind is all the better for it. There is a mellowness and calmness in life now, which was never there before. I am learning now how to be attached as well as detached, and mentally becoming my own master...

...I am happy, at peace with myself, and more of the Sannyasin than I ever was before. The love for my own kith and kin is growing less every day, and that for Mother increasing. Memories of long nights of vigil with Shri Ramakrishna under the Dakshineswar Banyan are waking up once more. And work? What is work? Whose work? Whom shall I work for?

I am free. I am Mother's child. She works. She plays. Why should I plan? What should I plan? Things came and went, just as She liked, without my planning...[58]

---

[57] SV Letters, p. 422; in this connection, see also his letter dated 20 April 1900, pp. 424-25.
[58] SV Letters, p. 421.

Vivekananda once said that his was the heart of a woman. But Swami Vivekananda had been saying, again and again, in his letters to his 'Madras boys' that India needed men with 'nerves of steel and muscles of iron'. 'Energy', 'manliness', 'force of character', 'strength', 'power of combined action', 'power of faith in one's self', 'not cowards but lions'—these were the words and phrases repeatedly being used in almost all his letters to them. Vivekananda was freely expressing his inner torments to his closest women friends and supporters, most of them American. The Swami allowed none of that in his letters to his gurubhais or to his Madras followers, not that he loved them less. To them, Swami Vivekananda was energy personified, urging them in heroic words to be *man*, strong and fearless, ready to lay down their lives in the service of India's downtrodden masses, putting aside all thoughts of personal salvation. He saw the social necessity of power; not power for its own sake, but to be employed in the selfless service to others. He detested cowardice; he despised softness of character; to him, weakness was a sin. In his letters to his Indian friends, he was often saying how India is full of these; and in profound reaction against them, he put the greatest emphasis on energy and power, quoting the Upanishad: 'This *Atman* is not to be attained by one who is weak.'

In this, but in this alone, Swami Vivekananda was not wholly unlike Nietzsche,[59] his senior contemporary, who, in a similar reaction against Christianity, had developed his philosophy of will to power. Nietzsche was a divided self, too, bearing upon his soul the visitations of two contrasting ideals, whose Greek symbols were Apollo and

---

[59] Born, 15 October 1844; died, 23 August 1900.

Dionysus. It was to that division—between the Apollonian ideal of self-knowledge and self-control and the Dionysian ideal of self-abandon and drunkenness—each pulling man with equal force but in opposite directions, that Nietzsche had traced the birth of tragedy. For that self-division, made his with tragic intensity, Nietzsche paid the price with his long years of madness. During his last twelve years, when he was lucid only rarely, he would sign his letters sometimes as 'Apollo', at other times as 'Dionysus'. But, unlike Swami Vivekananda, Nietzsche did not suffer the tragic division in one man between love and power. Excepting his attachment to his sister Elizabeth, and a short attachment to Salome, Nietzsche, from what we know of him, seemed to have been incapable of love. Neither did he direct his philosophy of the will to power towards removing the suffering of the poor and the oppressed. To Nietzsche, power was an end in itself, 'the transvaluation of all values'. That was not the case with Swami Vivekananda even while he was emphasizing strength and manliness. To him, power by itself was not a value, much less the transvaluation of all values. Vivekananda recoiled from power and its logic, although his other self, the Swami, by all accounts of him, exuded power and its majesty—with this difference, that His Majesty's head never failed to bow wherever he saw the transvaluation of self, and its greatness and holiness.

From his spiritual heights, Swami Vivekananda found it neither impossible nor inconsistent to give his love to all those who had touched his life. He knew all about that stuff of Maya and its bondage. At no time did he give up, though, his capacity *to feel*—the concrete situation of a fellow human being. To him, suffering had not turned into a philosophical category. Suffering is a reality that is sensed; it is palpable. And so was his response to suffering, palpable and deeply *felt*. To the Buddha, *as he has come down to us*, suffering, *duhkha*, had a metaphysical cause which could be understood and, with that knowledge, overcome; to which there was a path. It required no *personal* response to it. His compassion was impersonal. To the New Buddha, as Josephine MacLeod believed Swami Vivekananda to be, suffering did not have metaphysical cause only: it was created also by social oppression, inequality, and tyranny of every kind. Wherever he saw suffering, he responded to it personally, a tangible response to a tangible person. The Buddha is not known to have ever wept at the suffering of another; Swami Vivekananda did. Which of the two is a higher response from a strictly philosophical point of view, I cannot judge. Speaking personally, I should have found the Buddha's impersonal compassion unbearable.

Between the necessity of power which is loveless, and love as the law of life in which there is no seeking of power, if Vivekananda had surrendered to love, he did not fail to see how maddening love could also be. So he alternated between love and his resentment of love. However, in every act of his, be it the smallest, he was *living* love and reserving his *resentment of love* for some of his letters to those very persons with whom he felt bound with the ties of love. Early in 1895 what he had written to Brahmananda and quoted previously, may again be quoted here:

All expansion is life, all contraction is death. All love is expansion, all selfishness is contraction. Love is therefore the only law of life. He who loves lives, he who is selfish is dying. Therefore love for love's sake, because it is the only law of life, just as you breathe to live. This is the secret of selfless love, selfless action, and the rest.

But on 23 December of the same year, he wrote to Sharat (Saradananda): 'Emotional natures like mine are always preyed upon by relatives and friends. This world is merciless.'[60] And on 25 July 1897, from Almora, to Marie Halboister, a young English (but French) admirer of his:

…I am so glad that you have been helped by Vedanta and Yoga. I am unfortunately sometimes like the circus clown who made others laugh, himself miserable!!

You are naturally of a buoyant temperament. Nothing seems to touch you. And you are moreover a very prudent girl, inasmuch as you have scrupulously kept yourself away from 'love' and all its nonsense. So you see you have made your good Karma and planted the seed of your lifelong wellbeing.

…I wish I had nobody to love, and I were an orphan in my childhood. The greatest misery in my life has been my own people—my brothers and sisters and mother etc. Relatives are like deadly clogs to one's progress, and is it not a wonder that people will still go on to find new ones by *marriage*?

He who is alone is happy. Do good to all, like everyone, but *do not love* any one. It is a bondage, and bondage brings only misery. Live alone in your mind—that is happiness. To have nobody to care for and never minding who cares for one is the way to be free.

I envy so much your frame of mind—quiet, gentle, light yet deep and *free*. You are already free, Marie, free already—you are Jivan-mukta. I am more of a woman than a man, you are more of a man than a woman. I am always dragging others' pain into me—for nothing, without being able to do any good to anybody—just as women, if they have no children, bestow all their love upon a cat!!!

---

[60] *SV Letters*, p. 274.

Do you think this has any spirituality in it? Nonsense, it is all material *nervous bondage*—that is what it is. O! to get rid of the thraldom of the flesh.[61]

On 12 December 1899, Vivekananda was writing to Sara Bull:

…My mistakes have been great, but everyone of them was from too much love. How I hate *love*! Would I never had any Bhakti! Indeed, I wish I could be an Advaitist, calm and heartless. Well, this life is done. I will try in the next. I am sorry, especially now, that I have done more injury to my friends than there have been blessings on them. The peace, the quiet I am seeking, I never found.

I went years ago to the Himalayas, never to come back: and my sister committed suicide, the news reached me there, and that weak heart flung me off from that prospect of peace!! It is the weak heart that has driven me out of India to seek help for those I love, and here I am! Peace have I sought, but the heart, that seat of Bhakti, would not allow me to find it. Struggle and torture, torture and struggle! Well, be it then, since it is my fate, and the quicker it is over, the better. They say I am impulsive, but look at the circumstances!!! I am sorry I have been the cause of pain to you, to you above all, who love me so much, who have been so, so kind. But it is done—was a fact. I am now going to cut the knot or die in the attempt.[62]

He signed this letter as 'Ever your son, Vivekananda'.

In the postscript to this letter, Swami Vivekananda added (among other things):

---

[61] *SV Letters*, pp. 361-62.
[62] Ibid., pp. 405-06.

...The end is getting very dark and very much muddled; well, I expected it so. Don't think I give in a moment...Yes, let the world come, the hells come, the gods come, let Mother come, I fight and do not give in. Ravana got his release in three births by fighting the Lord Himself! It is glorious to fight Mother.

All blessings on you and yours. You have done for me more, much more, than I deserved ever.[63]

On 20 February 1900, on hearing the previous day from Mary that her father, George W. Hale, his 'Father Pope', had passed away, Swami Vivekananda wrote to her from Pasadena:

Your letter bearing the sad news of Mr. Hale's passing away reached me yesterday. I am sorry, because in spite of monastic training the heart lives on, and then Mr. Hale was one of the best souls I met in life. Of course you are sorry, miserable, and so is Mother Church and Harriet and the rest, especially as this is the first grief of its kind you have met, is it not? I have lost many, suffered much, and the most curious cause of suffering when somebody goes off is the feeling that I was not good enough to that person. When my father died, it was a pang for months, and I had been so disobedient.

...Well, well, what shall I say to you, Mary? You know all the talks; only I say this and it is true—if it were possible to exchange grief, and had I a cheerful mind, I would exchange mine for your grief ever and always. Mother knows best.[64]

There was no lecturing here on the impermanence of life, no empty consolation, no impersonal compassion, but a personal offer of taking upon him her grief. With this yet another bereavement, Vivekananda's great sadness at the

---

[63] Ibid., p. 406.
[64] Ibid., pp. 409-10.

passing away of Haridas Viharidas Desai, of Pavahari Baba, and then of Goodwin, were resurrected in his loving heart. Sadness is always experienced as simultaneity, not as sequence.

Swami Vivekananda's self-division between *personal* and *impersonal* was quite marked, too. He was aware, as he said in one of his letters to his brother-monks: 'It is one of the attendant evils of name and fame that you can't have anything private.' He was aware, too, that the demands of power are wholly opposed to the demands of love; therefore, personal relationships are nearly always a difficult matter for one leading a movement. On 1 October 1897, from Srinagar, the Swami wrote to Margaret Noble on this subject:

...The great difficulty is this: I see persons giving me almost the whole of their love. But I must not give any one the whole of mine in return, for that day the work would be ruined. Yet there are some who will look for such a return, not having the breadth of the impersonal view. It is absolutely necessary to the work that I should have the enthusiastic love of as many as possible, while I myself remain entirely impersonal. Otherwise jealousy and quarrels would break up everything. A leader must be impersonal. I am sure you understand this. I do not mean that one should be a brute, making use of the devotion of others for his own ends, and laughing in his sleeve meanwhile. What I mean is what I am, intensely personal in my love, but having the power to pluck out my own heart with my own hand, if it becomes necessary, 'for the good of many, for the welfare of many', as Buddha said. *Madness of love, and yet in it no bondage. Matter changed into spirit by the force of love. Nay, that is the gist of our Vedanta.*[65]

---

[65] Ibid., p. 366.

This simultaneity of *personal* and *impersonal* in the same person, not only contrary but paradoxical, so that the one could be achieved only by being the other, began to trouble Margaret. Indeed, it troubled her greatly and she suffered in her relationship with Swami Vivekananda, her Master. In a letter to Josephine MacLeod she would be writing two years later, in 1900, she said:

...Anyway, I begin to see why this use of personal and impersonal has always perplexed and irritated me. These two terms like all others are only relative. No one can say where they apply in the case of another soul. In the end the whole has to be affirmed in every detail—who is to say what it is your destiny, or mine, to state? You see, when one speaks of the Impersonal, one is really thinking of all that is most deeply personal to *everyone*. Isn't it so?[66]

There was another level of the impersonal, of which Swami Vivekananda was speaking.

...The eternal, the infinite, the omnipresent, the omniscient is a principle, not a person. You, I, and everyone are but embodiments of that principle; and the more of this infinite principle is embodied in a person, the greater is he, and all in the end will be the perfect embodiment of that, and thus all will be one, as they are now essentially. This is all there is of religion, and the practice is through this feeling of oneness that is love.[67]

Just as the self-division in the Swami, between the demands of 'work' and his own nature, found varied expressions, so did the pain and suffering of Margaret Noble as Sister

---

[66] Letter dated 23 January 1900, from Chicago. *Nivedita Letters*, Vol. I, p. 306.
[67] In his letter dated 'May, 1896', from London, to Mary Hale. *SV Letters*, p. 294.

Nivedita. In the first place, he demanded of her, now that she had dedicated herself in the service of India, to work for the secular education of Indian women, that she be a different person from what she had hitherto been. Though Margaret Noble had come to work for the women of India in a spirit of the greatest respect for them, she naturally said about herself: 'I am English to the core.' He began to attack her *English-ness* first of all and then everything she had cherished until then. Her biographer Pravrajika Atmaprana mentions how, after her initiation on 25 March 1898, Swami Vivekananda had asked her, to what nation she belonged. Margaret Noble, now Sister Nivedita, answered: 'To the English nation'. Thereupon he attacked England and the English people; and Margaret rose in their defence.[68] He asked her to forget everything, her country, her past, her family, even her name. There was a struggle between the two, she, as strong and full of her Irish fire, as he was of the Vivekanandian fire, by now famous. That was in Almora in May–June 1898, Josephine MacLeod and Sara Bull, on their first visit to India, with them.

When the conflict between Swami Vivekananda and Nivedita turned into an emotional crisis, Joe, feeling increasingly protective of Nivedita, told him plainly that he was hurting and offending her. He listened to her, went away, and returning in the evening, said to Joe: 'You were right. There must be a change. I am going away into the forests to be alone, and when I come back I shall bring peace,' which is what he did. In the only two letters she wrote from Almora, both of them to her beloved friend

---

[68] Pravrajika Atmaprana, *Nivedita*, p. 45.

in England, Mrs Nell Hammond, Nivedita let nothing of the crisis be known, beyond saying: 'I cannot yet throw any of my past experience of human life and human relationships overboard. Yet I can see that the saints fight hard to do so—can they be altogether wrong?'[69]

But neither had Swami Vivekananda thrown overboard any of *his* past experience of human life and human relationships. Why did he attack Nivedita's declaration of her being English to the core when he was speaking of his own Indian-ness? What wrong was she doing in defending the England she had known with all its faults when Swami Vivekananda himself, described by her in one of her lyrical but accurate descriptions of him, 'was a born lover, and the queen of his heart was his motherland'?[70] Furthermore, why was his attitude different in the case of Josephine MacLeod, who later recalled his saying to her—'the only thing Swamiji ever said to me on myself'—'Always remember that your greatest asset is that you are an American and a woman.'[71] She added her belief:

If the finest Hindu and the finest Englishman meet—there is no quarrel—only respect! So let us try to intensify our nationality. Fancy, the failure I'd be—to try to be a Hindu woman! Not that I don't admire them tremendously—that dedication first to God, then to husband and family! Selflessness!—but I'm born of a daring race— *making*, not following, precedent.[72]

---

[69] Her letter dated 5 June 1898. *Nivedita Letters*, Vol. 1, p. 13.
[70] Nivedita, *My Master*, p.
[71] Prabuddhaprana, *Tantine*, p. 244.
[72] Ibid., p. 244. In a letter she wrote to one 'Mr. Cowsik' (Kaushik) whom she had met in Mysore, and who was a devotee of Sri Ramakrishna and Swami Vivekananda.

There was another crisis between Swami Vivekananda and Nivedita when the party went from Almora to Kashmir, a crisis that was in some ways even more serious. It occurred when he made a pilgrimage to the cave of Amarnath, Joe and Sara Bull staying behind, and Nivedita going with him. This time, in her letter of 7 August 1898 from Kashmir, she did candidly speak of it to Nell Hammond. That crisis consisted not in the externals of two different histories but in the *inwardness* of an experience from which Nivedita felt excluded. She saw that a great exaltation had come upon Vivekananda when, on 2 August, they were in the cave and stood in front of the sacred ice Shiva-linga. For fear of being overwhelmed, he came out of the cave after two minutes or so. *He* felt greatly exalted; *she* felt nothing. He had said to her, when they were in the cave, that he was dedicating her to Shiva. She wanted him to tell her what *that* meant, but he would say nothing. She wanted him to share with her the meaning of his great exaltation, and he would say nothing.

In her letter, Nivedita confided to Nell Hammond:

For him it was a wonderfully solemn moment. He was utterly absorbed though he was only there two minutes, and then he fled lest emotion should get the upper hand. He was utterly exhausted too—for we had had a long and dangerous climb on foot—and his heart is weak. But I wish you could see his faith and courage and joy ever since. He says Siva gave him Amar (immortality) and now he cannot die till he himself wishes it. I am so glad to have been there with him. That must be a memory for ever, mustn't it? —and he *did* dedicate me to Siva too—though it's not the Hindu way to let one share in the dedication—and since he told me so I've grown Hindu in taste with alarming rapidity.

I am so deeply and intensely glad of this revelation that he has had. But oh Nell dear—it is such terrible pain to come face to face with something which is all *inwardness* to someone you worship, and for yourself to be able to get little further than externals. Swami could have made it live—but he was lost.

Even now I can scarcely look back on those hours without dropping once more into their abyss of anguish and disappointment, but I know that I am wrong—for I see that I am utterly forgiven by the King and that in some strange way I am nearer to him and to GOD for the pilgrimage. But oh for the bitterness of a lost chance—that can never never come again. For I was angry with him and would not listen to him when he was going to talk.

...You see I told him that if he would not put more reality into the word Master he would have to remember that we were nothing more to each other than an ordinary man and woman, and so I snubbed him and shut myself up in a hard shell.

He was so exquisite about it. Not a bit angry—only caring for little comforts for me. I suppose he thought I was tired—only he *couldn't* tell me about himself any more! And the next morning as we came home he said 'Margot, I haven't the power to do these things for you—*I* am not Ramakrishna Paramahamsa.' The most perfect because the most unconscious humility you ever saw.[73]

But you know part of it is the inevitable suffering that comes of the different national habits. My Irish nature expresses everything, the Hindu never dreams of expression, and Swami is so utterly shy of priestliness, whereas I am always craving for it—and so on.[74]

Offering an explanation for Swami Vivekananda's harshness towards Nivedita, Pravrajika Prabuddhaprana, the biographer of Josephine MacLeod, says: 'Nivedita was

---

[73] *Nivedita Letters*, Vol. 1, pp. 18–19.
[74] Ibid., p. 19.

aggressive in her defence of Western values. Vivekananda sought to free her from these strong sentiments so that she could totally accept her role in India. He therefore began a course in Indianizing a Western worker.'[75]

Not only does this far from explain the *nature* of the conflict between the two and pass over the anguish Nivedita suffered in Almora, it does no justice to Swami Vivekananda either. When had he set out to 'Indianize' anybody who had come from the West to work for India? By all accounts, *never*. Moreover, in most of his letters to India, he was himself, *clearly and repeatedly*, exhorting his countrymen to inculcate several Western values needed for the regeneration of the Indian character, the very values Nivedita embodied as an Irish woman.

Neither is the biographer of Sister Nivedita, Pravrajika Atmaprana, any nearer the truth in saying: 'It was obviously a conflict of two strong personalities. The Swami was not a person to compromise his views or even adopt a gentler method of teaching; Nivedita had not the submissive nature to accept blindly and humbly all that was said.'[76]

But when did Nivedita expect Swami Vivekananda to 'compromise his views' if only to be gentler? That would have been a negation of her own passion for truth. And when did Swami Vivekananda demand of *anybody*, leave alone Nivedita, that he or she 'accept blindly and humbly all that was said'? He himself never did, not even in relation to Sri Ramakrishna, and greatly respected Nivedita's questioning spirit.

Atmaprana is, however, infinitely more understanding of the situation of Nivedita in relation to Swami Vivekananda

[75] Prabuddhaprana, *Tantine*, p. 47.
[76] Atmaprana, *Nivedita*, p. 46.

and of their conflicts when she says: 'Her depression and suffering were heightened by the fact that she had known the Swami since meeting him in London as a friend and a beloved leader, and had expected him to be ever so. But now his attitude showed indifference, impatience and even silent hostility.'[77]

The question is: *why* that silent hostility—*if* it was that at all?

Recording in his diary his long conversations with Josephine MacLeod in the May of 1927 concerning Swami Vivekananda, which touched on Nivedita as well, Romain Rolland offers another explanation:

Sister Nivedita was treated very harshly by Vivekananda during the early days. He humiliated her about her English character— calling her proud and calculating. Maybe in this way he defended himself against the worshipful passion Nivedita had for him. Because it seems she had for him the lover's adoration which our friend Miss Slade showed for Gandhi. But between Gandhi and Miss Slade there was a distance of thirty years; between Vivekananda and Nivedita there were only five or six. And though the sentiment of Nivedita had always been of absolute purity, maybe Vivekananda understood the danger. He rebuked her without sparing her and would find fault with everything she did. Crushed and in tears, she would go back to the arms of Miss MacLeod. Finally the latter made some remark to Vivekananda in this regard which struck him. He said he would meditate on it and from that time completely changed his manner and was more gentle with her. But he was not

---

[77] Ibid., p. 46.

a man to tolerate the passions people had for him nor to treat them with fatherly compassion as Gandhi did.[78]

Apart from the manifest error of the statement that the Swami would find fault with *everything* Nivedita did, the main part of this explanation does not touch the core either. That Nivedita had for Swami Vivekananda worshipful adoration is undeniable. *She herself said so*. 'I suppose the fact is that anyone can see that I worship him—and that's the truth.'[79] That she craved for the *personal*, she said that too. 'Oh dear how I love and worship him! I wish he'd ask me to cut my heart out and give it to him.'[80] But from that alone, by what logic could one draw the inference that the Swami understood 'the danger' and, by being harsh to her, was 'defending himself' from the 'worshipful passion' of a woman? There were other women who, like Nivedita, had worshipful attitude towards the Swami; also, as in the case of Nivedita, the difference in their age was not much either. What special danger to him could then there have been from Nivedita? The truth is that the Swami did not ever entertain, even remotely, the notion that there *could* be any.

Besides, who can interpret the meaning of how one *looks* at another? In one of her letters from Ridgely Manor to Joe, Nivedita said:

---

[78] Reproduced in Prabuddhaprana, *Tantine*, p. 216 and also in Romain Rolland, *The Life of Vivekananda*, p.138, *fn*.2, with some alterations by him, not to the substance but to the language of his earlier entry into his diary which Prabuddhaprana has cited.

[79] Nivedita to Josephine MacLeod, letter dated 30 March 1899, from Calcutta. *Nivedita Letters*, Vol.1, p. 96.

[80] Ibid., Vol. 1, pp. 189-90.

...Someone criticised me to Olea (Sara Bull's daughter) for looking at Swami when he was talking, and I heard of it in due course. Of course I could not helping (*sic*) thinking of it next time he talked, and trying to look elsewhere. And then I found the secret of avoiding Mrs. Johnson's eyes. In every face except his, you come up against a barrier, and have to keep outside, and look at the front of the house. But look at him, and you seem to be gazing through open portals straight into the Infinite. Is this because he is so little conscious of himself?[81]

As to the Swami's harshness towards Nivedita, it must always be kept in mind that he was no less harsh, indeed very much more, to his brother-monks and to Alasinga Perumal. On 12 December 1899, Swami Vivekananda had written to Mrs Sara Bull:

You are perfectly right. I am brutal, very indeed...I am very sorry I use harsh language to my boys; but they also know I love them more than anybody else on this earth...I am a fighter and must die fighting, not give way—that is why I get crazy at the boys. I don't ask them to fight, but not to hinder my fight.'[82]

However harsh his scolding, they all knew, Nivedita most of all, its seemingly paradoxical source—love.

The truth is that Swami Vivekananda saw much more of himself in Nivedita than in any other Western woman friend and supporter of his. He saw in her the same rejection of injustice, oppression, the degradation of one human being by another, the same passion for freedom, the same concern with social evils—these burned in Nivedita's Irish

---

[81] Her letter dated 27 October 1899 to Josephine MacLeod. *Nivedita Letters*, Vol. I, p. 224.
[82] Letter dated 12 December 1899. *SV Letters*, p. 405.

heart as fiercely as they did in his. She quickly saw that the question of education for women was related to what she called 'the other question'—of nationalism, from which the Swami was shying away. One part of him clearly saw that, indeed, as a necessity which required political freedom and therefore political action but another part of him saw with even greater clarity that 'nationalism' was not the way to the regeneration of India either. He was fighting in her what he was fighting in himself. Besides, he saw in her the same selfless giving nature, the same *personal*, which he knew to be the core of his person as well. The difference between others and her was that *she* was now a member of the Ramakrishna Order, a *naishtik brahmacharini*.[83] And the rules of that context, as far as personal relationships were concerned, were different. Swami Vivekananda submitted to them, for he had made them himself; Vivekananda was a man who had never lived limited by 'rules' or by 'context'. Vivekananda was simultaneously craving peace and freedom that was ever his, but was circumscribed by 'work' and by 'organization' that Swami Vivekananda had made *his* and which entailed fighting. Swami Vivekananda lived in *history* and its conflicting demands; Vivekananda floated in *transcendence* and its joyful freedom. Nivedita understood and worshipped Swami Vivekananda; she was baffled and puzzled by Vivekananda.

In the month of May 1894, with all that calumny heaped upon him, Swami Vivekananda was feeling obliged to vindicate himself in the eyes of his closest friends and supporters,[84] while Vivekananda was tormented by

---

[83] In this context, read her two letters dated 30 March 1899 to Josephine MacLeod, *Nivedita Letters*, Vol. I, pp. 95–99; and dated 26 March 1899, to Sara Bull, Ibid., pp. 93–94.

[84] See the previous chapter of this book.

having to do so; for self-vindication is self-humiliation as well. To his 'Adhyapakji', Professor John Wright, while the Swami was writing:

…I am morally bound to afford you every satisfaction, my kind friend; but for the rest of the world I do not care what they say— the Sannyasin must not have self-defence…I do not care for the attempts of the old missionary; but the fever of jealousy which attacked Mazoomdar gave me a terrible shock, and I pray that he would know better—for he is a great and good man who has tried all his life to do good. But this proves one of my Master's sayings: 'Living in a room covered with black soot—however careful you may be—some spots must stick to your clothes.' So—however one may try to be good and holy—so long he is in the world, some parts of his nature must gravitate downwards.

Vivekananda was adding:

I was never a *missionary*, nor ever would be one—my place is in the Himalayas. I have satisfied myself so far—that I can with a full conscience say, 'My God, I saw terrible misery amongst my brethren; I searched and discovered the way out of it, tried my best to apply the remedy, but failed. So Thy will be done!'[85]

But Swami Vivekananda knew that his place was not in the Himalayas. He wept at the sight of pain and suffering in the human universe, which he made his own. Vivekananda longed with increasing intensity for the universe beyond, which he knew to exist.

What I have called the 'self-division' of Swami Vivekananda, Romain Rolland calls it the 'double impress':

---

[85] *SV Letters*, p. 97.See also *SV New Discoveries*, Vol. 2, p. 95.

Even from his appearance it was possible to infer that although absolute detachment bathed the heights of his mind, the rest of his body remained immersed in life and action. His whole edifice bears this double impress: the basement is a nursery of apostles of truth and social service who mix in the life of the people and the movement of the times. But the summit is the *Ara Maxima*, the lantern of the dome, the spire of the cathedral, the Ashrama of all Ashramas, the Advaita built on the Himalayas, where the two hemispheres, the West and the East, meet at the confluence of all mankind in absolute Unity.[86]

From Ridgely Manor, 18 October 1899, Nivedita wrote a long letter to Josephine MacLeod,[87] in which she described the scene there, which included her account of the conversations with the Swami. Among many other things, she wrote:

At lunch on Friday, the King talked again about Sri R.K. He abused himself for being filled and poisoned with the Western reaction of those days, so that he was always looking and questioning whether this man was 'holy' or not. After 6 years he came to understand that He was *not* holy, because He had become *identified with holiness*. He was full of gaiety and merriment—and he had expected the 'holy' to be so different![88]

During that conversation, Sara Bull mentioned how '...her husband was never sensitive about criticism of his music—that he expected, he knew it was not perfect. But on road-engineering he felt deeply, and could be flattered!'
    Nivedita continued her narration:

---

[86] Romain Rolland, *The Life of Vivekananda and the Gospel*, p. 314.
[87] *Nivedita Letters*, Vol. I, pp. 214–19.
[88] Ibid., Vol. 1, p. 215.

Then, in our amusement, we all teased Swami for his carelessness about his religious teacherhood, and vanity about his portrait-painting (he has produced three or four portraits of me which others say are a libel even on me, but which just delight himself— sweet King!)—and he suddenly woke up and said—'You see there is one thing called Love—and there is another thing called Union. And Union is greater than Love.

'I do not *love* Religion. I have become identified with it. It is my life. So no man loves that thing in which his life has been spent, in which he really has accomplished something. *That which we love is not yet ourself.* Your husband did not *love* music for which he had always stood. He loved engineering in which as yet he knew comparatively little. This is the difference between Bhakti and Gnan. And this is why Gnan is greater than Bhakti.'[89]

By the same reckoning we can say that Swami Vivekananda did not *love* India—he was *identified* with India in its noblest philosophy and its wretched degradation alike, in its Vedantic gospel of equality and liberty and its social practices of inequality and oppression. Both produced in him two sets of contrary emotions. He was not a '*patriot*', he was *patriotism* personified; just as Sri Ramakrishna was not 'holy', he was *holiness* personified. When one is identified with holiness and living it, one can be full of merriment and laughter, as Sri Ramakrishna was, which often baffled many because they had very limited notions of what a holy man or woman is like, or, worse, what he or she *ought* to be. Similarly, when one is patriotism personified one fearlessly speaks of the causes of degradation, as Swami Vivekananda had been doing, often vehemently. Hence, his divided language while speaking of India.

---

[89] Ibid., Vol. 1, p. 216.

Then Vivekananda breaks in for he was not limited to what the Swami was identifying with. Much vaster in his inner self than 'patriotism' and 'religion', with perfect ease he went beyond even *them*. Hence 'the double impress'. In his letter of 7 August 1895, from New York, he was writing to E.T. Sturdy:

Neither numbers, nor powers, nor wealth, nor learning, nor eloquence, nor anything else will prevail, but *purity, living the life*, in one word, *anubhuti*, realization.

...Doctrines have been expounded enough. There are books by the million. Oh for an ounce of practice!

...Doubtless I do love India. But every day my sight grows clear. What is India, or England, or America to us? We are the servants of that God who by the ignorant is called MAN. He who pours water at the root, does he not water the whole tree? There is but one basis of well-being, social, political, or spiritual—to know that I and my brother are *one*. This is true for all countries and all people.[90]

More or less at the same time, in his letter of August 1895, to Alasinga he wrote: 'Truth is my God, the universe my country.'[91] Again, on 9 September 1895, from Paris: 'I know my mission in life, and no chauvinism about me. I belong as much to India as to the world, no humbug about this...What country has any special claim on me? Am I any nation's slave?'[92] And in yet another letter, 2 May 1895, Vivekananda spoke: 'Love makes the whole

---

[90] *SV Letters*, p. 248.
[91] Ibid., p. 244.
[92] *SV Letters*, p. 257.

universe as one's own home.'[93] These sentiments were always present in Vivekananda simultaneously with everything Swami Vivekananda was saying and doing in the West and India in the earlier years of his mission, from 1893 to the end of 1896, and became more prominent in his teachings during his second visit to the West, between July 1899 and October 1900.

While he was at Almora in May-June of 1898, Josephine MacLeod and Sara Bull with him, Swami Vivekananda experienced how a particular place could be simultaneously associated with sad news and spiritual exhilaration. It was at Almora, during his parivrajaka years that he had heard of his sister committing suicide, a deep emotional blow to him.[94] Again, it was now at Almora that he was told of the passing away of Pavahari Baba[95] whom he revered next to Sri Ramakrishna, and of Goodwin he loved so much. These were two other deep emotional blows to him. When Joe gave him the news of Goodwin's death at Ootacamund, he took it calmly; only 'He looked for a long time out upon the snowcapped Himalayas without speaking and presently he said, "My last public utterance is over."' In his letter of 5 May 1898 to her, Goodwin had given to Josephine MacLeod his estimate of Indian society which he had seen quite closely:

When I came to India I need not say what my feelings were with regard to Swamiji, but I have been here 16 months, and I have completely come round to your point of view. I will do anything for him *personally*, but I simply do not care a pin for anything

---

[93] Ibid., p. 224.
[94] Read again Chapter 5 of this book.
[95] Read again Chapter 3 of this book.

else. If I do any of his work it will be merely because *he* wishes it.

...I realise more and more every day that the Swami is not a Hindu—as Hindus go because everything must be judged by the sum-total, and the sum-total of India is meanness, and petty scheming, and *not* religion.[96]

Goodwin died less than a month thereafter, on 2 June, not yet twenty-eight. The Swami wrote the following tribute to him:

With infinite sorrow I learn the sad news of Mr. Goodwin's departure from this life, the more so as it was terribly sudden and therefore prevented all possibilities of my being at his side at the time of death. The debt of gratitude, I owe him, can never be repaid and those who think they have been helped by any thought of mine, ought to know, that almost every word of it, was published through the untiring and most unselfish exertions of Mr. Goodwin. In him I have lost a friend true as still, a disciple of never-ending devotion, a worker who knew not what tiring was and the world is less rich by one of those few who are born, as it were, only to live for others.[97]

Vivekananda bitterly exclaimed, 'As if it would not be one's right and duty to fight such a God and slay Him for killing Goodwin! And Goodwin, if he had lived, could have done so much!'[98] From this, one can imagine the depth of his grief over Goodwin departing. Since that feeling would have seemed inconsistent in a sannyasin, as it had seemed

---

[96] *SV New Discoveries*, Vol. 4, p. 495-96. For more on Goodwin, see pp. 488–95, 496–98.
[97] Published in *The Prabuddha Bharata*, August 1898. See *Vivekananda in Indian Newspapers*, p. 611-12.
[98] Prabuddhaprana, *Tantine*, p. 49.

to Pramadadas Mitra of Varanasi on seeing the Swami grieved by the passing away of Balaram Bose and hearing of the fatal illness of Surendranath Mitra,[99] the Swami explained to the ladies: 'Sri Ramakrishna, while seeming to be all *bhakti* (devotion) was really all *jnana* (knowledge), but he, himself, apparently all *jnana*, was full of *bhakti* (and that there he was apt to weaken).'[100]

If 'weakening' that was, it was the greatest strength of Swami Vivekananda, the reason why he had touched countless hearts and had touched them so deeply. If one is incapable of feeling the sorrow of one's self, one can never feel the sorrow of the *other*. Earlier in this chapter we saw Vivekananda bitterly resenting his loving nature, resenting 'love' itself, and wishing he were a 'heartless Advaitist'. But those who took him even for a day in their homes felt ever afterwards that the universe of Love had flowed in.

In the same summer of 1898, at Almora, Aswini Kumar Datta, the eminent patriot of nineteenth-century Bengal, had come calling. He asked the monastic novice, the brahmachari, acting as the doorkeeper of the Swami's room, 'Is Naren Datta here?' The brahmachari answered, rather saucily, 'There is no Naren Datta here. He died long ago. There is only Swami Vivekananda here.' Aswini Kumar answered back, 'I have come here not to meet Swami Vivekananda but Paramahamsa Dev's Narendra.' The novice repeated his earlier answer, which irritated the great man. On hearing some sounds outside his room, the Swami called the novice inside and asked him what the matter was, and the answer he gave to Aswini Kumar was reported. 'Oh what *have* you done! Just show him

---

[99] Read again Chapter 3 of this book.
[100] Prabuddhaprana, *Tantine*, p. 49.

in.' The eminent visitor recalled that once when he visited Sri Ramakrishna, the saint had asked him to have a conversation with his Narendra, which on that day he could not but had promised that one day he would. He came to redeem that promise: 'the Master's words cannot be in vain.' During their conversation, Aswini Kumar addressed him at one point as 'Swamiji'. And Swamiji immediately shot back, 'When did I become a "Swami" to you? I am still the same Narendra. Call me by that name.'[101]

Some biographies of Swami Vivekananda mention that in 1901, after his return from his second visit to the West, 'Swami Vivekananda took his mother on a pilgrimage to some sacred places in Bihar and East Bengal.' It was not 'Swami Vivekananda' but Narendranath Datta, the eldest son of Bhubaneswari Devi, who had taken his mother on a pilgrimage, which gave him deep satisfaction because it had made her so very happy, travelling with her son. On 26 January 1901, from the Belur Math, he wrote to Sara Bull:

I am going to take my mother on pilgrimage next week. It may take months to make the complete round of pilgrimages. This is the one great wish of a Hindu widow. I have brought only misery to my people all my life. I am trying at least to fulfil this one wish of hers.[102]

In this letter to Sara, he spoke also of what was yet another emotional blow to him:

…The gloom has not lifted with the advent of the new century, it is visibly thickening. I went to see Mrs. Sevier at Mayavati. On

---

[101] This event is narrated in *The Life*, pp. 574-75.
[102] *CWSV*, V, p. 154. This letter is not included in *Letters of Swami Vivekananda*. See also *CWSV*, VII.

my way I learnt of the sudden death of the Raja of Khetri. It appears he was restoring some old architectural monument at Agra, at his own expense, and was up some tower on inspection. Part of the tower came down, and he was instantly killed.[103]

In what was perhaps his last letter to Raja Ajit Singh, written on 14 June 1899, the Swami had said: 'May you be protected from all dangers and may all blessings ever attend you!'[104]

In the next few letters to Sara, he told her more. On 2 February: '...Mrs. Sevier is expected here soon—*en route* to England. I expected to go to England with her, but as it now turns out, I must go on a long pilgrimage with my mother.[105] On 29 March, from Dacca: '...My mother, aunt and cousin came over five days ago to Dacca, as there was a great sacred bath in the Brahmaputra river...I am going to take my mother and the other ladies to Chandranath, a holy place at the easternmost corner of Bengal.'[106]

Simultaneously he wrote a stern letter to Shashi (Ramakrishnananda), who had set up in Madras the first Centre of the Ramakrishna Order:

---

[103] Ibid., p.154. Also to Mary Hale, his letter dated 18 May 1901, p. 160, and again 5 July, 1901, p. 166. It was in his falling from a tower of the tomb of Emperor Akbar, at Sikandra, that Raja Ajit Singh had died. 'Thus we sometimes come to grief on account of our zeal for antiquity. Take care, Mary, don't be too zealous for your piece of Indian antiquity.' Marie Louise Burke says, *SV New Discoveries*, Vol. 6, p. 262, that *CWSV* obscures the meaning by turning *Italian* into *Indian*. 'In view of the context and the situation, *Italian* is surely what Swamiji wrote, Mary having married a rich Italian, much older in age than she, and the Swami lightheartedly cautioning her!'

[104] Ibid., p. 150.

[105] *CWSV*, V, p. 156.

[106] Ibid., p. 158.

I am going with my mother to Rameswaram, that is all. I don't know whether I shall go to Madras at all. If I go, it will be strictly private. My body and mind are completely worked out; I cannot stand a single person. I do not want anybody. I have neither the strength nor the money, nor the will to take up anybody with me. Bhaktas of Guru Maharaj or not, it does not matter. It was very foolish of you even to ask such a question. Let me tell you again, I am more dead than alive, and strictly refuse to see anybody. If you cannot manage this, I don't go to Madras. I have to become a bit selfish to save my body.

Let Yogin Ma and others go their own way. I shall not take up any company in my present state of health.[107]

The Swami's relationships consisted of three distinct groups: with his brother-monks of Sri Ramakrishna; with his ardent followers in Madras; and with his Western friends and supporters. In all of them, one dominant trait of his personality, an inheritance from his father Bisvanath Datta, was manifest—his fierce independence which was, however, not loveless. Now, whatever punishment human society may inflict upon anybody truly independent, such a person inflicts a punishment upon himself or herself in the first place. For the needs of independence are, seemingly at least, incompatible with the needs of relationship. Swami Vivekananda carried within himself both with a tragic intensity, which few could understand. There was in him the simultaneity of strong independence that spoke the language of love with a childlike dependence that spoke the language of freedom.

---

[107] Ibid., p. 155. This letter bears no date.

Furthermore, his work was located in the framework of nineteenth-century India, with the encounter of Western civilization, Western Christianity and British imperialism joining hands, and the diverse Indian responses to them full of irreconcilable contradictions.[108] The Swami saw that only too clearly.[109] But now it was not 'work', it was his message, the message of the *living* Vedanta, which was not limited to India. It was not 'organization' as much as reaching out in the human universe of even greater contradictions. Vivekananda saw, furthermore, that 'work and 'organization' swallow the message, and even before that happens, swallow the teacher. He was now seeing far beyond. In his letter of 25 March 1900, from San Francisco, he wrote to Nivedita:

I am much better and am growing very strong. I feel sometimes that freedom is near at hand, and the tortures of the last two years have been great lessons in many ways. Disease and misfortune come to do us good in the long run, although at the time we feel that we are submerged for ever.

I am the infinite blue sky; the clouds may gather over me, but I am the same infinite blue.

I am trying to get a taste of that peace which I know is my nature and everyone's nature. These tin-pots of bodies and foolish dreams of happiness and misery—what are they?

---

[108] See my *Dharma, India and the World Order*, 'Modern Indian Perceptions of India and the West', pp. 151–339.

[109] It will be a great mistake to perceive Swami Vivekananda only through some spiritual haze, ignoring his concerns with what British rule was doing in India; but it will be a greater mistake to perceive him and his work only, or even mainly, as the counter-challenge of Hinduism. To those who do the first, I suggest that they read, to take only one example, his letter of 30 October 1899, written to Mary Hale, from Ridgely Manor during his second visit to the West. *SV Letters*, pp. 394–96.

My dreams are breaking. Om Tat Sat![110]

Three days later, but actually simultaneously, he was writing to Mary Hale:

I am attaining peace that passeth understanding, which is neither joy nor sorrow, but something above them both. Tell Mother that. My passing through the valley of death—physical, mental—last two years, has helped me in this. Now I am nearing that *Peace*, the eternal silence. Now I mean to see things as they are, everything in that peace, perfect in its way. 'He whose joy is only in himself, whose desires are only in himself, he has *learnt* his lessons.' This is the great lesson that we are here to learn through myriads of births and heavens and hells—that there is nothing to be asked for, desired for, beyond one's self. 'The greatest thing I can obtain is myself.' 'I am free', therefore I require none else for my happiness. 'Alone through eternity, because I was free, am free, and will remain free for ever.' This is Vedantism. I preached the theory so long, but oh, joy! Mary, my dear sister, I am realizing it now every day. Yes, I am. 'I am free.' 'Alone, alone, I am the one without a second.'[111]

P.S. Now I am going to be truly Vivekananda. Did you ever enjoy evil? Ha! ha! you silly girl, all is good! Nonsense. Some good, some evil. I enjoy the good, and I enjoy the evil. I was Jesus, and I was Judas Iscariot; both my play, my fun. 'So long as there are two, fear shall not leave thee.' Ostrich method? Hide your heads in the sand and think there is nobody seeing you! All is good! Be brave and face everything, come good, come evil, both welcome, both of you my play. I have no good to attain, no ideal to clench up to, no ambition to fulfil; I, the diamond mine, am playing with pebbles, good and evil; good for you, evil,

---

[110] *SV Letters*, p. 416.
[111] Ibid., pp. 417-18.

come; good for you, good, you come too. If the universe tumbles round my ears, what is that to me? I am Peace that passeth understanding; understanding only gives us good or evil. I am beyond, I am peace.'[112]

This 'Postscript' will remain, I believe, among the profoundest of all postscripts ever written.

In the enormous mass of works on Swami Vivekananda, hardly anything is written about Vivekananda's inner torments, his passing through what he called 'the valley of death'.[113] Let us hear Nivedita's description of them in her letter of 4 November 1899 to Joe, written from Ridgely Manor, Joe having gone away to attend to her dying brother at the home of Mrs Roxie Blodgett in Los Angeles:

...On Thursday evening, Swami came down for a cigar or something, and found Mrs. Bull and myself in earnest talk. So he sat down too—of course. One could see that he was troubled and for the first time he talked of the two years foretold to him, of defection and disease and treachery—and of how it was growing thicker today than ever. Laughingly, he said he supposed the last month would be worst. He spoke of E.T.S. (Sturdy) and of the Indian troubles—and he said he found himself still the Sannyasi—he minded no loss—but he *could* be hurt through personal love. Treachery cut deep. S. Sara had almost tears in her eyes when she came into my room after, and sat talking of it for an hour. She

---

[112] Ibid., p. 418.
[113] In his letter dated 28 March, 1900, from San Francisco, to Mary Hale.

prays that we may be able, during this last month, to surround him with Peace.[114]

...He had said something to S. Sara, and indeed again in that night-talk of the fact that he is guided and protected in his *work*, but all that is personal turned to ashes. If Sri Rama Krishna and Mother did not protect him in these hardest trials of life, which of us would not turn our backs on Them all, and go down to Hell with him? It almost made me hate the Mother for a minute, but I could not lose the feeling of amusement.[115]

...Such a wail I have listened to since lunch—that I fled to my room to cry. Then he followed me and stood at the door a minute, and revealed still more of the awful suffering. Oh Swami! Swami! He had asked so little of the Mother! Only that 2 or 3 he loved should be kept happy, and good and pure...[116]

Nivedita decided that, for the next month or so, she would 'worship only Siva, and pay no attention to the Mother. That is my protest.'[117]

In the same letter, Nivedita wrote:

I ought to tell you—and forgot—how he was talking in the old way about escaping from the world, He has been reciting the hatred of Fame and Wealth all his life, but he is only now beginning to understand what it really means. It is becoming unbearable. 'Where am I now!' he said, turning to me suddenly with such an *awful* look of lostness on his face. And then he began to repeat something—'And so to Thou—Ramakrishna—(with a pause) I betake myself. For in Thy feet alone is the Refuge of man.' Such a moment! Darling—I longed for you there.

'This body is going anyway. It shall go with hard tapasya—

---

[114] *Nivedita Letters*, Vol. 1, p. 225.
[115] Ibid., p. 225.
[116] Ibid., p. 227.
[117] Ibid., p. 225.

I will say 10000 Om a day—and with fasting. Alone, alone by the Ganges—in the Himalayas—saying Hara Hara, The Freed One, The Freed One. I will change my name once more, and this time none shall know. I shall take the initiation of sannyasa over again—and it shall be for this—and I will never never come back to anyone again.'

And then again that lost look, and the awful thought that he had lost his power of meditation. I have lost all—lost all—for you Mlechhas! And with that a smile—and a sigh—and the turning to go away.

Yum dearest, we can help no one. There is a space at last between each two atoms and *none* ever touches the other. Is there *no* way of circumventing, of conquering these terrible impossible laws? Can we not *somehow* find a way to mitigate all this for him? No way at all?[118]

Sara Bull found the way. Deeply sensitive to the inner torments of her 'son' Vivekananda, and herself troubled as a result, she now advised him to 'choose the freedom of the sannyasin and be done with organization and ambition'. Bringing together the facts relating to this most significant but completely ignored turn in his life, Prabuddhaprana says: 'Sara, who had been the person to urge Swami Vivekananda to accept these methods of formality in his organisation of the Ramakrishna Order's activities, was now asking him to quit. There was probably, no one else in this relation to the Swami who could have done so.'[119]

---

[118] Ibid., pp. 227-28.
[119] Prabuddhaprana, *Saint Sara*, pp. 375-76. She quotes the letter Sara wrote to the Swami, p. 375. That letter is quoted also in Marie Louise Burke, *SV New Discoveries*, Vol. 6, pp. 164-65.

Yes, there was; and he was in a far more intimate relation to the Swami—Vivekananda.

With the same intensity as Vivekananda was expressing his inner withdrawal, the Swami Vivekananda, on this second visit to the West, was working hard to spread the message of the Vedanta in a language never heard before. But he was not wholly free to do that either. The financial difficulties at the Belur Math were acute, for the local municipality was taxing it out and the monks at the monastery were often going without food. His need to earn money by lecturing was very nearly desperate but he was not getting much from his lectures, although large numbers came to hear him. The Swami wrote to Sara Bull that he must therefore return to the Math, for his presence was necessary to straighten things out. But Vivekananda was writing to her: 'It is becoming clearer to me that I lay down all concerns of the Math and for a time go back to my mother.' That was once again his announcement that it was time for him to return to his true self, but was being silenced by the Swami. Not for long, though.

Something else was now beckoning Vivekananda, a different call from a different land, a call that was not of his motherland, nor of her people, nor of disciples, nor of friends—but a call from beyond them all. He knew he did not have many months more to live; something else was demanding his attention—a pure inwardness, a journey within, to which he invited no one, from which no one was excluded.

On 18 April 1900, from Alameda, California, Vivekananda wrote to Josephine MacLeod, his 'Joe':

...Work is always difficult: pray for me Joe that my works stop for ever, and my whole soul be absorbed in Mother. Her works, She knows.

...I am well, very well mentally. I feel the rest of the soul more than that of the body. The battles are lost and won. I have bundled my things and am waiting for the great deliverer.

'Shiva, O Shiva, carry my boat to the other shore.'

After all, Joe, I am only the boy who used to listen with rapt wonderment to the wonderful words of Ramakrishna under the Banyan at Dakshineswar. That is my true nature, work and activities, doing good and so forth are all superimpositions. Now I again hear his voice; the same old voice thrilling my soul. Bonds are breaking—love dying, work becoming tasteless—the glamour is off life.

...I am glad I was born, glad I suffered so, glad I did make big blunders, glad to enter peace. I leave none bound, I take no bonds. Whether this body will fall and release me or I enter into freedom in the body, the old man is gone, gone for ever, never to come! The guide, the Guru, the leader, the teacher, has passed away; the boy, the student, the servant, is left behind.

...The sweetest moments of my life have been when I was drifting; I am drifting again—with the bright warm sun ahead and masses of vegetation around—and in the heat everything is so still, so calm—and I am drifting languidly—in the warm heart of the river! I dare not make a splash with my hands or feet—for fear of breaking the marvellous stillness, stillness that makes you feel sure it is an illusion!

Behind my work was ambition, behind my love was personality, behind my purity was fear, behind my guidance the thirst of power! Now they are vanishing and I drift. I come! Mother, I come! In Thy warm bosom, floating wheresoever Thou takest me, in the voiceless, in the strange, in the wonderland, I come—a spectator, no more an actor.

Oh, it is so calm! My thoughts seem to come from a great, great distance in the interior of my own heart. They seem like faint, distant whispers, and peace is upon everything, sweet, sweet peace—like that one feels a few moments just before falling into sleep, when things are seen and felt like shadows—without fear, without love, without emotion. Peace that one feels alone, surrounded with statues and pictures—I come! Lord, I come!

The world *is*, but not beautiful nor ugly, but as sensations without exciting any emotion. Oh, Joe, the blessedness of it! Everything is good and beautiful; for things are all losing their relative proportions to me—my body among the first.[120]

Joe carried this letter in her handbag; and whenever she felt overburdened, she took it out, read it, and felt healed.[121] Time had turned the paper on which the letter was written yellow; but the yellow of the passage of time had made the words shine all the more.

---

[120] *SV Letters*, p. 422-23. It was in this letter that he wrote about the problems Abhedananda had created at the New York Vedanta Society.
[121] In 1939, eighty years old, that is what she told Nikos Kazantzakis, the famous Greek novelist, to whom she was introducing Swami Vivekananda. See Prabuddhaprana, *Tantine*, p. 277.

12

Swami Vivekananda's Last Benediction

As early as 26 June 1895, at the height of Swami Vivekananda's spectacular fame and his quietly working spiritual influence in the West and in India, Vivekananda, his other self, had written to Mary Hale:

The more the shades around deepen, the more the ends approach, and the more one understands the true meaning of life, that it is a dream; and we begin to understand the failure of everyone to grasp it, for they only attempted to get meaning out of the meaningless. To get reality out of a dream is boyish enthusiasm. 'Everything is evanescent, everything is changeful'—knowing this, the sage gives up both pleasure and pain and becomes a witness of this panorama— (the universe)—without attaching himself to anything.

...Desire, ignorance, and inequality—this is the trinity of bondage.

Denial of the will to live, knowledge, and same-sightedness is the trinity of liberation.

Freedom is the goal of the universe.

'Nor love nor hate, nor pleasure nor pain, nor death nor life, nor religion nor irreligion: not this, not this, not this.'[1]

It was in Cairo in November 1900 that on a sudden impulse, with which Josephine MacLeod was familiar, Swami

---

[1] In his letter dated 26 June 1895, to Mary Hale. *SV Letters*, p. 240.

Vivekananda said to her that he wanted to return to India. Until then it was presumed that, at the end of that famous trip to Egypt, he would return with them to America. And Joe said to him: 'Yes, go.' But he had no money to pay his passage back to India. Emma Calve said to him: 'Why Swamiji, if it is only that, I'll pay your fare; it is nothing. But why do you want to leave us?' Moved almost to tears by her love and generosity, he said to Emma: 'I want to go back to India to die and I want to be with my brothers (his brother-monks).' 'But Swamiji, you cannot die, we need you.' Then he said to her that he would die on 4 July. She bought him a first-class ticket for his voyage back to India. When they all came to say farewell to him, Emma had a clear feeling that she would never see him again.[2]

Joe was again in India in February 1901, on her way to Japan, from where she returned to Calcutta on 6 January 1902. She had brought with her the well-known Japanese artist, Kakuzo Okakura, whom she admired greatly, and wanted him to meet Swami Vivekananda. They stayed at the Belur Math. Okakura wanted to visit the places associated with the Buddha, and the Swami accompanied him and Joe on their visit to Bodh Gaya and Varanasi, even though his health was not at all good. Those journeys were also his own last physical salutation to the Buddha and to the city that had meant so much to him in the journey of his life.

In April 1902, Joe spent two hours with her friend, alone, in his room at the Math. She recalled later:

At Belur Math one day, while Sister Nivedita was distributing prizes for some athletics, I was standing in Swamiji's bedroom at the Math,

---

[2] All this was later recorded by Madame Emma Calve in her memoirs.

at the window, watching, and he said to me, 'I shall never see forty.' I, knowing he was thirty-nine, said to him, 'But, Swami, Buddha did not do his great work until between forty and eighty.' But he said, 'I delivered my message and I must go.' I asked, 'Why go?' and he said, 'The shadow of a big tree will not let the smaller trees grow up. I must go to make room.'

Afterwards I went again to the Himalayas. I did not see Swami again.[3]

Joe later left for London to attend the coronation of King Edward VII.

As I said, I never was a disciple, only a friend, but I remember in my last letter to him in April 1902, as I was leaving India—I was never to see him again—I distinctly remember writing in this good-bye letter the one sentence, 'I swim or sink with you.' I read that over three times and said, 'Do I mean it?' And I did. And it went. And he received it, though I never had an answer.[4]

Swami Vivekananda's last benediction, as it were, was reserved for Nivedita, his spiritual daughter, to whom he had simultaneously been harsh *and* loving, indifferent *and* very close. Nivedita spent half a day on 2 July with Swami Vivekananda. Although he himself was fasting on that day, he served her lunch.

He insisted on serving me (but this is not for repetition to others), fanning me while I ate, washing my hands for me and so on. I said—'Swami, I *hate* you to do this. I should do it for *You*.' Then he laughed and said in his daring way—'But Jesus washed the feet

---

[3] Josephine MacLeod in *Reminiscences*, p. 242.
[4] Ibid.

of His disciples.' It was on the tip of my tongue to say—'But then, that was the last time.' Thank Heaven, I did not.[5]

On 4 July 1902, at nine in the night, Swami Vivekananda passed into eternity. He was not yet forty.

The next day his mortal body, through which he had been teaching his universal gospel of Vedanta as love but had suffered equally, was given over to Agni, the God of Fire. Something else happened, too—yet another benediction of Swami Vivekananda, his last assurance of love, to his spiritual daughter Nivedita, and, as she thought it to be, also his last letter to Joe that 'he would not have allowed to be lost in the post'.

I said to Swami Saradananda seeing a certain cloth covering the bed-top—'Is *this* going to be burnt? It is the last thing I ever saw Him wear!' Swami Saradananda offered it to me there, but I would not take it. Only I said 'If I could only cut a corner of the border off for Yum!' But I had neither knife nor scissors, and the seemliness of the act would have been doubtful—so I did nothing. At 6 O'clock—or was it 5?—my first letter told you, I think it was 6—as if I were twitched by the sleeve. I looked down, and there, safe out of all that burning and blackness, there blew to my feet the very two or three inches I had desired out of the border of the cloth. I took it as a Letter from Him to you, from beyond the grave. I *cannot* believe that he has allowed it to be lost in the post![6]

---

[5] Her letter dated 28 August 1902, to Nell and Eric Hammond. *Nivedita Letters*, Vol. I, p. 499.
[6] Her letter dated 14 September 1902, to Josephine MacLeod. *Nivedita Letters*, Vol. I, p. 505.

On 10 July, Nivedita wrote to Mary Hale, giving the details of the last day of his life:

You have heard of Swamiji's death on Friday evening last, the 4th of July, at 9. Perhaps you already know that he was ill all through the winter, and indeed ever since reaching India from Egypt. But during the last months and weeks he has been improving remarkably and though none of the older Swamis thought there could be a permanent cure, yet it did not seem at all improbable that he would recover sufficiently to go to Japan and work this autumn. On Friday itself he worked very hard, spending more than 3 hours in meditation, and teaching and talking to one and another all day. At ½ past four a special message reached Calcutta from him that he had never felt so well. About that time, he went out for a walk and walked two miles—a great deal here. Then he came into his room and dismissed everyone. He wanted to meditate. After about an hour, he was tired, and lay down, calling a boy to fan him. Half an hour later, a trembling of the hand, crying as if in a dream, and some irregular breathing made the lad call the house—but when they reached his side, he was already gone. Everything points to great Samadhi. He left everything in order. Everything at peace and in the moment of his greatest strength, quietly, of his own will, he left us.[7]

'Do you realise how ideally great the last scene has been?' Nivedita wrote a week later to Josephine MacLeod. 'Quietly to put the body down as a worn-out garment at the end of an evening meditation!'[8]

---

[7] *Nivedita Letters*, Vol. I, p. 478. See also her letter to the Hammonds, cited above, in which she gave the same details of Swami Vivekananda's last day, pp. 498–99.

[8] Her letter dated 16 July 1902. *Nivedita Letters*, Vol. I, p. 481.

What Sri Ramakrishna had said about Narendranath, we can say about Swami Vivekananda: 'He has lighted the fire. Now it doesn't matter whether he stays in the room or goes out.'[9]

That fire has been burning for more than a hundred years.

---

[9] M—*The Gospel*, entry dated 19 August 1883, p. 217.

Index

(*Note*. In this index, 'SV' denotes Swami Vivekananda; and where abbreviated, 'Sri RK' denotes Sri Ramakrishna. Several names are arranged under their first names. Thus, Bhubaneswari Devi Datta, SV's mother, and not 'Datta, Bhubaneswari Devi'. Alasinga Perumal, and not 'Perumal, Alasinga'. In most other cases, the customary practice has been followed. Concepts, such as 'Absolute', and Sanskrit words are in italics. This Index is a detailed road map to what is in this book and where, but only that. A road map is no substitute for travelling on the road.)

Adbhutananda, Swami (Rakturam, Latu), a direct disciple of Sri Ramakrishna, 84.

adhikara-vada, brahmanical theory of 'entitlement according to caste hierarchy' SV strongly condemns (*see* Swami Vivekananda).

advaita, philosophy of non-duality, as oneness of all life, SV advocates throughout (*see* under Swami Vivekananda).

Advaitananda, Swami (Gopal Sur, Elder Gopal), a direct disciple of Sri Ramakrishna, 84.

Ajit Singh, Raja of Khetri, inseparable from SV's life story, and their close relationship, 125-26; his reverence for SV, and SV's love for him, 125, 141, 143; gives SV, at that time 'Satchidananda', the name 'Vivekananda', *Swami Vivekananda* is born in May 1893 at Khetri, and its irony, 85-6, 143; meets SV's travel cost to America (1893), 145, and SV visits him prior to his departure, 141-43; escorts SV up to Jaipur, arranges an evening of entertainment where SV meets another teacher of his, a dancing girl, he will never forget, 144; to him alone SV turns, seeking financial help for his mother, Bhubaneswari Devi (*q.v.*), 125, and in that regard his two anguished letters to, 362-63 ; makes certain that SV's mother would get from Khetri Raj Treasury Rs.100 every month as long as she lived, 363;

—SV deeply sad at the death of, in a freak accident (1901) at Agra, 126, 395-96;

—SV's letters from America to, 99-100, 101, 125-26, 186, 251-52, 292; his last letter to, 396.

Akhandananda, Swami (Gangadhar Ghatak, Gangadhar), a direct disciple of Sri Ramakrishna, 84; SV nurses him in his illness at Hrishikesh, 94, 148-49; and SV's emotional bond with, 94, 147;

—SV's letters to, 147, 327, 330, 349, 350-51.

Alasinga Perumal, most prominent among those, some of them householders, who gather round SV (January1893) in Madras, 136-37; goes from door to door to raise money to send SV to Parliament of Religions (*q.v,*) in Chicago (*q.v.*), 136, 138; SV's close relationship with, 136, 227, 229-30, but ignored in all biographies of SV, 136-37; Sundararama Iyer's (*q.v.*) tribute to, 137-38; in Bombay, to see SV off and give him money he had collected, 145;

—some of SV's most stirring letters from America are written to, 102, 108, 111, 136, 146, 158-59, 161, 163, 178-79, 182, 193,

Belur Math, final place for the monks of Sri Ramakrishna, and irony in the building of, with money given by three *women*, 83; SV with some young students of Calcutta and his spontaneous giving to one of them at, 128-29; before leaving on his second visit to America (1899), SV's talk at, 333; acute financial difficulties at, 402-3; Josephine MacLeod's last visit (April 1902) to SV at, 407-8.

bhakti (*See* Ramakrishna Paramahamsa and Swami Vivekananda).

Bhairavi Brahmani, a woman of great beauty and learning, Sri Ramakrishna's teacher in the path of tantra, 27; defends him when genuineness of his trances questioned, 27;

Bhubaneswari Devi Datta, SV's mother, xv, and her family,1-3; her portrait, 9-10, her complaint to Lord Shiva when SV too difficult to manage as a child, 9; till his last day SV remains attached to, xvii, 8, 154-55, and why *that* requires special attention, 155-57; SV never ceases to acknowledge publically what he owes to, making him what he is, xvii, 1, 10, 243-44; receives same acknowledgement (1894) from some American women,10-11; close relationship between mother and son, 8-9; her complaint against her daughters, 15; visits the ailing Sri Ramakrishna, who asks her to take Narendra (SV) back home, 61, 81; is visited by Haridas Viharidas Desai (*q.v.*), Dewan of Junagadh, and SV is deeply touched, 154; Sister Christine's (*q.v.*) portrait of, 10, 155; Sara Bull's tribute to, 241-42; SV's tribute to, 243; SV deeply worried what effect the slanderous stories about him, circulated in Calcutta by Pratap Chandra Mazoomdar (*q.v.*) would have upon, 244; SV's greatest inheritance from, 'Never compromise with truth, come what may', 9, 16, 45, 256; suffers anxiety and pain on account of her other two sons, Mahendranath (*q.v.*) and Bhupendranath (*q.v.*), 306; SV writes to Ajit Singh, Raja of Khetri, seeking financial help for, 362-63; SV's conversation with Nivedita concerning, 363-64; SV borrows from Math account to build a small house for, and live with, 365; is taken on pilgrimage (1901) by SV, himself in poor health, 395-96.

Bhupendranath Datta (Dr.), SV's youngest brother, *fns*.1 & 2 at p.1; *fn*. 3 at p.2; *fn*. 6 at p.3; author of *Swami Vivekananda Patriot-Prophet—A Study*, see *fn.* 2 at p.1; provides details of Datta family, with names, not to be found elsewhere, 1-3, 4-5, 15, and rest of Ch.1 with relevant *fns.*; seldom mentioned in standard biographies of SV, 3; defends his father's liberal views and disposition, 6-7; describes his mother Bhubaneswari Devi's visit to the ailing Sri Ramakrishna, 61; fragments SV's concerns and sayings in exclusive light of socialism,

encounters in Salem, Massachusetts, open hostility of, 169; enraged because their accounts of India and Hinduism proved false by SV, and their funding by Americans reduced considerably as a result, 221, regard SV as an enemy to be destroyed, and their campaign of slander against him, its climax in Detroit (1894), 221-22, 231; SV has a fight with a Presbyterian on the stories, Hindu mothers throwing their babies to crocodiles in rivers and some such, being spread by, 256.

Christine, Sister (Christine Greenstidel), of Detroit, hears SV in Detroit first, and her recollection of it, 286; travelling long distance with her friend Mary C. Funke (*q.v.*), arrives at Thousand Island Park and what she says to SV, 285-86; is accepted for his work in India, 293; crosses Atlantic to receive SV at Tilbury Dock on Thames (1899) on his second visit to West, 334;

—her reminiscences of SV and of what he tells her about what he owed to his father and mother, 8, 9-10, 155;

—SV's letter to, 360.

Cornelia Conger, granddaughter of John B. and Emily Lyon (*q.v*) with whom SV stayed during Parliament of Religions days, and her reminiscences of SV, 187-88, 226.

Dakshineswar, and Kali temple, *place* most intimately connected with Sri Ramakrishna and his wife Sri Sarada Devi who lived there, and with Narendranath Datta, Swami Vivekananda in making, 23-4; atmosphere of honest spiritual inquiry and not merely discourse at, 45-6, but also of wit and laughter, 55, 67-8, 70; see remaining pages of Ch.2 mainly; 220; and numerous other pages in this book.

Datta, Aswini Kumar, eminent patriot of nineteenth-century Bengal, visits Almora, asking for Sri Ramakrishna's 'Narendra' and not 'Swami Vivekananda', and what follows, 394.

Datta, Durgaprasad, SV's grandfather, a rich lawyer of Calcutta, renounces the world when twenty-five, abandoning his wife Shyamasundari Devi (*q.v.*) and a young son, Biswanath, SV's father, and vanishes in Varanasi (*q.v.*) 3-5, 60 (*See* also Varanasi);

Datta, Rammohan, SV's great-grandfather, managing clerk and associate of an English lawyer in Calcutta, 3.

Desai, Haridas Viharidas, Dewan of Junagadh ('Dewanji'), gave SV his love and care and faith in his destiny, and SV's close relationship with, and gratitude to, 143, 146, 154, 252, 282; visits SV's mother in Calcutta and SV is deeply touched, 154; SV's deep sadness on hearing at Thousand Island Park news of the death of, 282, 285;

   —SV's letters to, 103, 143, 154, 179-80, 194, 207, 230.

Deussen, Paul, Professor, German Indologist, famous for his work on Upanishads and Vedanta (*q.v.*), SV meets, at Kiel, talking with him in Sanskrit, 309-10; takes SV to visit some places in Germany and Holland, and later meets him in London, 310.

Dhammapada, SV's invocation of, 149-50.

Dharmapala, a Buddhist from Ceylon (now Sri Lanka), represents Buddhism at Parliament of Religions, and, upset by SV's criticism of historical Buddhism, his malicious attack on him, while receiving from him his love and friendship, 268.

dialogue, with one's *self* an essential pre-condition of, with the *other* (*see* Swami Vivekananda).

Duff, Alexander, a British missionary to India, and his abusive statement on Hinduism, 112 and *fn.* 82 at that page.

Dutcher, Mary Elizabeth, a devout Methodist, organizes (summer 1895) a retreat for a select few at Thousand Island Park to hear and be with SV, 282; all her beliefs shaken to their roots on hearing SV at her cottage, her consequent inner turmoil, which he understands, 287.

Ellis, Ruth, a friend of Sara Bull, writes to her about SV expressing to her many times his deepest appreciation of Sara, 253.

Emma Calve, Mme., French singer of repute, becomes devoted to SV, in Paris to hear SV at a Congress of History of Religions, 336; takes SV on a tour of Egypt thereafter, Josephine MacLeod with them, 337; and her account of that incident in Cairo when SV stood in front of a prostitute and wept, 248-49; SV's tribute to, 337; on SV suddenly deciding to cut short that trip and return to India but said he had no money, buys a first-class ticket for his voyage back, and has a feeling she will never see him again, 406-07.

Farmer, Sarah, organizes Greenacre Conference on inner unity of all religions, and on Sara Bull offering money to SV for his Indian work, he suggests she gives that money to, for her Greenacre Conference work instead, 280-81; and SV's tribute to, 281;

   —SV's letter to, 281.

Katyayani, elder sister of Sri Ramakrishna, 22.

Kazantzakis, Nikos, Greek novelist, to whom Josephine MacLeod was introducing SV (1939), *fn.*121 at p. 405.

Keshab Chandra Sen, founder and leading light of Brahmo Samaj, visits Sri RK at Dakshineswar often, and their conversations full of wit and humour, 55.

Kierkegaard, Soren, his idea of authentic Christianity as *feeling* Jesus Christ contemporaneously, and his criticism of the Church and pronouncement on Christendom, for which he is expelled from the Church, xxvi, 267-68.

Kiranbala, SV's other younger sister, 2.

Kripananda, Swami (Leon Landsberg), a brief sketch of, 274, 276; in relation to SV, from worshipful adoration to its reversal, 275-76, SV affected by neither, 276; writes to Sara Bull, 274-75; is initiated by SV into full sannyasa, 276, 285 (*see* also Thousand Island Park); turns against his guru, but SV's grace and love for him unaltered, 276; and Sara Bull's continued kindness to, 242;

—SV's letter to, 313.

Leggett, Betty (formerly Sturges), comes with her sister Josephine MacLeod, and with them Francis Leggett, to hear SV in New York, 277; her two children from her previous marriage, Alberta and Hollister; and her marriage to Francis, in Paris (August), SV present as a witness, and its extraordinary significance, 293-94; continues courting kings and queens, neglecting emotional bonds of marriage, and drifts apart from Francis, 295; their love for SV and financial support to his 'work' in America and India abide, as does his love for them, 295;

—Francis, a very rich businessman of New York, invites SV to Ridgely Manor after hearing his talk, 277-78, beginning of a deep friendship between SV and, 278; his marriage to Betty Sturges, 293-94; always held SV to be the greatest man he had ever met, 295; Betty and, after their honeymoon, join SV in London, 295; does much to nurture New York Vedanta Society, is disgusted with Abhedananda disrupting its smooth functioning, and resigns its presidentship, 366-67, 368; and SV's attitude to that whole affair, 369;

—SV's letter to, 245-46.

house of, and its explanation, 311-12; comes to India with SV, 321, 366; after donating the entire money with which the land for Belur Math was bought, criticizes everything Indian, SV and his brother-monks most of all, and Burke's comment on, 334 & *fn.* 200 at that page, 366, and Nivedita on the desertion of, *fn.*10 at p. 366.

Munshi Jagmohanlal, private Secretary of Raja Ajit Singh, comes to Madras to fetch SV and bring him to Khetri, 141; escorts SV up to Bombay, on instructions from the Raja buys a first-class ticket on S.S. *Peninsular* for SV's voyage to America, presents him a new silk robe and a handsome purse, and sees him off, 143-45.

Narasimhachariar ('G.G'), one of SV's 'Madras boys';

—SV's letter to, 185.

Narendranath Datta (Narendra, Naren): *see* Swami Vivekananda.

Nell Hammond, Mrs., (*see* Nivedita).

neti, famous postscript of Upanishad, repeated twice, in describing Reality, wrongly translated as 'it is not *this*' when the formation of the word '*na+iti*' clearly means 'it is not this *alone*', 'not yet complete' (the description), to be added in making judgements about the self and the *other* and also at the end of each chapter in this book, xxviii.

New York, another *place* of great importance in SV's life and 'work' in America, referred to under different entries.

Nietzsche, senior contemporary of SV; SV's self-division not wholly unlike the self-division of, but a fundamental difference between SV and, 371-72.

Nikhilananda, Swami, translates into English as *The Gospel of Sri Ramakrishna*. 'M''s *Sri Sri Ramakrishna Kathamrita*: see *fns.*2 at pp.1-2, 16 at p.9, 3 at p.22, 8 at p.24, 56 at p.60, 10 at p.137, 10 at p.163; and 335.

Niranjanananda, Swami (Nitya Niranjan Sen, Niranjan), a direct disciple of Sri Ramakrishna, 84-85;

Nirmalananda, Swami (Tulsi Charan Dutta, Tulsi), a direct disciple of Sri Ramakrishna, 85;

Nivedita, Sister (Margaret Elizabeth Noble, Margot), of Wimbledon, xviii; the name of, with those of Josephine MacLeod and Sara Bull, 'the Trinity', inseparable from SV, 279; meets SV in London (1895) at a talk

—SV arrives in Chicago weeks before, learns of problems, 161, is introduced to Professor John Henry Wright of Harvard who ensures SV included as a delegate to, 164-65;

—opens 11 September 1893, Chicago, the scene, extraordinary response to SV's speech and to him at, reported extensively in newspapers, 175-82; SV writes to Prof. Wright, 176-77, to Alasinga Perumal, 178-79, and to Haridas Viharidas Desai, 179-80, describing; and SV's speech on concluding day of, 180;

—SV's perceptions of, 'was my first step', 180-81, 184; was 'a heathen show' meant to prove Christianity's superiority over other religions, 185-86, Archbishop of Canterbury refuses to send anyone to represent Church of England, holding Christianity cannot be equated with other religions and sit on same platform, 185; still SV's high praise for,178, 184, 186.

Pavahari Baba, the great saint of Ghazipur SV reveres next to Sri Ramakrishna who had heard of, *fn*.97 at p.121; SV's (during his wandering years) complex relationship with, and attachment to, 119-22, his brother-monks wrongly perceive as disloyalty to Sri Ramakrishna and, irritated by their attitude, SV's stern admonition to them, 121-22; SV's tribute to, 122; at Almora SV hears of the death of, 392.

personal and *impersonal, see* Nivedita.

Porbandar, birth place of Mahatma Gandhi, during his wandering years SV at (1891), and irony of, 131-32.

Prabuddhaprana, Pravrajika (Leona Katz), and her *Tantine, The life of Josephine MacLeod: Friend of Swami Vivekananda,* and *Saint Sara: The Life of Sara Chapman Bull, the American Mother of Swami Vivekananda,* both indispensable for meeting SV, ix-x; xviii-xix, and *fns.* 4 & 5 at p. xix; cited at many places in this book.

prakriti, Nature, climate, SV's initial indifference to, an imagined conversation between them, 209-10; makes him equip himself for American, 210; SV describes to a brother-monk (Ramakrishnananda) American, 211-12; SV joyfully accepts diversity of, 216, never advocated that joys of, be dissolved in thick broth of *Brahman*, 'Absolute', 216.

Premananda, Swami (Baburam Ghosh, Baburam), a direct disciple of Sri Ramakrishna, 85; one of those who spoke of SV's reverence for Pavahari Baba as disloyalty to Sri RK, goes to Ghazipur to bring SV back who, irritated by his attitude, sends him away, 121.

Purusha and *prakriti*, '*Uncreated*' and '*Created Nature*', two main concepts of Samkhya philosophy: Dr. Sarkar (laughingly) administers to his patient Sri Ramakrishna two globules of medicine as, 70; SV's imagined declaration, 209. (*See* also Ramakrishna Paramahamsa and Sarkar, Dr. Mahendra Lal.)

Raghumani Devi, SV's grandmother, mother's mother; her youngest grandson Bhupendranath's portrait of, 15-6.

Ramkumar, elder brother of Sri Ramakrishna, 22; comes to Calcutta and opens a school there, 22, agrees to act as priest of Rani Rasmani's Kali temple at Dakshineswar, 24, also *fn*.8 at that page.

Ramabai, Pandita, a Brahmin widow converted to Christianity, 165; SV's first lecture in America (not at Parliament of Religions) at Boston Ramabai Circle, giving a picture of Hindu widows in contrast to that painted by, incurring their hostility, 165, ladies of Ramabai Circle join Christian missionaries in slandering SV, 224.

Ramakrishna Paramahamsa, Sri (Gadadhar Chattopadhyaya), born at Kamarpukur (18 February 1836), 22, also *fn*.4 at that page, in highly orthodox brahmin family; two elder brothers and two sisters, 22; comes to Calcutta to live with his elder bother Ramkumar, 22-3; is absorbed in quest of God-realization, falls ill, returns to Kamarpukur, is married to Saradamani, 23; returns to Calcutta and during Ramkumar's illness and after his death, appointed priest at Kali temple at Dakshineswar, lives in a small room there, 24;

—intoxicated with love of Divine Mother Kali, feels her *presence* in everything, 25, even in a cat he feeds with food meant as offering to Deity, scandalous to many and his explanation, 54; sees Divine Mother even in a wicked man, 54; laughs and weeps and dances and sings in ecstasy of God, 25, 67, becomes known for these but even more for his childlike nature and affection for all, 25; ordinary men and women of all faiths, many poor but earnest, come in hundreds to see, 25, 56, and their different perceptions of, from 'stark mad' to 'divinely inspired', 25, but all touched by his sincerity and loving manners, 56;

— no sectarian saint, against dogmatism, travels different roads of religious faith, tantra, Vaishnava bhakti, Vedanta, 27, Islam when he even dresses like a Muslim and does namaz thrice daily (his own description), 28, worships Jesus Christ, 28-9, Buddha, Jain Tirthankaras and Sikh Gurus, 29, and his conclusion by direct

announces his first endeavour is to start a Math for women, which did not mean monasticism for women but their education, 196; lays the rule that women's Math shall be absolutely independent, and no man shall dictate to a woman, nor a woman to a man, 197; declares that women will work out their destines better than men can do for them, all mischief to women has come because men undertook to shape the destines of women, 197; see also 328-29, 330-31;

—unlike the Buddha, his *ishta*, 327-28, and Sri RK, his Master, 33-4, his highest regard for woman as redeemer of civilization, 327, 330; the most passionate voice for Indian women, xxiv; his *living* Vedanta inseparable from his passionate concern for living Durgas, women of India, 331;

—praises American women highly, 195;

—makes a sharp distinction between 'religion' and 'society' and contrasts India with West in those terms, 198-200, which examined, 201;

—and what may be called *Testament of Swami Vivekananda*, 202-05;

—opens dialogue as much with Hinduism as with Christianity, dialogue of the self with the self within the self, 205-07; is the strongest Hindu challenge to what Hindus had turned religion into, 206-07; no salesman of 'Hinduism', or of any other *ism*, rather a scourge of all *isms*, 235; no sectarian monk, nor a missionary of Hinduism, teaching truths that are universal, 296;

—his devastating response to the criticism of orthodox Brahmins that in West he was eating meat, 215-16, also 212-13, compares Kshatriyas, generally meat eaters, with Brahmins as regards sharing of knowledge, 216;

—and all that about his remaining sexually chaste: collective evidence of all those Western women who knew him intimately, not a trace of the sexual in his intimate relationships with them, he had gone beyond it naturally, 34-5; his confession to Emily Lyon of having had 'the greatest temptation of his life in America', on her asking. 'Who is she, Swami?', his answer (laughingly): 'Organisation', 187-88, 226; far too great a person to be measured by the yardstick of sexual chastity alone, 245; his selflessness, concern for others, freedom and liberty to others, trust, childlike simplicity, honesty to himself and others, and his power to awaken deeper self of another